Writing Outside the Lines

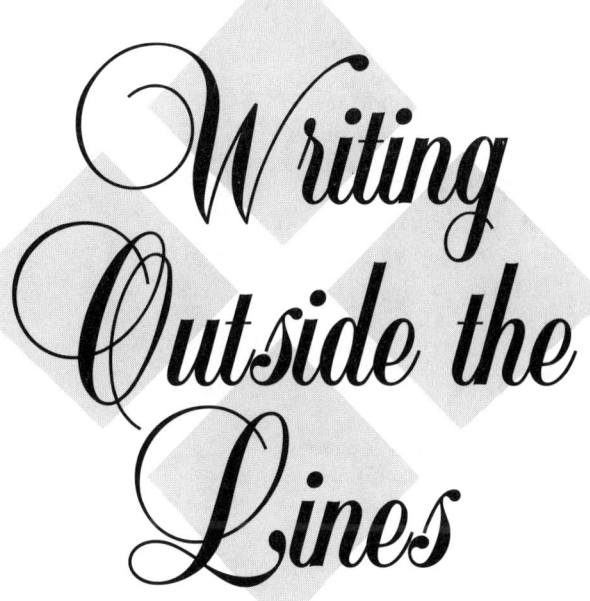

Writing Outside the Lines

Stories of Literacy

Martha Marinara
University of Central Florida

Peggy Ellington
Wesleyan College

Allyn and Bacon
Boston   London   Sydney   Tokyo   Singapore

Vice President: *Eben W. Ludlow*
Series Editorial Assistant: *Grace Trudo*
Executive Marketing Manager: *Lisa Kimball*
Composition and Prepress Buyer: *Linda Cox*
Manufacturing Buyer: *Suzanne Lareau*
Cover Administrator: *Linda Knowles*
Editorial-Production: *Modern Graphics, Inc.*
Electronic Composition: *Modern Graphics, Inc.*

Copyright © 2000 Allyn & Bacon
A Pearson Education Company
Needham Heights, Massachusetts 02494

Internet: www.abacon.com

All rights reserved. No part of the material protected by this copyright notice may be reproduced or utilized in any form or by any means, electronic or mechanical, including photocopying, recording, or by any information storage and retrieval system, without written permission of the copyright owner.

Library of Congress Cataloging-in-Publication Data

Marinara, Martha, 1956–
  Writing outside the lines : stories of literacy / Martha Marinara, Peggy Ellington.
    p.   cm.
  ISBN 0-205-30510-5
  1. College readers. 2. English language—Rhetoric Problems, exercises, etc. 3. Literacy Problems, exercises, etc. 4. Readers—Literacy. I. Ellington, Peggy, 1951–. II. Title.
PE1417.M42125 1999
808'.0427—dc21
                                                                99-39135
                                                                    CIP

Credits for this book appear on pages 337–340, which constitute an extension of this copyright page.

Printed in the United States of America
10 9 8 7 6 5 4 3 2 1   04 03 02 01 00 99

Contents

❖

Why we wrote this book, a sort of Preface   ix

How to use this book, a note to students   xv

Each selection is accompanied by Prereading Reflection, Final Reflection, After You Read Consider and Suggestions for Writing

School Literacy   1

Learning to Use Language   2

Jane Smiley, *The Consequences, from* Moo   4

Harold Rosen, *Comrade Rosie Rosen*   10

John McPherson, *Close to Home*   17

Johnny Connors, *The Man That Spelt "Knife" Was a Fool*   20

Katherine Grigg, *Frustration*   25

Tiffany Gay, *Sugar, Spice, and Everything Nice*   28

Langston Hughes, *Theme for English B*   33

Mike Rose, *I Just Wanna Be Average*   36

William Stafford, *At a Small College*   46

Evelyn Freedman, *Ready for Anything*   49

Bill Hall, *Toothmarks in the Table of Time*   55

Collaborative Assignments for School Literacy   58

v

Work Literacy 61

Writing and Work 62

Tim O'Brien, *The Things They Carried* 64

Susan Orlean, *Beautiful Girls* 81

Abraham Verghese, *From My Own Country* 95

Michelle Cook, *The Great Blueberry War* 104

Elizabeth Berg, *Nurse Wonder* 108

Tillie Olsen, *I Stand Here Ironing* 116

Nancy Sommers, *I Stand Here Writing* 125

Ben Hamper, *I, Rivethead* 136

Jessica Marinara, *Christmas for the Colorblind* 150

Sandra Cisneros, *First Job* 157

Chris Llewellyn, *March 25, 1911* 160

Melissa Graham, *A World Painted John Deere Green* 166

Collaborative Assignments for Work Literacy 172

Home Literacy 173

Kitchen Table Talk 174

Les Wade, *Grandma's Fruitroom* 177

Marti S. Baker, *Circle of My Womanhood* 180

Shirley Brice Heath, *Talk Is the Thing* 186

Fannie Flagg, *Preface from* Fannie Flagg's Original Whistle Stop Cafe Cookbook 193

Whitney Otto, *Instructions No. 3* 199

Kim King, *Grandmother's Kitchen, My Classroom* 204

Jeanne Leiby, *Why I Read* 208

J. Nozipo Maraire, *From* Zenzele, A letter for My Daughter 211
Pat Rushin, *Zoo Welcomes New Arrival* 216
Jenny Joseph, *Warning* 227
Chang-rae Lee, *From* Native Speaker 229
Eudora Welty, *Wordstruck* 235

Collaborative Assignments for Home Literacy 242

Alternative Literacy 246

Other Literacies 247

Lillian Hellman, *Turtle* 249
Alice Marriott, *The Whole Pot* 261
Leonard Kriegel, *Graffiti: Tunnel Notes of a New Yorker* 270
Timothy Guidera, *Bowl's Eye View* 278
Jane Martin-Brown, *Paths of Loss and Liberation* 285
Rita Nachtmann, *From* Pee Wee and the Wheelman 289
Mary Sterner Lawson, *Reading Faces* 299
Libby Bailey, *I Am What I Am* 302
Nancy Hemingway, *The Bracelet* 305
Dorothy Allison, *From* Bastard Out of Carolina 316
bell hooks, From *Bone Black* 329
Fernando La Rosa, *The Man* 332

Suggestions for Group Literacy Work 334

Credits 337

Why we wrote this book, a sort of Preface

❖

> You must keep your promises to us!
>
> —Frank Baum, *The Wizard of Oz*

  We wrote this book because we wanted to share our stories about being nontraditional students. We both raised children and worked fulltime while squeezing classes, studying, reading, and writing in to every spare minute. Juggling and balancing on a tightrope became the metaphors for our everyday routines. We both often wondered how many parents make their own school lunch at the same time they make their children's; how many parents give up a night out in order to have money to buy books. We both reached a moment of self-enlightenment when we realized that browsing in bookstores had become a leisure time activity. Slowly, our lives changed, our families changed, we changed. We developed different aesthetic and social values, became more politically active, and more tolerant of different cultures and people. Like all nontraditional students, there are similarities to our stories, although the details—what makes us individuals—make our stories very different.

  A few years ago, before beginning my early morning composition class, I listened to several of my students discussing "naked beer slides." When I asked what they were, the students were incredulous at my ignorance. "Oh, come on," one of them said. "You were a freshman once."

  Well, yes, I was, but when I was a freshman for the second time around I was twenty-seven, had two demanding daughters, worked full-time in a small grocery store, and was never invited to a naked beer slide. I had spent a total of thirteen years working on my undergraduate degree in English and then, because stacking apples, pears, and tomatoes in those appealing perfect pyramids is more mind numbing than it looks, I threw bank account and caution to the winds, quit my job, began teaching creative writing at a small university (I was qualified because I had published two poems and one short story and the department was desperate), and began work on my masters degree. I finished that degree when I was thirty-four, moved to Pennsylvania, and started work on a doctorate in composition, rhetoric and critical theory, where my students were horrified to learn that they were being taught by someone who had been a cashier and a waitress, someone who had done something rather than read books in the library. When I took my first full-time teaching position, degree still tightly rolled in its long mailing tube, I was acutely aware that if I had stayed at the grocery store I would probably be produce manager and making lots more money than I was teaching writing. But I still wouldn't be invited to a naked beer slide.

What does it mean to be an adult learner? A nontraditional student? Graduate studies did teach me to look critically at any word with *"non"* in front of it because it sets up the root word as a standard, something to be measured against. Traditional becomes the preferred choice; any other choice is secondary. Being a nontraditional student means carrying a constant load of anxiety, just waiting for some professor to look at you sadly and say, "Really, you should have gone to Technical College and studied welding." It means constantly wondering (especially while studying algebra) why you aren't welding by day so you can relax at night, play with your dog, watch *Ally McBeal* and *The X-Files*, eat nachos, finish off a six-pack of Rolling Rock. It means juggling priorities: dropping out one quarter because you need the tuition money to buy a new refrigerator, skipping English class to attend your daughter's piano recital, studying instead of sleeping, forcing yourself to actually smell your morning coffee before you gulp it down, cooking dinner while reading *Othello*, missing all the blockbuster summer movies. It means that somewhere along the way you've decided that education is more important than new clothes, a vacation, a sane life. (My oldest daughter said to me after I had finished the final corrections on my thesis, "Can we have something for dinner now besides hot-dogs?") It means always looking towards the future, putting away your books for an evening, and hugging your daughter and making her linguini with clam sauce because the present is already part of that future.

———— ❖ ————

Six years ago, I became a tutor for a thirty-one-year-old nonreader who had just finished serving yet another stint in one of Georgia's institutions of correction. More than anything else, Donald wanted to read. And he worked harder at the learning than anyone I had ever known. After two years, I decided it was time for him to find out how well he was doing. I arranged for him to speak to a group of local high school students. At that time, I attended their class once a week and offered writing and reading workshops outside of their typical skill and drill setting. But after two months, I was again noticing signs that the initial restlessness was resurfacing. So I thought perhaps another point of view would reenergize our group.

What Donald did that day was more than reenergizing. And it all began with an empty journal. Thirty eyes stared up at the blank journal pages, and fifteen accompanying mouths dropped open as Donald said, "This is what life is like when you're a nonreader in a reading world." From that point, my student held my fifteen high school seniors captivated. They listened to his story, asked questions, and began to understand the gift that reading gave to each of them.

After the fifty-five minutes were over, Donald raced outside for a cigarette and some air. He began to unwind and talked nonstop while I drove him back to his job. "I was so scared, but I did it. I think they liked what I said, don't you?" He rushed on without waiting for an answer. "I tried the journal idea on my mom last night, and she thought it was dumb, but the kids got it, didn't they? I could do this again. Maybe this is a new career for me. Do you think they noticed my shaking? Do you think they know how hard this was? Do you think I made a difference for them?"

What could I answer to my student and my friend? He had just walked into a southwest Georgia high school English class and, as he put it, "knocked the socks off fifteen cocky seniors." As a teacher, I knew just how hard that was to do. I didn't answer, just smiled and bobbed my head while I silently planned next week's reading lesson. During that lesson time, I knew we would relive his experience in front of that class. We would relive the questions about how he measured and cut carpet, laid Formica and tile, remodeled kitchens and baths without knowing how to read. And it was then that I would help him see that being literate did not just mean that he could go into a library, pick up any book, and read it. Being literate meant working within his own world, doing what needed to be done. It meant using a variety of experiences to gain competency. And Donald was competent. In fact, when it came to remodeling, he was more competent than I had ever been. But he valued what I was able to do, not what he was. My job, at that point, was to help him recognize the value of what he could do that I, and many others, could not.

Donald felt as I had many years before when I came back to college thirteen years, four children, and one pending divorce after I had started. I was ill prepared, I thought, to compete with the other students in the classroom, students who were much younger than I, much quicker, much smarter. These students did not work eight hours before they came to class; they probably didn't get up at 3 A.M. to find quiet time to study and write; they certainly didn't have children almost their age to take care of and support in more than monetary ways. I shudder now to think of the time I spent feeling "less than." And it wasn't until several years had passed and I was in graduate school that I began to appreciate my own literacy and life knowledge when I overheard two professors talking. Part of their conversation surprised me:

"I'm excited, several of my students are older. And you know that always makes for a more interesting discussion."

"To say nothing of the papers you'll get to read. Man, you lucked out."

I could not believe what I had heard. Professors valued returning students because of the experiences and the literacies that they brought with them to the classroom. That was the beginning of my commitment to returning students, and perhaps, although I did not know it then, it was the beginning of my commitment to this textbook as well.

We both teach adult learners to write within an academic setting. Sometimes referred to as *nontraditional students* and more often now as *return to college students*, adult learners bring a wealth of life learning and knowledge to our classrooms. Unfortunately, their knowledge and experience does not easily correlate with college subjects such as biology, algebra, Western civilization, and first-year composition. This disaffection with their own knowledge partly results from the way college curriculums are structured. General education requirements contain knowledge and skills that every student needs to learn in the same way to succeed in their major courses and to reach their goal of being college educated. First-year composition, most often part of the general education requirements, usually introduces academic writing: what it is, what it looks and sounds like. Students are expected to assimilate new knowledge rather than make connections with past experiences.

Another reason for this disaffection, and the reason we have written this book, is that many adult learners are not provided the opportunity to reflect on, claim, and rename their own learning. Adult learners are quite used to articulating what they know about writing in terms of their lack of formal preparation. They readily perceive the different arenas in which their histories as learners are played—school, work, and home. Within these three constructs of themselves as learners, the "school self" is usually the deficit model that falls short of some ideal knower, writer, and learner. But the language of "school literacy" is not the only language we have to talk about writers and writing. The language of adult learners resonates with cultural and social dynamics, but they are not always asked to look at and to write about the richness of their lives and themselves as literate in those areas that formal education has yet to claim. When given opportunities to connect different knowledge and literacies, adult students can reintegrate themselves as learners and knowers, building on what they already know and do best to both critique and gain control over the learning conditions in their universities.

One of our friends, Irene, recently received a master's degree from a large research university in the northeast. While attending classes and writing her thesis, she called us frequently for emotional and academic support. At one point she was told that her thesis topic—relationships of power within the management structures of long-term care facilities—wasn't academic enough. For the past six years, my sister has been a nursing supervisor at a long-term care facility. One of the problems she encounters at work concerns the attitudes of RNs toward health aides (who have considerably less formal education and make considerably less money), which in turn causes increased tension between the staff and the clients they serve. Irene initiated a series of workshops aimed at increasing the health aides' knowledge of caregiving and thereby enhancing their sense of professionalism. She hoped to raise the health aides' self-respect and help them achieve the respect of the RNs. At the same time Irene was initiating these workshops, her political consciousness was raised by the texts she was reading in her graduate classes. For her thesis, she proposed to study these power inequities in depth and propose a solution. Irene was guided toward another topic and eventually received her degree, but she still feels that one of the most important things she learned in graduate school is that what she does every day for a living is not intellectually valuable. Unfortunately, Irene's story isn't unique.

Our students' stories—about their schooling, their work, and their homes and families—inspire this book. We wanted to create a vehicle that places value on and works with the knowledge and experience that students bring to our classrooms. Because our students' stories are often the site of conflict and tension, integrating their narratives with texts that are labeled *academic* helps students negotiate the borders between work and school, past and present, self and other. Our purpose in writing this text was to place students' vast knowledge and academic knowledge into the same space so that student writers could question not only what they are learning, but why and how.

Connecting the classroom with "real life" means teaching students to take uncomfortable risks, to develop a critical perspective toward their education, and to recognize the power relations that allow them to speak in particular ways. Most important, it means encouraging them to develop public and private voices by reflecting on their lives and negotiating their connections to the lives of others.

How to use this book, a note to students

Writing Outside the Lines: Stories of Literacy asks you to make connections between your classroom experiences and home experiences, between your work lives and your school lives, between your past and present. Rather than chapters, the readings are divided into categories that mirror the situations in your lives, those that provide learning opportunities—school, work, home, and everywhere else. The readings included within the specific sections combine various writing strategies intended to encourage you to write about a particular author's unique perspective on his or her world and, in the process, write about the world through your own unique perspective. We want you to interpret these readings by retrieving similar memories of events, people, or places as those you are reading about. When these connections happen, you can begin to compare your experiences, reactions, or understandings (the known) with those of the author (the unknown). With these comparisons come a greater understanding and awareness of our world and the people in it along with the opportunity to critique the world through writing. Every selection provides opportunities prior to the reading, within the reading, and after the reading that prompt these comparisons.

Prior to each reading, we provide a "Prereading Reflection" prompt to help you construct a framework for what you are about to read. In Harold Rosen's *Comrade Rosie Rosen*, for example, the author recalls a time when his mother left her comfortable world to enter a world less familiar to her—his school. She does this to ensure that her son has the educational opportunities that he is entitled to. Prior to reading, you are asked to remember a time when a parent or adult figure fought for your rights.

After the initial "Prereading Reflection," each piece of writing incorporates several opportunities for you to compare your own experiences to those presented by the author. There is also room in the margins for you to write your own questions or comments on sections that inspire, worry, annoy, confuse, or interest you as you read. Returning to the Rosen work, the first reflective prompt asks you to think back to a time when you found yourself somewhere you weren't wanted and then asks you to remember where you found the courage to remain in that place.

After each reading, you are asked to reflect on the reading one final time. In the Rosen essay, the author shares his pride in his mother because she is different from other mothers he knows, while you are asked to speculate on whether his mother's difference might also have caused him to feel an emotion other than pride.

After the reading, small group or whole class discussion questions are provided to allow opportunities for you to share and expand your reflections with your class and to examine the particular piece of writing from other perspectives. For example, Harold Rosen begins his piece with an experience that occurs when he is eleven; he next recalls two experiences, one that occurs when he is eight, and the other when he is only seven. You and the other students in your class are asked to consider how his presentation might confuse readers who are comfortable with a standard chronological approach to a narrative.

After you have had the opportunity to reflect, to respond, and to engage in conversations with other readers, some suggestions for writing are provided. These suggestions at times call for a traditional essay format, such as writing about a time when you were proud of a family member. Or the prompts may suggest another type of writing, such as a prospective student's profile based on evaluation of marketing plans for institutions in your areas or a revision of the ending of an essay, scene, or story that allows a writer to explore "what might have happened if . . . ." In each case, the suggestions serve as springboards that provide another way for you to approach the writing.

As writers, we've attempted to include opportunities to experience various forms of writing, each of which has the potential for life beyond mere completion of an assignment for a grade. We suggest writing letters to editors, managers, or board members seeking changes in policies or positions or praising efforts for a job well done. Some suggestions are designed to tap into your creativity, such as creating character sketches, writing poems, or constructing collages of photographs that share a common theme and incorporate short, vivid descriptions. Other suggestions include opportunities that combine research strategies and creativity by asking you to seek information from outside sources and share the information through panel discussions, debates, and pamphlets.

Finally, at the end of the text, are "Suggestions for Group Literacy Work." These list collaborative activities that invite students to join with others of similar interests to continue the connections each has made individually. Ideas include considering each member's cultural history as handed down through some activity or hobby that involves members of the family (for example, cooking, woodworking, participating in sports). Then individually or as a group, you are asked to trace the roots of this involvement and share the information with the entire class in a poster presentation format. Or group members might visit a local nursing or assisted care home several times. While there, they would collect stories from the residents. Then using the stories, they might focus on a consistent theme within the stories (for example, going to war, dating, jobs, or education) and share both the theme and versions of the stories with other class members in writing or orally.

From the beginning through the end of each section, the connections made by readers and writers are emphasized. The connections help you conceptualize what you bring to the reading, to your classes, to other class members, and to the world in which you live. Connections and comparisons of what you already know to what you are learning provide the basis for critical thinking about a book, a course, a field of study, or a life. We invite you to share your connections with others so that all learners in your classes benefit from the knowing that has gone on around and beyond their worlds.

School Literacy

People who go to college are incredible. We go to classes. We read and absorb and are comprehensively tested on heavy amounts of various materials. We sleep very little. We often think of the past and want to go back. We know we cannot, and soon we won't want to. We all had separate lives, families, backgrounds, pasts. We live totally different from how we used to live. We are frustrated and sometimes want to give up, but we never stop trying, and our friends won't let us. We keep going, because above all else, we never stop learning, growing, changing, and, most important, dreaming.

—Stacy E. Dare

LEARNING TO USE LANGUAGE

It's fun to have fun, but you have to know how.

—Dr. Seuss

Sometimes after I've taught a particularly lively class, one in which everyone talked with each other and sometimes even laughed, I hear a voice from my childhood. The voice is from Dr. Seuss's *The Cat in the Hat*, but it is not the voice of the cat who only wants the children to enjoy themselves. I hear the voice of "the fish in the pot," who acts as a powerless parent substitute or possibly Sally and her brother's conscience, telling me "NO, no, no." My uneasiness comes in part from my own story of schooling, a story where learning was a serious business (even recess had rules and was carefully monitored), and in part from that strong, cultural voice that tells me how teachers are supposed to behave. Unfortunately, I learned how teachers are supposed to behave from some of my teachers; I'm still unlearning those behaviors.

My own story of schooling begins in kindergarten where I was confronted with a totally alien culture. I come from a large family, and anyone who has many siblings knows that extra friends are nice but unnecessary; your playmates are already built into your life. And no matter how badly I might have treated my brothers and sisters, they couldn't take their toys and go home. So not only did I actually have to learn to get along with others when I reached school, I also was confronted with social activities I had never seen before. The first time one of my classmates received birthday spankings, I was horrified. I vowed never to let my teachers know when my birthday came around.

I experienced my first crush in kindergarten. Madeline had long red hair and was the most fascinating person I had ever met. Madeline could speak and write in French. As someone who was just learning to form neat letters with a large pencil and read in English, I found her bilingual abilities enormously appealing. I managed to sit next to her every day (before I learned to get along with others I was very skilled at pushing other children out of my way), and I constantly asked her questions about herself and her life. She remained my friend until the early spring when the class was tasked with making Easter cards for our mothers. I asked Madeline to help me write "the Easter bunny will bring you candy and a kiss" in French because I had not been too well behaved that week and wanted to impress my mother. Madeline told me how to spell each word and I carefully formed the letters. I completed the card with crayon drawings of bunnies and flowers and baskets full of candy. I knew my mother would be thrilled and probably cry and hug me.

My mother was thrilled, and she did cry and hug me although the words on the card had nothing to do with the Easter bunny. Instead, I had written (in French), "I love you. I adore you. What more do you want." I was very angry with Madeline and decided that I better hurry up and learn to read in every language that existed in the world so I wouldn't be taken advantage of again.

I didn't manage to learn every language, but after many years of schooling, I learned to write tolerably well in English. As you read through the following selections about schooling, keep in mind your own experiences as a student and the ideas you have already encountered. Mark down those passages that strike you as close to your own experience. These notes should become your own emerging text—the work you have already done as a reader, writer, and thinker intertwined with the work you are about to do. How have you broken out of your defined role as a student? How have you managed to fill that role? What moments in your schooling stand out for you? What moments were most satisfying? Most frustrating?

This section opens with an excerpt from Jane Smiley's *Moo*, a novel about faculty and students at a large university in the Midwest. In this chapter, four roommates "cocoon" in their room rather than face their classes, families, boyfriends, and missed assignments. The second piece in this section is "Comrade Rosie Rosen." In this essay, Harold Rosen tells us what happens when his mother enters an unfamiliar world to ensure that her son receives the education she believes he is entitled to. John McPherson's cartoons from his series *Close to Home* take a humorous look at college culture, and in "The Man That Spelt 'Knife' Was a Fool," we are confronted with Johnny Connors' desire to read and write in spite of his inability to attend school regularly, a desire so strong that he scours garbage dumps searching for things to read.

Katherine Grigg expresses her feelings about writing in "Frustration," and Tiffany Gay explores her growing feminism in "Sugar, Spice, and Everything Nice." In "Theme for English B," Langston Hughes speaks to his teacher about his assignment, and in the essay "I Just Wanna Be Average," Mike Rose tells about his story of moving in high school from a vocational track to a college prep track. William Stafford's "At a Small College" asks readers to think about life on a small, rural campus. Evelyn Freedman's "Ready for Anything" explores her emerging literacy and reasons for reading. Finally, in "Toothmarks in the Table of Time," Bill Hall relates his memories about his third-grade teacher.

Jane Smiley

The Consequences, from Moo

Jane Smiley grew up in St. Louis and graduated from Vassar in 1971. She attended graduate school in Iowa and in 1981 began teaching at Iowa State. In 1997, she moved to California, bought a ranch, and began raising horses. Despite her new lifestyle, she still finds time to write. Smiley won a Pulitzer Prize for A Thousand Acres *in 1991, which was followed by* Moo, *a hilarious look at life in an agricultural university in the United States. Her most recent work is* The All-True Travels and Adventures of Lidie Newton: A Novel *(1998).*

At first it was strange to think and write about something before you read it. But after a while it started to help me to read better.

—Kirsten McCarthy

Prereading Reflection

Write about a time when your academic efforts came into question or under scrutiny by your parents or another family member.

Mary had a fever of 102, and every time she tried to stand up, it felt as though chills were cascading down her body. So, she was lying in bed, covered up to her chin, with a cool washcloth on her forehead that Keri had put there as some sort of rural folk remedy. Nor would Keri allow her to take aspirin, hadn't she heard of Reye's syndrome? Only Tylenol, but they didn't have any Tylenol, so Keri had gone to get some.

Otherwise Mary would have left the room and gone to the lounge, in order to avoid listening to Sherri whine over the telephone to her mother and father, who had just received her midterm grades.

She whined, "It's really hard here. I wasn't exactly prepared."

> Do you agree that Sherri's parents have a right to show concern for her poor performance in class?

She whined, "I did learn things. I haven't been wasting time."

She whined, "I know it costs a lot. Geez, I know exactly how much it costs, for Christ's sake."

She whined, "I'm sorry. No, I haven't learned to talk that way from my roommates." She looked over at Mary and made a face. "I'm just frustrated, is all."

She whined, "I know it's a privilege you and Daddy didn't have. Well, I am sorry."

She whined, "I am. I really AM. I thought I sounded sorry. I tried to sound sorry." A pause. "Because I AM sorry!"

Mary's grades had not gone home, because she had gotten no F's or D's. She had even gotten a B– on her calculus test, which meant that statistically (in her calculus course, the computer grading system spit out a merciless curve) she was above the fiftieth percentile, which meant that more than 50 percent of the students had an even more tenuous grasp on calculus than she did, which was, in its way, almost frightening. At least it was if you had a fever of 102 and discrete, unpleasant ideas were rolling around in your head like steel pinballs, making a lot of noise and lighting up various feelings, all of them negative.

> Do you ever feel that you are the only one who doesn't "get" an idea from class?

Sherri whined, "Well, it's hard for everybody. Nobody did great, not even Diane. I don't see why you're so mad. Daddy isn't that mad, and he's the one who's paying."

> Do you ever have trouble explaining what you really mean?

She whined, "I know. I'm sorry. I AM sorry. I know. I know."

Sherri had gotten two F's and a C–, which meant that her grade average was .94, not even a D, and that if she didn't bring it up, didn't in fact double it, she would be out at the end of the semester.

Sherri whined, "Yes, my hair is red. I dyed it. Can we talk about that another time?"

She opened her little refrigerator and took out a pack of cigarettes. Then she brandished a mineral water in Mary's direction, but Mary shook her head. An open one that she hadn't been able to finish sat on the desk beside her bed.

Finally, Sherri whined, "Well, I AM going to do better, okay? I promise. I PROMISE. Okay, then. Okay, bye." She hung up and went over to the window, where she lit her cigarette. Between puffs, she held it out the partially opened window. When Mary assayed a little cough, she said, "I know, I know. Tobacco is bad for the soil, bad for

> Do you think or behave differently than many of your friends? What attracts you to them?

the workers, bad for the public health, and bad for the body. I'm a sucker." This litany, made up by Keri, was something the other girls had employed to persuade Sherri to stop smoking, but so far it hadn't worked.

She whined, "God! She just went on and on." Mary felt like her bed was rocking, or her head was sloshing. One or the other. One or the other. One or the other.

Sherri said, "You going to throw up again?"

"I don't know."

Sherri stubbed out her cigarette and ran for the bucket in the maintenance closet in the hall, where Diane had left it to dry after washing it out from the last time. She set it by the bed, then she felt the washcloth, which had heated up, and carried it over to the sink and wrung it out in cold water. She seemed to share this belief in the efficacy of the washcloth. She and Keri had been faithful and firm about keeping it on Mary's forehead. What with Mary's virus and Sherri's grades and some kind of snit Diane was in about Bob, the girls had been spending more time together and it hadn't been so bad, really. Okay, Mary admitted, they were taking the opportunity to hide out in their room, to not go forth in the various ways that demanded bravery of them, or at least fortitude. They were eating chicken soup made on a hot plate, and popcorn, and Cheez-it crackers, and tortilla chips with salsa. They were doing their hair and their nails and their laundry. They were turning down dates. Mary had even told Hassan not to come see her—he could give the stuffed grape leaves to somebody in married student housing made for her to Keri.

> Why does Mary view the roommates' present situation as positive or at least as not so bad?

> Have you ever shared a room with someone? What do you remember about the experience?

Keri had turned into the mom, and that was okay, too. She made the soup and the popcorn, picked dishes off the floor and washed them, took Mary's temperature, called Student Health for advice, set the example of how to huddle in close quarters by keeping her bed made and her clothes folded and put away. She had bought the mineral water. Soon she would be back with the Tylenol. The cocoon was warm and comfortable and private. Outside it was chilly and gray. Mary closed her eyes.

Sherri went over to the window and lit another cigarette. She held it out as far as she could, but it was starting to rain. She bent down and put her nose to the crack of the open window. The moist, cold air felt good on her hot cheeks, but she didn't want to go out into it. She didn't want to do anything but smoke and sit around. That was her problem.

She could see that Mary was falling asleep. It would be a perfect time to go over to her desk and at least read her English assignment, a relatively painless activity compared to the others. But she couldn't move, except to bend down from time to time and feel the outer chill. She knew this sloth was a sin, a sin to match all the others she had committed since coming to school—lust (she had slept with three different near-strangers, one of them twice), gluttony (she had gained at least five pounds going out for pizza after supper), covetousness (one of the guys she had slept with was going with a girl from her high school, and she'd only gotten interested in him because Doreen had always dated the cutest guys and made a big deal of it, which pissed her off), anger (every time her mother called), envy (she kept it quiet, but it circulated—Keri could eat anything, Mary had great clothes, Diane, at least until lately, had fallen into this great sex thing), and pride. Well, pride. Pride was what kept you from admitting you had any problems, even when everybody knew you did.

Where do you think Sherri's inability to work comes from?

The thing was, whether or not virtue was in fact its own reward, it did seem like sin was its own punishment.

It wasn't as if she didn't think about changing her ways. She did. But the thoughts came to her idly, without conviction. Just as now she thought idly about reading her English assignment, she often thought idly about stopping smoking, which she had, in fact, just started, and didn't like all that much, she thought idly about going to classes, she thought idly about going to the library, she thought idly about going to her computer station and accessing her geology problems. She thought idly about not taking two desserts when she went through the dinner line. The food in Dubuque House was good—everyone helped cook and one of the rewards of multiculturalism was a spicy and delicious diet. The thing was, she had let down completely. The thing was, every thought of her family served to show her a way to let down even further than she had suspected was possible. It seemed like every brick wall that she ran into, that was supposed to hurt her enough to shake her up and give her some conviction, just turned into a door and she passed through it into deeper inertia. She stubbed out her cigarette and lay back limply on Diane's bed.

Does attending college ever affect only the individual? What other people does it affect?

The thing was, one day last week when she'd gotten to her English class, the teacher and some of the students who always sat in the front row were laughing about a memo the teacher (whose name Sherri still wasn't quite sure of) had gotten in which the students were called "customers." Now it was true that Sherri had come in late, and also true that she owed the teacher two papers, so she hadn't wanted to attract the woman's attention any more than necessary, but she'd found the laughter confusing at first, then aggravating. When the teacher tried to widen the discussion by asking what the others thought about the difference between "students" and "customers," Sherri had maintained the same appearance of benign ignorance and noncommittal good will that the other freshmen had, but that didn't mean that she didn't have an opinion. In fact, they all had the same opinion, which they expressed to one another after class—if they were paying all this money, then they must be customers, and if they were customers, then why was that particular English teacher so bo-o-o-ring? Factory reject? Candidate for manufacturer's recall? Obsolete model? Was the total tedium of their class due to mechanical failure or pilot error? Well, it had made them all laugh afterward in the hall outside of class. But now, limp on her bed, Sherri decided it wasn't funny. The fact was, she wasn't getting what she was paying for, which was—what? She couldn't define it, exactly. But she knew this limp, irritable feeling well enough. It was the sensation of consumer dissatisfaction, and it was sooooo annoying.

Do you buy into the "customer" argument? What do you "purchase" when you pay tuition?

The sound of Mary rustlings arid gagging roused her. She jumped up and ran across the room, managing to catch the washcloth before it fell into the bucket. She held Mary's forehead and patted her back and tried not to look at the bucket.

Final Reflection

How have you changed since coming to your college or university?

At first, I hated talking in class, but when I got interested I couldn't stop.
—Steve King

❖ *After You Read, Consider*

1. Do you agree that students should be treated as customers? What would the contract between "buyer" and "seller" contain? What kinds of consumer rights and privileges would students have?

2. If students were treated as customers, how might the educational system change? How might students change?

3. How does a specific professor or particular subject affect your assessment of whether the time spent in class is exhilarating or boring?

Writing draft after draft after draft after draft (OK, I'm exaggerating) was very frustrating until I began to see how my ideas changed for the better.
—A. Mehenson

❖ Suggestions for Writing

1. Evaluate the marketing plans used to attract students to various institutions in your area. Based on your evaluation, construct a profile of the type of student who might choose to attend these institutions.

2. Rewrite the final three paragraphs of the chapter to incorporate a response by Sherri to her English teacher's question. Then explain your revision by answering the question yourself.

3. Using examples from your present educational experience, illustrate how students are viewed in your institution. How do professors "read" students?

Harold Rosen

Comrade Rosie Rosen

Harold Rosen is an Emeritus Professor in the Department of English, Media and Drama at the Institute of Education, University of London. He is the author of Language and Class *(1986) and* Stories and Meanings *(1988), has coauthored several books, and has also published many papers and articles on English teaching and language in education. His current interest is the role of narrative in education, and he volunteers as a storyteller in schools.*

I hated writing in my journal. I never managed to like it, but I did find a lot of ideas in there for my papers.

—Mike Thompson

Prereading Reflection

Write about a time when a parent or adult figure fought for your rights.

I was eleven, sitting on a hard chair, looking at the man across the desk. He looked weary, perhaps even cross. My mother was sitting on a chair next to me. She too was looking across the desk at the man. I thought I could detect the glint of battle in her eye, but the man hadn't noticed. He wasn't looking at either of us but down at the buff-coloured folder which he frowned at while he was opening it.

Think back to a time when you felt that you were somewhere you weren't wanted. Where did you find the courage to stay?

We had ended up in this room after crossing Westminster Bridge. From the north side you gaze across the river at County Hall. I had seen it from there several times—a very important building, very governmental, solid, expensive, closed. I had never wondered what went on in it. I don't think I knew that they governed London from there and I certainly didn't know that somewhere in there they governed my education. As we crossed the bridge County Hall expanded, spreading its long facade right along the South Bank of the river. There seemed to be no way into its white coldness. How did anybody get in? Was there a special side door for nobodies? This was not going to be easy. But my mother was not touched by doubt. I could tell by her walk and the hold of her head. She led me round to the back without hesitation. Had she been here before? We went up wide steps into a high entrance hall. Uniformed men asked her business and one gave her directions like a policeman. We trekked up wide staircases into a labyrinth of expensive wood, along paneled corridors, our shoes clacking on polished parquet. We were, I felt sure, in enemy territory. County Hall men and women passed us about their business, intent, silent. I found them sinister.

My mother found the room we wanted. Its ordinariness came as a surprise—drab walls, well-worn lino, a few stacks of files on the floor, books and pamphlets leaning crazily on a set of shelves. A tray of papers on the desk was overspilling a little. I would have liked to be away from there, back on my side of the river, walking freely along the Embankment, taking in boats, bridges, public gardens and saunterers.

The man across the desk looked up and gazed at my mother without saying a word. Teachers do that, I thought. It's how they get on top of you from the word go. My mother wore for the occasion her best black gloves, a newish grey hat and a fox fur. Gloves, hat, fur—she was putting on the style. The man began talking in a rusty voice, affecting infinite patience and civility, cultivated in dealing with the lower orders, especially those from the East End. I heard heavy condescension and controlled insolence. I worried desperately. My scholarship to the grammar school was at stake.

—Before I hear what you have to say, Mrs. Rosen, and I shall do, rest assured, you simply must understand I have noted all the details. I have read your letter most carefully. I see from the form you've filled out that you and your husband became U.S. citizens in 1913. I am very sorry to tell you that makes the boy an alien. You won't have read the regulations, of course. Oh, so sorry, you have? Well, they are very clear, aren't they? We are obliged to see that all conditions are met before we can . . . .

—Just a minute, just a minute. No one has asked me about what happened to my citizenship after I came back to England in 1922. You certainly haven't, have you? I reclaimed my British citizenship in 1924 after they changed the law. There's quite a few things which concern this scholarship which I've not been asked about.

—Mrs. Rosen, we have checked the details very thoroughly.

—You haven't got all the details so how can you have checked them?

> Rosen's mother has the necessary information to support her position. How has being prepared helped you in the past?

At this point she took out of her bag a little sheaf of papers. I marveled at her composure. The deskman made an attempt to speak but my mother, certain she had the initiative, cut him off.

—No, no. Don't rush me. Are you in a hurry? Let's go through these papers one by one. And you should know that my local councillor, Mr. Silver, will be coming to see you and my MP, Mr. John Scurr, tells me he'll be writing to you.

> Why is the official's attitude changing? How does Rosen's mother force him to see her differently?

The official's manner was changing. Not that he became affable, but he was no longer dismissive and patronising. I had by now shed all my discomfort and sat revelling in my mother's aplomb. I was sure I'd get that scholarship.

I had heard my mother confronting officialdom before—across desks and counters and on our own doorstep. I loved the ways in which she could hold her own with the best of them, just as I winced when I heard nervous old folk struggling for English words to cope with men and their pens and papers and well-timed ways of looking over the tops of their glasses. I admit fully that I thought my mother was something special for all sorts of reasons, some of which don't look very good now. Yes, I know too that mothers are special to their children who are loved by them, defended by them and who are always there. But that's not what I mean at all. I was, I suppose, what I can only call a mother snob, inflated ridiculously by all the ways in which she was different from the Jewish mums who surrounded me. First of all she was born in England, right there in Stepney, not in Minsk, Vilna or Odessa. It followed that she'd been to school in England and after getting a job as a cashier in a large grocer's shop in Aldgate she took extra classes at the People's Palace so she spoke Real English. In the family it sounded

> Rosen is proud both that his mother differs from and resembles others of her ethnic heritage. How does he reconcile this tension? How do you reconcile this kind of tension in your own life.

Jewish. After all, you can't speak of Passover, a barmitzvah, how to make cheese blintzes without throwing in a few Yiddish and Hebrew words and phrases and even direct translations from Yiddish. But my mother could drop all that very easily and posh up her English when the occasion demanded it. When she sometimes overdid it and made her lips look different my pride went sour on me. Usually I took great pleasure in her sounding so English, believing that it was mostly this which gave her the confidence to cross the frontiers of the ghetto to go to theatres and meetings and to take us on trips into the country. I was pleased she didn't speak to me in Yiddish and I indecently discarded it totally as soon as I could. To me her English made her a cut above, several cuts.

At eight I knew she was the cleverest woman in the world. If not in the world then at least between Gardiner's Corner and Burdett Road. I knew, too, that she'd read millions of books—Whitechapel Library was one of her haunts. She had quite a few old books on the shelves of a small battered bookcase in her bedroom, bought, I suppose, for pence from market stalls or in fundraising bazaars. Once I could read I used to puzzle over the titles. So many of them seemed perversely opaque—*Hypatia, Quo Vadis, Pygmalion, Erewhon, Anti-Dubring, The Ragged Trousered Philanthropists* and *King of the Schnorrers*. I had gradually come to the conclusion that she knew every word in the English language. I used to sit on the floor and read when she was in bed in the morning. Once I was struggling through *Robinson Crusoe* because someone had given it to me as a birthday present and because it was brand new with a brilliant red cover, in the middle of which was pasted a picture of Robinson himself bare foot and thatched all over. But inside the print was too small, the black and white illustrations murky and the language elusive. The compensation was that if there was a word I couldn't understand I'd ask my encyclopaedic mother.

—Mum, what's an ague? (I pronounced it to rhyme with plague.)
—A what? Something wrong there. Read the sentence out to me.
—'I was stricken with an ague'.
—Ah, I see, you should say ay-gue. It means a fever.

I was seven. I was sitting for the umpteenth time in a large seedy room in Cable Street. A crowd of men and women were sitting on an assortment of battered old chairs under a blue-grey swirl of reeking cigarette and pipe smoke. Against one flaking wall was propped the red banner with a yellow hammer and sickle in the middle of it. Down one end Milly was making lemon tea on an old black stove and serving portions of cheesecake. I was reading *Film Fun* and getting impatient for my mother to get me some of that cheesecake. These were The Comrades at a meeting of The Party in what were always called The Premises. That evening we'd struggled through the damp of Cable Street, across the puddles of the smelly yard and joined The Comrades.

I knew in a half-truculent way that there was not going to be much in this for me. From time to time I looked up from my comic and tried to listen to the very serious men and women. Not easy. Each speaker took a long time and there

Were you ever at an important "adult" meeting that you could not understand? Do you now understand what the meeting was about? How did this happen?

was very little I could understand. Out there, nobody else talked like this, pointing didactic fingers and punching the air. I knew some of them very well for they often came to the house to deliver "literature" (I had trouble with that word for a long time). When they did, they talked like everyone else—mostly. A few of them gave me their time and joked and told me stories and one of them sang Yiddish songs. Tobias, whom I had heard speaking like an avenging angel, gave me a copy of William Morris's *News from Nowhere* and wrote in it, "The fault, dear Brutus, lies not in our stars but in ourselves that we are underlings." I couldn't make much of that at the time. Keep it till later, he had said. One day he arrived with a cardboard box full of volumes of an out-of-date encyclopaedia—I think it was Harmsworth's. Volume Seven was missing but we sat together looking at the pictures and he kept up an instructive patter.

> Have you ever reread something that you didn't understand as a child but did as an adult? What specifically caused the change besides maturity?

—You'll see. Some day this will help you with your studies. It's all in here.

They were shoved higgledy-piggledy in the cupboard on the landing outside my bedroom and I often pulled out a volume and turned the pages. I liked Tobias, even when he was orating at The Premises. This evening as usual the argot which so bewitched them was rolling out. They spoke of the dictatorship of the proletariat, surplus value, the balance of class forces, the crimes of the bourgeoisie. There were dark denunciations of class traitors and deviationists. My mother could speak this language, too. She was at a table at the front of the meeting as Branch Secretary with four other Comrades. After the meeting, long after I had finished my cheesecake and some lemonade, she stayed behind to plan leafleting, a poster parade, canvassing—activities which I'd sometimes be drawn into and be given a placard to hold or a tin to shake. Before The Comrades left The Premises they stopped to take some pamphlets from the piles on the trestle table. My mother took some too. They were as baffling to me as the speeches. They were called things like "The Final Crisis of Capitalism," "The Ninth Plenum of the Comintern," "The Soviet Path to Peace." I used to look for the ones with pictures. There were always pictures of men in jail—The Twelve Class War Prisoners (in England), The Meerut Prisoners (in India), Tom Mooney (in the U.S.), marchers with slogan banners, strikers outside their factories and confrontations with police. They became the dominant icons of my childhood and my mother was in the thick of all this. Look at her speaking and them listening. What a woman!

My friends' mothers were not like that, loveable though I found them, plumply installed in their kitchens with their magic recipes, overflowing with affection. They were always good to me, stroked my

Have you ever been "schlepped" to places that seemed peculiar to your friends? How did the experience affect you?

hair and found me noshy tit-bits. They clearly thought *life* must be hard for a little boy whose mother was always schlepping him to meetings. All the same, if there was trouble with a landlord they were round to our house like a shot.

Final Reflection

The author shares his pride in his mother. Clearly, she is different from other mothers he knows. Do you suppose her differences ever caused him emotions other than pride? Why?

I liked hearing what other people thought about the readings.

—Susan Mikolos

❖ *After You Read, Consider*

1. Rosen's mother is able to adjust her language to her situation. How do that skill and her choice of reading assist her and her son?

2. The author speaks first of a time when he was eleven, and then a time when he was eight, and finally a time when he was seven. How might presenting the information this way confuse the reader?

3. Rosen's mother is a member of the Communist party. How does your perception of what communism is or who a communist is affect how you read this essay?

I don't know if I'll ever be able to finish a paper. Everytime I thought I was done, I thought of something else.

—Katie Morrison

❖ *Suggestions for Writing*

1. Compare a member of your family with a member of another family you know well. Rather than just telling what is different about them, write about why they are different and how their difference affects your life.

2. Rosen makes a point of telling us that his mother is different from the "Jewish mums" even though she is from the East End. Rosen's mother, because she was born in London and had some education,

could "posh up" her speech, forcing bored bureaucrats to pay attention to her concerns. Think of a time when a social difference made your life more difficult or made it hard for you to solve a problem. Analyze how labels may impact how an individual is viewed by society.

3. Write a narrative about a time when you were proud of a family member. How did this family member's actions change your perspective on your relationship with your school, neighborhood, work, or the rest of your family?

John McPherson

Close to Home

John McPherson is the cartoonist and creator of the syndicated cartoon panel Close to Home, *which appears daily in seven hundred newspapers worldwide, including* The Washington Post, The Los Angeles Times, The Houston Chronicle, *and* The Tokyo Times. *McPherson has published ten collections of his* Close to Home *cartoons and illustrated the children's book* The Barber of Bingo (1997). *Before becoming syndicated, McPherson worked as a freelance cartoonist for seven years.*

❖

Prereading Reflection

Write about a time you entered a new culture without knowing the rules that governed it.

Freshman Lisa Dubner hadn't caught on to the fact that most college classes are held every other day.

When you are a new member of a class, do you feel comfortable asking questions or seeking clarification from a student or teacher?

17

After awhile, my journal helped me focus my ideas.

—Jennifer Ayers

The size of some university libraries can be pretty intimidating to first-year students.

Libraries are resources for your education. What, if anything, about a library intimidates you? Librarians often say, "We are here to help you; just ask." Have you ever asked for help in a library? What happened?

Reflections should be like mirrors of what you are thinking.

—Jennifer Ayers

Final Reflection

Refer back to your prereading reflection. What lesson proved most useful in allowing you to successfully navigate through your new experience?

Class discussion gave me a chance to hear what other people were thinking.

—Tim Morgan

❖ *After You Read, Consider*

1. What unwritten rules have you discovered since coming to your college or university?

2. When you begin a new class, what are you most concerned about? How do you work through that concern?

3. Learning the layout of a library is time-consuming, as is learning how to search out material. How do you schedule your time when planning initial research sessions in a new library?

❖ *Suggestions for Writing*

1. Write a humorous essay focusing on a school experience (for example, registering for classes, applying for financial aid, eating cafeteria food, offering up excuses for missing class).

2. Create a pamphlet for new students at your institution. Prior to formalizing your advice, collect information from a variety of students.

3. Write a letter to your institution's president, director of admissions, financial aid representative, or cadre of advisors that offers insight into some of the questions left unasked by new students enrolling in your school.

Johnny Connors

The Man That Spelt "Knife" Was a Fool

Johnny Connors grew up an Irish gypsy, one of the thousands who still travel about the outskirts of European society in covered wagons. Like the children of many U.S. agricultural workers who must follow the harvests, gypsy children often are unable to attend school for very long. Connors's struggle to read and write took him from classrooms to rubbish dumps. He eventually did learn to read and write, and his story appears in the book Gypsies *by Jeremy Sanford (1972).*

I liked being able to write before I read. It was like a warm-up really.
— Margaret Montgomery

Prereading Reflection

Based on the title, what do you predict that this essay will be about?

About four weeks had passed and I could write my name JOHN.
And nearly every minute during the day I would be saying, "ZABQAZXOUWZ. ACB792Y14MN2Q," and so on.
I would sing it all day, "ABCDEFGHIJKLMNOPQRSTUVWXYZ."
Six weeks had passed and I could tell the time of the clock myself.
That was six weeks at night-school. Then the Nun asked me, would I like to go to a real classroom with little girls, because it was a girls' school. I said I would, so the next day for the first time in my life I was in a classroom. When the girls of the class saw me I could hear them whispering to one another; "He is a gyppo."
I was nearly mad. I shouted, "Ah, shut up your big mouths." I know it was wrong of me to treat young ladies that way, but they had started it.

After a while that day I got settled down to the class. And then I asked the teacher, "Could I go to the toilet?"

"Yes, John, go right ahead out to the yard."

I went into the toilet and I bolted one of the doors, and two girls came in. It was a girls' toilet I was in.

"Hurry on, Mary, and pull your bloomers up when you leave."

I made a burst for the door and my trousers tripped me up. I ran out the gate of the school. As I was going out I met the Reverend Mother.

"What's wrong, John?" said the Reverend Mother.

"Those girls followed me into the toilet, the dirty things. They should be ashamed of themselves." I could see a smile on the Reverend Mother's face.

"You go back to your class, John, and I will sort it all out."

> Can you think of a time when you were ashamed? How did this shame feel? Did you fight back?

I was ashamed of my life. Then it was playtime and the girls came to like me. I would skip with them, play ball with them. They became great pals of mine. The big bully girls were afraid of me, because when the big bully girls would bully the little girls I would stop them.

There was one big girl: I christened her Young Elephant. She was a very fat girl and she would bump into the little girls and the little girls would fall flat on their faces. So one day she was bullying all the other little girls. "Hold on there, you overgrown young elephant, don't be pushing any of the little girls." So from that day onwards she never pushed any of the little girls, and if she tried to the little girls would say, "I will get John to call you more names."

I really enjoyed being at school. But the police and corporation gave my Daddy three days' notice and I had to leave school.

> Have you ever moved during a school year? What problems resulted?

That night when I came back to the wagon, my Daddy said, "Johnny, tomorrow is your last day at school."

"What?" I said, "I am not going to stop going to school."

"Well, if you don't you will have to follow the wagons a very long road."

"Why?" I said.

"Because we are being shifted on Saturday."

I could not sleep that night, I was fed up.

The next morning I went to school, and I told the teacher that this was my last day at school. She was very upset.

"Why must you stop going to school, John?" said the teacher.

"Because we are getting shifted."

"Oh, I am sorry to hear that, John."

At playtime all the girls gathered round me, "Please don't leave, John."

Some of them was crying.

That evening I was forced to say good luck to all.

I was a very happy little boy and I wanted to go to school and I would not be able to go to school. So I said to myself, "I will learn myself how to read proper." Every sweet-paper with writing on it I would collect them all day. Tea bags, sugar bags and butter wrappers. I would stay at shop windows reading everything that was in the windows. And big words like "Palmolive," I would split them up, Pal-mo-live. And "Corporation," Cor-por-ation. The only words that had me beat were medical words. "Physician" was a killer. I did really lose my temper with that word PHYSICIAN. What really was making me angry was that words like PHYSICIAN, LAMB or KNIFE had silent letter words, and I would say to myself the man that spelt KNIFE was a fool.

Have you ever wanted to learn a skill this much?

When I would be sent to the shops on errands, I would be hours reading everything in the shop. My Mammy often told me to get Lyons' tea. Instead I would get some other strange brand of tea so as I could read the strange words on the packet. Because I knew every word on the Lyons' tea packet.

Can you think of times in your life when being able to read was a matter of survival?

The same way when my Daddy would send me for cigarettes. He would say to me, "Make sure you get Woodbines," and I would say, "Maybe they have no Woodbines, what kind will I get if they have no Woodbines?" My Daddy would say, "Get any kind." I would get the strangest packet of cigarettes the shop had in stock so as I could read the writing on the packet. And if I was beaten at a word, I would go back into the shop and ask the person in the shop what the word meant. There were times people got angry with me over me asking so many questions. And they would simply say, "Buzz off, you are a nuisance." Sweets with strange wrappings was the sweets I liked very much, even if they were horrible sweets. I don't think I ever enjoyed a sweet in them times, because I was not interested in the sweets, the wrapping was what I got more enjoyment out of. In other words, strange things were more helpful to me.

Also milestones, finger-posts, and most of all the rubbish-dumps were my teacher. When I would see a dump I would rather collect the old newspapers, comics and books out of the dump than go to the movies. Furthermore, I had

How did "the hard way" that Connors learned to read make what he learned different from what he would have learned in school?

been locked up on many occasions by the police and convicted for taking old books and papers and educational articles of my own choosing from dumps. So you could say I paid the hard way for the little bit of knowledge I have.

> *I never had to think so much when I was reading.*
> —S. Patrowski

Final Reflection

Why was learning to read so important to Connors? What did he hope to gain with this ability?

> *I thought if you asked "why" during class discussion one more time, I was going to scream. Sorry.*
> —Maryanne Ellison

❖ *After You Read, Consider*

1. Does Connors's writing style enhance or inhibit your ability to understand this piece? How does his writing style help you understand how he learned to read?

2. Discuss the importance of reading or ponder the message of this essay.

3. Referring back to your reflection, did this story hold any surprises for you?

> *Each time I write, I feel a little lighter.*
> —Allen Steerman

❖ *Suggestions for Writing*

1. Consider a time when you wanted to stay in a place but had to leave. When writing about that experience, explore how the move affected your education. Did you find it easier or harder to learn after you moved? Were there some things you learned because of the experience of moving? Some educational experiences you may have lost?

2. Do parents have a responsibility to provide the means for their children to secure an adequate education? How do parents make decisions about whether an education is adequate?

3. Compare Connors's formal educational experience with another writer's educational experience that you've read about in this text or another text. How did the writers' educational experiences shape the lives they had as adults? Their choice of careers? Where they lived?

Katherine Grigg

Frustration

Katherine Grigg was born and raised in Orlando, Florida. She received her BA in English and is currently working on her MA in Creative Writing at the University of Central Florida. Her goal after graduating is to write the next best-seller and become fabulously wealthy. Aside from that, she plans to pursue teaching and editorial work.

Prereading Reflection

Reflect and write about what the process of writing is like for you. Don't spend too much time narrating how you write. Rather, write about how you feel when you write.

Syllables spaz on the page,
bouncing from margin to margin
like a hyper-caffeinated pinball. I try to
grasp the slippery globes, only to
have them arc out of reach
just as my fingers
brush their blackened edges.
Thwarted, I go to the closet and pull out
my favorite box of letters (all polished
and shiny for just such an occasion) I
open the box and deeply inhale the
articulate aroma, stroke the
curves, flick the jutting tips, then
pick up the careful stacks and scatter
them in front of
me, moving, shuf-
fling, shifting, until I paste
a phrase together. The lone sentence
struggles erect, momentarily, then

Why is the energy of language so frustrating for this writer?

List all the verbs the writer uses to describe the act of writing. Make another list that describes how these words make you feel.

collapses on the page,
laboring for a nourishing
breath. I try
again, praying for a Red Sea-parting
epiphany of life-altering words to appear,
but I get only brine, and the syllabic stick
vanishes with a whiff of fishy air.
Now I conjure
an ominous pocked cauldron, crack my
knuckles, and direct all God-power to
my fingertips. The sky
blackens, Muses wail, my skull glows
with effort, when
a single leaden dot thuds on the ground,
leaving only
a dent of drivel. Motherfu . . .
I empty my arsenal of expletives on the screen with
machine-gun ferocity and dance in the vicious blaze.

> What is different about the energy conveyed in the words at the end of this poem?

Sometimes I thought and rethought so much that I didn't know what I thought.

—Julie Barnett

Final Reflection

Is there anything about this writer's description of her writing process that mirrors yours? How is your writing process different from Grigg's?

❖ After You Read, Consider

1. The writer expresses great frustration, even anger, at what she perceives as an inability to write what she wants to say. But, in fact, she is quite articulate in describing her frustration and anger. What do you make of this contradiction?

2. Where does the writer's reference "Red Sea-parting" come from? Where and when did you learn this? How would you explain this reference to someone who had never heard it before?

3. At one point the writer mentions a "box of letters." She is talking about alphabet letters from which she wants to form words and sentences, but what if she also meant a box of correspondence she had

written or received from others. How could reading old letters help someone to write?

I like being able to connect how I think with what I'm writing about.
—Anne Klein

❖ *Suggestions for Writing*

1. Think of all the different things you have written: shopping lists, thank you notes, letters, school assignments, lab reports, memos, research papers. Are some harder to write than others? Why? Does the writing format or the person you are writing to make the writing more or less difficult? Write an essay in which you consider different writing projects you have completed. Discuss why some were more enjoyable to write than others and why some gave you more satisfaction as a writer.

2. Write a poem about writing. Describe how it feels to write. Then discuss those feelings in an essay and tell your readers why you chose certain words or arranged your lines in a particular way.

Tiffany Gay

Sugar, Spice, and Everything Nice

> *Tiffany Gay, a senior at Armstrong Atlantic State University, is native to Savannah, Georgia. She is pursuing a degree in English with Teacher Certification. She hopes to teach middle grades or high school English. She is an avid reader and writer and also sings in a local group.*

> I liked writing in my journal and taking notes. It was a lot like doodling. I just didn't like to have to put my ideas into essays.
>
> —Kate Fellow-Smith

Prereading Reflection

Write about a specific event, gift, expectation, or reaction that helped define the role you fill within your family.

From birth, female children are forced into confining roles. The girls are swathed in pink blankets, frills and dolls. Even our nursery rhymes present females as subservient and helpless. The beautiful, incapable female is presented to us forever waiting to marry her "Prince Charming" or crying out for her "Knight in Shining Armor" to rescue her. Just what are little girls made of? Girls are drenched in the stereotype that girls are just what the old adage says, *sugar, spice, and everything nice*. When a young girl does something deemed improper by social construct, they are slapped with the age old statement that good girls don't do those types of things. Adrienne Rich argues in *When We Dead Awaken: Writing as Re-Vision* that "Re-Vision—the act of looking back, of seeing with fresh eyes, of entering an old text from a new critical direction—is for women more than a chapter in cultural history: it is an act of survival.

Do you believe the "knight in shining armor" myth is still perpetuated? Why or why not?

Until we can understand the assumptions in which we are drenched we cannot know ourselves" (35). Rich calls for women to examine the culture in which they are confined. Women must challenge the roles constructed by the patriarchal society in which they live. Rich challenges women to look at "how our language has trapped as well as liberated us, how the very act of naming has been till now a male prerogative, and how we can begin to see and name—and therefore live—afresh" (35). We must make a way for females to break out of the stereotypical roles that are attached to their gender. We must challenge women to be their own person—strong and independent.

From childhood, I was aware of the roles that I was expected to fill. As I grew, the stereotypes that pervade our culture became more and more apparent to me. I could see the passive roles that society had prepared for me to fill. My parents expected me to do well in school, go to college, get a job, get married, and have children. My husband's role would be to act as the provider for our family and head of the household. My dreams of going to graduate school to pursue a Masters and ultimately a doctorate were not taken seriously by family or my fiance until just recently. It wasn't until recently that I truly examined my position in life and realized that I needed to make changes. Adrienne Rich writes, "I have hesitated to do what I am going to do now, which is to use myself as an illustration. For one thing, it's a lot easier and less dangerous to talk about others . . . " (38). Rich's piece challenged me to examine my life and the female roles I was passively submitting to.

What stereotypical roles assigned to women do you recognize?

Up until a week ago, I was engaged to be married. My destiny was to fill the stereotypical mold of wife, mother, and teacher, following in the footsteps of my older sister. However, deep inside I knew that I was denying longings that were central to who I am. I have always longed to pursue a doctoral degree in Southern Literature and to teach college. This thirst for knowledge was such an integral part of my identity, but it was being suppressed by the roles I was expected to fill. The idea of being a wife at twenty-one brought me no joy. The man I was betrothed to marry was a suitable mate for me. He was a hard worker, a Christian, and a friend of my family. However, the differences in our intellects and his lack of ambition denied my heart, my soul, and my mind a feeling that I longed for. I always pictured myself married to a man who had the same academic ambitions as myself. I pictured myself marrying an intellectual equal, but I truly felt that I would be ostracized by family and friends if I broke off this engagement. Planning had begun and the

What do you believe would have happened to the author or her intended spouse had she decided to marry?

engagement had already been announced. Yet, deep in my soul I knew that I could not marry this man. He neither stimulated me intellectually nor emotionally. For some time I felt as Rich describes it, that my conflict was a "failure of love in myself" (42).

Ultimately, I realized that my lack of enthusiasm about filling the traditional female role was not a failure on my part, but a triumph. For the first time in my life, I realized that I could revise the roles that I had been expected to fill. While I may one day choose to be a wife and mother, there are other pursuits and dreams I have yet to pursue. I came to the realization that I could challenge the stereotypical role of the woman. I decided that I would not be the woman Rich describes in her poem "The Loser." I affirmed that I will not have my imagination and beauty "chafed ... into use" (41). A woman should not have to deny her passions—intellectual or otherwise. I would not fill the subservient, needy role that I was doomed to fill: "But to be a female human being trying to fulfill traditional female functions in a traditional way is in direct conflict with the subversive function of the imagination" (42). I chose not to fulfill the role of wife in a relationship with a partner who neither encouraged nor understood my need for academic pursuit. I was unwilling to let my true self be mired down in traditional female roles that I did not wish to fill.

> What are some traditions that might bind you to a specific role or course of action?

> Have you ever read anything that changed the way you think about yourself and your relationships?

While my decision may not have been totally driven by an assertion of my womanhood, it did give me a new found perspective on the roles of women in our society. As Rich argues, women need "not to pass on a tradition but to break its hold over us" (35). Women need to redefine the patriarchal society that surrounds them. Women need to challenge the language that confines us. Women are constantly suffering from the sickness of the double standard that pervades our society. This standard is apparent from the highest elevation of our social construct to the lowest derogatory terms used in our society. If a woman indulges passion, she is a slut. If a man indulges passion, he is a stud. It is the age old stereotype that plagues the female race. Even the few derogatory terms that are applied most exclusively to men are demeaning to women. The obscenities "son of a bitch" and "bastard" are ultimately offensive to the mother of the one to which it is directed. Even the most derogatory terms I could conjure for men, ultimately defame the mother not the man. Our society is flooded with

> Has your gender affected your choice of career? Do you think your educational experiences are different because you are male or female?

female stereotypes. From children's stories and nursery rhymes to the "encouraging" of female students toward certain subjects, the traditional female roles are reinforced on a daily basis in our society.

The reinforcement of traditional female roles is carried out on a daily basis in our educational systems. Young girls are encouraged to play with dolls while young boys are encouraged to play cops and robbers. Courses in our high schools such as home ec and childcare are dominated by female students. The reinforcement of female stereotypes became even more apparent to me while participating in a practicuum for an education class. The Eleventh grade high school English class, which I was observing, was reviewing Emily Dickinson's "Heart! We Will Forget Him." During the class discussion, a young man called out that this was nothing but girl poetry. The feelings of loss and longing and love are not gender specific. Yet, the sentimental expression of these feelings is viewed as female. This point became even more poignant to me while doing an oral report on Kate Chopin's *The Storm* in my American Literature class in college. Chopin's short story was deemed a *Harlequin* romance by a male reader in the class due to its true depiction of a female's realization of long awaited passion. *Harlequin* or true to the female experience?

What would happen if females began to completely redefine what is female? What would happen in our patriarchal society if "slut" now become a positive descriptor for a woman? Women need to revise the role of the female in our society. Women are confined to gender roles that were largely perpetrated by a society of males. They are fulfilling roles deemed appropriate for them by men. Women need to assert their imagination and their power. Women need to break out of the role or subject of poetry and literature and become "luxury for man and . . . as the painter's model and the poet's muse" (35). In our society today it is becoming more and more apparent that the "creative energy of patriarchy is fast running out; what remains is its self-generating energy for destruction. As women we have our work cut out for us" (49).

> What would happen if traditional female roles changed? What would the world be like?

WORK CITED

Rich, Adrienne. "When We Dead Awaken: Writing As Re-vision." In *On Lies, Secrets, and Silence: Selected Prose 1966–1978*. New York: Norton, 1979.

Reflection is explaining your response. It makes you dig deeper. You can't just say anything.

—Maureen Meehan

Final Reflection

What are some stereotypes that accommodate the vision you have of yourself? Consider how you would feel if these conventions suddenly disappeared.

> *I really don't like that many people in the class seem to have nothing to say during class, but can't stop talking when I'm ready to go home.*
>
> —Steve Tilson

❖ After You Read, Consider

1. Does formal education guarantee intellectual equality? Can someone who lacks a formal education still be deemed an intellectual equal? Why or why not?

2. Can you recall a class in high school or college that worked to break through gender stereotypes?

3. What children's books or stories can you recall that work to sustain gender stereotypes?

> *OK, I KNOW this was a writing class, but don't you think we wrote way too much?*
>
> —Chris Peterson

❖ Suggestions for Writing

1. The author's voice throughout the piece remains strong and definitive. Analyze this essay in terms of word choice, language, organizational patterns, or other rhetorical strategies to determine whether the author's argument is effective.

2. Rewrite a fairy tale of your choice that reverses or modifies typical gender roles.

3. Visit a toy store to compare the toys sold and the marketing methods employed to attract sales. Then identify manufacturers who appear committed to breaking down gender stereotypes. Write an essay in which you analyze how toys support or break gender stereotypes.

Langston Hughes

Theme for English B

Langston Hughes was born in Joplin, Missouri, in 1902. When Langston was seven or eight he went to live with his grandmother, who told him wonderful stories about Frederick Douglass and Sojourner Truth and took him to hear Booker T. Washington. She also introduced him to The Crisis, edited by W. E. B. Du Bois, who wrote The Souls of Black Folk (1903), young Langston's favorite book. The sights and sounds of Harlem inspired him more than his classes in engineering and eventually he quit school. Hughes continued writing through the 1930s and the 1940s, speaking for the poor and homeless black people who suffered during the Great Depression. His work combines verse form with the rhythms of spirituals and blues.

I do need to say that writing in my journal got really really tedious. Sometimes I had nothing to say.

—Kevin McGuire

Prereading Reflection

Think about the essays you write for school. What audience are you writing for? How hard is it to write for readers you do not know personally?

The instructor said,

Go home and write
a page tonight.
And let that page come out of you—Then, it will be true.

Does this assignment sound difficult? What do you think the instructor wants? Is writing, even in answer to a simple question, ever simple?

I wonder if it's that simple?
I am twenty-two, colored, born in Winston-Salem.

I went to school there, then Durham, then here
to this college on the hill above Harlem.
I am the only colored student in my class.
The steps from the hill lead down into Harlem,   Why is Hughes giving
through a park, then I cross St. Nicholas,   us directions to his
Eighth Avenue, Seventh, and I come to the Y,   room? What is he
the Harlem Branch Y, where I take the elevator   trying to tell his
up to my room, sit down, and write this page: instructor?

It's not easy to know what is true for you or me
at twenty-two, my age. But I guess I'm what
I feel and see and hear, Harlem, I hear you:
hear you, hear me—we two—you, me, talk on this page.
(I hear New York, too.) Me—who?
Well, I like to eat, sleep, drink, and be in love.
I like to work, read, learn, and understand life.
I like a pipe for a Christmas present.
or records—Bessie, bop, or Bach.

I guess being colored doesn't make me *not* like
the same things other folks like who are other races.
So will my page be colored that I write?   The page is not colored, but
Being me, it will not be white.   still Hughes feels there is a
But it will be   difference in how his language
a part of you, instructor.   looks on the page. What is that
You are white—   difference?
yet a part of me, as I am a part of you.
That's American.
Sometimes perhaps you don't want to be a part of me.
Nor do I often want to be a part of you.
But we are, that's true!
As I learn from you,
I guess you learn from me—

Reflecting means thinking again and again about what you read or write.
—Brenda Woods

Final Reflection

How difficult is it to write about your feelings and experiences for an audience outside of your own culture?

❖ After You Read, Consider

1. Hughes is trying to make something happen with his poem, to reach his audience in some way. What do you think he wants us to learn?

2. Hughes writes, "It's not easy to know what is true for you or me," and yet that is the assignment he has been given: *"let that page come out of you— / Then, it will be true."* The instructor makes it sound easy and straightforward, but what do you think?

3. In the last line of his poem, Hughes claims that his instructor will learn from him. What does he expect his instructor to learn?

> *Oh, no, I used to think, not another paper assignment. I will admit that sometimes I did swear, but I always learned something.*
> —Peter M. Markman

❖ Suggestions for Writing

1. Hughes writes, "You are white— / yet a part of me, as I am part of you / That's American." How does Hughes define *American*? How do you define yourself as *American*? Write an essay in which you discuss how your definition works or doesn't work with Hughes's definition.

2. Is there a particular place that you think defines who you are? Describe the place and tell how it reflects you and your life.

3. Is part of Hughes's job as a student to let his teacher know who he is? Why is this important to Hughes? Do we learn from our teachers, or is education more like sharing ideas? Write an essay in which you explain why Hughes thinks he must teach his instructor about his culture.

Mike Rose

I Just Wanna Be Average

> Mike Rose grew up in Los Angeles in the 1950s in a poor neighborhood. Mistakenly placed in the vocational track in high school, "a dumping ground for the disaffected," Rose used his indifference as a defense against learning. Encouraged by his tough, caring biology teacher, Rose switched to the college prep track, graduated in 1966 from Loyola University, and earned a PhD in Education from the University of California at Los Angeles. Rose, now a professor at UCLA, directs the UCLA Writing Program. This excerpt from his book Lives on the Boundary (1989) tells the story of his struggles with education.

❖

Journal writing is the closest I have ever come to automatic writing.
—Anne Morgan

Prereading Reflection

Make a list of the courses you took in high school. Did any of them prepare you for work? What kind of work?

❖

My rhapsodic and prescientific astronomy carried me into my teens, consumed me right up till high school, losing out finally, and only, to the siren call of pubescence—that endocrine hoodoo that transmogrifies nice boys into gawky flesh fiends. My mother used to bring home *Confidential* magazine, a peep-show rag specializing in the sins of the stars, and it beckoned me mercilessly; Jayne Mansfield's cleavage, Gina Lollobrigida's eyes, innuendos about deviant sexuality, ads for Frederick's of Hollywood-spiked heels, lacy brassieres, the epiphany of silk panties on a mannequin's hips. Along with Phil Everly, I was through with counting the stars above.

Budding manhood. Only adults talk about adolescence budding. Kids have no choice but to talk in extremes; they're being wrenched and buffeted, rabbit-punched from inside by systemic thugs. Nothing sweet and pastoral here. Kids become ridiculous and touching at one and the same time: passionate about the trivial, fixed before the mirror, yet traversing one of the most important rites of passage in their lives—liminal people, silly and profoundly human. Given my own expertise, I fantasized about concocting the fail-safe aphrodisiac that would bring Marianne Bilpusch, the cloakroom monitor, rushing into my arms or about commanding a squadron of bosomy, linguistically mysterious astronauts like Zsa Zsa Gabor. My parents used to say that their son would have the best education they could afford. Maybe I would be a doctor. There was a public school in our neighborhood and several Catholic schools to the west. They had heard that quality schooling meant private, Catholic schooling, so they somehow got the money together to send me to Our Lady of Mercy, fifteen or 50 miles southwest of Ninety-first and Vermont. So much for my fantasies. Most Catholic secondary schools then were separated by gender.

> Why do some people forget what it was like to be young?

> Do you think you get different kinds of education from different schools? Why?

> Did you spend a lot of time traveling to school? What did you learn on your bus or car rides?

It took two buses to get to Our Lady of Mercy. The first started deep in South Los Angeles and caught me at midpoint. The second drifted through neighborhoods with trees, parks, big lawns, and lots of flowers. The rides were long but were livened up by a group of South L.A. veterans whose parents also thought that Hope had set up shop in the west end of the county. There was Christy Biggars, who, at sixteen, was dealing and was, according to rumor, a pimp as well. There were Bill Cobb and Johnny Gonzales, grease-pencil artists extraordinaire, who left Nembutal-enhanced swirls of "Cobb" and "Johnny" on the corrugated walls of the bus. And then there was Tyrrell Wilson. Tyrrell was the coolest kid I knew. He ran the dozens like a metric halfback, laid down a rap that outrhymed and outpointed Cobb, whose rap was good but not great—the curse of a moderately soulful kid trapped in white skin. But it was Cobb who would sneak a radio onto the bus, and thus underwrote his patter with Little Richard, Fats Domino, Chuck Berry, the Coasters, and Ernie K. Doe's mother-in-law, an awful woman who was "sent from down below." And so it was that Christy and Cobb and Johnny G. and Tyrrell and I and assorted others picked up along the way passed our days in the back of the bus, a funny mix brought together by geography and parental desire.

Entrance to school brings with it forms and releases and assessments. Mercy relied on a series of tests, mostly the Stanford Binet, for placement, and somehow the results of my tests got confused with those of another student named Rose. The other Rose apparently didn't do very well, for I was placed in the vocational track, a euphemism for the bottom level. Neither I nor my parents realized what this meant. We had no sense that Business Math, Typing, and English-Level D were dead ends. The current spate of reports on the schools criticizes parents for not involving themselves in the education of their children. But how would someone like Tommy Rose, with his two years of Italian schooling, know what to ask? And what sort of pressure could an exhausted waitress apply? The error went undetected, and I remained in the vocational track for two years. What a place.

Is vocational education a dead end as Rose claims?

My homeroom was supervised by Brother Dill, a troubled and unstable man who also taught freshman English. When his class drifted away from him, which was often, his voice would rise in paranoid accusations, and occasionally he would lose control and shake or smack us. I hadn't been there two months when one of his brisk, face-turning slaps had my glasses sliding down the aisle. Physical education was also pretty harsh. Our teacher was a stubby ex-lineman who had played old-time pro ball in the Midwest. He routinely had us grabbing our ankles to receive his stinging paddle across our butts. He did that, he said, to make men of us. "Rose," he bellowed on our first encounter; me standing geeky in line in my baggy shorts. " 'Rose'? What the hell kind of name is that?"

Did any of your teachers ever ridicule you? What did you learn from these encounters?

"Italian, sir," I squeaked.

"Italian! Ho. Rose, do you know the sound a bag of shit makes when it hits the wall?"

"No, sir."

"Wop!"

Sophomore English was taught by Mr. Mitropetros. He was a large, bejeweled man who managed the parking lot at the Shrine Auditorium. He would crow and preen and list for us the stars he'd brushed against. We'd ask questions and glance knowingly and snicker, and all that fueled the poor guy to brag some more. Parking cars was his night job. He had little training in English, so his lesson plan for his day work had us reading the district's required text, *Julius Caesar*, aloud for the semester. We'd finish the play way before the twenty weeks was up, so he'd

Why do you think the teacher didn't assign another play? What did the students learn from reading the play out loud in class?

have us switch parts again and again and start again: David Snyder, the fastest guy at Mercy, muscling through Caesar to the breathless squeals of Calpurnia, as interpreted by Steve Fusco, a surfer who owned the school's most envied paneled wagon. Week ten and Dave and Steve would take on new roles, as would we all, and render a water-logged Cassius and a Brutus that are beyond my powers of description.

Spanish I—taken in the second year—fell into the hands of a new recruit. Mr. Montez was a tiny man, slight, five foot six at the most, soft-spoken and delicate. Spanish was a particularly rowdy class, and Mr. Montez was as prepared for it as a doily maker at a hammer throw. He would tap his pencil to a room in which Steve Fusco was propelling spitballs from his heavy lips, in which Mike Dweetz was taunting Billy Hawk, a half-Indian, half-Spanish, reed-thin, quietly explosive boy. The vocational track at Our Lady of Mercy mixed kids traveling in from South L.A. with South Bay surfers and a few Slavs and Chicanos from the harbors of San Pedro. This was a dangerous miscellany: surfers and hodads and South-Central blacks all ablaze to the metronomic tapping of Hector Montez's pencil. One day Billy lost it. Out of the corner of my eye I saw him strike out with his right arm and catch Dweetz across the neck. Quick as a spasm, Dweetz was out of his seat, scattering desks, cracking Billy on the side of the head, right behind the eye. Snyder and Fusco and others broke it up, but the room felt hot and close and naked. Mr. Montez's tenuous authority was finally ripped to shreds, and I think everyone felt a little strange about that. The charade was over, and when it came down to it, I don't think any of the kids really wanted it to end this way, They had pushed and pushed and bullied their way into a freedom that both scared and embarrassed them.

Rose went to a very diverse school. How could the teachers have made this "dangerous miscellany" easier?

Students will float to the mark you set. I and the others in the vocational classes were bobbing in pretty shallow water. Vocational education has aimed at increasing the economic opportunities of students who do not do well in our schools. Some serious programs succeed in doing that, and through exceptional teachers—like Mr. Gross in *Horace's Compromise*—students learn to develop hypotheses and troubleshoot, reason through a problem, and communicate effectively—the true job skills. The vocational track, however, is most often a place for those who are just not making it, a dumping ground for the disaffected. There were a few teachers who worked hard at education; young Brother Slattery, for example, combined a stern voice with

Why does Rose refer to problem solving as a "true job skill"?

weekly quizzes to try to pass along to us a skeletal outline of world history. But mostly the teachers had no idea of how to engage the imaginations of us kids who were scuttling along at the bottom of the pond. And the teachers would have needed some inventiveness, for none of us was groomed for the classroom. It wasn't just that I didn't know things—didn't know how to simplify algebraic fractions, couldn't identify different kinds of clauses, bungled Spanish translations—but that I had developed various faulty and inadequate ways of doing algebra and making sense of Spanish. Worse yet, the years of defensive tuning out in elementary school had given me a way to escape quickly while seeming at least half alert. During my time in Voc. Ed., I developed further into a mediocre student and a somnambulant problem solver, and that affected the subjects I did have the wherewithal to handle: I detested Shakespeare; I got bored with history. My attention flitted here and there. I fooled around in class and read my books indifferently—the intellectual equivalent of playing with your food. I did what I had to do to get by, and I did it with half a mind.

> Why did Rose's course of study encourage mediocrity? Is that a goal of some kinds of education? Why?

But I did learn things about people and eventually came into my own socially. I liked the guys in Voc. Ed. Growing up where I did, I understood and admired physical prowess, and there was an abundance of muscle here. There was Dave Snyder, a sprinter and halfback of true quality. Dave's ability and his quick wit gave him a natural appeal, and he was welcome in any clique, though he always kept a little independent. He enjoyed acting the fool and could care less about studies, but he possessed a certain maturity and never caused the faculty much trouble. It was a testament to this independence that he included me among his friends—I eventually went out for track, but I was no jock. Owing to the Latin alphabet and a dearth of *R*s and *S*s, Snyder sat behind Rose, and we started exchanging one-liners and became friends.

> Why does Rose spend a lot of time describing all his friends to us? Why does he think it is important for us to know his friends?

There was Ted Richard, a much-touted Little League pitcher. He was chunky and had a baby face and came to Our Lady of Mercy as a seasoned street fighter. Ted was quick to laugh and he had a loud, jolly laugh, but when he got angry he'd smile a little smile, the kind that simply raises the corner of the mouth a quarter of an inch. For those who knew, it was an eerie signal. Those who didn't found themselves in big trouble, for Ted was very quick. He loved to carry on what we would come to call philosophical discussions: What is courage? Does God exist? He also loved words, enjoyed picking up big ones like *salubrious* and *equivocal* and using them in our conversations—laughing at himself as the word hit a chuckhole rolling off his tongue. Ted didn't do all that well in school—baseball and parties and testing the courage he'd speculated about took up his time. His textbooks were *Argosy* and *Field and Stream*, whatever newspapers he'd find on the bus stop—from the *Daily Worker* to pornography—conversations with uncles or hobos or businessmen he'd meet in a coffee shop, *The Old Man and the Sea*. With hindsight, I can see that Ted was developing into one of those rough-hewn intellectuals whose sources are a mix of the learned and the apocryphal, whose discussions are both assured and sad.

And then there was Ken Harvey. Ken was good-looking in a puffy way and had a full and oily ducktail and was a car enthusiast . . . a hodad. One day in religion class, he said the sentence that turned out to be one of the most memorable of the hundreds of thousands I heard in those Voc. Ed. years. We were talking about the parable of the talents, about achievement, working hard, doing the best you can do, blah-blah-blah, when the teacher called on the restive Ken Harvey for an opinion. Ken thought about it, but just for a second, and said (with studied, minimal affect), "I just wanna be average." That woke me up. Average?! Who wants to be average? Then the athletes chimed in with cliches that make you want to laryngectomize them, and the exchange became a platitudinous melee. At the time, I thought Ken's assertion was stupid, and I wrote him off. But his sentence has stayed with me all these years, and I think I am finally coming to understand it.

Ken Harvey was gasping for air. School can be a tremendously disorienting place. No matter how bad the school, you're going to encounter notions that don't fit with the assumptions and beliefs that you grew up with—maybe you'll hear these dissonant notions from teachers, maybe from the other students, and maybe you'll read them. You'll also be thrown in with all kinds of kids from all kinds of backgrounds, and that can be unsettling—this is especially true in places of rich ethnic and linguistic mix, like the L.A. basin. You'll see a handful of students far excel you in courses that sound exotic and that are only in the curriculum of the elite: French, physics, trigonometry. And all this is happening while you're trying to shape an identity, your body is changing, and your emotions are running wild. If you're a working-class kid in the vocational track, the options you'll have to deal with this will be constrained in certain ways. You're defined by your school as "slow"; you're placed in a curriculum that isn't designed to liberate you but to occupy you, or, if you're lucky, train you, though the training is for work the society does not esteem; other students are picking up the cues from your school and your curriculum and interacting with you in particular

Rose explains that school is more difficult for working-class students. Why does he believe this is so?

ways. If you're a kid like Ted Richard, you turn your back on all this and let your mind roam where it may. But youngsters like Ted are rare. What Ken and so many others do is protect themselves from such suffocating madness by taking on with a vengeance the identity implied in the vocational track. Reject the confusion and frustration by openly defining yourself as the Common Joe. Champion the average. Rely on your own good sense. Fuck this bullshit. Bullshit, of course, is everything you—and the others—fear is beyond you: books, essays, tests, academic scrambling, complexity, scientific reasoning, philosophical inquiry.

The tragedy is that you have to twist the knife in your own gray matter to make this defense work. You'll have to shut down, have to reject intellectual stimuli or diffuse them with sarcasm, have to cultivate stupidity, have to convert boredom from a malady into a way of confronting the world. Keep your vocabulary simple, act stoned when you're not or act more stoned than you are, flaunt ignorance, materialize your dreams. It is a powerful and effective defense—it neutralizes the insult and the frustration of being a vocational kid and, when perfected, it drives teachers up the wall, a delightful secondary effect. But like all strong magic, it exacts a price.

My own deliverance from the Voc. Ed. world began with sophomore biology. Every student, college prep to vocational, had to take biology, and unlike the other courses, the same person taught all sections. When teaching the vocational group, Brother Clint probably slowed down a bit or omitted a little of the fundamental biochemistry, but he used the same book and more or less the same syllabus across the board. If one class got tough, he could get tougher. He was young and powerful and very handsome, and looks and physical strength were high currency. No one gave him any trouble.

I was pretty bad at the dissecting table, but the lectures and the textbook were interesting: plastic overlays that, with each turned page, peeled away skin, then veins and muscle, then organs, down to the very bones that Brother Clint, pointer in hand, would tap out on our hanging skeleton. Dave Snyder was in big trouble, for the study of life—versus the living of it—was sticking in his craw. We worked out a code for our multiple-choice exams. He'd poke me in the back: once for the answer under A, twice for B, and so on; and when he'd hit the right one, I'd look up to the ceiling as though I were lost in thought. Poke: cytoplasm. Poke, poke: methane. Poke, poke, poke: William Harvey. Poke, poke, poke, poke: islets of Langerhans. This didn't work out perfectly, but Dave passed the course, and I mastered the dreamy look of a guy on a record jacket. And something else happened. Brother Clint puzzled over this Voc. Ed. kid who was racking up 98s and 99s on his tests. He checked the school's records and discovered the error. He recommended that I begin my junior year in the College

Prep program. According to all I've read since, such a shift, as one report put it, is virtually impossible. Kids at that level rarely cross tracks. The telling thing is how chancy both my placement into and exit from Voc. Ed. was; neither I nor my parents had anything to do with it. I lived in one world during spring semester and when I came back to school in the fall, I was living in another.

Have you ever moved to a new school or made a change from one class to another? How difficult was this for you?

Switching to College Prep was a mixed blessing. I was an erratic student. I was undisciplined. And I hadn't caught onto the rules of the game: Why work hard in a class that didn't grab my fancy? I was also hopelessly behind in math. Chemistry was hard; toying with my chemistry set years before hadn't prepared me for the chemist's equations. Fortunately, the priest who taught both chemistry and second-year algebra was also the school's athletic director. Membership on the track team covered me; I knew I wouldn't get lower than a C. U.S. history was taught pretty well, and I did okay. But civics was taken over by a football coach who had trouble reading the textbook aloud—and reading aloud was the centerpiece of his pedagogy. College Prep at Mercy was certainly an improvement over the vocational program—at least it carried some status—but the social science curriculum was weak, and the mathematics and physical sciences were simply beyond me. I had a miserable quantitative background and ended up copying some assignments and finessing the rest as best I could. Let me try to explain how it feels to see again and again material you should once have learned but didn't. You are given a problem. It requires you to simplify algebraic fractions or to multiply expressions containing square roots. You know this is pretty basic material because you've seen it for years.

Is it ever possible to do this much "catch-up" work in learning? Is there some course of study you are not pursuing because you feel it is too late?

Once a teacher took some time with you, and you learned how to carry out these operations. Simple versions, anyway. But that was a year or two or more in the past, and these are more complex versions, and now you're not sure. And this, you keep telling yourself, is ninth- or even eighth-grade stuff. Next it's a word problem. This is also old hat. The basic elements are as familiar as story characters: trains speeding so many miles per hour or shadows of buildings angling so many degrees. Maybe you know enough, have sat through enough explanations, to be able to begin setting up the problem: "If one train is going this fast . . . " or "This shadow is really one line of a triangle . . . then:" "Let's see . . . " "How did Jones do this?" "Hmmmm." "No." "No, that won't work." Your attention wavers. You wonder about other things: a football game, a dance, that cute new checker at the market. You try to focus on the problem again. You scribble on paper for a while, but the tension wins out and your attention flits elsewhere. You crumple the paper and begin daydreaming to ease the frustration. The particulars will vary, but in essence this is what a number of students go through, especially those in so-called remedial classes. They open their textbooks and see once again the familiar and impenetrable formulas and diagrams and terms that have stumped them for years. There is no excitement here. *No* excitement. Regardless of what the teacher says, this is not a new challenge. There is, rather, embarrassment and frustration and, not surprisingly, some anger in being reminded once again of longstanding inadequacies. No wonder so many students finally attribute their difficulties to something inborn, organic: "That part of my brain just doesn't work." Given the troubling histories many of these students have, it's miraculous that any of them can lift the shroud of hopelessness sufficiently to make deliverance from these classes possible.

> *What moments strike me when I read—that's what I write down and think about.*
>
> —Susan Pavlakos

Final Reflection

How was your own high school experience different from Rose's? Are there similarities?

❖ *After You Read, Consider*

1. When did Rose change his perspective on education? How did this change come about?

2. What is Rose's attitude toward his teachers?

3. What social beliefs does Rose develop from his exposure to vocational education?

> *I found I always had to write at least two drafts to make sense out of what I was thinking.*
>
> —Susan Moneri

❖ *Suggestions for Writing*

1. How does your experience of class roles support the ideas about education that Rose relates? Write an essay in which you describe where

and how you came to find out that everyone does not live the same way. How does the recognition of class roles affect your notions of democratic or public education?

2. What boundaries do you see being crossed in Rose's essay? How easy was it for Rose to cross these boundaries? Is it that easy for everyone? Write an essay in which you describe a border crossing of your own.

3. What goals did you have when you began high school? Do you think you learned enough to achieve these goals? What should you have studied? How well did high school prepare you for what you are learning now? Write an essay in which you analyze your high school academic experience as preparation for college.

William Stafford

At a Small College

William Stafford was born in Hutchinson, Kansas, in 1914. In 1944, he married Dorothy Hope Frantz and they had four children. He taught English for thirty years at Lewis and Clark College in Oregon. Stafford authored sixty-seven books, the first of which, West of Your City *(1960), when he was forty-six. In 1963, he received the National Book Award for* Traveling in the Dark *(1962). Named Oregon's Poet Laureate in 1975, his work continues to touch the lives of his readers. Stafford died in 1993.*

Prereading never made much sense to me until I realized that I needed some way to think before I began reading.

—Steve Tilson

Prereading Reflection

Think and write about the differences you would expect to experience attending a small college as opposed to a major university.

Words jut forward out of the stone:
"Follow me and I will make you
fishers of people." On the great still earth,
suddenly, this once in your life, you find
your place, alone, where hills and fields
can surround silence; and here for an instant
you rest. All purposes wait: the running
after next effort, the hope and regret.

Without asking, you came. Over the years
succession of days passed, each a mouth
demanding attention. Strong arms
pushed you. Over hills and around corners

> Who does the writer refer to when he talks about "fishers of people"?

the wind carried views toward you and away.
The sky that watches you now arched over.

How can perceptions of events be carried toward or away from you?

Darkness floods forward. Soft on the open
playing fields a bell intones
what it can of serenity. In the still night
your life hurries on, a vault with a jewel
hidden inside. Enveloped by your times,
you stare ahead along the dark road.
You remember to breathe, to stand on the earth again.

What does the "jewel hidden inside" refer to?

> *I always asked myself, "How did what I read connect to me personally."*
> —Margaret Meehan

Final Reflection

After reading and thinking about this poem, refine how a student's experience might be affected by the size of the college, the landscape, whether the campus is urban or rural. How could the location and size of a school affect how you learn?

❖ *After You Read, Consider*

1. What are the strongest images in this poem? Why do you choose these particular images?

2. Poetry is believed to have levels of meaning. Can you identify different meanings in the poem? Why or why not?

3. What does the author mean when he writes, "You remember to breathe, to stand on the earth again"?

> *I still write to try out new ideas and resolve internal conflicts.*
> —Fran Hanson

❖ *Suggestions for Writing*

1. Using the surroundings of the classroom, write a descriptive paper about one or more of your teachers. Consider the images in the poem as you choose what to include in the essay.

2. Think of a particular school that you once attended. How has attending that school affected your educational experiences? Tell the story of

what you learned from what surrounded your educational experience there.

3. Take a careful look at the college you are attending now. Try to "read" the campus. What do the buildings and landscape say about the education there? What do they say about you as a student? Write an essay that describes the campus, being careful to connect your description with a "reading" or analysis of the campus.

Evelyn Freedman

Ready for Anything

Evelyn Freedman started college when she was forty-seven years old after spending the years before as a wife, mother, and Girl Scout leader. She lived in many different locations with her husband, an officer in the air force, and their daughter. In the Girl Scouts, she went from being a Girl Scout leader to holding many council leadership positions, such as summer camp director and council trainer. When she wrote this essay, she was a full-time sophomore in college pursuing a degree in communication.

Prereading Reflection

Reflect on who you are, your past experiences, family background, place of birth, and gender. How did those particular experiences influence how you read?

Christopher Robin was sitting outside his door, putting on his Big Boots. As soon as he saw the Big Boots, Pooh knew that an Adventure was going to happen, and he brushed the honey off his nose with the back of his paw, and spruced himself up as well as he could, so as to look Ready for Anything.
—From Winnie-the-Pooh

My earliest recollections of reading are all about A. A. Milne's wonderful stories and all the marvelous adventures of Pooh and his friends. Surrounding those stories are the many memories of my Dad. Nearly every night of my childhood he would *perch* himself on the edge of the bed and opening a book he would begin to read, the rhythms of his voice inspiring and fueling my imagination. It was through him that my desire to read grew and it was by his side that I learned how letters form words and words form ideas that capture our imagination.

> When you were a child, what books did you read most often?

49

I can hardly remember a time when I couldn't read. For me, books were always full of promise. Books were my window to a larger world—a world beyond my family, friends, and relatives. Books held out the promise of discovery, and adventure—the on button to my imagination. In my childhood home, books were everywhere... uncensored and always available for exploration, entertainment, and self-enhancement. I loved to read! And, every time I read there was the excitement and anticipation of an adventure waiting to happen.

Do you remember learning to read? What was this experience like?

Kindergarten was where I began to learn that there were rules and hidden agendas about books and how you should read. I also began to learn that there were rules about behavior, dress, and learning that were different for girls and boys. My kindergarten was pretty stereotypical: boy toys on one wall, girl toys on the other, low tables and chairs in the middle, teacher's desk at the front. One of the most intriguing objects in that room was a low white shelf of picture books. That shelving was behind the teacher's desk and strictly out of bounds to little hands. Another off limits area was the boys' toys, and those toys were awesome! Full size wooden blocks and trucks that moved. The only thing that moved on the girls' side of the room was a carpet sweeper and baby carriage! I also seem to have a dim recollection of everything being pink. Needless to say the boys' side of the room was like Mecca to a girl always "Ready for Anything." The only trouble was that if you were a girl you could only enter Mecca if the boys were through with it... like they wanted to play with a pink carpet sweeper!

Do you remember school rules that were different from the rules you learned at home?

I was a discipline problem from the start. I didn't stay on the girls' side and I wouldn't take a nap. My largest offense was that the teacher would find me under a desk or in a corner reading the holy picture books! I graduated kindergarten with a label in-cor-re-ga-bull. I didn't know what the word meant but I understood from the tone of adults' voices that it wasn't good. I began then a habit that I continue today ... I started to keep lists of words that I didn't understand so I could find out about them later.

Each successive year in school I collected more words I tried to understand: po-tent-all, un-so-she-bal, un-mot-t-vated, etcetera. There were some bright spots. I was always the best reader in class, but it was boring; and the books were too simple. In grammar school I began to learn that books held a different purpose and it wasn't fun and adventure! Reading had become a test for what you could remember. It didn't matter if the information was too boring to push your on button, and God forbid if you asked too many questions! I kept trying to improve the stories, like, what if Dick, Jane, and Spot went up the hill and through a magic portal to India. In school, imagination became labeled daydreaming which was, unfortunately for me, a punishable offense. I learned early on that teachers didn't care why I read; they only cared about what I could regurgitate. I learned how in the first weeks of each school year I could read my textbooks, and then put them away, only to review a chapter right before a test. It was in this way that I passed through school reading only what was required to pass. I did, however, discover that textbooks could be a source of fun and adventure if you read the author's notes and references at the back of the book. The promise was still there, if you followed the trail of self-discovery contained in the references. The library became my source for answers, and I spent many hours there happily following textbook reference trails and losing myself in the geography of far off places.

Did you ever daydream during class? Why do you think you did?

What kinds of research have you done? Did it all take place in the library?

Does everyone learn to hate school or certain subjects at some point? Why do you think that happens?

By the sixth grade I had learned to hate school, but I had also learned to start questioning why things were the way they were. For one thing, I have a younger sister, and she never seemed to have the same problems conforming that I did. Why was I different? Didn't we have the same parents? Weren't we being brought up in the same house? Why could I turn my nightmares into adventures, and for her nightmares only brought terror? What had caused our life experiences to be so different? Why had I, by the sixth grade, learned that if you raised your hand in class you were showing off, while she had learned to wait until called on? How come, if we were sisters and had the same parents, I was the daughter who could do no right, and she was the daughter who could do no wrong? And there was another big why . . . Why, if my best friend Paul and I did the same things, was I the only one who got punished? Why didn't Mr. Pettie smack the boys' hands with a ruler for sloppy writing?

The how I read started back then; I read to answer the question why. It's because I wanted to know more than just what the word incorrigible meant. I wanted to know why someone would label a person with that word instead of another. I still want to know! I believe that what I read and how I read grew out of these past experiences. Today I read my textbooks in much the same way as I did back in Junior and Senior High, except that now I read them three times: once, for a general sense of what they contain; the second time for specific content; and the third time rereading specific chapters before a test to refresh my memory. I still take a special interest in the author's notes and references, and it is not unusual for me to read many related books or to research who the author is, or was, searching for a deeper insight into what he or she was trying to convey. I want to know more than what the author said; I still want to know why the author believed what he or she said.

There are three publications that I read whenever possible, the *New York Times Book Review*, the *New Yorker*, and *Scientific American*. I had never thought of it before, but I suppose I read the *New Yorker* to exercise the right half of my brain, and *Scientific American* to exercise the left. All of these publications hold the same promise of discovery and adventure that those early childhood stories did, and best of all, the right article can still push the on button to my imagination. I still love reading, and I still love following reference trails to other books and articles that help me try to answer the why questions.

Here is an example of one of my most recent trails which leads right back to those "why" questions I raised in grammar school, like "Why are my sister and I so different?" and "Why does your gender affect how you are socialized?" My copy of the *New Yorker* arrives and I begin by reading the Comment and The Talk of the Town sections. Next I skim the articles to see which ones interest me. I hold the Fiction section and cartoons in reserve for when I need an escape from reality. I leave for last The Critics section, making mental notes of books or films on which I want to follow up. In the August 17 edition, the article "Do Parents Matter?" by Malcolm Gladwell, immediately catches my eye. In his article, Mr. Gladwell seems quite intrigued by the fact that a suburban New Jersey grandmother has developed a new theory on child development. He spends a lot of space in his article informing the reader about how Judith Rich Harris has developed her theory. He does this by articulating her life story. The article made me curious to find out what other people thought about Ms. Harris's theory. Why has this theory sent psychologists reeling and what implications does it have on the nature/nurture debate? The reference trail leads me to two more articles: one in the February 1998 edition of *Psychology Today*, titled "The Power of Peers," and the other, in the September 7, 1998 edition of *Newsweek* titled "The Parent Trap." Here's the gist of Ms. Harris's theory (I quote Sharon Begley from the *Newsweek* article): "Nothing parents do will affect a child's behavior, mental health, ability to form relationships, sense of self-worth, intelligence or personality. What genes don't do, peers do." Okay, I'm beginning to

> Does it matter if you care about what you are researching or reading? How could purpose make a difference for you?

see why everybody is all fired up, especially developmental psychologists and sociologists; after all, their bread and butter are dependent on the nurture side of the argument, but why should I care? The question leads me to investigate and search for Ms. Harris's theory written in her own words. I find her manuscript in the 1995, Vol. 102, No. 3, edition of *Psychological Review*.

> Why do you think Freedman made these particular connections when she was reading? What was she hoping to find?

It's not my intent here to analyze Ms. Harris and her theory or to explain what conclusions I reached about her theory. I've only used her story to illustrate how I read and for what reasons I read. I read for the promise ... the promise of discovery, adventure, and imagination unfettered. It is my attempt to get beyond the what of a subject and to discover the why, so that ... I can be "Ready for Anything."

My ideas sometimes meander and loop back like a river. That's why I like the reflections. They didn't have to be real coherent.

—Michael Smith

Final Reflection

Why is it important for Freedman "to get beyond the what of a subject"?

I liked the discussions we had in class. They were more like conversations.

—Kevin Gary

❖ *After You Read, Consider*

1. How does Freedman connect her early experiences with reading to her experiences with reading now?

2. It sounds as if Freedman is doing research on child raising when she discusses her reading habits. How are reading habits connected to methods for research?

3. How can education make one "ready for anything"?

Writing has never been easy for me, but the comments about my essays from other students in the class at least gave me some encouragement.

—Tiffany Lewis

❖ Suggestions for Writing

1. Freedman opens with a quotation from A. A. Milne's *Winnie-the-Pooh*. Write an essay in which you explain why she chose this quotation and how it reflects the importance of reading and writing in her life.

2. Write an essay in which you discuss your favorite childhood books. Why were these books important to you? What did you learn from them?

3. Write your own literacy narrative. What early reading and writing experiences do you remember? How did you feel about yourself as a reader and writer? What is your attitude toward writing? Where do you think this attitude comes from?

Bill Hall

Toothmarks in the Table of Time

Bill Hall is the editorial page editor of the Lewiston Morning Tribune *in northern Idaho. "Toothmarks in the Table of Time" appeared in* The Sandwich Man *(1988), a collection of essays that portray his membership in the "sandwich generation," the meat that provides nourishment to both younger and older family members. Hall is the father of six children and the grandfather of ten cats, two hyperventilating dogs, one goat, one runty burrow, one chicken, one Japanese car, and seven small human beings.*

❖

Prereading Reflection

Write about a time when you lost someone or something important in your life.

❖

Footprints on the sands of time are nothing compared with toothmarks in a table.

But the toothmarks were missing. Sharon had sent a battered coffee table to be refinished and the refinisher had done the job too well. The refinisher had wiped away not only the irrelevant scratches and the meaningless dents but a significant set of tiny toothmarks.

It was little Marcie's mouth that had munched its mark into that cherry wood a generation before, an incredibly strong little jaw to leave such an enduring impression on the wood and on the world. A kid with a set of chompers like that could come in handy at Christmas when you get ready to crack the walnuts.

Do you have furniture in your home that family members have "marked"? What sorts of memories do the marks invoke?

Marcie is Sharon's niece and was but a babe the day she adorned the table with proof of the only two teeth she had. Over the years, the mark became a treasure, as such marks do. Sharon could never see the sun glint off those two precise little dents without thinking of that pint-sized table chomper, Marcie, and laughing.

And so she could have kicked herself that she forgot the tiny toothmarks when she sent the table off to the furniture refinisher. She didn't think about having the marks preserved until too late. The table came home, flat and smooth and as rich as cherry wood can be, but with its memories sanded off.

And what a potent polish they used when they restored that coffee table. It not only subdued one of Sharon's memories but it restored one of mine. It brought back a bitter-sweet time in my third grade classroom, a troubled classroom where the children didn't understand what was amiss.

The teacher was worn and sometimes mean. She was a competent teacher, filling young minds rather readily with times tables and geography and those other square pegs of hard-cornered, third grade knowledge that do not cram gently into round little heads. And she was kind most of the time but there were days when she would grow moody. There were days when she was clearly miserable about something, that melancholy woman. There were days when she would cloud over.

Why do you suppose that Hall can remember the details of his third grade teacher so vividly?

She would be lost in some distant preoccupation far from the classroom. And of course, with the teacher all but officially absent, we would get rowdy, so rowdy finally that our foolishness would bring her back from that sad place she was in.

Then her mood would swing rapidly to anger and she would come down hard on young heads. She was not a bad woman, but frankly I feared her at first, the way you fear the unknown, the unpleasantly unpredictable.

One day, she made an ill-behaved boy bend over so that she might give him a swat with a flimsy wooden yardstick, a routine punishment not considered excessive at the time. As she brought the strip of cheap pine down on his backside, it shattered into three pieces and, for some freaky reason, flew high in the air.

She began laughing. So did we all, including the boy being punished. In fact, she laughed so hard that her upper plate actually fell out on the wooden floor with a clunk. We held our breaths at first.

But her sense of humor overshadowed her embarrassment and she laughed all the more. Relieved, we joined her in that laugh, too. And she was gasping with mirth as she left the room, teeth in hand, heading for the rest room to wash those choppers before stuffing them back into her mouth.

Has a teacher ever laughed at her- or himself in one of your classes? Why?

We felt a little better about her after that. After that, we seemed to warm to her.

And then one day she read us the Eugene Field poem, "Little Boy Blue," that rather maudlin verse about the toy soldier and the toy dog who linger forever, gathering rust and dust, waiting for the little boy who left them on the shelf.

She explained the poem to us, saying the little boy had died and the toys were never removed from the shelf because the mother couldn't bear to disturb them.

These things happen, she said. "I lost a little boy. He left his handprint on his bedroom window and I've never been able to wash that window."

Things went rather better in the class after that, and not just because we were touched by what she told us, but because we were also flattered that she had paid us the great compliment of treating us like adults, like friends, telling us her troubles, albeit in a roundabout way. And though that class had got off to a rather dreary start, she and the third grade are today mostly a pleasant memory.

Have you had a teacher who has treated you like a friend, an equal, sharing triumphs or tragedies?

Such memories can be maintained in the grain of your mind if not in the surface of your coffee table. And all is not lost with coffee tables either. Treasured dents and significant toothmarks are replaceable. Marcie is a grown woman now. But she can always drop by some day and put the bite on the coffee table for old time's sake.

And there is more than one way to leave your mark. The kids in that third grade classroom those many years ago never met their troubled teacher's lost son. But his small hand touched our lives that year as surely as it touched a pane of glass.

Reflecting is like memories of reading.

—Angie Mikell

Final Reflection

How can losing someone or something help people discover another someone or something in their lives?

Sometimes it's difficult to talk right after you've read something, so I didn't always like class discussion.

—Tiffany Lewis

❖ *After You Read, Consider*

1. Has a teacher ever shared a personal story with you? How did the sharing impact you or your learning in the classroom?

2. Hall frames his essay with an experience that happens much later in his life and then concludes the essay with the same experience. What does this technique help the reader understand about the moment he is writing about?

3. Can you recall a class that started off poorly and ended well? What caused the change?

The ideal paper may never exist, but the process of writing became more important to me.

—Cecelia Molares

❖ *Suggestions for Writing*

1. Write an essay that details something you've lost or found in your life. Show your readers how and why this loss or discovery was significant to you.

2. Write an essay that discusses the effects of teachers and students sharing personal stories in the classroom. When is this a useful learning experience? When is it not?

3. Choose a piece of writing that you consider humorous. It could be a poem, story, or newspaper column. Write an essay that examines how that piece of writing uses humor. What did you learn from the writer's humor? How did you learn it?

Collaborative Assignments for School Literacy

1. With a group of three to four people, visit several college and/or high school campuses in your area. Take detailed notes about the building designs, the landscaping, the layout of the campus and main buildings, the names of the buildings, the signage, and the academic services. As a group, carefully discuss the various aspects of each campus. What do these details tell you about the colleges and the students who attend them?
2. In a small group or as a class, view several movies about education, students, and teachers such as *Stand and Deliver, Educating Rita, Dead Poets Society,* or *The Wall.* Discuss how these films portray students, schools, learning, and teaching. What do the students and teachers learn in each of these flims?
3. Individually take notes that describe the classroom you are sitting in and include everything you can see, hear, and feel that might affect how you learn. Include for example the shape of the room, position of the desks, color of the walls, whether or not the room has windows. As a class, compare your notes and discuss whether or not the room encourages or inhibits learning. What can you learn from your classroom besides the subject matter?
4. In small groups, list several alternatives to formal education such as going to museums or malls, seeing films or plays, watching cooking shows on television, playing with small children, visiting a friend in the hospital, or browsing in a bookstore. As a class, discuss what you might learn from each of these experiences and why the knowledge might be important to your growth as an individual.
5. In small groups, spend some time looking through the web pages of different kinds of colleges. Discuss why a college might advertise itself in a particular way. Discuss which colleges you are attracted to and why.

Work Literacy

Work is the means by which people construct their material and imaginative lives.

—Maggie Hume

Writing and Work

I want to be with people who submerge in the task, who go into the fields to harvest . . .
move in a common rhythm when the food must come in or the fire be putout
—Marge Piercy

My parents didn't believe in giving any of us an allowance. They did believe that all their children should help around the house and the yard; my mother thought we should work to prove we were part of the family, and my father just believed it was good for us. "Anyway," he'd say, "why do you think I had all these kids?" So I grew up doing laundry, changing sheets, cooking large dinners, sweeping floors, babysitting—along with my four sisters, I learned all the possible girl jobs—and my brothers mowed the lawn, raked leaves, painted, washed the family station wagon, and cleaned out the garage three or four times a year. I have friends that still don't think much of my parents because they didn't let us sleep late on Saturday mornings and never let us watch more than one cartoon.

My first paying job was very important to me because it got me out of the house (and away from making school lunches in the evenings) and made it possible to stay out past my usual curfew. I worked at a Dairy Queen, and while it was disappointing to find out why the chocolate coating stayed on the ice cream cone, to this day I can still remember how proud I felt to be able to make the little curl on top of the mound of soft ice cream. It wasn't long before I found that cleaning up and feeding people at work wasn't much different than doing it at home. Because my boss had to answer to the health department (an institution my mother threatened us with whenever she looked in our rooms), cleaning up at work was actually harder than cleaning up at home. But there was one important difference: a paycheck. Now I had some independence because I could buy my own clothes and go out with my friends without asking for money from my parents.

Most of the work I do now is no longer physical—I get paid to teach and write—but still I often find myself exhausted at the end of the day. When I write, I take frequent breaks to pick up my house, wash the kitchen floor, or fold the laundry. I am not procrastinating (regardless of what my family thinks). I can think more clearly when I'm moving around, when my hands and my head are working at the same time.

I still feel good about myself when I repair a lamp, clean the kitchen floor, mow the lawn, or paint a room. There is something so satisfying about being able to stand back and look at something I've repaired, painted, or put together.

WRITING AND WORK

What is it about working with our hands that makes us feel human, useful, and part of a community? How do we define what is work? Why is some work considered harder than other work? Is it just how much we are paid that makes us valuable? What makes work satisfactory? What makes us enjoy or not enjoy our jobs?

These are some of the questions you might want to think about as you read through the selections in "Work Literacy." The section opens with Tim O'Brien's "The Things They Carried," a short story that chronicles a soldier's experiences in Vietnam. "Beautiful Girls" by Susan Orlean takes an uncomfortable and complex look at how beauty pageants are both liberating and oppressing.

Abraham Verghese's excerpt from *My Own Country* is about an infectious disease specialist's early encounters with patients with AIDS. He tries to come to some understanding about those infected with AIDS, the needs of their families, and all the deaths he encounters. "The Great Blueberry War" by Michelle Cook is a humorous look at a young girl's first paying job; in "Nurse Wonder" by Elizabeth Berg, a healthcare worker explains why she cares for the seemingly hopeless.

Tillie Olsen's "I Stand Here Ironing" tells the story of a working mother's love for her daughter as well as the guilt she feels for having to work as much as she did when her daughter was young. "I Stand Here Writing" by Nancy Sommers explains how a teacher connects her personal life and family with her life as a writing teacher. In "I, Rivethead," Ben Hamper takes an ironic look at working for a car manufacturer.

In "Christmas for the Colorblind," Jessica Marinara tells her readers about working, Christmas shopping, and killing a deer. "First Job" by Sandra Cisneros narrates how a young girl learns the unspoken rules at work from her co-workers. Chris Llewellyn's poem "March 25, 1911," looks at a historical tragedy and the plight of sweatshop workers; and, finally, in "A World Painted John Deere Green" Melissa Graham takes a broader view of working by analyzing how technology changes our culture, not always for the better.

Tim O'Brien

The Things They Carried

Born in 1946 in a small town in Minnesota, Tim O'Brien graduated with a BA in political science in one hand and a draft notice in the other. While he was against the war, he reported to service and soon found himself in Vietnam with the 3rd Platoon, A Company, 5th Battalion, 46th Infantry, stationed in My Lai a year after the massacre. Of this time he says he could feel evil in the place, "the wickedness that soaks into your blood and heats up and starts to sizzle." He returned from his tour in Vietnam with a Purple Heart and several publications to his credit. At that point, O'Brien began graduate studies at Harvard eventually leaving the school to become a newspaper reporter for the Washington Post. *Within one year, he had turned his attention to fiction.*

Prereading Reflection

Write about a possession that you always keep with you whether you are at home or away.

First Lieutenant Jimmy Cross carried letters from a girl named Martha, a junior at Mount Sebastian College in New Jersey. They were not love letters, but Lieutenant Cross was hoping, so he kept them folded in plastic at the bottom of his rucksack. In the late afternoon, after a day's march, he would dig his foxhole, wash his hands under a canteen, unwrap the letters, hold them with the tips of his fingers, and spend the last hour of light pretending. He would imagine romantic camping trips into the White Mountains in New Hampshire. He would sometimes taste the envelope flaps, knowing her tongue had been there. More than anything, he wanted Martha to love him as he loved her, but the letters were mostly chatty, elusive on the matter of love. She was a virgin, he was almost sure. She was an English major at Mount Sebastian, and she wrote

Have you ever saved written letters from someone? Why did you save them?

beautifully about her professors and roommates and midterm exams, about her respect for Chaucer and her great affection for Virginia Woolf. She often quoted lines of poetry; she never mentioned the war, except to say, Jimmy, take care of yourself. The letters weighed 10 ounces. They were signed Love, Martha, but Lieutenant Cross understood that Love was only a way of signing and did not mean what he sometimes pretended it meant. At dusk, he would carefully return the letters to his rucksack. Slowly, a bit distracted, he would get up and move among his men, checking the perimeter, then at full dark he would return to his hole and watch the night and wonder if Martha was a virgin.

The things they carried were largely determined by necessity. Among the necessities or near-necessities were P-38 can openers, pocket knives, heat tabs, wristwatches, dog tags, mosquito repellent, chewing gum, candy, cigarettes, salt tablets, packets of Kool-Aid, lighters, matches, sewing kits, Military Payment Certificates, C rations, and two or three canteens of water. Together, these items weighed between 15 and 20 pounds, depending upon a man's habits or rate of metabolism. Henry Dobbins, who was a big man, carried extra rations; he was especially fond of canned peaches in heavy syrup over pound cake. Dave Jensen, who practiced field hygiene, carried a toothbrush, dental floss, and several hotel-sized bars of soap he'd stolen on R&R in Sydney, Australia. Ted Lavender, who was scared, carried tranquilizers until he was shot in the head outside the village of Than Khe in mid-April. By necessity, and because it was SOP, they all carried steel helmets that weighed 5 pounds including the liner and camouflage cover. They carried the standard fatigue jackets and trousers. Very few carried underwear. On their feet they carried jungle boots—2.1 pounds—and Dave Jensen carried three pairs of socks and a can of Dr. Scholl's foot powder as a precaution against trench foot. Until he was shot, Ted Lavender carried six or seven ounces of premium dope, which for him was a necessity. Mitchell Sanders, the RTO, carried condoms. Norman Bowker carried a diary. Rat Kiley carried comic books. Kiowa, a devout Baptist, carried an illustrated New Testament that had been presented to him by his father, who taught Sunday school in Oklahoma City, Oklahoma. As a hedge against bad times, however, Kiowa also carried his grandmother's distrust of the white man, his grandfather's old hunting hatchet. Necessity dictated. Because the land was mined and booby-trapped, it was SOP for each man to carry a steel-centered, nylon-covered flak jacket, which weighed 6.7 pounds, but which on hot days seemed much heavier. Because you could die so quickly, each man carried at least one large compress bandage, usually in the helmet band for easy access.

What would you carry if you were in a stressful situation?

Because the nights were cold, and because the monsoons were wet, each carried a green plastic poncho that could be used as a raincoat or groundsheet or makeshift tent. With its quilted liner, the poncho weighed almost two pounds, but it was worth every ounce. In April, for instance, when Ted Lavender was shot, they used his poncho to wrap him up, then to carry him across the paddy, then to lift him into the chopper that took him away.

They were called legs or grunts.

To carry something was to hump it, as when Lieutenant Jimmy Cross humped his love for Martha up the hills and through the swamps. In its intransitive form, to hump meant to walk, or to march, but it implied burdens far beyond the intransitive.

> What makes all of the soldiers' possessions necessities? Are the photographs necessities? Why?

Almost everyone humped photographs. In his wallet, Lieutenant Cross carried two photographs of Martha. The first was a Kodacolor snapshot signed Love, though he knew better. She stood against a brick wall. Her eyes were gray and neutral, her lips slightly open as she stared straight-on at the camera. At night, sometimes, Lieutenant Cross wondered who had taken the picture, because he knew she had boyfriends, because he loved her so much, and because he could see the shadow of the picture-taker spreading out against the brick wall. The second photograph had been clipped from the 1968 Mount Sebastian yearbook. It was an action shot—women's volleyball—and Martha was bent horizontal to the floor, reaching, the palms of her hands in sharp focus, the tongue taut, the expression frank and competitive. There was no visible sweat. She wore white gym shorts. Her legs, he thought, were almost certainly the legs of a virgin, dry and without hair, the left knee cocked and carrying her entire weight, which was just over one hundred pounds. Lieutenant Cross remembered touching that left knee. A dark theater, he remembered, and the movie was *Bonnie and Clyde*, and Martha wore a tweed skirt, and during the final scene, when he touched her knee, she turned and looked at him in a sad, sober way that made him pull his hand back, but he would always remember the feel of the tweed skirt and the knee beneath it and the sound of the gunfire that killed Bonnie and Clyde, how embarrassing it was, how slow and oppressive. He remembered kissing her good night at the dorm door. Right then, he thought, he should've done something brave. He should've carried her up the stairs to her room and tied her to the bed and touched that left knee all night long. He should've risked it. Whenever he looked at the photographs, he thought of new things he should've done.

What they carried was partly a function of rank, partly of field specialty.

As a first lieutenant and platoon leader, Jimmy Cross carried a compass, maps, code books, binoculars, and a .45-caliber pistol that weighed 2.9 pounds fully loaded. He carried a strobe light and the responsibility for the lives of his men.

As an RTO, Mitchell Sanders carried the PRC-25 radio, a killer, 26 pounds with its battery.

As a medic, Rat Kiley carried a canvas satchel filled with morphine and plasma and malaria tablets and surgical tape and comic books and all the things a medic must carry, including M&M's for especially bad wounds, for a total weight of nearly 20 pounds.

As a big man, therefore a machine gunner, Henry Dobbins carried the M-60, which weighed 23 pounds unloaded, but which was almost always loaded. In addition, Dobbins carried between 10 and 15 pounds of ammunition draped in belts across his chest and shoulders.

As PFCs or Spec 4s, most of them were common grunts and carried the standard M-16 gas-operated assault rifle. The weapon weighed 7.5 pounds unloaded, 8.2 pounds with its full 20-round magazine. Depending on numerous factors, such as topography and psychology, the riflemen carried anywhere from 12 to 20 magazines, usually in cloth bandoliers, adding on another 8.4 pounds at minimum, 14 pounds at maximum.

All of the equipment is very heavy, but what things feel heavier?

When it was available, they also carried M-16 maintenance gear—rods and steel brushes and swabs and tubes of LSA oil—all of which weighed about a pound. Among the grunts, some carried the M-79 grenade launcher, 5.9 pounds unloaded, a reasonably light weapon except for the ammunition, which was heavy. A single round weighed 10 ounces. The typical load was 25 rounds. But Ted Lavender, who was scared, carried 34 rounds when he was shot and killed outside Than Khe, and he went down under an exceptional burden, more than 20 pounds of ammunition, plus the flak jacket and helmet and rations and water and toilet paper and tranquilizers and all the rest, plus the unweighed fear. He was dead weight. There was no twitching or flopping. Kiowa, who saw it happen, said it was like watching a rock fall, or a big sandbag or something—just boom, then down—not like the movies where the dead guy rolls around and does fancy spins and goes ass over teakettle—not like that, Kiowa said, the poor bastard just flat-fuck fell. Boom. Down. Nothing else. It was a bright morning in mid-April. Lieutenant Cross felt the pain. He blamed himself. They stripped off Lavender's canteens and ammo, all the heavy things, and Rat Kiley said the obvious, the guy's dead, and Mitchell Sanders used his radio to report one U.S. KIA and to request a chopper. Then they wrapped Lavender in his poncho. They carried him out to a dry paddy, established security, and sat smoking the dead man's dope until the chopper came. Lieutenant Cross kept to himself. He pictured Martha's smooth young face, thinking he loved her more than anything, more than his men, and now Ted Lavender was dead because he loved her so much and could not stop thinking about her. When the dustoff arrived, they carried Lavender aboard. Afterward they burned Than Khe. They marched until dusk, then dug their holes, and that night Kiowa kept explaining how you had to be there, how fast it was, how the poor guy just dropped like so much concrete. Boom-down, he said. Like cement.

In addition to the three standard weapons—the M-60, M-16, and M-79—they carried whatever presented itself, or whatever seemed appropriate as a means of killing or staying alive. They carried catch-as-catch-can. At various times, in various situations, they carried M-14s and CAR-15s and Swedish Ks and grease guns and captured AK-47s and Chi-Coms and RPGs and Simonov carbines and black market Uzis and .38-caliber Smith & Wesson handguns and 66 mm LAWs and shotguns and silencers and blackjacks and bayonets and C-4 plastic explosives. Lee Strunk carried a slingshot; a weapon of last resort, he called it. Mitchell Sanders carried brass knuckles. Kiowa carried his grandfather's feathered hatchet. Every third or fourth man carried a Claymore antipersonnel mine—3.5 pounds with its firing device. They all carried fragmentation grenades—14 ounces each. They all carried at least one M-18 colored smoke grenade—24 ounces. Some carried CS or tear gas grenades. Some carried white phosphorus grenades. They carried all they could bear, and then some, including a silent awe for the terrible power of the things they carried.

In the first week of April, before Lavender died, Lieutenant Jimmy Cross received a good-luck charm from Martha. It was a simple pebble, an ounce at most. Smooth to the touch, it was a milky white color with flecks of orange and violet, oval-shaped, like a miniature egg. In the accompanying letter, Martha wrote that she had found the pebble on the Jersey shoreline, precisely where the land touched water at high tide, where things came together but also separated. It was this separate-but-together quality, she wrote, that had inspired her to pick up the pebble and to carry it in her breast pocket for several days, where it seemed weightless, and then to send it through the mail, by air, as a token of her truest feelings for him. Lieutenant Cross found this romantic. But he wondered what her truest feelings were, exactly, and what she meant by separate-but-together. He wondered how the tides and waves had come into play on that afternoon along the Jersey shoreline when Martha saw the pebble and bent down to rescue it from geology. He imagined bare feet. Martha was a poet,

How does the pebble represent Cross's emotional baggage? How does this baggage become dangerous?

with the poet's sensibilities, and her feet would be brown and bare, the toenails unpainted, the eyes chilly and somber like the ocean in March, and though it was painful, he wondered who had been with her that afternoon. He imagined a pair of shadows moving along the strip of sand where things came together but also separated. It was phantom jealousy, he knew, but he couldn't help himself. He loved her so much. On the march, through the hot days of early April, he carried the pebble in his mouth, turning it with his tongue, tasting sea salt and moisture. His mind wandered. He had difficulty keeping his attention on the war. On occasion he would yell at his men to spread out the column, to keep their eyes open, but then he would slip away into daydreams, just pretending, walking barefoot along the Jersey shore, with Martha, carrying nothing. He would feel himself rising. Sun and waves and gentle winds, all love and lightness.

What they carried varied by mission.

When a mission took them to the mountains, they carried mosquito netting, machetes, canvas tarps, and extra bug juice.

If a mission seemed especially hazardous, or if it involved a place they knew to be bad, they carried everything they could. In certain heavily mined AOs, where the land was dense with Toe Poppers and Bouncing Betties, they took turns humping a 28-pound mine detector. With its headphones and big sensing plate, the equipment was a stress on the lower back and shoulders, awkward to handle, often useless because of the shrapnel in the earth, but they carried it anyway, partly for safety, partly for the illusion of safety.

On ambush, or other night missions, they carried peculiar little odds and ends. Kiowa always took along his New Testament and a pair of moccasins for silence. Dave Jensen carried night-sight vitamins high in carotene. Lee Strunk carried his slingshot; ammo, he claimed, would never be a problem. Rat Kiley carried brandy and M&M's candy. Until he was shot, Ted Lavender carried the starlight scope, which weighed 6.3 pounds with its aluminum carrying case. Henry Dobbins carried his girlfriend's pantyhose wrapped around his neck as a comforter. They all carried ghosts. When dark came, they would move out single file across the meadows and paddies to their ambush coordinates, where they would quietly set up the Claymores and lie down and spend the night waiting.

Other missions were more complicated and required special equipment. In mid-April, it was their mission to search out and destroy the elaborate tunnel complexes in the Than Khe area south of Chu Lai. To blow the tunnels, they carried one-pound blocks of pentrite high explosives, four blocks to a man, 68 pounds in all. They carried wiring, detonators, and battery-powered clackers. Dave Jensen carried earplugs. Most often, before blowing the tunnels, they were ordered by higher command to search them, which was considered bad news, but by and large they just shrugged and carried out orders. Because he was a big man, Henry Dobbins was excused from tunnel duty. The others would draw numbers. Before Lavender died there were 17 men in the platoon, and whoever drew the number 17 would strip off his gear and crawl in headfirst with a flashlight and Lieutenant Cross's .45-caliber pistol. The rest of them would fan out as security. They would sit down or kneel, not facing the hole, listening to the ground beneath them, imagining cobwebs and ghosts, whatever was down there—the tunnel walls squeezing in—how the flashlight seemed impossibly heavy in the hand and how it was tunnel vision in the very strictest sense, compression in all ways, even time, and how you had to wiggle in—ass and elbows—a swallowed-up feeling—and how you found yourself worrying about odd things: Will your flashlight go dead? Do rats carry rabies? If you screamed, how far would the sound carry? Would your buddies hear it? Would they have the courage to drag you out? In some respects, though not many, the waiting was worse than the tunnel itself. Imagination was a killer.

On April 16, when Lee Strunk drew the number 17, he laughed and muttered something and went down quickly. The morning was hot and very still. Not good, Kiowa said. He looked at the tunnel opening, then out across a dry paddy toward the village of Than Khe. Nothing moved. No clouds or birds or people. As they waited, the men smoked and drank Kool-Aid, not talking much, feeling sympathy for Lee Strunk but also feeling the luck of the draw. You win some, you lose some, said Mitchell Sanders, and sometimes you settle for a rain check. It was a tired line and no one laughed.

Henry Dobbins ate a tropical chocolate bar. Ted Lavender popped a tranquilizer and went off to pee.

After five minutes, Lieutenant Jimmy Cross moved to the tunnel, leaned down, and examined the darkness. Trouble, he thought—a cave-in maybe. And then suddenly, without willing it, he was thinking about Martha. The stresses and fractures, the quick collapse, the two of them buried alive under all that weight. Dense, crushing love. Kneeling, watching the hole, he tried to concentrate on Lee Strunk and the war, all the dangers, but his love was too much for him, he felt paralyzed, he wanted to sleep inside her lungs and breathe her blood and be smothered. He wanted her to be a virgin and not a virgin, all at once. He wanted to know her. Intimate secrets: Why poetry? Why so sad? Why that grayness in her eyes? Why so alone? Not lonely, just alone—riding her bike across campus or sitting off by herself in the cafeteria—even dancing, she danced alone—and it was the aloneness that filled him with love. He remembered telling her that one evening. How she nodded and looked away. And how, later, when he kissed her, she received the kiss without returning it, her eyes wide open, not afraid, not a virgin's eyes, just flat and uninvolved.

> How does Cross's imagination become a "killer"?

Lieutenant Cross gazed at the tunnel. But he was not there. He was buried with Martha under the white sand at the Jersey shore. They were pressed together, and the pebble in his mouth was her tongue. He was smiling. Vaguely, he was aware of how quiet the day was, the sullen paddies, yet he could not bring himself to worry about matters of security. He was beyond that. He was just a kid at war, in love. He was twenty-four years old. He couldn't help it.

A few moments later Lee Strunk crawled out of the tunnel. He came up grinning, filthy but alive. Lieutenant Cross nodded and closed his eyes while the others clapped Strunk on the back and made jokes about rising from the dead.

Worms, Rat Kiley said. Right out of the grave. Fuckin' zombie.

The men laughed. They all felt great relief.

Spook city, said Mitchell Sanders.

Lee Strunk made a funny ghost sound, a kind of moaning, yet very happy, and right then, when Strunk made that high happy moaning sound, when he went *Ahhooooo*, right then Ted Lavender was shot in the head on his way back from peeing. He lay with his mouth open. The teeth were broken. There was a swollen black bruise under his left eye. The cheekbone was gone. Oh shit, Rat Kiley said, the guy's dead. The guy's dead, he kept saying, which seemed profound—the guy's dead. I mean really.

> Even though they are at war, Lavender's death feels unexpected. Why?

The things they carried were determined to some extent by superstition. Lieutenant Cross carried his good-luck pebble. Dave Jensen carried a rabbit's foot. Norman Bowker, otherwise a very gentle person, carried a thumb that had been presented to him as a gift by Mitchell Sanders. The thumb was dark brown, rubbery to the touch, and weighed four ounces at most. It had been cut from a VC corpse, a boy of fifteen or sixteen. They'd found him at the bottom of an irrigation ditch, badly burned, flies in his mouth and eyes. The boy wore black shorts and sandals. At the time of his death he had been carrying a pouch of rice, a rifle, and three magazines of ammunition.

You want my opinion, Mitchell Sanders said, there's a definite moral here.

He put his hand on the dead boy's wrist. He was quiet for a time, as if counting a pulse, then he patted the stomach, almost affectionately, and used Kiowa's hunting hatchet to remove the thumb.

Henry Dobbins asked what the moral was.

Moral?

You know. *Moral.*

Sanders wrapped the thumb in toilet paper and handed it across to Norman Bowker. There was no blood. Smiling, he kicked the boy's head, watched the flies scatter, and said, It's like with that old TV show—Paladin. Have gun, will travel.

Henry Dobbins thought about it.

> What do you think the moral is?

Yeah, well, he finally said. I don't see no moral.

There it *is*, man.

Fuck off.

They carried USO stationery and pencils and pens. They carried Sterno, safety pins, trip flares, signal flares, spools of wire, razor blades, chewing tobacco, liberated joss sticks and statuettes of the smiling Buddha, candles, grease pencils, *The Stars and Stripes*, fingernail clippers, Psy Ops leaflets, bush hats, bolos, and much more. Twice a week, when the resupply choppers came in, they carried hot chow in green mermite cans and large canvas bags filled with iced beer and soda pop. They carried plastic water containers, each with a two-gallon capacity. Mitchell Sanders carried a set of starched tiger fatigues for special occasions. Henry Dobbins carried Black Flag insecticide. Dave Jensen carried empty sandbags that could be filled at night for added protection. Lee Strunk carried tanning lotion. Some things they carried in common. Taking turns, they carried the big PRC-77 scrambler radio, which weighed 30 pounds with its battery. They shared the weight of memory. They took up what others could no longer bear. Often, they carried each other, the wounded or weak. They carried infections. They carried chess sets, basketballs, Vietnamese-English dictionaries, insignia of rank, Bronze Stars and Purple Hearts, plastic cards imprinted with the Code of Conduct. They carried diseases, among them malaria and dysentery. They carried lice and ringworm and leeches and paddy algae and various rots and molds. They carried the land itself—Vietnam, the place, the soil—a powdery orange-red dust that covered their boots and fatigues and faces. They carried the sky. The whole atmosphere, they carried it, the humidity, the monsoons, the stink of fungus and decay, all of it, they carried gravity. They moved like mules. By daylight they took sniper fire, at night they were mortared, but it was not battle, it was just the endless march, village to village, without purpose, nothing won or lost. They marched for the sake of the march. They plodded along slowly, dumbly, leaning forward against the heat, unthinking, all blood and bone, simple grunts, soldiering with their legs, toiling up

> This paragraph is longer than the preceding ones. How does this affect your reading?

the hills and down into the paddies and across the rivers and up again and down, just humping, one step and then the next and then another, but no volition, no will, because it was automatic, it was anatomy, and the war was entirely a matter of posture and carriage, the hump was everything, a kind of inertia, a kind of emptiness, a dullness of desire and intellect and conscience and hope and human sensibility. Their principles were in their feet. Their calculations were biological. They had no sense of strategy or mission. They searched the villages without knowing what to look for, not caring, kicking over jars of rice, frisking children and old men, blowing tunnels, sometimes setting fires and sometimes not, then forming up and moving on to the next village, then other villages, where it would always be the same. They carried their own lives. The pressures were enormous. In the heat of early afternoon, they would remove their helmets and flak jackets, walking bare, which was dangerous but which helped ease the strain. They would often discard things along the route of march. Purely for comfort; they would throw away rations, blow their Claymores and grenades, no matter, because by nightfall the resupply choppers would arrive with more of the same, then a day or two later still more, fresh watermelons and crates of ammunition and sunglasses and woolen sweaters—the resources were stunning—sparklers for the Fourth of July, colored eggs for Easter—it was the great American war chest— the fruits of science, the smokestacks, the canneries, the arsenals at Hartford, the Minnesota forests, the machine shops, the vast fields of corn and wheat—they carried like freight trains; they carried it on their backs and shoulders—and for all the ambiguities of Vietnam, all the mysteries and unknowns, there was at least the single abiding certainty that they would never be at a loss for things to carry.

After the chopper took Lavender away, Lieutenant Jimmy Cross led his men into the village of Than Khe. They burned everything. They shot chickens and dogs, they trashed the village well, they called in artillery and watched the wreckage, then they marched for several hours through the hot afternoon, and then at dusk, while Kiowa explained how Lavender died, Lieutenant Cross found himself trembling.

He tried not to cry. With his entrenching tool, which weighed five pounds, he began digging a hole in the earth.

He felt shame. He hated himself. He had loved Martha more than his men, and as a consequence Lavender was now dead, and this was something he would have to carry like a stone in his stomach for the rest of the war.

All he could do was dig. He used his entrenching tool like an ax, slashing, feeling both love and hate, and then later, when it was full dark, he sat at the bottom of his foxhole and wept. It went on for a long while. In part, he was grieving for Ted Lavender, but mostly it was for Martha, and for himself, because she belonged to another world, which was not quite real, and because she was a junior at Mount Sebastian College in New Jersey, a poet and a virgin and uninvolved, and because he realized she did not love him and never would.

Like cement, Kiowa whispered in the dark. I swear to God—boom, down. Not a word.

I've heard this, said Norman Bowker.

A pisser, you know? Still zipping himself up. Zapped while zipping.

All right, fine. That's enough.

Yeah, but you had to see it, the guy just—

I heard, man. Cement. So why not shut the fuck *up*?

Kiowa shook his head sadly and glanced over at the hole where Lieutenant Jimmy Cross sat watching the night. The air was thick and wet. A warm dense fog had settled over the paddies and there was the stillness that precedes rain.

After a time Kiowa sighed.

One thing for sure, he said. The lieutenant's in some deep hurt. I mean that crying jag—the way he was carrying on—it wasn't fake or anything, it was real heavy-duty hurt. The man cares.

> Why is Kiowa's reaction to Cross's crying different from the others in his platoon?

Sure, Norman Bowker said.

Say what you want, the man does care.

We all got problems.

Not Lavender.

No, I guess not, Bowker said. Do me a favor, though.

Shut up?

That's a smart Indian. Shut up.

Shrugging, Kiowa pulled off his boots. He wanted to say more, just to lighten up his sleep, but instead he opened his New Testament and arranged it beneath his head as a pillow. The fog made things seem hollow and unattached. He tried not to think about Ted Lavender, but then he was thinking how fast it was, no drama, down and dead, and how it was hard to feel anything except surprise. It seemed unchristian. He wished he could find some great sadness, or even anger, but the emotion wasn't there and he couldn't make it happen. Mostly he felt pleased to be alive. He liked the smell of the New Testament under his cheek, the leather and ink and paper and glue, whatever the chemicals were. He liked hearing the sounds of night. Even his fatigue, it felt fine, the stiff muscles and the prickly awareness of his own body, a floating feeling. He enjoyed not being dead. Lying there, Kiowa admired Lieutenant Jimmy Cross's capacity for grief. He wanted to share the man's pain, he wanted to care as Jimmy Cross cared. And yet when he closed his eyes, all he could think was Boom-down, and all he could feel was the pleasure of having his boots off and the fog curling in around him and the damp soil and the Bible smells and the plush comfort of night.

After a moment Norman Bowker sat up in the dark.

What the hell, he said. You want to talk, *talk*. Tell it to me.

Forget it.

No, man, go on. One thing I hate, it's a silent Indian.

For the most part they carried themselves with poise, a kind of dignity. Now and then, however, there were times of panic, when they squealed or wanted to squeal but couldn't, when they twitched and made moaning sounds and covered their heads and said Dear Jesus and flopped around on the earth and fired their weapons blindly and cringed and sobbed and begged for the noise to stop and went wild and made stupid promises to themselves and to God and to their mothers and fathers, hoping not to die. In different ways, it happened to all of them. Afterward, when the firing ended, they would blink and peek up. They would touch their bodies, feeling shame, then quickly hiding it. They would force themselves to stand. As if in slow motion, frame by frame, the world would take on the old logic—absolute silence, then the wind, then sunlight, then voices. It was the burden of being alive. Awkwardly, the men would reassemble themselves, first in private, then in groups, becoming soldiers again. They would repair the leaks in their eyes. They would check for casualties, call in dustoffs, light cigarettes, try to smile, clear their throats and spit and begin cleaning their weapons. After a time someone would shake his head and say, No lie, I almost shit my pants, and someone else would laugh, which meant it was bad, yes, but the guy had obviously not shit his pants, it wasn't that bad, and in any case nobody would ever do such a thing and then go ahead and talk about it. They would squint into the dense, oppressive sunlight. For a few moments, perhaps, they would fall silent, lighting a joint and tracking its passage from man to man, inhaling, holding in the humiliation. Scary stuff, one of them might say. But then someone else would grin or flick his eyebrows and say, Roger-dodger, almost cut me a new asshole, *almost*.

There were numerous such poses. Some carried themselves with a sort of wistful resignation, others with pride or stiff soldierly discipline or good humor or macho zeal. They were afraid of dying but they were even more afraid to show it.

They found jokes to tell.

They used a hard vocabulary to contain the terrible softness. *Greased* they'd say. *Offed, lit up, zapped while zipping*. It wasn't cruelty, just stage presence. They were actors. When someone died, it wasn't quite dying, because in a curious way it seemed scripted, and because they had their lines mostly memorized, irony mixed with tragedy, and because they called it by other names, as if to encyst and destroy the reality of death itself. They kicked corpses. They cut off thumbs. They talked grunt lingo. They told stories about Ted Lavender's supply of tranquilizers, how the poor guy didn't feel a thing, how incredibly tranquil he was.

There's a moral here, said Mitchell Sanders.

They were waiting for Lavender's chopper, smoking the dead man's dope.

The moral's pretty obvious, Sanders said, and winked. Stay away from drugs. No joke, they'll ruin your day every time.

Cute, said Henry Dobbins.

Mind blower, get it? Talk about wiggy. Nothing left, just blood and brains.

They made themselves laugh.

There it is, they'd say. Over and over—there it is, my friend, there it is—as if the repetition itself were an act of poise, a balance between crazy and almost crazy, knowing without going, there it is, which meant be cool, let it ride, because Oh yeah, man, you can't change what can't be changed, there it is, there it absolutely and positively and fucking well *is*.

They were tough.

They carried all the emotional baggage of men who might die. Grief, terror, love, longing—these were intangibles, but the intangibles had their own mass and specific gravity, they had tangible weight. They carried shameful memories. They carried the common secret of cowardice barely restrained, the instinct to run or freeze or hide, and in many respects this was the heaviest burden of all, for it could never be put down, it required perfect balance and perfect posture. They carried their reputations. They carried the soldier's greatest fear, which was the fear of blushing. Men killed, and died, because they were embarrassed not to. It was what had brought them to the war in the first place, nothing positive, no dreams of glory or honor, just to avoid the blush of dishonor. They died so as not to die of embarrassment. They crawled into tunnels and walked point and advanced under fire. Each morning, despite the unknowns, they made their legs move. They endured. They kept humping. They did not submit to the obvious alternative, which was simply to close the eyes and fall. So easy, really. Go limp and tumble to the ground and let the muscles unwind and not speak and not budge until your buddies picked you up and lifted you into the chopper that would roar and dip its nose and carry you off to the world. A mere matter of falling, yet no one ever fell. It was not courage, exactly; the object was not valor. Rather, they were too frightened to be cowards.

By and large they carried these things inside, maintaining the masks of composure. They sneered at sick call. They spoke bitterly about guys who had found release by shooting off their own toes or fingers. Pussies, they'd say. Candy-asses. It was fierce, mocking talk, with only a trace of envy or awe, but even so the image played itself out behind their eyes.

They imagined the muzzle against flesh. So easy: squeeze the trigger and blow away a toe. They imagined it. They imagined the quick, sweet pain, then the evacuation to Japan, then a hospital with warm beds and cute geisha nurses.

And they dreamed of freedom birds.

At night, on guard, staring into the dark, they were carried away by jumbo jets. They felt the rush of takeoff. *Gone!* they yelled. And then velocity—wings and engines—a smiling stewardess—but it was more than a plane, it was a real bird, a big sleek silver bird with feathers and talons and high screeching. They were flying. The weights fell off; there was nothing to bear. They laughed and held on tight, feeling the cold slap of wind and altitude, soaring, thinking *It's over, I'm gone!*—they were naked, they were light and free—it was all lightness, bright and fast and buoyant, light as light, a helium buzz in the brain, a giddy bubbling in the lungs as they were taken up over the clouds and the war, beyond duty, beyond gravity and mortification and global entanglements—*Sin loi!* they yelled. *I'm sorry, mother-fuckers, but I'm out of it, I'm goofed, I'm on a space cruise, I'm gone!*—and it was a restful, unencumbered sensation, just riding the light waves, sailing that big silver freedom bird over the mountains and oceans, over America, over the farms and great sleeping cities and cemeteries and highways and the golden arches of McDonald's, it was flight, a kind of fleeing, a kind of falling, falling higher and higher, spinning off the edge of the earth and beyond the sun and through the vast, silent vacuum where there were no burdens and where everything weighed exactly nothing—*Gone!* they screamed. *I'm sorry but I'm gone!*—and so at night, not quite dreaming, they gave themselves over to lightness, they were carried, they were purely borne.

On the morning after Ted Lavender died, First Lieutenant Jimmy Cross crouched at the bottom of his foxhole and burned Martha's letters. Then he burned the two photographs. There was a steady rain falling, which made it difficult, but he used heat tabs and Sterno to build a small fire, screening it with his body, holding the photographs over the tight blue flame with the tips of his fingers.

Why does Cross burn Martha's letters? What has he decided?

He realized it was only a gesture. Stupid, he thought. Sentimental, too, but mostly just stupid.

Lavender was dead. You couldn't burn the blame.

Besides, the letters were in his head. And even now, without photographs, Lieutenant Cross could see Martha playing volleyball in her white gym shorts and yellow T-shirt. He could see her moving in the rain.

When the fire died out, Lieutenant Cross pulled his poncho over his shoulders and ate breakfast from a can.

There was no great mystery, he decided.

In those burned letters Martha had never mentioned the war, except to say, Jimmy, take care of yourself. She wasn't involved. She signed the letters Love, but it wasn't love, and all the fine lines and technicalities did not matter. Virginity was no longer an issue. He hated her. Yes, he did. He hated her. Love, too, but it was a hard, hating kind of love.

The morning came up wet and blurry. Everything seemed part of everything else, the fog and Martha and the deepening rain.

He was a soldier, after all.

Half smiling, Lieutenant Jimmy Cross took out his maps. He shook his head hard, as if to clear it, then bent forward and began planning the day's march. In ten minutes, or maybe twenty, he would rouse the men and they would pack up and head west, where the maps showed the country to be green and inviting. They would do what they had always done. The rain might add some weight, but otherwise it would be one more day layered upon all the other days.

He was realistic about it. There was that new hardness in his stomach. He loved her but he hated her.

No more fantasies, he told himself.

Henceforth, when he thought about Martha, it would be only to think that she belonged elsewhere. He would shut down the daydreams. This was not Mount Sebastian, it was another world, where there were no pretty poems or midterm exams, a place where men died because of carelessness and gross stupidity. Kiowa was right. Boom-down, and you were dead, never partly dead.

Briefly, in the rain, Lieutenant Cross saw Martha's gray eyes gazing back at him.

He understood.

It was very sad, he thought. The things men carried inside. The things men did or felt they had to do.

He almost nodded at her, but didn't.

Instead he went back to his maps. He was now determined to perform his duties firmly and without negligence. It wouldn't help Lavender, he knew that, but from this point on he would comport himself as an officer. He would dispose of his good-luck pebble. Swallow it, maybe, or use Lee Strunk's slingshot, or just drop it along the trail. On the march he would impose strict field discipline. He would be careful to send out flank security, to prevent straggling or bunching up, to keep his troops moving at the proper pace and at the proper interval. He would insist on clean weapons. He would confiscate the remainder of Lavender's dope. Later in the day, perhaps, he would call the men together and speak to them plainly. He would accept the blame for what had happened to Ted Lavender. He would be a man about it. He would look them in the eyes, keeping his chin level, and he would issue the new SOPs in a calm, impersonal tone of voice, a lieutenant's voice, leaving no room for argument or discussion. Commencing immediately, he'd tell them, they would no longer abandon equipment along the route of march. They would police up their acts. They would get their shit together, and keep it together, and maintain it neatly and in good working order.

He would not tolerate laxity. He would show strength, distancing himself.

Among the men there would be grumbling, of course, and maybe worse, because their days would seem longer and their loads heavier, but Lieutenant Jimmy Cross reminded himself that his obligation was not to be loved but to lead. He would dispense with love; it was not now a factor. And if anyone quarreled or complained, he would simply tighten his lips and arrange his shoulders in the correct command posture. He might give a curt little nod. Or he might not. He might just shrug and say, Carry on, then they would saddle up and form into a column and move out toward the villages west of Than Khe.

There is no real final reflection. We were always reflecting.

—Chris Neverson

Final Reflection

Revise your original reflective piece to include additional items you would carry. Consider physical, emotional, and intellectual baggage.

During class discussion, everyone talked—sometimes all at once—but I liked that the whole class got excited.

—Dan Morrison

❖ After You Read, Consider

1. How do the soldiers' possessions help you visualize who they are?

2. Kiowa carries mementoes from two worlds: an illustrated New Testament from his father, his distrust of the white man from his grand-

mother, his grandfather's hunting hatchet. How do his possessions frame his perceptions?

3. The list of things they carry creates a rhythm as the reader moves through the piece much like the rhythm in marching steps. How does such a technique work in this story? How does it add to your understanding?

> *I went from unwilling (and unable) to see, to a paper where I could finally see and wanted to show someone else.*
> —Heidi Robinson

❖ Suggestions for Writing

1. Write a biography of someone you know well by using his or her favorite possessions to describe his or her character.

2. Write your definition of war; then interview a number of former members of the military. In an essay, compare your concept of war and the perspectives of the people you interview.

3. Martha signs her letters "Love," but Lieutenant Cross knows she does not love him the way he loves her. In your essay answer the following: Why do they love each other differently? How is this difference shown in the story?

Susan Orlean

Beautiful Girls

Susan Orlean has been a staff writer at the New Yorker *since 1992. Her articles have also appeared in* Outside, Esquire, Rolling Stone, *and* Vogue. *She is the author of* The Orchid Thief *(1999) and* Saturday Night *(1990). Now a resident of New York City, Orlean was born in Cleveland, Ohio, and graduated from the University of Michigan.*

❖

Prereading Reflection

What makes someone physically beautiful? How important is physical beauty?

❖

The Holiday Inn in Prattville, Alabama, is on a grassy rise beside a wide gray highway across from a Waffle House and a McDonald's and several different places to buy gas. One Sunday this spring, the hotel lobby was especially crowded. Some of the people had come straight from church for Sunday lunch: mild-faced women in pastel dresses and men in gray suits and dull-blue ties; boys in white shirts and oxfords and girls in Sunday-school dresses and black Mary Janes. The rest of the people had come for the Universal/Southern Charm children's beauty pageant being held at the hotel. They were wearing stonewashed jeans or leisure outfits, and they were carrying babies or pushing strollers or rushing around leading little girls by the hand, and with a spare finger some of them were balancing hangers that held tiny dresses with ballooning skirts covered by dry cleaners' plastic bags. A few of the littlest babies were fussing. Mothers hurried through the lobby and bumped their strollers into other mothers' strollers. A miniature dress of green chiffon slid off its hanger and settled onto the carpet with a sigh, and as soon as the woman holding the empty hanger noticed it she yelled, "Nobody

Orlean very carefully sets up the scene for us. What does she want us to see?

move! *Don't step on that dress!*" Then a few three-year-olds started horsing around and squealing, and a cosmetic case slipped out of someone's hand, and, when it landed, out shot a dozen cylinder-shaped things—hair curlers, hairbrushes, lipstick tubes, eyeliner brushes—which rolled in every direction across the floor. A few fathers were sent back to the parking lot to retrieve the shoes or hat or Wet Ones or entry forms that had been left in the car by accident. One mother had spread her baby out on the lobby sofa and was changing her into a lavender Western outfit. In the ladies' room, small dresses and hats were hanging from every ledge they could hang from, and white anklet socks and white shoes and pairs of children's size-2 rhinestone-studded cowboy boots were scattered on the floor, and there was the tangy metallic smell of hot curling irons in the air. In the middle of the room, four women were adjusting the bows in their daughters' hair and smoothing blusher on their cheeks. Across from them, three other women were lined up elbow to elbow. Each one held a Great Lash mascara wand poised like a conductor's baton, and each was facing a lovely little girl in a glittering pageant dress sitting quietly in a sink.

I had never been to a beauty pageant before I went to Prattville. For the longest time, the world of children's beauty pageants was invisible to millions of people like me, who don't read *Pageant Life* and *Pageant World,* and don't plan their vacations around the big state finals, and don't have a little girl who has dozens of trophies and crowns and pageant banners in her room. Probably all of that would have remained invisible if someone hadn't murdered JonBenet Ramsey. Once the footage of her in pageant clothes and wearing makeup appeared on the TV news, the world of children's beauty pageants came into sight, and a horrible association was made—not just that a beauty-pageant girl was murdered but that the pageants themselves were depraved and had maybe even contributed to the murder in some way. It was as if you'd never heard of the game of football until the O.J. Simpson trial, and then you'd never be able to separate the crime from the game.

> What bias does Orlean admit to? Why does she let us know up front how she feels about beauty pageants?

But pageants have been taking place all over the country for decades, and in the South, especially, they are as common as barbecue. Pageants are held nearly every Sunday—Sunburst Pageants and Moonbeam Pageants and Miss American Starlet and Glamour Dolls USA Pageants—in meeting rooms at Holiday Inns and Comfort Inns and Best Westerns in places like Florence, Alabama, and Jackson, Mississippi, and Jackson, Tennessee. Every Sunday, pageants have been making winners and losers, inspiring and dashing hopes, wasting some people's money and making some little girls rich. As I left for

Alabama, I guessed that I would see some overcompetitive parents and some parents who would insist on winning even if their kids didn't want to be in a pageant—the same bad things you sometimes see at junior tennis matches and gymnastics meets. I knew that I wasn't going to enjoy seeing three-year-olds wearing eyeliner and crying when they weren't named Supreme Queen. But in spite of what most of the stories that followed JonBenet's murder led me to expect, what I saw in Prattville were not people like the Ramseys, with lots of money and mobility. They were ordinary people: they were dazzled by glamour, and they believed truly and uncynically in beauty and staked their faith on its power to lift you and carry you away. It may be embarrassing or naive to believe that being Miss America will lead you somewhere in life—unless it happens to be your life, or your daughter's life, and the working-class life that has been assigned to you and your baby feels small and flat and plain. There are only so many ways to get out of a place like Prattville. The crown you win on Sunday might be the chance for your beautiful baby to get a start on a different life, so that someday she might get ahead and get away.

If Orlean didn't see what she expected, then what does she see? Why does this complicate the issue for her? Why are these ordinary people somehow less culpable?

Darlene Burgess, who founded the Universal/Southern Charm International Pageant seventeen years ago, told me that ever since JonBenet, people who don't know anything about pageants are peering into the pageant world and then condemning it because they're shocked by the makeup and the dressy dresses and the sexy sophistication of some of the girls. There have been magazine stories and television shows about children's pageants before, but most of them have been for foreign press and TV, so this has really been the first time that the pageant world has been shoved into view. It's not that anyone has anything to hide; it's just that they feel scrutinized and criticized by people who haven't been to a single pageant—people who can't see how proud mothers are when their daughters win, and don't see how pageant people are practically a family, in which everyone knows each other and watches out for each other.

Darlene got into pageants purely by accident. She grew up on a farm in Arkansas in the fifties; her mother drove a grain truck, and Darlene lived on her own in town starting at the age of fifteen. She didn't know a thing about pageants and wouldn't have had the money to compete in them even if she had. When she got married, she and her husband Jerry, who was a pilot for Oral Roberts University, lived in Tulsa. They started their little girl, Becky, in dancing classes at the age of three. Becky was a natural onstage, and Darlene learned to coax out her best performances by waving a flyswatter at her. After a while,

Becky's dance teacher entered her in a competition that turned out to be part of a children's pageant. Becky came home that day with a trophy, and Darlene was hooked.

Darlene learned about pageants as she went along. One thing she learned was makeup. The dance teacher used some on the girls in their recitals, and Darlene didn't like it at first, but then she agreed that for pageants Becky needed it. "She was just so pale," Darlene said to me recently. "I just *had* to cake her. Otherwise, she would have been invisible onstage. If you have a baby who's a true blonde, not a browny-blonde, and you put her under those lights, it'll kill her." Darlene herself is tall and substantial and has fair skin and clay-colored hair. She wears big rimless glasses and warmup suits. She has an Arkansas accent, rolling and drawly, and a light, chiming laugh that can put you in an instant good mood. She is self-possessed and capable in a way that is slightly intimidating. When she needed a dress for Becky, she sewed one; when she saw that there was no good pageant-dress business in the area, she started one; when she discovered that no one manufactured mannequins small enough to use for her clients, she built one; and then, when she decided that the pageants Becky was entering were poorly run, she started her own. "I'd hear talk in dressing rooms," Darlene told me, "Like 'If they know you, you win; if they don't, you don't,' and then I was at a pageant and found out that one of the judges was the grandmother of one of the babies, and I thought, I'm going to do my own pageant and do it right." She picked a date, made up flyers, and rented a room. To break even, she had to attract at least fifty kids. She ended up with a hundred and twenty. After a few years, she was able to expand Southern Charm into North Carolina, Mississippi, New York, and Maryland, and she told me that she might soon be adding Virginia and Florida. In each state, Darlene appoints a director to run preliminary pageants and the state finals, and she herself takes care of the national finals. All beauty pageants are owned privately, and most use state directors, as Darlene does. State directors can make money running a pageant, but unless they own a system they need a full-time job. Recently, Darlene's Tennessee directors, a married couple, had to resign, because the man, a Baptist minister, had just got his own church and wasn't free on Sundays anymore.

How do beauty pageants make Burgess self-sufficient?

Stacie Brumit, Southern Charm's Alabama state director, arrived at the hotel around noon, loaded down with boxes and bags. The mothers in the lobby hurried with their daughters into a line that started in front of Stacie's registration table and curled down the hall and out the door. Stacie is round-faced and round-shouldered and has a bleached-blond pageboy. She was already heavily into pageants when she signed on to be Darlene's Alabama director—she had competed herself when she was little, and so far she has entered her two-year-old daughter, Brianna, in thirty, starting when Brianna was five months old. "I see how much being in them is giving Brianna, even at her age," she said. "I think she's going to be a great public speaker because of her pageant experience. She's learning poise. She's going to end up being . . . being like the President! I mean, he's not shaky when he's up there speaking." Before becoming a pageant director, Stacie worked at Wal-Mart. This was when she was expecting Brianna, and she says that even though directing a pageant is hard work, it's nothing compared with sitting on a stool out in the cold in front of a Wal-Mart greeting shoppers when you're six months pregnant and sick as a dog.

What do these mothers want for their daughters?

The kids in line to be registered ranged from six months old to almost but not quite four, and they were beautiful or cute or plain, and they were wearing white satin dresses covered with matching satin capes trimmed with feathers, and peach dresses with beaded bodices and heart-shaped cutouts in the back, and powder-blue dresses with leg-o'-mutton sleeves. The girls who were old enough to have some hair had it swept up, prom style, or left loose and sprayed into curvy shapes, and the bigger girls wore foundation, blusher, eye-shadow, and mascara, and the babies wore no makeup except maybe a little pink gloss on their lips. Some of the mothers wore attractive clothes and had their hair blown smooth, but many were too fat or too thin or looked tired and frayed next to their dazzling daughters. While the mothers were waiting to register, the fathers dawdled in the parking lot having a smoke. The babies napped, and the bigger girls practiced pageant modelling: eye contact with the judges; a wide smile showing one row of teeth; "pretty hands," which means holding your arms straight and slightly lifted, with your hands bent at the wrist and parallel to the floor; and "pretty feet," the pose for the beauty lineup, right heel pressed to left instep, toes wide and apart.

To put on a proper pageant, you need trophies and banners and crowns and plaques, and judges who aren't related to any of your contestants, and a master of ceremonies to run the event, and masking tape to make "X"s on the floor showing the kids where to do their modelling turns. If you're giving prize money, you need your prize money, but otherwise you don't need anything else—except in Tennessee and Arkansas, where directors need to post a ten-thousand-dollar bond. Tennessee instituted this practice about twenty years ago, after a pageant director in Nashville was shot and killed by her husband the night before one of her pageants and none of the contestants ever got their entry fees back. Some pageants are scams. Some issue bad checks to the winners or promise scholarships and never come through, and others say they will give you your prize money only if you come to another pageant, and by the time you do that you've spent more money than you would have ever won. There have been occasions when a pageant went bankrupt before any of the winners could collect their money but not before the pageant director had collected a lot of entry fees. Some pageants start late and are run sloppily, and the kids are kept up until all hours and are expected not to complain. Many pageants, though, like Universal/Southern Charm, have been around a long time and are considered quality pageants. Darlene Burgess is strict, and her rules are exacting:

> Contestants should stand still in lineup, no exaggerated poses. Mothers should have control of their child at all times. Baby through 6 years old should wear short dresses. Dresses do not have to be loaded with rhinestones. After 36 months of age, no waving or blowing kisses. Sportswear: This is a garment of your choice but should be dress sportswear such as a jumpsuit . . . something they would wear when dressing up, but not sports related. Black is a very good fashion color now. It is permissible in all age groups if the color is becoming to the contestant. Braces and Missing Teeth: This is just a part of growing up and as long as the contestant smiles and acts naturally you are not to count off. . . . This same principle applies to scratches and similar childhood mishaps. We expect our judges to conduct themselves in a ladylike (gentlemanly) fashion at all times. Judges, No Drinking at any time while you are at this pageant. No exceptions. You must keep in mind that this is a children's pageant and conduct yourselves accordingly.

In a stroller in the lobby was Nina from Montgomery, who had a tiny pink face and tiny gold earrings and a scramble of fine red hair. Her pageant dress was still on its hanger. She was napping in a pink sleep suit and a pair of Tweetie Bird shoes. Her mother, Kris Ragsdale, had a long dark braid and a steady, sobering gaze. While she talked, she moved Nina's stroller back and forth, the way you move a vacuum cleaner. Kris told me that she was eighteen and Nina was eight months old. She'd got into pageants this past winter, when she took Nina to the Jefferson Davis Pageant and the Christmas Angel Pageant in Montgomery at the urging of a friend. Kris had never been in a pageant when she was a kid. She mostly lived in foster homes or on her own since she was little, and she got married when she was sixteen. Her husband, James, was dressed in a loose heavy-metal-band T-shirt and an Orlando Magic hat, and he said he worked in Montgomery as a saw sharpener. "He's got a pretty good job," Kris said, rocking the stroller. "Still, I mean, we can hardly save a penny." Until recently, Kris and James shared an apartment with James's ex-girlfriend, James's little son, David, and

James's ex-girlfriend's daughter, to save on rent. It cost thirty-five dollars just to enter today's beauty competition, and there were extra fees to enter the contest for Most Photogenic, Most Beautiful, Best Dress, Dream Girl, and Western Wear. There was also the Supreme Special—fifty dollars for all categories except Dream Girl and Western Wear. The fees for national pageants are higher. It costs a hundred and seventy-five dollars to register for the Southern Charm national, and between fifty and a hundred dollars to enter each special category, like Superstar Baby, Talent, Additional Talent, and Southern Belle. Kris said she'd bought the Supreme Special for Nina today. "You save the money with the Supreme," she explained. "You don't get the Western Wear, but we don't do Western Wear with her yet anyway. The hats are too big for her." She lifted Nina out of the stroller and started changing her carefully into a stiff royal-blue dress. "My mom got this for me," Kris said. "It was guess how much. Sixty dollars reduced to forty."

A woman nearby who heard us talking came over and said to Kris, "Honey, you have to meet Joni Deal. She rents out all sorts of dresses and Western clothes and everything. She'll rent you something nice for the pageants." The woman was here with her granddaughter Rhiannon, who was named for a Fleetwood Mac song and was three years old and big for her age. Rhiannon had been in dozens of pageants and usually won everything except fashion. "We're doing something about that, though," her grandmother said. "We've got something really nice now for her dress. We're not talking about a Kathie Lee off-the-rack-from-Wal-Mart dress, either. I bought her a plain old dress, and then I went to the bridal section at a fabric store and bought a whole lot of trim and beading, and I got out that glue gun and did it myself." She looked at Kris and then said, "For us, losing is not an option."

"If we take Nina to the nationals, we're going to have to get her something that's more elegant," James said. "Something more frilly. The judges kill for frilly." In the meantime, Kris said, they had to save for future entry fees, although James hopes they will be able to find a local business that will sponsor Nina; someone told him that a business could claim beauty-pageant fees as a tax deduction. He mentioned that both Nina and David, his little boy, had been offered modelling contracts. "It sounded good," he said, "but it cost about six hundred and fifty dollars just to sign up, and then you had to buy all the makeup and the modelling kit, too, so we decided not to do it." He brightened for a moment. "Something good is definitely going to happen for Nina and David, I think," he said. "Nina's got the pageants, and my ex-girlfriend's talking to some guy right now at Extra Model Management who says he thinks he might be able to get a sitcom for David. That would really be great, but I think it would mean moving to New York, and I don't know how I feel about moving."

"It's hard doing pageants, because of the money, but it's worth it," Kris said. "I mean, everybody likes to show off their daughter, right?

> Why does Kris Ragsdale sacrifice so her daughter can be in pageants? What does she hope her daughter will gain from the experience? What does she hope she will learn?

It's fun for us, and she really enjoys it. It's mother-daughter time, and I know someday we won't have that as much. We're putting all her pageant pictures and scorecards in a scrapbook, so she can have it, and someday she'll be able to see it and all her trophies and say, 'Gee, I did that!' It gives her something she can be proud of."

The pageant was about to start, and Kris stood up and attached a bow to Nina's wisps of hair. Nina didn't have enough hair to hold a regular barrette, so Kris had devised something clever with a piece of a zipper she'd cut from a Zip-loc bag. She said she realized that some people might not like pageants, because they thought children shouldn't be exposed to competition this early in their lives, but she and James thought it would be good for Nina—it would give her a head start, especially if Nina wanted to try for Miss America someday. Kris said, "I know it's a lot of pressure, but, I mean, you know, you're under some kind of pressure your whole entire life."

Darlene likes her pageants to start with the babies, because they're at their best in the morning. "You have to do it that way," she said. "Babies just will not put up with an all-day pageant." The room for the competition looked festive. A blue-and-white Southern Charm banner was hanging on the back wall, and beside it was a table loaded with crowns and trophies of all different sizes. The crowns were as big as birthday cakes and were studded with rhinestones. The biggest ones cost almost two hundred dollars apiece. "When Becky was in pageants, she was always getting these so-so crowns," Darlene had complained to me. "I don't want that reputation, so I spend a fortune on my crowns."

The judges were two big-boned women with layered haircuts and soft faces. For a few minutes, they murmured to each other, and then looked at Stacie with solemn expressions and nodded. The mothers brought their babies forward one by one and held them facing out toward the judges, fluffing the babies' skirts into meringues of chiffon that billowed up and over the mothers' arms and the babies' dangling legs. Displayed this way, the babies looked weightless and relaxed and sublime, suspended in midair. The judges studied them and scored them in the individual categories while Stacie read introductions: "This is Cheyenne. Her hobbies are playing and cooing.... Her favorite food is pears.... Her favorite TV show is 'Barney.' She is sponsored today by her friends and family.... This is Kayle.... Her favorite food is macaroni and cheese.... Her hobby is exploring newfound things.... This is Taylor.... She loves

> How do you think the judges decide which baby is the most beautiful?

horseback riding and taking her baby cat, Patches, out for walks." One baby picked her nose during her moment at the judging table. Another flailed her arms at the balloons floating above the judges and started to cry. Kris bounced Nina and clucked at her until she finally cracked a gummy smile, but just at that moment both judges happened to look away. Everyone in the audience was standing and waving and aiming toss-away paper cameras at the babies onstage, and every time a camera flashed the crowns on the table flashed, too.

The older girls were divided into age groups of twelve to twenty-three months, twenty-four to thirty-five months, three- and four-year-olds together, five- and six-year-olds, and so on. Southern Charm accepts girls up to twenty-one years old, but the oldest girl at the Prattville pageant was probably seven. These older children walked onstage by themselves, and some of them even turned the way they were supposed to when they got to the masking-tape "X"s, and a few remembered to do "pretty hands" and "pretty feet" and the grimacing pageant-girl smile. The two-year-olds tended to wander. A blonde from Eclectic named Kendall stood twirling a piece of her hair around her finger and then roamed off the stage. Her mother was standing next to me, and she said that this would probably be Kendall's last pageant because she hated wearing dresses and was much happier barrel-racing her pony at home.

The Southern Charm rules say, "Remember, if you coach from the audience the child will not have eye contact with the judges and they will deduct points for not having eye contact." In spite of that, nearly all the parents were on their feet during the rest of the pageant, making wild hand signals to their daughters which meant "Smile" and "Blow a kiss at the judge" and "Smile much bigger." They pushed to the front of the room, nearly leaning over the judges' shoulders. It was as if someone had set them on a table and then tipped it forward. Just a few minutes after the pageant started, hardly anyone was left sitting in the back of the room.

Darlene has forty thousand people on her mailing list, and they are spread out all over the nation. JonBenet Ramsey was one of those names, although she never particularly stood out. Darlene says that in spite of what the papers have said not that many people in the pageant world had heard of JonBenet until she got killed. Right after the murder, Darlene looked up JonBenet's name on her computer and deleted it, so that the Ramseys wouldn't get any upsetting Southern Charm mail.

Darlene and Jerry Burgess live about ten miles from downtown Jackson, in an old farmhouse that has been renovated since the days when their daughter, Becky, was at home. (Becky is married and lives in Nashville, where she is studying to go to medical school, and she has a two-year-old daughter, who is just starting on the pageant circuit.) Now the Burgess house is pure pageant. In the outbuildings is a trophy shop and a silk-screening shop where the banners are made and a photography studio where Jerry shoots portfolios of contestants. In the basement is Glitz & Glamour, Darlene's mail-order pageant-dress business, and in the front room are four computers containing all the mailing lists, and eight video machines for copying Jerry's official tapes of the pageants, and Federal Express labels and boxes for the dozen or so Glitz & Glamour dresses and Southern Charm videos they ship out every day.

The phone rings all day without stopping, so it is nearly impossible to have an uninterrupted conversation with Darlene. One of the days I was in Jackson, I asked her why she thought people outside the pageant world objected to it so adamantly. "I don't know why they even have an opinion about it at all," she said. "I look at pageants like I look at any other hobby, like golf. I sure wouldn't hit a little white ball around on a lawn and I don't know why anyone else would want to, but that's their business and not mine. Hold on a minute."

"Hello, Glitz. . . . Yes, this is Darlene Burgess. . . . O.K., I can send you an entry form. How'd you find out about us? . . . Well, if you want to go to New York, that's a mini-national. Who's crowning in New York? Let me think. Oh, fiddle! Jerry, who's crowning in New York? Well, I can't remember. . . . So now give me your name and address."

Vicki Whitehead, who works at Glitz & Glamour part-time, came upstairs. "Darlene, I have a lady on the phone who has an eight-month-old she says is really tiny and she needs something very dainty for her to wear. And do we have any ultra-suede in an animal print in pink and black? Because I have a lady who's dying for some."

Another call for Darlene: "I see. . . . Do you have videos of her in pageants? O.K., send it and I'd be glad to critique it for you." Darlene covered the mouthpiece and said to me, "I'm offering to do it because this lady's up in Illinois and really needs help. They're not too pageant-wise up in places like Illinois. I really think the kids up North are afraid to compete with the kids down South. I remember once Becky said to me, 'Mom, the New York kids are beautiful, but they don't know how to model and they don't know how to dress.'"

When Darlene had a break from the phone, she said that nearly every day since JonBenet's murder she has been called by some reporter. So have most of the best-known coaches and the owners of the other big pageant systems. Since JonBenet, Darlene has had mothers tell her they weren't going to come to the pageants if reporters would be there, and some mothers have said they had stopped answering their phones because they were sick of being asked to comment on the murder. She is rankled by how dismissive non-pageant people are of everything that she loves about pageants and of how much they mean to these little girls. Some people in pageants have difficult lives and work hard all the time and lose out on a lot, but on any Sunday at a pageant somewhere they have their chance to win. This seems so obvious that Darlene thinks there must be some other reason that pageants have been so maligned. She has finally decided that people who don't appreciate children's pageants probably just don't have their own pretty little girls.

> Why is Darlene Burgess so surprised by the negative opinions about children's beauty pageants?

From all appearances, Darlene has been a very successful entrepreneur. It happens that most of her state directors are women, and many other pageant systems and pageant-related businesses, like the dress shops, are owned by women. Some of the best-known coaches are women, too. It seems odd that these are the very same women who are certain that a girl's best path in life is to learn how to look good onstage. It's as if they had never noticed that they've made something of themselves by relying on other talents.

The first day I was in Jackson, Darlene and I sat in her living room to watch some tapes of last year's Southern Charm national finals, while Jerry was in the other room labelling FedEx boxes with Glitz dresses inside, bound for Irving, Texas, and Lawrenceville, Georgia, and Leesville, Louisiana. To me, all the kids on the tape looked the same—cute, awkward, stiff in their frothy dresses, a little uncertain when they got to the "X"s on the stage. Most of them stared anxiously at their mothers for directions. Darlene used to judge pageants, and she still has a judge's eye: as we watched the tape, she pointed out winners and losers and which girls had pushy coaches and which girls were wearing makeup that didn't do justice to their skin tone. "This girl, she's beautiful, but her sportswear doesn't do a thing for her, it's too boxy," Darlene pointed out. "I don't like this one's hair all sprayed up like that. I swear, she looks like a Pentecostal! Oh, here's the Southern Belle category. You have to wear something that's historically accurate. My judges get so ticky about it that they'll come up onstage and check your dress and make sure you don't have any zippers. . . . Now, look at this baby with her belt sagging. I don't know why these mothers don't realize that a little Velcro under the belt would hold it up. Babies don't have any hips and they have that little potbelly, and a belt just isn't going to stay up on its own."

> Most of the judges and pageant directors seem to have very definite views about who is beautiful. How accurate do you think these are?

In her personal philosophy, Darlene doesn't like too much eyeliner, and this year she's going to allow only classic Miss America-style modelling in the Swimwear competition. She blames coaches for teaching sexy poses to the girls. "Ten years ago, it wasn't like this," she said. "Now, with the coaches, things are getting out of control." On her granddaughter, Shelby, she likes to see simple makeup and a gorgeous dress, and, since Shelby is doing well, this appears to be working. But some girls do need help to be really big in pageants, according to Darlene. They need coaching, they need advice on their clothes, and, in a few exceptional circumstances, they might even need surgery, although as a rule she doesn't approve. "There was one girl, about thirteen, and it was a special case," Darlene said. "She was a very pretty girl, except she had a really big old honker and it just killed her in the pageants. Even if she hadn't been a pageant child, she was actually better off with a new nose." She has seen kids who are miserable but have been pushed onstage by their mothers, and mothers who yell at their kids when they don't win, and kids falling asleep on their feet because the pageants went on late into the night. "I don't compete the kids at night, but some pageants do," she said. "I remember once Becky had to do her talent at one in the morning. One in the morning! She was exhausted! But the pageant directors insisted on going late. I think that's child abuse."

While we talked, Darlene got up to check the chicken in the oven and the fresh bread rising in her breadmaker for lunch. Before we ate, she wanted to show me the winners' speeches at last year's Southern Charm nationals. On the tape, a knock-kneed girl with tawny curls placed a rhinestone Supreme Queen crown on another girl's head. Then the new Supreme Queen started her speech: "I want to say thanks to the Lord Jesus Christ, and thanks to Jerry and Darlene, the directors of the pageant.... I want people to know that pageants are about the whole girl, not about who has the best makeup and hair."

> Do you think pageants are about the "whole girl"?

By the time the Western Wear competition began in Prattville, it was the end of the afternoon. The room was chaotic: people were coming in and out with snacks from a vending machine outside; a lot of the babies were fretting, and a few were yelling as if it were the end of the world. Stacie cast her eye on one of the loudest babies and said into her microphone, "Sounds like we got someone who's not ready for Western Wear!" I was sitting next to this particular loud baby, who was on her mother's lap, and a man behind us was the loud baby's grandfather. He tapped me on the shoulder. "What do you think of this?" he said, "I mean, they're exploiting these kids! Dressing them up, keeping them up all day!"

"Daddy, you're supposed to be supporting me, not criticizing me," the baby's mother said. "Look, it's our first pageant and probably our last, but I think it's good to try things. I don't know how I feel about spending so much money. But I like it. It's fun. It's just—Maybe she's not ready." She glanced at her daughter, who was about a year old and was dressed in a satin cowgirl outfit. The outfit looked scratchy. The baby was squirming and weeping. The man said, "Come on, look at her crying, Jeannie! I think it's crazy. And it's a waste of money besides."

Stacie Brumit had told me that she'd seen "a lot of mamas dragging their babies kicking and screaming onto the stage." She doesn't like that sort of thing, but she says that some children need extra encouragement. Even Brianna Brumit, who is a veteran, pulls back a little before she has to go onstage. "Once I get her up there, though, she's totally different," Stacie said. "She's just in another world. And it's special for me. For Brianna to go up and win Queen, that's the best thing in the world to me."

Nina Ragsdale didn't win Most Photogenic; when Kris asked the judges later, they told her that Nina's pictures needed to show more personality. Nina didn't win Dream Girl, which is based on pure facial beauty; that went to a baby with a peachy face and dark, sleepy eyes. She didn't win Most Beautiful, which is subtly different from Dream Girl, and she didn't win Best Dress; the judges said that blue didn't work for her and that Kris should get her something in turquoise or white. Then the final categories were announced. Nina didn't win Queen or Supreme Queen, and when there were hardly any prizes left to be given out my heart started sinking, but then Nina was named first runner-up and got a medium-sized trophy, and Kris had a moment in which to display her with the trophy on the stage. The baby who won Supreme Queen got a trophy that was taller than any of the children at the pageant. Someone called out, "Honey, if you live in a trailer you're in trouble! You won't be able to get that into your home!"

I went back to Alabama a few weeks later to see Nina in another pageant. This one was also at the Prattville Holiday Inn. The pageant was called Lil' American Beauty, and the trophies and the crowns and the backdrop were different, but the feeling in the air was the same. I recognized some of the kids from Southern Charm. There were only about a dozen girls, so the judging went fast and, just like at the first pageant, I could hardly bear to watch the crowning. Kris Ragsdale stood up there with Nina, who was asleep, her bow sliding out of her hair. The other mothers were also lined up with their babies, shifting them around in their arms like bags of groceries, and they had a little tightness in their faces as they waited to hear what the judges had to say. Most of the babies had curled up and were lost in the folds of their puffy dresses, and suddenly all I could really see were the mothers, wearing their plain outfits and their plain makeup, their husbands and parents standing a few feet away ready to take the picture they were all waiting for, of their beautiful daughters being crowned.

Final Reflection

How does the way a person looks affect your decisions about them?

> *Sometimes the class discussions got real heated, especially when people had strong opinions.*
>
> —Tim Morgan

❖ *After You Read, Consider*

1. What did you think of JonBenet Ramsey's murder before you read "Beautiful Girls"? How is this article about the Ramsey murder? How is it not?

2. Babies don't really have many choices; they do what their parents want them to. Would the age of the contestants make a difference in what you think about beauty pageants? Does it matter that the girls start so young?

3. Can participating in a beauty pageant really give a young girl poise and confidence?

> *I never did learn to like writing, but I found I liked the thinking and arguing that went with it.*
>
> —Chris Bakers

❖ *Suggestions for Writing*

1. At the end of her piece, Orlean shows the contestants fading into the background so that all she could "really see were the mothers, wearing their plain outfits and their plain makeup." Write an essay that explains what is happening in this final scene. How does Orlean feel about these mothers? Why can't she bear to watch the crowning?

2. Beauty pageants have helped some women start their own businesses and gain financial security, but at the same time the pageants place most of the emphasis for individual success on physical beauty. Write an essay in which you explore this contradiction.

3. As evidenced by Orlean's article, what do beauty pageants represent about work? Write an essay in which you explore the issue of beauty and the ethics of work.

Abraham Verghese

From My Own Country

Abraham Verghese is Professor of Medicine and Chief of Infectious Diseases at Texas Tech Health Sciences Center, El Paso, Texas. He is a graduate of the Iowa Writers' Workshop, and his writing has appeared in the New Yorker, Granta, The North American Review, Sports Illustrated, Story *and many medical journals, including the* Annals of Internal Medicine *and the* American Journal of Medicine. *He lives in El Paso, Texas.*

--- ❖ ---

I'm keeping my journal.

—Anne Rogers-Smith

Prereading Reflection

Recall a time when a close friend or family member was very ill.

--- ❖ ---

Bobby Keller called me in the office as I was about to leave for home. He sounded shrill and alarmed.

"Doc? Ed is *very* sick! He is *very, very* short of breath and running a fever. A hundred and three. Dr. Verghese, he's turning blue on me."

"Bobby, call the emergency ambulance service—tell them to bring you to the Johnson City Medical Center."

Ed Maupin, the diesel mechanic, had had a CD4 count of 30 the previous week when I had seen him in clinic; Bobby Keller's was 500. At that visit, Ed's oral thrush had cleared up but he was still feeling tired and had been missing work. When I had examined Ed, the lymph nodes in his neck, which had been as big as goose eggs, had suddenly shrunk: I had thought to myself that this was either a good sign or a very bad sign; his immune system had either given up the fight or successfully neutralized the virus. The latter was unlikely.

Bobby, at that visit, had looked well and continued to work in the fashion store. I hoped now that Bobby's description of the gravity of the situation was just histrionics.

I was at the Miracle Center well ahead of the ambulance. Soon it came roaring in, all its lights flashing. When the back door opened, I peeked in: Ed's eyes were rolled back in his head, and he was covered with a fine sheen of sweat. Despite the oxygen mask that the ambulance crew had on, his skin was the color of lead. His chest was making vigorous but ineffective excursions.

Bobby, who had ridden in the front, was scarcely able to stand up. His face was tremulous; he was on the verge of fainting.

"Don't put him on no machines, whatever you do," Bobby begged me. "Please, no machines."

"Why?"

"Because that's what he told me. He doesn't want it."

"When did he tell you? Just now?"

"No. A long time ago."

"Did he put it in writing? Does he have a living will?"

"No..."

> Do you feel like an outsider in the presence of medical professionals? Do you have problems making your desires about your health care known?

In the emergency room, I stabilized Ed as best I could without intubating him. I took his oxygen mask off momentarily and looked at his mouth. His mucous membranes were loaded with yeast again—it had blossomed in just a week. But I was examining his mouth to try to decide how difficult it would be to intubate him. His short, receding lower jaw, which the beard concealed well, could make this a tricky intubation. I asked him to say "aaah." He tried to comply: his uvula and tonsils just barely came into view, another sign that he would be a tough intubation.

Ideally, an anesthetist would have been the best person to perform intubation. But I didn't want to call an anesthetist who, given the patient, might or might not be willing to do this procedure. Time was running out.

> Why wouldn't an anesthetist be willing to do the procedure? Should a doctor have a right to refuse to treat a patient?

Ed was moaning and muttering incomprehensibly; his brain was clearly not getting enough oxygen. His blood pressure was 70 millimeters of mercury systolic over 50 diastolic. This was extremely low for him, because he had baseline hypertension. His cold, clammy extremities told me that the circulation to his arms and legs had shut down in an effort to shunt blood to the brain; even so, what blood got to the brain was not carrying enough oxygen. Ed's chest sounded dull in the bases when I percussed it; on listening with my stethoscope, he was wet and gurgly. The reason he was not oxygenating his blood was clear: his lungs were filled with inflammatory fluid. I ordered a stat chest x-ray and arterial blood gases. I had only a few minutes before I had to either breathe for him, or let him go. I needed more guidance from Bobby as to Ed's wishes.

I had an excellent nurse assisting me; she had already started an IV and brought the "crash cart." The respiratory therapist was administering oxygen and had an Ambu bag ready. I asked them to get goggles and masks in addition to their gloves, and to get a gown, mask and gloves ready for me. They were to put theirs on and wait for me. The curtains were pulled and Ed's presence was largely unnoticed in the bustle of the ER. An orthopedist was putting a cast on an individual in the next room, and patients were waiting in the other cubicles.

I came out to the waiting room, but Bobby was not there!

I hurried outside.

Bobby and three other men and one woman were near the ambulance entrance, smoking. The men bore a striking resemblance to Ed Maupin—the same sharp features, the slightly receding chin. One of them, the oldest, wore a green work uniform. I recognized his face as a familiar one, someone who worked in an auto parts store where I had ordered a replacement bumper for the rusted one that had fallen off my Z. Bobby Keller, still trembling, introduced me to Ed's brothers, all younger than Ed. The woman was the wife of one of the brothers.

"Bobby," I asked, "can I tell them what's going on?"

"Tell them everything," Bobby said, the tears pouring down uncontrollably, his body shaking with sobs.

I addressed the brothers: "Ed is very sick. A few months ago we found out he has AIDS." (There was no point in trying to make the distinction between HIV infection and AIDS. If Ed had not had AIDS when I saw him in the clinic, he most certainly did now.) "Now he has a bad pneumonia from the AIDS. I need to put him on a breathing machine in the next few minutes or he will die. I have a feeling that the pneumonia he has can be treated. If we put him on the breathing machine, it won't be forever. We have a good chance of getting him off. But Bobby tells me that Ed has expressed a desire *not* to be put on the machine."

The assembled family turned to Bobby who nodded vigorously: "He did! Said he never wanted to be on no machines."

The family was clear-eyed, trying to stay calm. They pulled hard at their cigarettes. The smoke rose quietly around their weathered faces. They looked like a Norman Rockwell portrait—small-town America's citizens in their workclothes in a hospital parking lot, facing a family crisis. But this situation was one that Norman Rockwell hadn't attempted, one he had never dreamed of. I felt they were fond of their oldest brother, though perhaps disapproving of his relationship with Bobby. Yet judging by how they had all been standing around Bobby when I walked out, I didn't think they had any strong dislike for Bobby—it was almost impossible to dislike him. They had had many years to get used to the idea of Bobby and Ed, the couple, and it was only the idea, I sensed, that they had somehow not accepted.

"We need to discuss this," the older brother said.

"We have no time, I need to go right back in," I said.

They moved a few feet away from Bobby and me. I asked Bobby, "Do you have power-of-attorney or anything like that to make decisions for Ed?" Bobby shook his head.

Why does Ed's family leave Bobby out of the decision-making process? What does this indicate?

We looked over to where the family was caucusing. The oldest brother was doing all the talking. They came back.

"We want for you to do everything you can. Put him on the breathing machine, if you have to."

At this a little wail came out of Bobby Keller and then degenerated into sobs. I put my hand on Bobby's shoulder. He shook his head back and forth, back and forth. He wanted to say something but could not find a voice.

The oldest brother spoke again. His tone was matter-of-fact and determined:

"*We* are his family. *We* are legally responsible for him. We want you to do *everything* for him."

We are his family. I watched Bobby's face crumble as he suddenly became a mere observer with no legal right to determine the fate of the man he had loved since he was seven years old. He was finally, despite the years that had passed and whatever acceptance he and Ed found together, an outsider.

I took him aside and said, "Bobby, I have to go on. There is no way for me not to at this point. There's a really good chance that I can rescue Ed from the pneumonia. If I thought it would only make Ed suffer, I wouldn't do it. If this is *Pneumocystis*, it should respond to treatment."

Bobby kept sobbing, shaking his head as I talked, fat tears rolling off his eyes onto the ground, onto his chest. He felt he was betraying Ed. He could not deliver on his promise.

I had no time to pacify Bobby or try to convince him. I rushed back in. Ed looked worse. As I went through the ritual of gowning and masking (it was reassuring to have rituals to fall back on, a ritual for every crisis), it struck me that the entire situation had been in my power to dictate. All I had to do was to come out and say that the pneumonia did not look good, that it looked like the end. *I* mentioned the respirator, *I* offered it as an option. I could have just kept quiet. I had, when it came down to the final moment, given Ed's brothers the power of family. Not Bobby.

But there was no time to look back now.

I leaned down to Ed's ear and explained what I was about to do. He showed no sign of understanding. He was expending tremendous amounts of energy to breathe.

I stood behind Ed with the endotracheal tube in my right hand and the laryngoscope in the other. I put Xylocaine jelly on the tip of the endotracheal tube. We lowered the head of the stretcher, extended Ed's head over the edge.

I had the nurse now give Ed an intravenous bolus of 20 milligrams of Valium. An anesthetist might have used a curarelike paralyzing agent. In a few seconds, Ed's breathing ceased altogether.

The respiratory therapist gave him a few brisk breaths of oxygen from the squeeze bag and stepped away. I inserted the laryngoscope blade into his mouth and heaved up on the tongue. I could not see the vocal cords and could only barely see the epiglottis. I pushed the tube past the epiglottis, giving the tube some torque, hoping to steer it into the voice box and down the trachea. It went in too easily and I knew I had missed.

I pulled out and we bagged him with the squeeze bag again. I was talking to myself: *Come on Abe; hamsters are ten times as difficult as this, and you have intubated 260 hamsters at last count.* Another voice in my head replied: *This ain't no hamster.*

Ed was a deeper shade of blue now. If I didn't do it in the next try, we were going to have to call an anesthetist. Or call a Code Blue. The second time and I still did not see the vocal cords. But this time I felt the tube grate against the tracheal rings, just as with my hamsters. I listened over first one side of the chest and then the other while the respiratory therapist pumped air into the tube. I could hear good breath sounds on both sides; we had secured an airway and the tube was sitting in perfect position, just above the carina, where the trachea divides into the left and right bronchi.

It had been a while since I had intubated anyone myself; usually there were layers of interns and residents and students who fought for and did all the procedures. I was pleased with our success. The nurse patted me on the back.

"Did you know," I asked her, in the glow of my postprocedural success, "that intubation was invented by a physician named O'Dwyer as a lifesaving measure in diphtheria? It's therefore an infectious diseases procedure!"

"Yeah, right," she said, unimpressed. "I'll keep that in mind. Next time we have a trauma case that needs intubation we'll call in an infectious diseases consult."

I went upstairs with Ed to the intensive care unit. Now I wrote orders for the settings on the ventilator that would optimally oxygenate Ed's lungs. I put him on a 100 percent inspired oxygen concentration (in contrast to the 21 percent oxygen concentration we normally breathe) and dialed in the rate and the volume of each breath the ventilator would deliver. I wrote an order to have an arterial blood oxygen measurement made in half an hour to allow me to cut back on the oxygen if at all possible; pure oxygen in high concentrations is damaging in and of itself. I wrote orders for intravenous fluids and for laboratory tests. I felt better about Ed in the ICU than I had with Scotty Daws. I had inherited Scotty Daws and in retrospect it had been a no-win situation. Ed was the best sort of patient to bring to the ICU. Someone who I thought would perhaps walk out of there.

Pneumocystis pneumonia is easy to diagnose if you get a good specimen of sputum. Secretions obtained by washing out a segment of lung during bronchoscopy—so-called bronchoalveolar lavage or BAL—are ideal, but even an ordinary sputum, as long as it is not grossly contaminated with saliva, can serve almost as well.

Since Ed had a tube going down into his trachea, breathing for him, it was simple enough to squirt some saline down it and then suck it back out with a catheter.

I carried the specimen down to the lab, made some smears of it on glass slides, then looked at them under the microscope after staining them for bacteria and TB. I saw only an outpouring of inflammatory cells and little else. To see *Pneumocystis carinii* requires a special stain called a silver stain. It would take a day for the pathology department to complete the stain and give me the definitive word on what it showed. The fact that I saw nothing but pus cells on my simple stains—no TB, no bacteria—suggested that this was *Pneumocystis*. I began Ed on trimethoprim-sulfamethoxazole, or Bactrim, the drug of choice for this organism.

The only cases of *Pneumocystis* pneumonia I had ever seen were in persons with AIDS. This was unique to my generation of infectious diseases physicians: we had all come of age in the era of AIDS.

But *Pneumocystis* had a long history before AIDS made it a household word. Epidemics of *Pneumocystis* swept through Europe in the 1940s. They occurred primarily in premature infants in orphanages, in the setting of overcrowding and malnutrition.

After the war years, the organism began to manifest only in select patients with immune-compromising conditions such as leukemia or after long-term cortisone administration. St. Jude Children's Hospital in Memphis, at the other end of the state from us, had accrued tremendous experience with this disease by virtue of their patient population—children with leukemias.

Why is the writer giving us all this background about pneumocystis? Why would this information be important to our understanding?

How are we to view this organism? As an invader from outside? Or an opportunist from within? To give a rat *Pneumocystis* pneumonia, all you have to do is give the rat cortisone—a potent suppressor of the immune system—and the rat then *spontaneously* develops *Pneumocystis* infection. By contrast, Betty and I had to pour staphylococci in massive doses down the hamster trachea to produce infection with staphylococci. The rat experiment suggests that *Pneumocystis* is present in low numbers in the lung at all times. The *Pneumocystis* that at this moment was filling up Ed's lungs lives in my lungs and in yours. The constant vigilance of the immune system keeps it in check. Immune suppression by steroids or, as in Ed's case, AIDS results in unchecked multiplication of this organism.

I sought out Bobby Keller in the ICU waiting room. His eyes were red and puffy from crying. I tried to explain what I had done so far. Bobby listened perfunctorily to what I had to say about *Pneumocystis* and the amount of oxygen Ed required. It was clear he felt Ed's time had come and that we had gone beyond a threshold of intervention that Ed had not wanted to cross.

When I got home it was after midnight. Steven was in our bed. Rather than disturb them, I went to Steven's room and crawled into his bed.

It felt as if my head had just touched the pillow when my beeper went off. It was from the ICU at the Miracle Center. An intern was calling to say that Ed's heart had gone into a malignant and chaotic rhythm. A Code Blue was in progress.

"What time is it?" I asked.

"Four thirty in the morning," he said.

"How long has the code been going on?"

"Five minutes. And there has been no sign of his heartbeat coming back."

"Keep going, I'll be right there. Ask the nurses to call in his lover and the family and have them wait in the quiet room."

In the ICU, a furious Code Blue was in progress. All the bustle and activity *around* Ed was in contrast to the activity *in* Ed's body: there was no heartbeat, and only the forceful chest compression by the intern was sending blood around. I reviewed the code chart: everything I would have done had been tried: calcium, epinephrine, bicarbonate. I waved everyone off, thanked them, and we pulled out the tube from Ed's trachea. Ed now looked peaceful, asleep.

In a few minutes there was no one in the room but an ICU nurse and myself. She was a night nurse I had seen around, but never worked with. She was picking up the debris from the code. She was dressed for a shuttle mission—gloves, gown, mask, goggles. This was not inappropriate, as during the Code Blue there was potential for splashing.

I said to her, by way of small talk, "I'm surprised that his heart should have quit so quickly. I really thought I could cure the pneumonia, wean him off the respirator, get a few more meaningful months or even years of life for him."

She stopped what she was doing, looked at me and said, affecting nonchalance: "Well they're *all* going to die, aren't they? There's not much point to this."

> Would you want this nurse to take care of your family member?

She left the room before I could think of an appropriate reply.

I was furious.

I wanted to ask her what the "point" was in the ninety-year-old patients that they played with in the unit for days until they were brain dead, all the while running up a huge bill that we, the taxpayers, would pay? Right at that moment there was a patient in the ICU whom we were sending up for dialysis three times a week when there was no hope of any other organ in the body recovering.

I wanted to ask her if *she* was in the same boat, would she like an extra year of life, or would she opt to leave the world right away? And for that matter, weren't we ALL going to die one day? Did she think her job was to solely take care of immortals?

I calmed myself. "Pick and choose your battles, Abe," I said to myself. In a way she had been baiting me; anything I said back to her would have been a self-fulfilling prophecy for her. It would prove my lack of objectivity. Besides, I *had* failed in this instance. Ed's corpse was proof of my failure.

When I stepped out of the room, I saw her with some other nurses at the nurses' station. She had surely finished telling them about our little encounter. I bade them all good night.

Bobby Keller and the Maupin family were in the quiet room. It was very difficult for me to go in there and tell them Ed had died. Bobby cried. His sobs were big and wrenching. Ed's brothers covered their eyes or turned their heads away from me. The eldest came over and shook my hand and thanked me. Bobby came out with, "Praise the Lord, his suffering is over," and walked alone toward the door.

The next day the pathology report of the bronchial washing from Ed's lung came back. The specimen had been loaded with the saucer-shaped, dark-staining *Pneumocystis*. At this point, of course, it hardly mattered. Ed was dead.

I thought of funerals I had been to in Johnson City where the grieving widow was escorted to the memorial service by friends and family. Tears and hugs, happy memories, casseroles and condolences. Who would comfort Bobby Keller, I wondered.

Final Reflection

Should a doctor be as involved with his or her patients and their families as the narrator is?

> *When we talked about AIDS, the class discussion was very emotional. Some people cried.*
> —Margaret Whiting

❖ *After You Read, Consider*

1. Given what Bobby says about Ed's wishes, do you agree with the way the doctor presents Ed's medical condition to his family?

2. How does the author's description of the family—"They looked like a Norman Rockwell portrait—small-town America's citizens in their workclothes in a hospital parking lot, facing a family crisis"—prepare you for the brother's reaction to Ed's condition?

3. The family responds, "*We* are his family. *We* are legally responsible for him. We want you to do *everything* for him." How would this response likely have differed if this had been a heterosexual couple who lived together? A married couple?

> *Some subjects are difficult to write about, even when they don't affect you directly.*
> —Tina Marshall

❖ *Suggestions for Writing*

1. After caring for Ed, an ICU nurse tells the narrator, "Well they're *all* going to die, aren't they? There's not much point to this." The narrator decides not to respond to her comment. Write a letter responding to this nurse's comments.

2. Write an essay in which you explore the topic of living wills. How might a living will have changed the outcome of this story? How might a living will have allowed Bobby to carry out Ed's last wishes?

3. Write an essay in which you explore the issue of infectious diseases such as AIDS and the caring or uncaring response of the medical community. Do health workers have the right to refuse to treat someone with a highly infectious disease?

Michelle Cook

The Great Blueberry War

Michelle Cook picked various kinds of berries during summer vacations until old enough to drive, then joined the army and eventually migrated to Georgia. She lives in the Atlanta area with her loving housemistress, Salad Shooter, the inspiration for her forthcoming novel, How to Raise a Fat, Spoiled Cat Who Will Awaken You with Loud Demands for Wet Food at 5 AM.

Prereading Reflection

Write about your first job.

Ker-sploosh! There is no sound in the world quite like that of a ripe blueberry exploding on the face of someone you've hurled it at. For a nine-year-old, it's about as much fun as a snowball fight. No, more fun, because blueberries leave this wonderful tint to the skin for days afterward. There is no better place to experience a blueberry fight than while working at a blueberry farm. During the summer of 1981, I gained and lost my first job at a berry farm in a period of two days, and I learned a whole lot about the do's and don'ts of the work world.

My older sister Sabrina and I had been hanging out all summer, getting tired of jumping bike ramps. We wanted something more. Something that brought in that all-important item: money. So when we heard the local blueberry farm was hiring pickers, we grabbed a couple of Sabrina's friends, Sandy and Margie, and biked the mile and a half out to the farm. The foreman looked us over carefully, and then said that I was too small for the work. I insisted loudly to him that while I might be short, I could work as hard as anyone. I wanted that 25 cents per bucket. To a worldly kid of nine, earning up to two dollars a day was a veritable fortune. It meant the freedom to buy and eat all the junk food I wanted. The foreman looked at me, sighed, and said I could come in to work.

> When you were young, how much money seemed like a substantial amount?

After the foreman told us to return at 7:00 AM the next day, we rode back to our fort in the woods. The four of us bragged for hours about what we were going to do with our fortunes. Sabrina, being the eldest, tried to convince us that we needed to pool our money together and do something really big, like build a new fort deep in the woods where the big kids couldn't find it and chase us out when they wanted to go necking. After much cajoling, I finally agreed that a kissing-free fort would be worth it. Kissing was so gross and disgusting. Who would want to swallow someone else's spit?

The next morning, each of us carrying a lunch bag, we rode out to face the world of the legitimately employed. Upon arriving, each of us were told where to lock our bikes, given a bucket, and shown to our respective rows of bushes. The first two hours were easy. Pick a handful of berries, eat half, and dump the rest in your bucket. After that, we began to sicken of berries, and starting yelling insults at each other through the dense rows. By lunchtime, everyone was tired and angry.

I didn't eat much of my lunch; a morning of scarfing blueberries had ruined my appetite. After our breaktime was over, we were herded back to our rows. Back to the toil and drudgery of manual labor. I don't know who threw that first berry, but when it squashed against the back of my head, I got angry. I asked the kid next to me, a true veteran of three whole weeks in the field, if it was okay to return fire. He informed me that the teenagers supervising us didn't care, provided that we didn't hit them and used only rotten berries. As he was telling me this, an entire barrage of berries came flying over from the bush that Sabrina lurked behind.

Yelling for him to cover my back, I dove around the corner of the row. Imagining I was a commando sneaking up silently upon the enemy, I attacked from behind. Smash! An entire handful of rotten berries poured juice from Sabrina's hair down the back of her neck. Before she could retaliate, someone blew a whistle and yelled that it was time to turn in berries and go home.

Have you ever been involved in a game like this? What happened?

By the next morning, I had pretty much forgotten the attack on Sabrina. But she had not. Little did I know she had been plotting revenge the entire night. And before we had been in the fields for an hour, she exacted it.

Yelling to me that she wanted to show me a huge tree frog she had found, she put the plan into motion. I wandered over, looked at her, and then asked where the frog was. She mumbled something, and I was attacked from behind. One of her friends threw a bucket over my head so that I couldn't see, and Sabrina proceeded to shove a handful of squashed berries down the front of my pants. Fighting them off, I yanked the bucket from my head and dived at her. And the fight was on. I don't recall much during the fight, only that it seemed like everybody was in on one side or another. Blueberries rained down like manna from heaven. I was having so much fun, I didn't notice that everyone had stopped suddenly.

Lifting my arm to launch another assault, it was stopped in midswing by the huge hand of the foreman. Looking down at me (at that point he seemed at least nine feet tall), he told me in no uncertain terms that my sister and I were fired. Taking our cards that kept track of our pickings, he informed us that we had made just under a dollar each. He took the money from his pocket, handed it to us, and told us to leave.

> Have you ever been fired from a job?

By the time the popsicle man came by that afternoon, Sabrina and I had mended our fences. We spent our earnings wisely—she on her favorite tutti-frutti bar, and I on the super fudge bomb.

That first job taught me many things about myself and my future in the work world. The most important thing for me is that I need to be able to have fun at work. If work becomes monotonous, I begin to screw off somehow and lose my job. This has been true all along, in every job I have ever held. I also learned a few fine points that have come in handy in the work world too. First off, if you consume most of your pickings before they get counted, you get only one fudge bomb instead of the two you could have had. Secondly, I learned how to launch and coordinate an assault on an enemy position, a bit of knowledge that proved useful later in my employment as a soldier. And the most important lesson I learned was this: if you are going to screw off at work, don't do it within hearing or eyesight range of the boss.

Final Reflection

Write about a job that remains a pleasant memory. Why did you like this job?

> *I always tried to hide during class discussions, but you wouldn't let me.*
>
> —Tina Christenson

❖ *After You Read, Consider*

1. What lessons have you learned from past jobs? How have these lessons affected the way you work now?

2. How did you spend your first paycheck?

3. Do you agree or disagree with the practice of hiring children to pick fruit or do other tasks?

I feel certain I have what it takes to be a good writer, I just need more balance.
—Margaret Phifer

❖ Suggestions for Writing

1. Create a classified advertisement that announces your idea of a perfect job. Include benefits, salary, and location.

2. Write a narrative that relates your most memorable work experience.

3. Write an essay in which you explore how the skills you possess fit a particular career.

Elizabeth Berg

Nurse Wonder

Elizabeth Berg has worked as a registered nurse, a lead singer in a rock band, a waitress, a hotel information clerk, an actress in an improvisational theater group, and a secretary.

In 1985, she entered an essay contest in **Parents Magazine** *and won. For seven years thereafter, she wrote personal essays and short stories for many magazines, including* **Redbook,** *the* **New York Times Magazine,** *and* **New Woman.** *During that time, she was nominated for a National Magazine Award. She also wrote and delivered essays on Special Reports Television and on* **Chronicle,** *a television news magazine in Boston. In 1992, she published her first book,* **Family Traditions.** *Since then, she has written five novels and is at work on another. Berg thinks fondly of all the jobs she had except for the time she had to wash chickens in a hospital cafeteria.*

❖

Being allowed to write what I thought about was really important to me. I liked making connections between my life and what we were reading.

—Tina Lewis

Prereading Reflection

Write about a time you or someone you know faced a seemingly hopeless medical situation.

❖

Wanda has Jay today. She is filling up the basin for a bed bath when I come in the room. I hold out my hand, introduce myself.

"Yes, I know your name," she says. "We talk about you sometimes." Then, hastily, "Nicely."

I wonder what that means.

"I can bathe him if you're busy," I tell her.

She puts the basin on the bedside stand, pours some oil in it.

"That's okay. We have a lot of help today. I've only got five others. They're done already."

I look at my watch. Nine-thirty.

Wanda lowers the head of Jay's bed, begins to wash his face. She is tender, thorough. She makes a little mitt of the washcloth so water doesn't drip off the ends. You don't always see that. Most times Jay's face gets scrubbed like a kitchen floor. But Wanda is the kind of nurse who takes her training seriously, the kind who won't hold dirty linen against her uniform, the kind you see washing her hands in the little sink out in the hall many times a day. I sit down in the chair, watch her. She's a very pretty girl, honey-blond hair pulled back into a braid, clear blue eyes, cheeks a nice pink color without the assistance of makeup. She wears tiny gold hoops in her ears. Her uniforms have flowers embroidered here and there—you have to look closely, because it's white on white. I wonder if she does it herself.

"You're new, huh?" I say.

"I've been here about three weeks now. I used to work at St. Mary's. In the oncology unit."

"You didn't like that?"

She turns around. "Oh, no. I loved it. They had a problem with my . . . Well, the truth is I got fired."

> Why does Wanda admit she was fired? What does she hope to gain by being candid?

I stifle an impulse to leap up and grab the washcloth away from her. Instead, I begin watching her more carefully.

"I'll tell you about it," she says. "It wasn't for incompetence or anything. But for now, just let me . . . I'd like to just pay attention to him."

"Of course."

She turns back to Jay, starts talking to him in a low, friendly voice. Her new car, she's talking about. Five speed. Moves out. Smells like leather, though there's none in the car. Paid sticker price, couldn't help it. And then how her garden has been planned, what vegetables she and her husband will harvest in the summer. "You'll be out of here by then, of course," she tells him. "I'll bring some tomatoes over to your house; you can make your kids some BLTs. Your daughters are beautiful, Jay." I lean back in my chair, and one-twentieth of my brain says wearily, "Say thank you, Jay."

> Why does Wanda spend so much time talking to Jay? Who benefits from her talk?

When she gets to his hand, Wanda exercises each finger independently, then moves all of them together. Yes, that's right. She's doing it right. I'll go get a cup of coffee.

In the day room, I see Flozell sitting by the window with Johnny. And then see that a baby is lying in his lap. I stop, stare, then go up to him. When he sees me coming, he pulls the blanket down from a tiny, sleeping face. The baby is beautiful, curly eyelashes, a dimpled chin, hands resting across a chest not much bigger than a silver dollar. "Who's this?" I whisper.

"My daughter!" he says. Not in a whisper. The baby startles, then stills. "Premature, but she out the hospital now. She fine."

"What's her name?" I ask.

"Tanesha," Johnny says, at the same time that Flozell says, "Name is Jacqueline, after you know who."

"My ass," Johnny says, with what I can only describe as a kind of misplaced elegance. She speaks quietly, down her nose, as though she is saying, "Indeed." She is quite beautiful, really; and so petite, she can't be over 5'1". I wonder how she created this baby with Flozell. Surely he didn't lie on top of her. He'd kill her. She is dressed in a floral print polyester dress, ruffles along the bottom and the top. A black leather jacket rests on her lap. Beside her, a huge black purse gapes open, revealing a pack of cigarettes, a gold cosmetics bag, a key ring with a rose captured in a plastic heart. "I'm the one had this baby and I'm the one named her. It's on her birth certificate. I called her 'Tanesha.' Ain't nothing he can do about it."

" 'Cept call her Jacqueline," he says. "That's just what I intend to do, call her Jac-que-line."

Johnny chews her gum for a while, swinging her crossed leg and watching him with slit-eyed affection. Then, "You call her that, she stare right into space. She ignore you. You ain't around enough to have no influence on her."

Flozell looks down at the sleeping face. His lower lip is pushed out. He is pouting magnificently.

"How's your husband?" Johnny asks me.

"He's being bathed," I say, as though that answers the question. Johnny nods, looks down at her purse, sad for me. The first time I met her, she asked, "What's wrong wid your man?" She was wearing large hoop earrings and I remember staring at one of them when I told her. She blinked, then said, "Whew, Lord!" She reached out for my arm, squeezed it.

"I just came in here for coffee," I tell her. "Can I get you some?"

"No thanks," she says, and then, to Flozell, "Give me that baby back now."

"Not yet," he says. "No."

What does Johnny's smiling signify?

"Sheeeit." Johnny resettles herself in her chair, smiling so widely I can see the gold repair on one of her back molars.

I fill a plastic cup half full of the day room's awful coffee, carry it back to Jay's room. Wanda is pulling his covers over him. "All done," she says. The odor of ironed sheets is in the air. Everything in his room has been straightened, cleaned. The bottles on top of his nightstand are lined up, the telephone dusted.

I walk over, kiss his cheek, put my hand on the top of his head, look closely into his face. "Jay," I say. "I'm here."

I wait a moment, then straighten, look over at Wanda. She is standing by the door, watching me.

Why is it important what Wanda thinks? Why does the narrator need her assurance?

"So what do *you* think?" I say.

"I think all things are possible," she says. "I think what we don't know about medicine is as vast as outer space. Is that what you meant?"

"Yes. Thank you."

She opens the door. "I'll be right back. I need to hang his feeding."

I sit on the bed, take Jay's hand. "Breakfast time, Jay. What do you want?"

As if I didn't know. Regular coffee in his regular cup at his regular table. He has a cup that has a Corvette on it. The picture of the white '56 has nearly faded away. We went to look at Corvettes once. Jay sat behind the wheel, and I watched him from the front of the car. It was a new one. I told him I didn't like it, that it looked like a Dustbuster, but I did like it, mostly for the way Jay's face looked when he turned on the headlights and they came flipping up out of the body of the car. I thought, when those kids are done with college, we're taking out a loan and buying one of these. Even if we have bifocals.

"I just saw Flozell's baby," I tell Jay. "He has a baby! And she's so beautiful. You remember when Sarah was born and the doctor told you to tell me what sex she was? And you weren't quite sure, because the umbilical cord confused you?" I smile down at him. If I try, I can imagine that his eyes are only closed to hear me better. "We were supposed to have a fancy dinner, but it was too late at night," I say. "So they brought us all the stuff they could find from the little kitchen there, remember? We got toast and jelly . . . Jell-O, graham crackers . . . what else? I don't know, it didn't matter, everything tasted wonderful. And I remember you had some apple juice and you started to toast Sarah, you held this little flowered paper cup up to her and started to say something and then you just started crying and then I started crying. Everybody cries about babies, huh, Jay? Maybe we should have another one." I say things like that sometimes, and then immediately feel as though some bottom has dropped out, as though I'm driving along and the road suddenly disappears. And I am sitting there, suspended in black space, my hands fiercely clenching the steering wheel as though I still had some control. I shouldn't say things like that.

Wanda comes in carrying Jay's feeding and I get out of the way, go to sit in the corner. After the stuff starts dripping in, she pulls an extra chair up to sit beside me. "I'd like to tell you what happened, why I got fired."

"You don't have to."

"I want to."

"All right." Actually, I do want to know.

"I was working nights," she says. "There was a woman who was dying. Irene was her name, sweet woman, and she had these sandals she kept at the side of the bed. They were so small. She never used them, she was too weak to get up, she just wanted them there. I think she thought maybe if she kept them there, she'd get to use them again. And I also think it was a way for us to know her—you know, a way of her saying, 'Look, I wasn't always a patient lying here in this bed. I went shopping. These are the shoes I picked out.'"

She looks at me, and I nod.

"Anyway," Wanda says, "she was in a lot of pain. I'd been taking care of her for a long time, a few weeks; every time I was on. I had her. I knew this was going to be the night that she died. After a while, you can just tell.

"It was really busy when you worked nights, you had at least eleven patients, you didn't ever have time to sit with any of them. I went in to see her as often as I could, I increased her morphine drip, I turned her and rubbed her back, but it wasn't enough. She was really restless. She asked me to put her on the floor. I said I couldn't do that. She said, Why not, she wanted to be on the floor, she was so sick of the bed, it was making her feel crazy to be in that bed. She wanted to be on the floor where there was more room. So I said, Fine, and I put a bunch of blankets down and got an aide to help me and we put her on the floor. And she smiled at me and said thank you. And the next time I came in she had died. I called the resident to pronounce her, and he said, What the hell was she doing on the floor? And I told him. He told someone else, and the next time I came to work they told me to punch out, I was fired."

She smiles ruefully at me, shrugs. "And that was it. They were not interested in any explanations. They didn't care that the other nurses all tried to defend me. They didn't care that all my evaluations had been excellent."

Do you think Wanda should have been fired?

I don't know what to think about what she has told me. I don't think what she did was wrong, yet it doesn't seem quite right, either. Suppose Jay woke up and asked her to put him on the floor. Suppose I walked in and found him there, wouldn't I be angry? But he would say, "No, Lainey, I asked for this." Unless he was dead. Suppose I came in and he was dead on the floor. Wouldn't I be angry? Even if I knew he'd asked to be put there? I don't know. I don't know. I don't want to think about it.

"What made you become a nurse?" I ask Wanda.

"Oh well, I wanted . . . I had a need to express my compassion. I wanted to help." She looks carefully at my face. "I care for people. They don't always let you show that."

"No."

She leans back, sighs. "I'll tell you, nursing school was murder. Once we were learning about hearts, and the instructor held up a beef heart—that's what we had to study, a heart from a cow, only the medical students got to look at a human heart. But anyway, he stuck his finger through a valve to show us the connection between the atrium and the ventricle, then wiggled it a little like he was playing a game, and I passed out. Not because it was gross. Because it was unholy. I understood we needed to learn. But I thought we should learn with reverence. I mean, there was a cow, born to a mother cow, living on the earth, and now here was that cow's heart in the hand of a human who was making fun of it."

What is Wanda saying about the human heart? How is this incident connected to her reasons for becoming a nurse?

"Yes," I say, as though I know exactly what she is talking about. And I sort of do.

Do you have someone you respond to in this way?

"From the time I first started nursing," she says, "patients would do things for me they wouldn't do for other nurses."

"Like what?"

"Well, once I took care of this woman psychiatrist who'd been horrible to all the other nurses, she was really hard to get along with. She wouldn't let anyone bathe her, and she was bedridden, believe me, she needed to get bathed. By the end of the day, I'd washed her. Turned out she was embarrassed to have anyone see her feet. Isn't that amazing? I mean, the tenderness of that?"

I smile.

"And then when I was just an aide, a woman who'd had a colostomy picked me to be the one to ask about sex. She told me to close the door and then she said, 'What about my husband? How does one have sex with this thing?' She was quite formal, you know, a very rich woman, lying in bed in her turquoise negligee, her face all made up. 'How does *one* have sex?' I was sort of scared, but I knew she needed me to tell her something. I knew she wouldn't ask anyone else. So I said, 'Well, you just take off the bag and tape a little cotton square over the stoma. And then you forget about it. Because that's not what he's making love to.' And then I asked her what was so attractive about the original exit, anyway. You know. A stoma is no worse than an asshole, was my opinion."

She leans forward again, speaks softly. "I'm just trying to tell you I know what you're doing with all these things around your husband— his clothes, the kids' drawings, all the things you bring in from home. And the way you talk to him, read to him. I support you one hundred percent. I think it really helps."

Do you believe the children's drawings benefit Jay?

I look back at her, and my heart feels like a full bucket, hanging heavy in my chest. "Do you really?"

"Yes."

"The kids have started doing it too," I tell her. "They tell him little stories. Well, the younger one, Amy, does. Sarah's still not sure. But she's starting to come around. Last time we visited she told him she'd gotten an *A* on a test just before we left. She sort of yelled it from the middle of the room. I hope it's okay. I hope it's not . . . I don't know, damaging or anything for them."

"I think it's fine. I think it's a good way for them to feel like they're doing something too. And may I tell you something? I also think you should take care of yourself. You can crack up a little when these things go on for so long. You've got to bring a healthy self in here. That will help him most. He needs to feel your strength. And you need to do what you have to to keep it."

"Well, yes, I know. I know that. In fact, I just wanted to see him this morning, and then I'm going away all day. To a farm, with my neighbor and our children. To relax."

"Good."

I pick up my purse, pull it tight against my belly. "So, do you . . . honestly now, do you really think there's a chance he'll come home?"

"I absolutely do."

"Yes. Well, I believe it too. I don't know that anyone else does, though."

"You'd be surprised. When I told you we talk about you, that's because we admire you."

I put my hands over my face, start to cry. Wanda puts her hand on my shoulder, speaks softly. "We're going to get him back to you, Mrs. Berman."

I nod, sniff loudly. "Please call me 'Lainey.' "

"Okay. You know what the nurses where I used to work called me?"

"What?"

" 'Wonder.' "

"Oh. That's good."

"Yes, I thought so, too." She stands up. "Go out to the country. Have a good time. And don't worry, we'll take care of him."

I come out into the hall, close the door quietly. I'm a little nervous.

I wonder if I've said too much. I feel as though I've unzipped myself and handed my shy insides to a nurse named Wonder. If that was a mistake, it's too late now.

Final Reflection

If a family member or good friend was in a coma, how would you respond during hospital visits?

> *You know, sometimes we did talk about a subject for too long.*
> —Christopher Adams

❖ *After You Read, Consider*

1. If you were in a coma, how would you like others to treat you?

2. Was Wanda justified in putting the former patient on the floor?

3. How would taking breaks away from a chronic patient increase the health and well-being of the visitor or caregiver?

> *I believe a person does much better work when she does something she likes.*
> —Mary Thomas

❖ *Suggestions for Writing*

1. Prepare a presentation for a hospital governing board or ethics committee defending Wanda's response to her patient's request to be placed on the floor.

2. Research how treatment for patients suffering from traumatic brain injuries has changed in the last decade. Report the findings in a pamphlet or newsletter whose audience would be family and friends of such patients.

3. Based on research, prepare and conduct a workshop detailing how friends and family members can most effectively support the spouse or children of an individual who suffers a traumatic brain injury.

Tillie Olsen

I Stand Here Ironing

"I Stand Here Ironing" *comes from* Tell Me a Riddle *(1961), a story collection that won the O. Henry Award for Fiction in 1961. Olsen was born in Nebraska in 1912 and dropped out of high school during the Depression. Public libraries were her college. After some early publications, Olsen devoted twenty years to her family as a working-class wife and mother. Only at the age of forty could she find the time to resume writing. Her other published works include* Yonnondio: From the Thirties *(1979).*

❖

Reflecting always helps me write. I appreciated the time we spent in class writing reflections.

—Maryann Morgan

Prereading Reflection

Think back to a time when a choice you had to make for another person turned out to be a bad one.

❖

I stand here ironing, and what you asked me moves tormented back and forth with the iron.

"I wish you would manage the time to come in and talk with me about your daughter. I'm sure you can help me understand her. She's a youngster who needs help and whom I'm deeply interested in helping."

"Who needs help." Even if I came, what good would it do? You think because I am her mother I have a key, or that in some way you could use me as a key? She has lived for nineteen years. There is all that life that has happened outside of me, beyond me.

And when is there time to remember, to sift, to weigh, to estimate, to total? I will start and there will be an interruption and I will have to gather it all together again. Or I will become engulfed with all I did or did not do, with what should have been and what cannot be helped.

She was a beautiful baby. The first and only one of our five that was beautiful at birth. You do not guess how new and uneasy her tenancy in her now-loveliness. You did not know her all those years she was thought homely, or see her poring over her baby pictures, making me tell her over and over how beautiful she had been—and would be, I would tell her—and was now, to the seeing eye. But the seeing eyes were few or nonexistent. Including mine.

I nursed her. They feel that's important nowadays. I nursed all the children, but with her, with all the fierce rigidity of first motherhood, I did like the books then said. Though her cries battered me to trembling and my breasts ached with swollenness, I waited till the clock decreed.

Why do I put that first? I do not even know if it matters, or if it explains anything.

Why do you think the narrator is telling us about her daughter's childhood?

She was a beautiful baby. She blew shining bubbles of sound. She loved motion, loved light, loved color and music and textures. She would lie on the floor in her blue overalls patting the surface so hard in ecstasy her hands and feet would blur. She was a miracle to me, but when she was eight months old I had to leave her daytimes with the woman downstairs to whom she was no miracle at all, for I worked or looked for work and for Emily's father, who "could no longer endure" (he wrote in his goodbye note) "sharing want with us."

I was nineteen. It was the pre-relief, pre-WPA world of the depression. I would start running as soon as I got off the streetcar, running up the stairs, the place smelling sour, and awake or asleep to startle awake, when she saw me she would break into a clogged weeping that could not be comforted, a weeping I can hear yet.

After a while I found a job hashing at night so I could be with her days, and it was better. But it came to where I had to bring her to his family and leave her.

How did the narrator feel about not being able to financially care for her daughter?

It took a long time to raise the money for her fare back. Then she got chicken pox and I had to wait longer. When she finally came, I hardly knew her, walking quick and nervous like her father, looking like her father, thin, and dressed in a shoddy red that yellowed her skin and glared at the pockmarks. All the baby loveliness gone.

She was two. Old enough for nursery school they said, and I did not know then what I know now—the fatigue of the long day, and the lacerations of group life in nurseries that are only parking places for children.

Except that it would have made no difference if I had known. It was the only place there was. It was the only way we could be together, the only way I could hold a job.

And even without knowing, I knew. I knew the teacher that was evil because all these years it has curdled into my memory, the little boy hunched in the corner, her rasp, "why aren't you outside, because Alvin hits you? that's no reason, go out, scaredy." I knew Emily hated it even if she did not clutch and implore "don't go Mommy" like the other children, mornings.

She always had a reason why we should stay home. Momma, you look sick, Momma. I feel sick. Momma, the teachers aren't there today, they're sick. Momma, we can't go, there was a fire there last night. Momma, it's a holiday today, no school, they told me.

But never a direct protest, never rebellion. I think of our others in their three-, four-year-oldness—the explosions, the tempers, the denunciations, the demands—and I feel suddenly ill. I put the iron down. What in me demanded that goodness in her? And what was the cost, the cost to her of such goodness?

What do you think it cost the narrator's daughter to be "good" and accept her situation?

The old man living in the back once said in his gentle way: "You should smile at Emily more when you look at her." What *was* in my face when I looked at her? I loved her. There were all the acts of love.

Why couldn't others read the narrator's working as "acts of love"?

It was only with the others I remembered what he said, and it was the face of joy, and not of care or tightness or worry I turned to them—too late for Emily. She does not smile easily, let alone almost always as her brothers and sisters do. Her face is closed and sombre, but when she wants, how fluid. You must have seen it in her pantomimes, you spoke of her rare gift for comedy on the stage that rouses a laughter out of the audience so dear they applaud and applaud and do not want to let her go.

Where does it come from, that comedy? There was none of it in her when she came back to me that second time, after I had had to send her away again. She had a new daddy now to learn to love, and I think perhaps it was a better time.

Except when we left her alone nights, telling ourselves she was old enough.

"Can't you go some other time, Mommy, like tomorrow?" she would ask. "Will it be just a little while you'll be gone? Do you promise?"

The time we came back, the front door open, the clock on the floor in the hall. She rigid awake. "It wasn't just a little while. I didn't cry. Three times I called you, just three times, and then I ran downstairs to open the door so you could come faster. The clock talked loud. I threw it away, it scared me what it talked."

She said the clock talked loud again that night I went to the hospital to have Susan. She was delirious with the fever that comes before red measles, but she was fully conscious all the week I was gone and the week after we were home when she could not come near the new baby or me.

She did not get well. She stayed skeleton thin, not wanting to eat, and night after night she had nightmares. She would call for me, and I would rouse from exhaustion to sleepily call back: "You're all right, darling, go to sleep, it's just a dream," and if she still called, in a sterner voice, "now go to sleep, Emily, there's nothing to hurt you." Twice, only twice, when I had to get up for Susan anyhow, I went in to sit with her.

Now when it is too late (as if she would let me hold and comfort her like I do the others) I get up and go to her at once at her moan or restless stirring. "Are you awake, Emily? Can I get you something?" And the answer is always the same: "No, I'm all right, go back to sleep, Mother."

They persuaded me at the clinic to send her away to a convalescent home in the country where "she can have the kind of food and care you can't manage for her, and you'll be free to concentrate on the new baby." They still send children to that place. I see pictures on the society page of sleek young women planning affairs to raise money for it, or dancing at the affairs, or decorating Easter eggs or filling Christmas stockings for the children.

They never have a picture of the children so I do not know if the girls still wear those gigantic red bows and the ravaged looks on the every other Sunday when parents can come to visit "unless otherwise notified."—as we were notified the first six weeks.

Oh it is a handsome place, green lawns and tall trees and fluted flower beds. High up on the balconies of each cottage the children stand, the girls in their red bows and white dresses, the boys in white suits and giant red ties. The parents stand below shrieking up to be heard and the children shriek down to be heard, and between them the invisible wall "Not To Be Contaminated by Parental Germs or Physical Affection."

There was a tiny girl who always stood hand in hand with Emily. Her parents never came. One visit she was gone. "They moved her to Rose College," Emily shouted in explanation. "They don't like you to love anybody here."

She wrote once a week, the labored writing of a seven-year-old. "I am fine. How is the baby. If I write my leter nicly I will have a star. Love." There never was a star. We wrote every other day, letters she could never hold or keep but only hear read—once. "We simply do not have room for children to keep any personal possessions," they patiently explained when we pieced one Sunday's shrieking together to plead how much it would mean to Emily, who loved so to keep things, to be allowed to keep her letters and cards.

Each visit she looked frailer. "She isn't eating," they told us.

(They had runny eggs for breakfast or mush with lumps, Emily said later, I'd hold it in my mouth and not swallow. Nothing ever tasted good, just when they had chicken.)

> **What did her daughter's convalescence in the country cost them both?**

It took us eight months to get her released home, and only the fact that she gained back so little of her seven lost pounds convinced the social worker.

I used to try to hold and love her after she came back, but her body would stay stiff, and after a while she'd push away. She ate little. Food sickened her, and I think much of life too. Oh she had physical lightness and brightness, twinkling by on skates, bouncing like a ball up and down up and down over the jump rope, skimming over the hill; but these were momentary.

She fretted about her appearance, thin and dark and foreign-looking at a time when every little girl was supposed to look or thought she should look a chubby blonde replica of Shirley Temple. The doorbell sometimes rang for her, but no one seemed to come and play in the house or be a best friend. Maybe because we moved so much.

There was a boy she loved painfully through two school semesters. Months later she told me how she had taken pennies from my purse to buy him candy. "Licorice was his favorite and I brought him some every day, but he still liked Jennifer better'n me. Why, Mommy?" The kind of question for which there is no answer.

> **Have you ever done anything that you knew was wrong to win someone else's approval or attention?**

School was a worry to her. She was not glib or quick in a world where glibness and quickness were easily confused with ability to learn. To her overworked and exasperated teachers she was an overconscientious "slow learner" who kept trying to catch up and was absent entirely too often.

I let her be absent, though sometimes the illness was imaginary. How different from my now-strictness about attendance with the others. I wasn't working. We had a new baby, I was home anyhow. Sometimes, after Susan grew old enough, I would keep her home from school, too, to have them all together.

Mostly Emily had asthma, and her breathing, harsh and labored, would fill the house with a curiously tranquil sound. I would bring the two old dresser mirrors and her boxes of collections to her bed. She would select beads and single earrings, bottle tops and shells, dried flowers and pebbles, old postcards and scraps, all sorts of oddments; then she and Susan would play Kingdom, setting up landscapes and furniture, peopling them with action.

Those were the only times of peaceful companionship between her and Susan. I have edged away from it, that poisonous feeling between them, that terrible balancing of hurts and needs I had to do between the two, and did so badly, those earlier years.

> Do you have siblings? Are they very different from you? Do you ever get jealous of them?

Oh there are conflicts between the others too, each one human, needing, demanding, hurting, taking—but only between Emily and Susan, no, Emily toward Susan that corroding resentment. It seems so obvious on the surface, yet it is not obvious. Susan, the second child, Susan, golden- and curly-haired and chubby, quick and articulate and assured, everything in appearance and manner Emily was not; Susan, not able to resist Emily's precious things, losing or sometimes clumsily breaking them; Susan telling jokes and riddles to company for applause while Emily sat silent (to say to me later: that was *my* riddle, Mother, I told it to Susan); Susan, who for all the five years' difference in age was just a year behind Emily in developing physically.

I am glad for that slow physical development that widened the difference between her and her contemporaries, though she suffered over it. She was too vulnerable for that terrible world of youthful competition, of preening and parading, of constant measuring of yourself against every other, of envy. "If I had that copper hair," "If I had that skin...." She tormented herself enough about not looking like the others, there was enough of the unsureness, the having to be conscious of words before you speak, the constant caring—what are they thinking of me? without having it all magnified by the merciless physical drives.

Ronnie is calling. He is wet and I change him. It is rare there is such a cry now. That time of motherhood is almost behind me when the ear is not one's own but must always be racked and listening for the child cry, the child call. We sit for a while and I hold him, looking out over the city spread in charcoal with its soft aisles of light. "*Shoogily*," he breathes and curls closer. I carry him back to bed, asleep. *Shoogily*. A funny word, a family word, inherited from Emily, invented by her to say: *comfort*.

In this and other ways she leaves her seal, I say aloud. And startle at my saying it. What do I mean? What did I start to gather together, to try and make coherent? I was at the terrible, growing years. War years. I do not remember them well. I was working, there were four smaller ones now, there was not time for her. She had to help be a mother, and housekeeper, and shopper. She had to set her seal. Mornings of crisis and near hysteria trying to get lunches packed, hair combed, coats and shoes found, everyone to school or Child Care on time, the baby ready for transportation. And always the paper scribbled on by a smaller one, the book looked at by Susan then mislaid, the homework not done. Running out to that huge school where she was one, she was lost, she was a drop; suffering over the unpreparedness, stammering and unsure in her classes.

There was so little time left at night after the kids were bedded down. She would struggle over books, always eating (it was in those years she developed her enormous appetite that is legendary in our family) and I would be ironing, or preparing food for the next day, or writing V-mail to Bill, or tending the baby. Sometimes, to make me laugh, or out of her despair, she would imitate happenings or types at school.

I think I said once: "Why don't you do something like this in the school amateur show?" One morning she phoned me at work, hardly understandable through the weeping: "Mother, I did it. I won, I won; they gave me first prize; they clapped and clapped and wouldn't let me go."

Now suddenly she was Somebody, and as imprisoned in her difference as she had been in anonymity.

She began to be asked to perform at other high schools, even in colleges, then at city and statewide affairs. The first one we went to, I only recognized her that first moment when thin, shy, she almost drowned herself into the curtains. Then: Was this Emily? The control, the command, the convulsing and deadly clowning, the spell, then the roaring, stamping audience, unwilling to let this rare and precious laughter out of their lives.

Afterwards: You ought to do something about her with a gift like that—but without money or knowing how, what does one do? We have left it all to her, and the gift has as often eddied inside, clogged and clotted, as been used and growing.

She is coming. She runs up the stairs two at a time with her light graceful step, and I know she is happy tonight. Whatever it was that occasioned your call did not happen today.

"Aren't you ever going to finish the ironing, Mother? Whistler painted his mother in a rocker. I'd have to paint mine standing over an ironing board." This is one of her communicative nights and she tells me everything and nothing as she fixes herself a plate of food out of the icebox.

She is so lovely. Why did you want me to come in at all? Why were you concerned? She will find her way.

She starts up the stairs to bed. "Don't get me up with the rest in the morning." "But I thought you were having midterms." "Oh, those," she comes back in, kisses me, and says quite lightly, "in a couple of years when we'll all be atom-dead they won't matter a bit."

She has said it before. She *believes* it. But because I have been dredging the past, and all that compounds a human being is so heavy and meaningful in me, I cannot endure it tonight.

> The narrator summarizes her whole story in this paragraph. How does this paragraph affect the way you read her character?

I will never total it all. I will never come in to say: She was a child seldom smiled at. Her father left me before she was a year old. I had to work her first six years when there was work, or I sent her home and to his relatives. There were years she had care she hated. She was dark and thin and foreign-looking in a world where the prestige went to blondeness and curly hair and dimples, she was slow where glibness was prized. She was a child of anxious, not proud, love. We were poor and could not afford for her the soil of easy growth. I was a young mother, I was a distracted mother. There were the other children pushing up, demanding. Her younger sister seemed all that she was not. There were years she did not want me to touch her. She kept too much in herself, her life was such she had to keep too much in herself. My wisdom came too late. She has much to her and probably nothing will come of it. She is a child of her age, of depression, of war, of fear.

Let her be. So all that is in her will not bloom—but in how many does it? There is still enough left to live by. Only help her to know—help make it so there is cause for her to know—that she is more than this dress on the ironing board, helpless before the iron.

Think, think, think, think, think.

—Donna Kelly

Final Reflection

Write about a time a child or family member asked you to stay with them but other commitments forced you to go somewhere else.

❖ *After You Read, Consider*

1. The narrator feels remorse for some of the choices she was forced to make to ensure that she and her children survived. Is this remorse justified?

2. Do you believe first-born children have a harder life than children who come later?

3. Can you think of a way other than monetary that the mother could have helped her daughter develop her talent?

❖ *Suggestions for Writing*

1. Conduct a panel discussion with a number of single mothers about the problems of single parenting.

2. Find out about child support services in your area. Report your findings in a pamphlet or newsletter to a group of first-time mothers.

3. Rewrite this story from Emily's point of view.

Nancy Sommers

I Stand Here Writing

Nancy Sommers finds the details of life—the smell of cardamom, coriander, and cayenne, for instance, or the notes her daughters pin to the refrigerator—the kind of living, breathing primary sources she wants to write about. Writing about her own life, trying to connect the personal with the academic, requires her to figure out what is at stake, both intellectually and personally, in the language and ideas she cares about. Sommers is the Sosland Director of Expository Writing at Harvard University, where she directs the freshman writing program and the Harvard Study of undergraduate writing.

❖

Reflections give me a chance to express my feelings and ideas in a way that doesn't have to be public opinion.

—Ivana Rubric

Prereading Reflection

How many ways do you use writing each day? Do the different purposes for each writing act make the process different each time?

❖

I stand in my kitchen, wiping the cardamom, coriander, and cayenne off my fingers. My head is abuzz with words, with bits and pieces of conversation. I hear a phrase I have read recently, something about "a radical loss of certainty." But, I wonder, how did the sentence begin? I search the air for the rest of the sentence, can't find it, shake some more cardamom, and a bit of coriander. Then, by some play of mind, I am back home again in Indiana with my family, sitting

> Do all writers have conversations in their heads? How can these conversations become part of the writing process?

around the kitchen table. Two people are talking, and there are three opinions; three people are talking, and there are six opinions. Opinions grow exponentially. I fight my way back to that sentence. Writing, that's how it begins: "Writing is a radical loss of certainty." (Or is it uncertainty?) It isn't so great for the chicken when all these voices start showing up, with all these sentences hanging in mid-air, but the voices keep me company. I am a writer, not a cook, and the truth is I don't care much about the chicken. Stories beget stories. Writing emerges from writing.

The truth. Has truth anything to do with the facts? All I know is that no matter how many facts I might clutter my life with, I am as bound to the primordial drama of my family as the earth is to the sun. This year my father, the son of a severe Prussian matriarch, watched me indulge my daughters, and announced to me that he wished I had been his mother. This year, my thirty-ninth, my last year to be thirty-something, my mother—who has a touch of magic, who can walk into the middle of a field of millions of clovers and find the *one* with four leaves—has begun to think I need help. She sends me cards monthly with four-leaf clovers taped inside. Two words neatly printed in capital letters—GOOD LUCK!! I look at these clovers and hear Reynolds Price's words: "Nobody under forty can believe how nearly everything's inherited." I wonder what my mother knows, what she is trying to tell me about the facts of my life.

What does this writer think is the difference between truth and facts?

When I was in high school studying French, laboring to conjugate verbs, the numerous four-leaf clovers my mother had carefully pressed inside her French dictionary made me imagine her in a field of clovers lyrically conjugating verbs of love. This is the only romantic image I have of my mother, a shy and conservative woman whose own mother died when she was five, whose grandparents were killed by the Nazis, who fled Germany at age thirteen with her father and sister. Despite the sheer facts of her life, despite the accumulation of grim knowable data, the truth is my mother is an optimistic person. She has the curious capacity always to be looking for luck, putting her faith in four-leaf clovers, ladybugs, pennies, and other amulets of fortune. She has a vision different from mine, one the facts alone can't explain. I, her daughter, was left, for a long time, seeing only the ironies; they were my defense against the facts of my life.

In this world of my inheritance in which daughters can become their fathers' mothers and mothers know their daughters are entering into a world where only sheer good luck will guide them, I hear from my own daughters that I am not in tune with their worlds, that I am just like a 50s mom, that they are 90s children, and I should stop acting so primitive. My children laugh uproariously at my autograph book, a 1959 artifact they unearthed in the basement of my parents' home. "Never kiss by the garden gate. Love is blind, but the neighbors ain't," wrote one friend. And my best friend, who introduced herself to me on the first day of first grade, looking me straight in the eye—and whispering through her crooked little teeth "the Jews killed Jesus"—wrote in this autograph book: "Mary had a little lamb. Her father shot it dead. Now she carries it to school between two slices of bread."

My ten-year-old daughter, Rachel, writes notes to me in hieroglyphics and tapes signs on the refrigerator in Urdu. "Salaam Namma Man Rachaal Ast" reads one sign. Simply translated it means "Hello, my name is Rachel." Alex, my seven-year-old daughter, writes me lists, new lists each month, visibly reminding me of the many things I need to buy or do for her. This month's list includes a little refrigerator filled with Coke and candy; ears pierced; a new toilet; neon nail polish and *real* adult make-up.

Why does her daughter find lists important? Why doesn't she just tell her mother what she wants?

How do I look at these facts? How do I embrace these experiences, these texts of my life, and translate them into ideas? How do I make sense of them and the conversations they engender in my head? I look at Alex's list and wonder what kind of feminist daughter I am raising whose deepest desires include neon nail polish and *real* adult make-up. Looking at her lists a different way, I wonder if this second child of mine is asking me for something larger, something more permanent and real than adult make-up. Maybe I got that sentence wrong. Maybe it is that "Love (as well as writing) involves a radical loss of certainty."

Love is blind, but the neighbors ain't. Mary's father shot her little lamb dead, and now she carries it to school between two slices of bread. I hear these rhymes today, and they don't say to me what they say to my daughters. They don't seem so innocent. I hear them and think about the ways in which my neighbors in Indiana could only see my family as Jews from Germany, exotic strangers who ate tongue, outsiders who didn't celebrate Christmas. I wonder if my daughter Rachel needs to tell me her name in Urdu because she thinks we don't share a common language. These sources change meaning when I ask the questions in a different way. They introduce new ironies, new questions.

I want to understand these living, breathing, primary souces all around me. I want to be, in Henry James's words, "a person upon whom nothing is lost." These sources speak to me of love and loss, of memory and desire, of the ways in which we come to understand something through difference and opposition. Two years ago I

How does Sommers connect all the different parts of her life in writing?

learned the word *segue* from one of my students. At first the word seemed peculiar. Segue sounded like something you did only on the Los Angeles freeway. Now I hear that word everywhere, and I have begun using it. I want to know how to segue from one idea to the next, from one thought to the fragment lying beside it. But the connections don't always come with four-leaf clovers and the words GOOD LUCK neatly printed beside them.

My academic need to find connections sends me to the library. There are eleven million books in my University's libraries. Certainly these sanctioned voices, these authorities, these published sources can help me find the connections. Someone, probably some three thousand someones, has studied what it is like to be the child of survivors. Someone has written a manual on how the granddaughter of a severe Prussian matriarch and the daughter of a collector of amulets ought to raise feminist daughters. I want to walk into the fields of writing, into those eleven million books, and find the one book that will explain it all. But I've learned to expect less from such sources. They seldom have the answers. And the answers they do have reveal themselves to me at the most unexpected times. I have been led astray more than once while searching books for the truth.

Once I learned a lesson about borrowing someone else's words and losing my own.

I was fourteen, light years away from thirty-something. High school debate teams across the nation were arguing the pros and cons of the United States Military Aid Policy. It all came back to me as I listened to the news of the Persian Gulf War, as I listened to Stormin' Norman giving his morning briefings, an eerie resonance, all our arguments, the millions of combative words—sorties—fired back and forth. In my first practice debate, not having had enough time to assemble my own sources, I borrowed quote cards from my teammates. I attempted to bolster my position that the U.S. should limit its military aid by reading a quote in my best debate style: "W. W. Rostow says: 'We should not give military aid to India because it will exacerbate endemic rivalries.'"

Under cross-examination, my nemesis, Bobby Rosenfeld, the neighbor kid, who always knew the right answers, began firing a series of questions at me without stopping to let me answer:

"Nancy, can you tell me who W. W. Rostow is? And can you tell me why he might say this? Nancy, can you tell me what 'exacerbate' means? Can you tell me what 'endemic rivalries' are? And exactly what does it mean to 'exacerbate endemic rivalries'?"

I didn't know. I simply did not know who W. W. Rostow was, why he might have said that, what "exacerbate" meant, or what an "endemic rivalry" was. Millions of four-leaf clovers couldn't have helped me. I might as well have been speaking Urdu. I didn't know who my source was, the context of the source, nor the literal meaning of the words I had read. Borrowing words from authorities had left me without any words of my own.

> What is Sommers trying to teach us here about how our voices fit in with the words of others?

My debate partner and I went on that year to win the Indiana state championship and to place third in the nationals. Bobby Rosenfeld never cross-examined me again, but for twenty years he has appeared in my dreams. I am not certain why I would dream so frequently about this scrawny kid whom I despised. I think, though, that he became for me what the Sea Dyak tribe of Borneo calls a *ngarong*, a dream guide, someone guiding me to understanding. In this case, Bobby guided me to understand the endemic rivalries within myself. The last time Bobby appeared in a dream he had become a woman.

I learned a more valuable lesson about sources as a college senior. I was the kind of student who loved words, words out of context, words that swirled around inside my mouth, words like *exacerbate, undulating, lugubrious,* and *zeugma.* "She stained her honour or her new brocade," wrote Alexander Pope. I would try to write zeugmas whenever I could, exacerbating my already lugubrious prose. Within the English department, I was known more for my long hair, untamed and untranslatable, and for my long distance bicycle rides than for my scholarship.

For my senior thesis, I picked Emerson's essay "Eloquence." Harrison Hayford, my advisor, suggested that I might just get off my bicycle, get lost in the library, and read all of Emerson's essays, journals, letters. I had picked one of Emerson's least distinguished essays, an essay that the critics mentioned only in passing, and if I were not entirely on my own, I had at least carved out new territory for myself.

I spent weeks in the library reading Emerson's journals, reading newspaper accounts from Rockford and Peoria, Illinois, where he had first delivered "Eloquence" as a speech. Emerson stood at the podium, the wind blowing his papers hither and yon, calmly picking them up, and proceeding to read page 8 followed by page 3, followed by page 6, followed by page 2. No one seemed to know the difference. Emerson's Midwestern audience was overwhelmed by this strange man from Concord, Massachusetts, this eloquent stranger whose unit of expression was the sentence.

As I sat in the library, wearing my QUESTION AUTHORITY T-shirt, I could admire this man who delivered his Divinity School Address in 1838, speaking words so repugnant to the genteel people of Cambridge that it was almost thirty years before Harvard felt safe having him around again. I could understand the Midwestern audience's awe and adulation as they listened but didn't quite comprehend Emerson's stunning oratory. I had joined the debate team not to argue the U.S. Military Aid Policy, but to learn how to be an orator who could stun audiences, to learn a personal eloquence I could never learn at home. Perhaps only children of immigrant parents can understand the embarrassing moments of inarticulateness, the missed connections that come from learning to speak a language from parents who claim a different mother tongue.

As an undergraduate, I wanted to free myself from that mother tongue. Four-leaf clovers and amulets of oppression weighed heavy on my mind, and I could see no connection whatsoever between those facts of my life and the untranslatable side of myself that set me in opposition to authority. And then along came Emerson. Like his Midwest audience, I didn't care about having him whole. I liked the promise and the rhapsodic freedom I found in his sentences, in his invitation to seize life as our dictionary, to believe that "Life was not something to be learned but to be lived." I loved his insistence that "the one thing of value is the active soul." I read that "Books are for the scholar's idle time," and I knew that he had given me permission to explore the world. Going into Emerson was like walking into a revelation; it was the first time I had gone into the texts not looking for a specific answer, and it was the first time the texts gave me the answers I needed. Never mind that I got only part of what Emerson was telling me. I got inspiration, I got insight, and I began to care deeply about my work.

Today I reread the man who set me off on a new road, and I find a different kind of wisdom. Today I reread "The American Scholar," and I don't underline the sentence "Books are for the scholar's idle time." I continue to the next paragraph, underlining the sentence "One must be an inventor to read well." The second sentence doesn't contradict the one I read twenty years ago, but it means more today. I bring more to it, and I know that I can walk into text after text, source after source, and they will give me insight, but not answers. I have learned too that my sources can surprise me. Like my mother, I find myself sometimes surrounded by a field of four-leaf clovers, there for the picking, waiting to see what I can make of them. But I must be an inventor if I am to read those sources well, if I am to imagine the connections.

Why do you think Sommers reads Emerson differently from when she was an undergraduate?

As I stand in my kitchen, the voices that come to me come by way of a lifetime of reading, they come on the waves of life, and they seem to be helping me translate the untranslatable. They come, not at my bidding, but when I least expect them, when I am receptive enough to listen to their voices. They come when I am open.

If I could teach my students one lesson about writing it would be to see themselves as sources, as places from which ideas originate, to see themselves as Emerson's transparent eyeball, all that they have read and experienced—the dictionaries of their lives—circulating through them. I want them to learn how sources thicken, complicate, enlarge writing, but I want them to know too how it is always the writer's voice, vision, and argument that create the new source. I want my students to see that nothing reveals itself straight out, especially the sources all around them. But I know enough by now that this Emersonian ideal can't be passed on in one lesson or even a semester of lessons.

Many of the students who come to my classes have been trained to collect facts; they act as if their primary job is to accumulate enough authorities so that there is no doubt about the "truth" of their thesis. They most often disappear behind the weight and permanence of their borrowed words, moving their pens, mouthing the words of others, allowing sources to speak through them unquestioned, unexamined.

At the outset, many of my students think that personal writing is writing about the death of their grandmother. Academic writing is reporting what Elizabeth Kübler-Ross has written about death and dying. Being personal, I want to show my students, does not mean being autobiographical. Being academic does not mean being remote, distant, imponderable. Being personal means bringing their judgments and interpretation to bear on what they read and write, learning that they never leave themselves behind even when they write academic essays.

> How does Sommers define autobiography? Why is this an important definition for students?

Last year, David Gray came into my essay class disappointed about everything. He didn't like the time of the class, didn't like the reading list, didn't seem to like me. Nothing pleased him. "If this is a class on the essay," he asked the first day, "why aren't we reading real essayists like Addison, Steele, and Lamb?" On the second day, after being asked to read Annie Dillard's "Living Like Weasels," David complained that a weasel wasn't a fit subject for an essay. "Writers need big subjects. Look at Melville. He needed a whale for *Moby-Dick*. A weasel—that's nothing but a rodent." And so it continued for a few weeks.

I kept my equanimity in class, but at home I'd tell my family about this kid who kept testing me, seizing me like Dillard's weasel, and not letting go. I secretly wanted him out of my class. But then again, I sensed in him a kindred spirit, someone else who needed to question authority.

I wanted my students to write exploratory essays about education, so I asked them to think of a time when they had learned something, and then a time when they had tried to learn something but couldn't. I wanted them to see what ideas and connections they could find between these two very different experiences and the other essays they were reading for the class. I wanted the various sources to work as catalysts. I wanted my students to find a way to talk back to those other writers. The assigned texts were an odd assortment with few apparent connections. I hoped my students would find the common ground, but also the moments of tension, the contradictions, and the ambiguities in those sources.

David used the assigned texts as a catalyst for his thinking, but as was his way, he went beyond the texts I offered and chose his own. He begins his essay, "Dulcis Est Sapientia," with an account of his high school Latin class, suggesting that he once knew declensions, that he had a knack for conjugations, but has forgotten them. He tells us that if his teacher were to appear suddenly today and demand the perfect subjunctive of *venire*, he would stutter hopelessly.

About that Latin class, David asks, "What is going on here? Did I once know Latin and forget it through disuse? Perhaps I never learned Latin at all. What I learned was a bunch of words which, with the aid of various ending sounds, indicated that Gaius was either a good man delivering messages to the lieutenant or a general who struck camp at the seventh hour. I may have known it once, but I never learned it." The class never gave David the gift of language. There was something awry in the method.

What is learning? That's what David explores in his essay as he moves from his Latin lesson to thinking about surrealist paintings, to thinking about barriers we create, to Plato, to an airplane ride in which he observed a mother teaching her child concepts of color and number, all the time taking his readers along with him on his journey, questioning sources, reflecting, expanding, and enriching his growing sense that learning should stress ideas rather than merely accumulating facts and information.

David draws his essay to a close with an analysis of a joke: A man goes to a cocktail party and gets soused. He approaches his host and asks, "Pardon me, but do lemons whistle?"

The host looks at him oddly and answers, "No, lemons don't whistle."

"Oh dear," says the guest, "then I'm afraid I just squeezed your canary into my gin and tonic."

David reflects about the significance of this joke: "One need not be an ornithologist to get the joke, but one must know that canaries are yellow and that they whistle.... What constitutes the joke is a connection made between two things ... which have absolutely nothing in common except for their yellowness. It would never occur to us to make a comparison between the two, let alone to confuse one with the other. But this is the value of the joke, to force into our consciousness the ideas which we held but never actively considered.... This knocking down of barriers between ideas is parallel to the process that occurs in all learning. The barriers that we set ... suddenly crumble; the boundaries ... are extended to include other modes of thought." Learning, like joking, David argues, gives us pleasure by satisfying our innate capacity to recognize coherence, to discern patterns and connections.

David's essay, like any essay, does not intend to offer the last word on its subject. The civilizing influence of an essay is that it keeps the conversation going, chronicling an intellectual journey, reflecting conversations with sources. I am confident that when David writes for his philosophy course he won't tell a joke anywhere in his essay. But if the joke—if any of his sources—serves him as a catalyst for his thinking, if he makes connections among the sources that circulate within him, between Plato and surrealism, between Latin lessons and mother-child lessons—the dictionaries of *his* life—then he has learned something valuable about writing.

> What is significant to Sommers about David's writing, about the connections he makes between jokes and learning?

I say to myself that I don't believe in luck. And yet. Not too long ago Rachel came home speaking with some anxiety about an achievement test that she had to take at school. Wanting to comfort her, I urged her to take my rabbit's foot to school the next day. Always alert to life's ironies, Rachel said, "Sure, Mom, a rabbit's foot will really help me find the answers. And even if it did, how would I know the answer the next time when I didn't have that furry little claw?" The next day, proud of her ease in taking the test, she remained perplexed by the one question that seized her and wouldn't let go. She tried it on me: "Here's the question," she said. "Can you figure out which of these sentences cannot be true?"

(a) We warmed our hands by the fire.
(b) The rain poured in and around the windows.
(c) The wind beckoned us to open the door.

Only in the mind of someone who writes achievement tests, and wants to close the door on the imagination, could the one false sentence be "The wind beckoned us to open the door." Probably to this kind of mind, Emerson's sentence "Life is our dictionary" is also not a true sentence.

But life *is* our dictionary, and that's how we know that the wind can beckon us to open the door. Like Emerson, we let the wind blow our pages hither and yon, forcing us to start in the middle, moving from page 8 to page 2, forward to page 7, moving back and forth in time, losing our certainty.

Like Emerson, I love basic units, the words themselves, words like cardamom, coriander, words that play around in my head, swirl around in my mouth. The challenge, of course, is not to be a ventriloquist—not to be a mouther of words—but to be open to other voices, untranslatable as they might be. Being open to the unexpected, we can embrace complexities: canaries and lemons, amulets and autograph books, fathers who want their daughters to be their mothers, and daughters who write notes in Urdu—all those odd, unusual conjunctions can come together and speak through us.

The other day, I called my mother and told her about this essay, told her that I had been thinking about the gold bracelet she took with her as one of her few possessions from Germany—a thin gold chain with three amulets: a mushroom, a lady bug, and, of course, a four-leaf clover. Two other charms fell off years ago—she lost one, I the other. I used to worry over the missing links, thinking only of the loss, of what we could never retrieve. When I look at the bracelet now, I think about the Prussian matriarch, my grandmother, and my whole primordial family drama. I think too of Emerson and the pages that blew in the wind and the gaps that seemed not to matter. The bracelet is but one of many sources that intrigues me. Considering them in whatever order they appear, with whatever gaps, I want to see where they will lead me, what they tell me.

With writing and with teaching, as well as with love, we don't know how the sentence will begin and, rarely ever, how it will end. Having the courage to live with uncertainty, ambiguity, even doubt, we can walk into all of those fields of writing, knowing that we will find volumes upon volumes bidding *us* enter. We need only be inventors, we need only give freely and abundantly to the texts, imagining even as we write that we too will be a source from which other readers can draw sustenance.

Final Reflection

How do you connect the different kinds of writing you do? How does each text both shape and tell your life?

❖ *After You Read, Consider*

1. Reread the way Sommers opens her essay, the combination of spices, chicken, family, and ideas. How does the sentence "Writing is a radical loss of certainty" work within this mix?

2. Why does Sommers tell us about her family? What do her family members have to do with her writing about teaching? About academic ideas?

3. At one point, Sommers mentions the "embarrassing moments of inarticulateness" she faced as the child of immigrants. Yet, she never appears ashamed of her parents and is in fact proud of them. Have you had moments like this with your own family?

It would be hard for me to wake up each morning knowing I had to read and write things I didn't care about.
—Carol DeLinno

❖ Suggestions for Writing

1. In many ways, Sommers's essay is a search for connections between academic life and home, teaching and parenting, the past and the present. Write an essay in which you explore the connections you must make in your own life between work and home, school and family.

2. Sommers spends several paragraphs writing about sources, voices, and borrowing words, but her discussion is most certainly not a lecture about plagiarism. Write an essay in which you discuss why Sommers includes this discussion.

3. Find a recipe that has been in your family for a long time. Write an essay in which you describe the origin of the recipe and why this dish is important to your family.

Ben Hamper

I, Rivethead

Ben Hamper had worked at General Motors for six years when he wrote this essay. By the time he left his position on Rivet Line #1, he had been laid off five times in five years as a part of the GM shutdowns. His story is told in Roger and Me, *Michael Moore's movie about the GM pullout in Flint, Michigan.*

Prereading Reflection

Have you ever taken a job you didn't particularly like just because you had or felt you had no other options? Write about what this experience was like.

I knew in the tenth grade that I would become a shoprat. It was more an understanding of certain truisms found in my hometown than any form of game plan I might have been hatching. In Flint, Michigan, you either balled up your fists and got career motivated the moment the piano quit banging the commencement theme or, more likely, you'd still be left leanin' when the ancestors arrived to pass along your birthright. Here, kid, fetch.

At least up until recently, that's the way it worked. All roads led to General Motors in Flint. Father and son, sister and brother, each of 'em swingin' through the gates to play follow-the-earner.

What kind of legacy is Hamper showing us?

The pattern began to dissolve with the cutbacks and technological gains of the early '80s. All of a sudden, trying to find an application for work at General Motors was like searching out buried treasure. It's now to a point where Flint youths can no longer entertain "shoprat" as a career option. The evolution of the critter appears at end, and unless I somehow manage to knock up a GMF spot-welding robot, I rather doubt I'll ever see any of my offspring inside the factory.

I almost didn't make it in myself. After high school, I wasted four prime earning years running around with my tongue stuck out at the smokestacks. I painted apartments. I swept floors. I got married and divorced. As long as I had my birthright stowed in my back pocket, I felt relatively safe in delaying destiny.

During this period, I would often-times get drunk and park by one of the factories just to watch the fools pile out at quit time. I hated the looks on their faces. I would sit there with a can of beer in my lap and try to focus in on one alternative career goal. There weren't any. All I ever came back to was the inevitable self-admission that I didn't want to do *anything*. And around these parts, that's just chicken-shit slang for "What time does the line start up on Monday?"

> Hamper admits he has no career goals. How does this admission shape your assessment of him?

To be accurate, I hired in on a weekend. General Motors was in the midst of one of its boom-boom quota years, so reinforcements were being called in on Saturdays, Sundays, Salad Days—anytime was the right time. It was also the first time I could ever remember being asked out on a Saturday night by a Corporation.

Before we were to begin working, the group I was hiring in with was instructed to meet for physical examination in the plant hospital. We were a sluggish-looking crew. There were about 20 of us all together—each person chain-smoking and staring at the floor, waiting in silence to be pronounced fit for active drudgery. I had a hunch that there wasn't a marketable skill amongst us.

The urine test was up first. We were each handed a small vial and told to line up for the restroom. The guy in front of me kept looking over his shoulder at me. When it was his turn, he spun around and asked if it would be all right if I donated a little of my urine for his vial. He seemed to be undergoing a mild panic attack. Apparently, the fear was that the Company might look down upon any prospective serf who was incapable of bringing forth the pee when it mattered most. No piss, no job, ingrate!

"I just can't go right now," the guy moaned.

I didn't care much for the idea of passing my piss around with a total stranger. It didn't seem like a solid career move. Besides, for all either of us knew, I might be holding on to a bad batch. I had a background of hepatitis. My formative years were spent wolfing down a wide variety of menacing chemicals. I drank like a sieve. Heck, I never even wiped off the seat in public bathrooms. Who'd wanna take a crapshoot on the chance that any of that might come floating to the surface of their corporate dossier?

Evidently, this guy. He returned from the john and, true to his word, the vial he held before me was completely empty. "C'mon," he said, "just a squirt. I'll pay you for it."

> **How do you feel about Hamper selling his urine?**

Christ, that did it. "Gimme the thing," I groaned. It probably wasn't the most noble act of giving one had ever made in behalf of a needy Union brother, but somehow it sure seemed like it at the time.

We were almost through with our urine samples when a member of our group, a late arrival, walked in to the hospital and began to speak with our overseer. I could sense the guy was in deep trouble. He kept apologizing over and over—something to do with getting messed up in traffic and being detained. Judging by his performance, I doubted that he was lying.

It didn't matter. The man with the clipboard wasn't buying a single word. He stood there shaking his head from one side to the other—just another maggot in a short-sleeve shirt, deputized to protect the status quo. He did his job well.

"You were told to be prompt," he spouted. "There can be *no exceptions.*"

The realization that he'd blown his big audition seemed to overwhelm the late guy. He looked down at the floor, his voice started breaking, and, right there in front of everyone, he began to cry. It all came spillin' out—what was he gonna tell his family and who would understand? For the sons and daughters of the assembly line, 1977 wasn't the best of years to go fumblin' the family baton.

> **Why does Hamper tell us the fate of the job candidate who was late? Later he is jealous of him. Why might he exhibit this emotion?**

We stood there clutching our little vials of piss as they escorted him out. We had been on time. We were going to build trucks for Chevrolet. The man with the bow tie and clipboard had written down all of our names. Our friend had been ten minutes late. He had proven himself undeserving of a hitch on the screw train. There could be no exceptions.

Now and again, I'll find myself still thinking about the late guy. It'll be one of those terribly humid shifts when the parts just aren't going together right and the clock begins to take two steps back for every step forward. Exhausted and desperate, I'll begin to see him over by the pool table in the tavern across the street. He'll have a cold beer in his hand and a grin a mile wide. I imagine myself walking up to him with my safety glasses, my locker key, and my plastic identification badge held out in my hand. "Here, it's all yours, buddy."

Immediately, the jukebox will stop playing. Everyone in the bar turns toward me and begins to laugh. The late guy slips his arm around the waitress and they both start shaking their heads. "We already started," he'll say. "There can be no exceptions."

I was assigned to the cab shop, an area more commonly known to its inhabitants as "the Jungle." Lifers will tell you that on a scale from one to ten—with one representing midtown Pompeii and ten being GM Chairman Roger Smith's summer digs—the Jungle rates about a minus-six.

It wasn't difficult to see how they had come up with the name for the place. Ropes, wires, and assorted black rubber cables drooped down and entangled everything. Sparks shot out in all directions—bouncing in the aisles, flying into the rafters and even ricocheting off the natives' heads. The noise level was deafening. It was like some hideous unrelenting tape-loop of trains having sex. I realized instantly that, as far as new homes go, the Jungle left a lot to be desired. Me Tarzan, you fucked.

> How does Hamper's description of the cab shop serve to justify his attitude towards working for GM?

I had been forewarned. As our group was being dispatched at various drop points throughout the factory, the guy walking beside me kept mumbling about our likely destination. "Cab Shop," the prophet would say. "We're headed for Cab Shop." I somehow wondered if this meant we would be building taxis.

The group would trudge on, leaving a few workers in each new area. We stopped by the Trim Line. The Axle Line. The Frame Line. The Fender Line. The Receding Hairline. When we arrived at the Motor Line, my friend with the bashful bladder hopped off. "Thanks," he said. It was kinda strange. All we had in common was a small, worthless vial of urine. "Have a nice career," I offered.

Soon, all but two rookies had been planted—the prophet and me. We took a freight elevator upstairs, and when the gate opened, my companion moaned loudly: "Goddamn, I knew it. The bastard's lettin' us off in Cab Shop." By this point, I couldn't have agreed with the guy more. Our overseer was the epitome of bastard. On top of that, he made for one lousy Johnny Appleseed. There could be no exceptions.

"Here you are, boys—the Cab Department. In this area you are advised to wear clothing made from a nonflammable fabric. Also, you will need to purchase a pair of steel-toed work boots, available at fair cost in the shoe store next to the workers cafeteria. Good luck, boys."

It turned out that the prophet would be working right across from me. His name was Roy and he'd come to Flint from Oklahoma to live with his brother and find work in the factory. Just your basic "Grapes-of-Wrath-run-aground-in-the-Pizza-Pizza Generation" story line, I suppose.

Our jobs were identical: install splash shields, pencil rods, and assorted nuts and bolts in the rear end of Chevy Blazers. To accomplish this, we worked on a portion of the line where the cabs would rise up on an elevated track. Once the cabs were about five feet off the ground, we'd have to duck inside the rear wheel wells and bust a little ass. Standing across from each other in those cramped wheel wells always reminded me of the two neighbors in the Right Guard commercial who met every morning in their communal medicine cabinet. "Hi, Guy! Care for a scoop of sealer on that pencil rod?"

We adjusted to the heat and grew accustomed to the noise. After a while, we even got used to the claustrophobia of the wheel wells. The idea that we were being paid handsome wages to mimic a bunch of overachieving simians suited us just dandy. In America there was nothing to accomplish as long as the numbers on your pay stub tumbled out in a sequence that served to justify your daily dread.

The one thing we couldn't escape was the monotony of our new jobs. Every minute, every hour, every truck, and every movement totaled nothing but a plodding replica of the one that had gone before. The monotony especially began to gnaw away at Roy. When the lunch horn sounded, we'd race out to his pickup and Roy would start pulling these enormous joints from a glove box. His stash was incredible. "Take one," he'd offer. Pot made me nervous, so I would stick to beer or slug a little whiskey.

> Have you ever had a monotonous job? What did you do to relieve the tedium?

The numbing process seemed to demand more every night. We'd go out to the truck and Roy would start burning two joints at once. Now and then, he'd slip down a hit of acid. "I don't know if I'm gonna make my 90 days," he'd tell me. Ninety days was the minimum amount of service required for a worker to apply for sick leave. It was all part of Roy's master plan: reach 90 days' seniority, round up a reliable quack, feign some mysterious injury and, with all the paperwork in order, semi-retire to an orbit of disco bars, women, and cocktails. The old Ozzie Nelson work ethic festering over and over in the hearts of the young.

Roy never did make his 90. To those who were on hand during his last days of service, it came as no real surprise. We all realized that Roy was cracking up.

First there was the incident involving the sacrificial rodent. Roy had managed to capture this tiny mouse that had been sneaking around under one of the stock bins. He built an elaborate little house for the creature and set it on his workbench. He fed it. He gave it water. He built windows in the house so that his pet could "watch me doin' my job." Any worker who passed through the area was summoned over and given a personal introduction to the mouse. For all the world, it seemed like a glorious love affair.

I could never figure out whether it was because of the dope or the drudgery or some unseen domestic quarrel, but things sure switched around in a hurry after each lunch break. Roy would rush through each job, run back to his workbench, and start screaming at the mouse through the tiny cardboard windows. He insisted that the mouse was mocking the way he performed the job. He ranted and raved. He began shaking the house. Keep in mind that, throughout all of this, we were still somehow managing to build 'em *"Chevy Tough!"*

Finally, it was over. Roy grabbed the mouse by the tail and stalked up the welder's platform. He took a brazing torch, gassed up a long blue flame, and right there in the middle of Jungleland, incinerated his little buddy at arm's length.

> Why does Hamper tell us about the rodent incident?

It didn't get any better. The day before he quit, Roy approached me with a box-cutter knife in his glove. His request was that I take the blade and give him a slice across the back of his hand. He felt flat sure that this ploy would land him a few days off the job.

I had to refuse. Once again, it didn't seem like a solid career move. Roy went on to the other workers where he received a couple of charitable offers to cut his throat, but no dice on the hand. He sulked back to his job.

After a half-dozen attempts on his own, Roy finally got himself a gash. He waited until the blood had a chance to spread out a bit and then went dashing off to see the boss. The damage was minimal. A hunk of gauze, an elastic bandage, and a slow, defeated shuffle back to the wheel wells.

After that day, I never saw Roy again. Personnel sent down a young Puerto Rican guy to help me do the Right Guard commercial and the two of us put in our 90 days without much of a squawk.

The money was right, even if we weren't.

The layoffs grabbed me in 1980. If you have a deep-rooted fear of standing in an unemployment line like I did, I advise that you do everything in your power to hang on to your job. Heap your employer with phony plaudits, offer to baby-sit his kids, gulp amphetamines and perform the work load of ten servants. If you have to, get down on all fours and smooch his dusty wing-tips anew with sheen. In your spare time go to church, pray to Allah, pray to Buddha, plead with Zeus, beg of Jah, implore the graces of whichever deity landed the '69 Mets a pennant to keep your little butt in the sling and outta the Michigan Employment Security Commission (MESC) logjam of human languish. No, this is not the place to be if you get clammy in a crowd.

First off, the MESC has no windows. Once you pop through the doors, it's like entering a holding tank for sodden sumo wrestlers. You're required to check in at the front desk where a nice little old lady (who appears to have been a teenager during the Spanish-American War) will put a red check next to your appointment time and ask you if you have any paperwork to turn in. Always answer no or you will be detained for a time approximately the same as was needed to build the Pyramids. Paperwork makes these people freeze, reducing them to slow-motion voyagers across the tar pits of eternity. If you have paperwork to hand in, wait until you are absolutely *commanded* to present it and then give weighty consideration to the benefits of suicide.

After your card has been checked at the front desk, you will be instructed to fall into line. Being a shoprat, the most popular of jobless hacks, I have my choice of line 10, 11, or 12, and without fail I always choose the wrong one. My method is to give a quick glance into the eyes of the prospective claims people and somehow determine just which one is herding them out the fastest. Sometimes I'll choose the stiff old man. Sometimes the pretty young woman. Sometimes the evil lady who looks like Agnes Moorehead ripped from the grave. The strategy never works. Either the pretty young woman gets bogged down with potential Romeos, the old guy has to go shuffling off to the can, or the huffy bat spends a half-hour gnawing on some piece of red tape gristle with some dunce who can't remember his age.

A friend of mine insists that the MESC has made a widespread effort to stock its ranks full of people with fetishes for dominance. Though I might hedge a bit on that assertion, it is true that many of its employees seem to delight in having you grovel, squirm, and plead total ignorance to their avalanche of legal brain boggle. They act as though you laid yourself off, that you have no intention of ever lifting another finger, that you're in a frantic rush to get back poolside to your bevy of naked stewardesses, that you hate this country and wanna take their money to buy explosives to lob at the governor's motorcade.

> How does Hamper feel about collecting unemployment? What is your attitude toward the unemployed?

Reading through their standard probes, I'm always tempted to give them a jolt:

> Q: "Have you received any income during the past two weeks?"
>
> A: "Yes, I was paid $10,000 to carry out a hit on a U.S. senator."
>
> Q: "Are you receiving any benefits from any other state?"
>
> A: "Yes, I am on a retainer fee from the state of New York as a producer of male prostitutes."
>
> Q: "Have you been able and available for work?"
>
> A: "No, I haven't. I've been too busy selling cocaine and have been too wasted to hear the phone even if it rang."

One thing about being stranded in the unemployment line that I find preferable to a line at a grocery store or movie is that no one speaks to you. Of course, there is always the exception like the guy a few weeks ago who must have mistook me for a chaplain, a social worker, or the future biographer of his life's stupid deeds. As we edged closer and closer to the claims desk, at a pace not discernible to the naked eye, I was treated to every fact of this bumpkin's existence—the kids, his taxes, the deep green hue of his lawn, the hunting dog, his asthma, his perceptions of Blanchard, Reagan, Poland, and the *A-Team*. What is it that makes people think that I have the slightest interest in what's going on in their lives? I hardly have any interest in mine.

Occasionally you'll see people get really irked over a development in their claim. The last time I was in for my check, the desk people dropped this big ugly bomb stating that because of blah-blah-blah (read: unlimited technical bullshit), the extended benefits program was being cut and that the majority of these jobless folks had run the old money meter bone dry. Believe me, this message was not received with cheers and beers—as proven by the fact that one enraged castoff, being of sound strength, if not entirely sound mind, saw fit to retreat to the MESC personnel parking lot, pull out a knife and proceed to play Zorro on the office worker's radials. He was apprehended and stashed in the pokey, where I guess he's pretty much accomplished his objective—the State is still gonna be footing his meal money.

The thing you want to avoid at all costs when visiting the unemployment office is to be detained in the section of seats over by the side wall. That is where they send you if you develop complications in your claim, if you need to file a new claim, if you act unappreciative, or if you go to the bathroom in your pants. If you are instructed to have a seat over in this dreadful limbo, it is advisable that you pack a hefty lunch, bring the complete works of your favorite authors, have your mail delivery halted, and prepare to wait, wait, wait. So far, I've been lucky to avoid taking up a perch in the Land That Time Forgot. What they do with these people is not apparent. Every now and then you see some wire-rimmed weasel in a suit coat poke his head out from beyond the partition and summon one of the waiting few to follow him.

Never, but never, have I ever seen people reappear once ushered in to the boundless back chambers of the MESC. At first I thought that they were merely ducking out a side exit, but casual research into this possible explanation has shown me that *there is no side exit.*

I take it now that this is how it ends. A silent trudge down a narrow hallway, led by a cranky claims executioner with cold eyes and blue lips. Finally having your benefits exhausted, you are a total nonentity. No one misses you. No one can see you. You disappear from the unemployment statistics. You no longer exist.

A miniature Auschwitz has been assembled far behind the clicking of the cashier's keys, far removed from the lazy shuffle of the fresh claimant's feet, off in back where you now only wait for the pellets to drop and the air to get red.

Oh, it could have been worse. You could have been burnt in a house fire. You could have been snagged in a plane prop. You could have been trampled at a Paul Anka concert. You could have had to go find a job.

I was fortunate to be called back to work just one week before my claim was to expire. In a roundabout way, I have only one man to thank for this swell turn of fate—Caspar Weinberger. It was this man's dogged lust for a few billion dollars worth of military trucks that reopened the doors and pumped new life into my sagging career as a shoprat.

Who could argue? When the call came in askin' if I'd like to come back and help assemble Ronnie's new Death Wagon, I was quick to respond. "Hell yes, I will go!" Conscientious objection might be a noble path on draft day, but I had to admit to having developed a strong desire to eat food every day, and I didn't think it would be an easy habit to break.

> Why is it difficult for Hamper to turn down the opportunity to work for GM again?

Back on the line I was reincarnated as a rivethead. The placement must have been the right one, because I've been at it now for six years.

The most important thing I've learned during my appointment to the Rivet Line is a new approach to job monotony. Rather than dreading the tedium that accompanies assembly labor, I've found that one should lie down and wallow in it. Let repetition be its own reward. The key is to grind your job down into a series of empty, vacant gestures. Chew on it until it becomes a flavorless pulp. Keep plowing the same daily rut. Reject change. Reject variety. Aspire to vegetation and dance that trance around.

Once this is accomplished, work on speed. Attempt to shave three seconds per month off your standard performance time. You must always remember that General Motors isn't paying you to think. They've got holes they need screws in, bolts they need nuts on. Goddamn it, give it to 'em! Fast, faster . . . *faster!*

You want an example of perfection? Well, I've mastered dead head velocity to such an accomplished level that, oftentimes, I must run down the line and examine a prior frame just to make sure that I performed my duties on it. Without fail, the job is always complete. It's proud moments like these when I know I have achieved total zombie nirvana. After all, how can you possibly dread an event that you're not even aware has happened?

> How does Hamper make "repetition its own reward"?

Working the Rivet Line is like being paid to flunk high school the rest of your life. An adolescent time warp that peddles report cards (line audit scores), awards stars (complimentary plastic coffee mugs with corporate logo), causes pimples (Carpal Tunnel Syndrome), and serves up detention (indefinite layoffs). (Carpal Tunnel Syndrome is bound to affect almost every rivethead sooner or later. The symptoms are easy enough to recognize: you wake up in the morning and your hands feel as though they were underwater. They tingle and feel uncomfortably thick. For an hour or so, it is impossible to write your name or even pick your nose with any semblance of style and grace.)

The parallel could also be stretched to include the fact that I've seen the same number of co-workers (three) sent home after wetting their pants as those sent home after mashing off a finger in a rivet gun. Sing it, Bonehead: "No more pencils, no more books, no more pinkies, we've got hooks!"

We even have our own version of the high school mascot. I wouldn't fib ya, honest. His name is Howie Makem—the "Quality Cat."

GM created Howie six years ago as the messianic embodiment of its new quality drive. A livin', breathin' propaganda vessel hired to spur the troops. Imagine it: "Slogans on free coffee cups just ain't gettin' it, Bill. My suggestion is that we give the men a kitty cat."

Howie stands about five-feet-seven. He has light brown fur, long synthetic whiskers, and a head the size of a Datsun. A very magical cat, he walks everywhere on his hind paws. Sadly, Howie was not entrusted with a dick.

Though it's been six years now, I still get spooked every time Howie appears on one of his rounds. I can never quite prepare myself for the sight of that gigantic corduroy cat's head bouncin' down the aisle, issuing me a quick thumbs-up signal and then disappearing back into the haze.

I will think to myself: *Someone* is in that head. *Someone* whose wife and kids lie sound asleep in another part of town while the stars shine down and the trucks pile up and Daddy haunts the halls in his kitty costume. *Someone* who was forced to go through 12 worthless years of the American Education System only to wind up jerry-riggin' the same old acid flashback for the benefit of a bunch of bleary-eyed screw jockeys with 12 o'clock shadow.

Why does Hamper have a problem with Howie Makem?

There should be exemptions for men who aspire to do nothing more than dress up as house pets in the middle of factories.

Another thought has occurred to me. If Howie Makem is allowed to roam the plant as the spiritual ambassador of the "Quality Concept," why isn't equal time being provided a likewise, embodied representative of GM's *foremost* preoccupation—the "Quantity Concept." For the sake of realism, Howie needs an alter ego. An elusive second self that would lurk amongst the shadows and pounce on any worker who dare cause a stoppage on the line.

I decided I might like the role. Through information passed on by a friend, I learned that Howie had a spare head stowed away somewhere in the audit area. It was my intention to swipe the spare noggin, paint the eyes a violent red, attach giant fangs to its over-bite, and carve the word QUOTA across its forehead.

With that accomplished, the "Quantity Cat" could set out to terrorize all those responsible for downtime. (How many times had I heard it: "For each minute the line is down, the Company loses another $10,000 income.") "Howie Takem" could ambush workers at stoplights. Park next to them in drive-ins. Claw their bedroom windows during the sex act. Growl at them from behind the Beer Nuts rack in Mark's Lounge.

Unfortunately, it didn't work out. I made it as far as locating the very closet where Howie stashed his head, but on each visit, the sucker was padlocked. My source tells me this is because the Quality people are taking no chances. Last winter, vandals made off with Howie's legs and torso and all the Quality folks are left with is a couple of disembodied cat heads collecting dust.

This part confuses me. Just because Howie (either version) no longer has a body, what's to stop him from putting on the head and performing his rounds in jeans or coveralls? The way I figure it—as long as you've got a head, you've got a Howie. Right?

It's silly, I make $12.82 an hour. When everything goes right, I have no idea what I'm doing. I retire in the year 2007. I'll believe anything.

It was Dave, ex-rivethead-turned-Door-Fit-Inspector at the Chevy Truck plant in Flint, who first suggested that we turn to the professional psychiatric world for input and guidance. He was having those nightmares again—the ones in which Roger Smith clutches the end of a limbo stick and plods around the living room on his knees while strange exotic birds hiss, moan, and defecate on stacks of old aluminum.

"Our health insurance will cover the whole shot," reasoned Dave. "It's just as legit as having a busted back. Besides, there may be some time off work in the deal or, at the very least, some get-happy drugs."

Time off work? Get-happy drugs? I didn't see much need for either. As usual, I had no idea of what I wanted, outside of a half-tank of gas, some cigarettes, a little pocket change, and a new copy of Alex Chilton's *Like Flies on Sherbet*. I assumed that having a good-paying job that I thoroughly despised verified my position as just another square-jawed care-free American. Dave disagreed: "I believe, more firmly than ever, that you need your head dipped."

We contacted a couple of local analysts—Dave's first-round selection being an eccentric German he summoned up from the yellow pages while browsing for "impressive-sounding surnames," and I, in turn, taking potluck from a scroll I had found lying around in the office of my family doctor.

After a couple of visits each, we compared findings. Dave's doctors pronounced him to be a top-notch manic-depressive (hardly a startling revelation considering the fact that if Dave were asked whether a glass of water on the counter was half-full or half-empty, he would probably reply, "Bone dry and swarming with leeches"). His shrink peeled off a prescription of lithium, suggested that a career move was in order, and pleaded with Dave never to buy a home in his subdivision.

My sessions were somewhat less frantic. According to my shrink, there were two main factors holding me back in life. He felt that I was prone to too much worry, agonizing over things that were beyond my control, and that it was a half-decent hunch that my life was being "controlled by Satan." (The session took on a religious tone once I admitted to being a failed Catholic.) I immediately reasoned that if the latter were true, then the former condition was hardly to be unexpected.

Dave and I aren't seeing psychiatrists anymore. As far as I know, Dave opted for liquor over lithium and is still fondling door jams one floor above me at Chevy Truck.

As for myself. I still worry about everything: hailstorms, dying pets, bad arteries, the Boston Celtics, phone bills, Madonna's marriage, and turning 30. Satan is *not* controlling my life! Bill Cullen is.

It's 11:35 P.M. and I return to the Rivet Line at GM Truck and Bus. I'm sitting on top of an overturned garbage pail next to my workbench. I have roughly one minute before the next truck frame arrives and I must resume my assembler's duties.

Fifty miles to the south, GM Chairman Roger Smith gnaws at a dish of pears while Johnny Carson unfolds the evening's monologue. Roger's wife is slouching next to him, painting her toenails. I'd guess that neither of them knows I am here pounding rivets.

In an hour and a half, the line'll shut down and I'll be out of here. If I worked in a burger joint or gas station, the boss and I would probably close up and go bowl a few rounds at Eastown Lanes.

But here at GM I've never even seen my Boss, Roger Smith, let alone commit ten pins with him. So I think its time we hit the bowling alley—just Smitty and I. Not my foreman. Not the plant manager. Not even my Union honcho, Owen Bieber, who'd probably have some brute with a MADE IN AMERICA tattoo on his biceps bury my face in the ball return.

> What does Hamper hope to gain by meeting Roger Smith?

Nope, it's gotta be Roger, or I ain't gonna dance.

He owes it to me is the way I got it figured, and I in turn owe it to all my proud ancestors—a dedicated bunch of shoprats if there ever were some. Consider this roll call: my old man worked for the Company. My grandpappy worked for the Company. My sweet little granny worked for the Company. My other grandpappy, God rest his assembler's soul, worked for the Company. I'm telling you damn near everybody who ever leased limb space on the ol' family sap worked for the Company, and if you're wondering what happened to my other granny—well, somebody had to stay back home and pack that army a lunch.

Including my nine years of service to GM, we're left staring at something like 126 years devoted to the General Motors Corporation. That's an incredible amount of time to be spent wondering what to do with the three-ten spare. Seven and a half centuries in dog years and all my clan has got to offer when they drag around the spotlight for show-and-tell is: a few ugly wristwatches, a shoe box fulla pension stubs, lien-free false teeth, and the scar that runs down my dear daddy's back. Excluding having my spine fused back together, I want all those things too! Plus ten frames of bowling with Rog.

What is Hamper's attitude towards his legacy?

I've approached a number of my co-workers regarding my bowling quest and not one of them has ever laughed at me. They all seemed to handle the subject with a genuine sense of concern. And fascination.

For instance, a recent conversation I had with one of my Rivet Line pals went like this:

"Wouldn't it be a nice gesture if, on occasion, you went out and had a couple beers with the Boss?"

"I'd do it."

"And," I continued, "don't you think that maybe inroads could be made toward tearing down the hostile relationship between Labor and Management if you and the Boss agreed to go bowling once a month?"

"Yeah, that might help," my pal admitted.

"Just you and Roger Smith taking time out and tipping a few Strohs."

"Well, it all depends," the guy hesitated.

"How's that?"

"Who the fuck is Roger Smith?"

It is now 1:30 A.M. And I won't be bowling with Roger tonight. The nights here crawl by indistinguishably from one another and every Thursday evening Roger sends me a check to show me what a good boy I've been.

Tomorrow I'll punch in and do it all over again. Once every hour an army truck will roll past on the line with its hood latch no doubt pointed at some poor rebel in El Salvador, Lebanon, or maybe Cleveland. I grab my gun and rivet a dual-exhaust tail pipe hanger to its ribs.

The bell rings, the line stops and I go out, sit in my car, and smoke Newport Menthol Kings until the lot clears. I rub out the last cigarette and go home to drink bourbon from a plastic mug emblazoned with the motto: "WE MAKE OUR OWN HISTORY—50 YEARS. UAW." This is the best I've felt all day.

If I last that long, I can retire in 21 years.

It's a living. Sorta.

Reflections assured my engagement.

—Ivana Rubric

Final Reflection

Have you ever made a major job change? How hard was it to make this change?

❖ *After You Read, Consider*

1. Is Hamper proud of being a "rivethead"? Is he proud of being able to survive his job?

2. What coping strategies does Hamper develop?

3. Why does Hamper believe that working at GM is his only option?

❖ *Suggestions for Writing*

1. Write an essay in which you explore all of Hamper's legacies. Include his attitudes towards work as well as his choice of careers. What did he inherit along with the opportunity to be a "shoprat"?

2. Explore the different career options in your area. Has the choice of possible careers changed so much that it isn't possible to have the same job your father or mother did? Write an essay in which you justify your chosen career.

3. What makes a job meaningful? In an essay, explore what kind of work is meaningful for you and your expectations about the work you hope to do someday.

Jessica Marinara

Christmas for the Colorblind

Jessica Marinara is a scholar, pizza architect, and warrior in the metaphorical battle to subvert the dominant paradigm. She presently has no free time. When she does, she writes letters to the editor, plays rugby, and paints her toenails. On graduation she intends to pursue a PhD in a valiant effort to place herself further in debt.

The more I wrote in my journal, the easier it was to write my essays.
—Linda McGuire

Prereading Reflection

Do you like to celebrate holidays?

There are no real seasons in the Deep South. The days simply melt into one another—a slowly turning kaleidoscope of sun and stars, rain clouds and wind. The few trees that lose their leaves do so in a slow drifting dance. Brittle and dark, they stand against the shifting gray sky, the Spanish moss clinging to them like the tatters of a burial gown.

> How does this scene make you feel?

Natives claim that Spring and Fall, no matter how ephemeral, really do exist, but as a person who played in crisp piles of leaves and watched the crocuses bloom in the snow, I know the truth. A year of weather in Georgia is like a life that only has a beginning and an end. The hot, moist summer birthing slowly slides into the cool dryness of the truly aged winter with an unnerving imperceptibility.

As a recent transplant to this state, I have learned to recognize the passing seasons by the garish icons of idealist holidays that adorn the houses of my neighbors—scampering pink Easter bunnies for Spring, American flags for Summer, grinning jack-o-lanterns for Fall, and jolly Santa Claus with his clan of elves for Winter.

Right now I'm caught in a whirlwind of Christmas retail hell. Thanksgiving dinner has just barely settled in my stomach and already I'm suffering from an advertisement induced case of Christmas shopping stress. There is no season scarier for a lapsed Irish Catholic who thinks too much. As far as I'm concerned, Santa Claus and Satan are both just big, red men who are fighting over the job of scaring Christian children into being good. Santa gets November and December, Satan gets the rest of the year.

Do you suffer from shopping stress during certain holidays or celebratory times?

Of course "The Season" isn't all bad. People become more liberal tippers at the bakery slash deli where I work. Even better than that, the customers start treating me more like a human being and less like their personal scapegoat. Granted, I'm only thinking that right now because the door is locked and the open sign is switched off. But I am still here, swishing a bleach sodden mop around on the floor, erasing the foot traffic of the day. This job should have come with an instruction manual:

Job Title: Food Service
Job Description: Must tolerate stupid co-workers and irate customers who are convinced that everything is your fault.
Pros: Free food and a paycheck
Cons: You will get no respect, even if you are the only one who can serve beef tongue without vomiting.
Prescription: Caffeine.

Can you relate to a job that includes this type of pro and con list?

But then again, every situation requires a new method of survival. This one is no different. I give the mop one last swish on the floor and then shove it and the heavy yellow bucket into the kitchen. Finished, I heave myself onto a stainless steel bakery table to take the weight off my feet.

"Ah, so Puck has come to talk to me," says Jeremy wiping sweat onto the shoulder of his ragged Dead shirt.

"You poor dear, were you lonely all by yourself in the kitchen?" I ask, giving him the mischievous dimpled grin that earned me my nickname. "But you have Slava and Alexi to talk to."

"Puck, they left three hours ago and besides they barely speak English."

What does her description of her co-workers reveal about Karen?

"And this makes them different from my co-servers how?" I ask wincing at the memory of the long line of crispy-haired Barbie dolls that I have been forced to train.

Jeremy sprinkles a handful of black snow onto a batch of poppy seed bagels and then slams the oven door closed.

"This job is making me crazy," he says. He runs around the kitchen in circles, a puppy frustrated with the endless chase after its own tail.

"Don't let it get to you. Instead of thinking of it as a means of survival, think of it as an outlet for your creative passions."

"First of all, Puck," says Jeremy as he engages in a lively jig with the dripping mop, "being a starving artist is highly overrated. And second of all, this isn't a bakery, it's a glorified Dunkin Donuts."

"It could be worse," pipes up a familiar voice. "You could be going to the mall like us."

My boyfriend Michael is lounging in the open back door wearing boots, jeans and a black T-shirt that says "Mutate and Survive" in big yellow letters. I give him a bear hug hello and put my fingers in his white-blond hair. Sometimes I can't figure out how the two of us ended up having so much in common. He was raised by a good Catholic woman and an ex-military father. I was raised by a radical feminist mother and a borderline paranoid father who is convinced the world is on the verge of collapse. Maybe our differences balance us out. Or maybe we're the only two people in the world warped enough to understand one another.

Why does Karen think their parentage makes them "warped" in some way?

The buzzer on the oven goes off; Jeremy sighs and disentangles himself from the mop. "You two kids have fun now."

Laughing, we leave him hurling steaming hot bagels into wire baskets.

"Michael, do we really have to do this?" I give him the most pitiful face I can muster while struggling into a heavy sweatshirt. He unlocks the passenger door to his truck and lets me in before getting in himself.

"Are you sure you don't want to put on some jeans," he asks, frowning at my cutesy, black uniform shorts.

"No. Now let's go before I change my mind."

I firmly believe that the mall and hell are completely synonymous places. In the sauna-like weather of each, jeans would be overkill. As usual Michael knows what I'm thinking and needs no further explanation.

Why doesn't Karen like malls? How do you feel about malls?

The mall is a veritable breeding ground for packs of prissy *prima donnas* who check their hair in every semi-reflective window they pass and schools of jingling grandmas in festive red and green sweatsuits. As predicted, it is at least a sweltering 95 degrees. We manage to buy gifts for my sister and both our mothers before the canned Christmas muzack and mechanical elves drive us into the parking lot.

"I think Nikki will like that shirt we got her. She likes green right?"

He weaves a complicated path to the truck. How he manages to find it in the sea of other vehicles is beyond me, but he does.

"Sweetheart, it's red."

"Oh."

How does the author feel about Michael's colorblindness?

Most of the time his colorblindness is unnoticeable; I almost never have to tell him what color things are. I think this season just messes with his perceptions. All that red and green must be a boring monotone for him.

"Do you want to go for a drive?" Michael asks before he even switches on the engine.

"Yeah, I could use some down time after all that."

It got dark while we were encased in the fluorescent fantasy land of shopping chaos and I feel like I am suffering from a major case of jet lag. I pull the rubber band out of my hair and let it down in dark waves that are much more comfortable than the severe ponytail it was in. Rolling down the windows, we cruise out of the luxury car infested parking lot and onto the highway. The rapidly cooling night air sneaks in its bony fingers, whipping our hair into tangles.

"City limits," Michael reads the passing sign aloud. "If we just passed the City Limits sign and the one for the nature preserve doesn't come up for another quarter mile, where are we?"

"If Savannah is hell and the preserve is heaven, then I guess that would put us in purgatory," I answer.

Michael squints into the darkness and steers around a gentle curve in the road. The soft glow of animal eyes peer at us from in between the trees. The tiny points of gold remind me of the strings of Christmas lights we left behind. Maybe the animals are having a party without us. If they are, we wouldn't know it. Only quiet surrounds the cocoon inside the truck.

Darting out of the surrounding blackness, a doe leaps onto the asphalt. Her unexpected movement, the raucous beauty of her four-legged *jette*, shatters our reverie.

Have you ever hit an animal with a vehicle?

Frozen in the glare of electrical sunshine, she shudders as Michael slams on the brakes. Instinctively, she bolts. Heading like a moth for the seductive glow of light, her body is slammed into the grill of the truck, head thrown back, white neck exposed.

I brace myself against the dash as we swerve, the dull thud of flesh against chrome a fading echo. The tires spit chunks of gravel as we pull onto the shoulder.

"Oh, baby, please be all right." Michael's words become a silent litany.

We crouch by her body in the wet grass on the side of the road. Her muscles are pulled into taut cords underneath the soft tan of her pelt. Michael presses a hand to her side and another to her throat. I wait in silence. *She has such long eyelashes.*

"She's gone," Michael rubs her side. "I'm so sorry." He chokes on the words.

"Ya'll all right?" a voice calls out.

There is a uniformed man heading towards us. I glance behind him, across the street to two sparkling yellow fire engines. I hadn't realized where we were.

"Hit a deer," Michael says, blowing too much breath into the words.

"They'll dart out in front of you that way," the fireman says.

Kneeling beside us, he puts his hand on the deer's throat, feeling again for a pulse of life that isn't there.

"We'll put 'er in the truck and drive 'er up under the light so's we can get a look at 'er."

The fireman lifts her, two huge fists wrapped around her spindly legs. Her head falls slack, white ears pointed at the ground. Her body makes a quiet rasping sound as it slides across the bedliner. I fumble with the door handle and clamber awkwardly into the truck. The piercing yellow light from the fire station settles over us, over the deer, as we back into the lot. Outside again, I wrap my arms around myself and shiver.

There is blood coming out of her ears. Fine webs that map the tiny variations of soft pink flesh. Her teeth are sunk into her tongue; pain a way of clinging to life.

"She's so small," Michael says quietly.

"This here's a full grown deer. They don't get much bigger than this 'cause there's so many of them."

The fireman pauses and says nothing for a long moment. He is probably trying to think of something comforting to say.

> How do you feel about the firefighter's question?

"Ya'll want the meat?" he asks finally. "I can clean 'er up right now for ya. I'm goin' deer hunting in the morning."

I want to tell him that I don't eat meat, not even fish, but I can't. I begin to feel too full of words.

"Nah, man," Michael shakes his head. "I couldn't eat a deer I hit."

"If ya really don't want 'er I'll take 'er. I usually don't eat what people have hit, but this one's still warm."

I realize that he is trying not to waste a life that is not his. I am still angry.

"Yeah, she's yours if you want her." Michael lifts the doe out of the truck and lays her on the cement slab in front of the fire engine. I stare at the empty truck as the voices of Michael and the fireman rise and fall behind me. I make no effort to understand them.

The doe has left behind a small puddle of thick blood. Under the lights it shines like a ruby. My birthstone. The two men walk back towards me. Michael sees the blood and asks the fireman if he has a towel or something, anything.

Why can Michael see that the deer's blood is red?

"I've never seen such red blood," Michael mutters at the same time as the fireman says, "Yeah, hold on a minute."

He picks up a garden hose that has been lying impotent in the grass a few steps away. Michael and I glance at each other while the fireman turns on the water. As he sprays the blood out of the bed the spray hits me. I don't move out of the way. Her blood is red, red to someone who cannot see it, red to someone who cannot stop seeing it.

"Your truck OK?" asks the fireman after turning off the spigot.

"Yeah, I think I lost a rim though."

"I'll go get it."

He heads off down the driveway searching the trees with a flashlight. Michael walks over to the doe and crouches beside her. Reaching down he closes her eyes and then walks back towards me. I fight the urge to flinch as he puts an arm around my shoulders and his hand in my hair. I don't want him to touch me; he has death on his hands.

"She didn't suffer, Karen."

The fireman comes back victorious, the bent rim in one hand.

"You all right?" he finally asks me.

I nod dumbly.

Michael and the fireman shake hands. There is nothing else to do but leave, so we do.

"I'm sorry. I really am. I tried to avoid her."

"I know it wasn't your fault. I didn't see her either." I slide across the seat and kiss his shoulder.

On the way home we drive down a street lined with Christmas decorations. Grinning reindeer lit up in lights.

Final Reflection

Based on your initial reflection, write about a time when you experienced an unpleasant incident during a favorite season or holiday.

> *It is a lot harder to talk about images in stories. Everyone in class seemed to interpret them differently.*
>
> —Susan Thompson

❖ *After You Read, Consider*

1. Why is Michael's colorblindness important to the telling of this story?

2. Karen flinches when Michael puts his arm around her after he's come from the dead deer. What do you believe she's feeling but has no words to express?

3. The narrator refers to her co-workers simply as Barbie dolls, yet she goes into great detail when describing the deer. Why do you suppose she chooses that technique?

❖ *Suggestions for Writing*

1. The fireman offers Michael and Karen the meat from the deer. When they turn it down, he offers to take the meat himself. Write an editorial supporting or protesting his actions.

2. The author is a vegetarian. She and Michael are on their way to a nature preserve. How might these facts be used to interpret her reactions to the death of the deer? Write an essay in which you explore her feelings.

3. Michael and Karen react very differently to the deer's death. Karen's imagination causes her to see the deer's blood and think of her own birthstone, to notice the deer's eyelashes, to be too angry to speak. Michael, although he doesn't want to eat the deer, is more practical as he thinks to clean up the blood and find his rim. Write an essay in which you explore how gender might play a part in their reactions.

Sandra Cisneros

First Job

Throughout Sandra Cisneros's childhood, her Mexican American mother, Mexican father, six brothers, and she moved between Mexico City and Chicago, which never allowed her time to get settled in one place. Her loneliness from having no sisters and few friends drove her to bury herself in reading. In high school, she wrote poetry and was the literary magazine editor, but, according to Cisneros, she didn't really start writing until her first creative writing class in college in 1974. Cisneros realized that she needed to write what she knew and adopted a writing style that was purposely opposite that of her classmates. Five years after receiving her MA from the writing program at the University of Iowa, she returned to Loyola University in Chicago, where she had previously earned a BA in English, to work as an administrative assistant. Prior to this job, she worked in the Chicano barrio in Chicago teaching high school dropouts. Through these jobs, she gained more experience with the problems of young Latinas.

Prereading Reflection

Write about co-workers who are older than you. How are their attitudes toward work different than yours?

It wasn't as if I didn't want to work. I did. I had even gone to the social security office the month before to get my social security number. I needed money. The Catholic high school cost a lot, and Papa said nobody went to public school unless you wanted to turn out bad. I thought I'd find an easy job, the kind other kids had, working in the dime store or maybe a hotdog stand. And though I hadn't started looking yet, I thought I might the week after next. But when I came home that afternoon, all wet because Tito had pushed me into the open water hydrant—only I had sort of let

> How old do you think the narrator is? What is she telling you about her experience?

him—Mama called me in the kitchen before I could even go and change, and Aunt Lala was sitting there drinking her coffee with a spoon. Aunt Lala said she had found a job for me at the Peter Pan Photo Finishers on North Broadway where she worked and how old was I and to show up tomorrow saying I was one year older and that was that.

What does the narrator learn about work before she even gets there?

So the next morning I put on the navy blue dress that made me look older and borrowed money for lunch and bus fare because Aunt Lala said I wouldn't get paid 'til the next Friday and I went in and saw the boss of the Peter Pan Photo Finishers on North Broadway where Aunt Lala worked and lied about my age like she told me to and sure enough I started that same day.

In my job I had to wear white gloves. I was supposed to match negatives with their prints, just look at the picture and look for the same one on the negative strip, put it in the envelope, and do the next one. That's all. I didn't know where these envelopes were coming from or where they were going. I just did what I was told.

It was real easy and I guess I wouldn't have minded it except that you got tired after a while and I didn't know if I could sit down or not, and then I started sitting down only when the two ladies next to me did. After a while they started to laugh and came up to me and said I could sit when I wanted to and I said I knew.

When lunch time came I was scared to eat alone in the company lunchroom with all those men and ladies looking, so I ate real fast standing in one of the washroom stalls and had lots of time left over so I went back to work early. But then break time came and not knowing where else to go I went into the coatroom because there was a bench there.

I guess it was time for the night shift or middle shift to arrive because a few people came in and punched the time clock and an older Oriental man said hello and we talked for a while about my just starting and he said we could be friends and next time to go in the lunchroom and sit with him and I felt better. He had nice eyes and I didn't feel so nervous anymore. Then he asked if I knew what day it was and when I said I didn't he said it was his birthday and would I please give him a birthday kiss. I thought I would because he was so old and just as I was about to put my lips on his cheek, he grabs my face with both hands and kisses me hard on the mouth and doesn't let go.

What would you do at this point?

Final Reflection

Write an ending to this story in which the narrator is allowed to respond to the older man's behavior.

❖ After You Read, Consider

1. Why does Aunt Lala tell the narrator to lie about her age? Why would her parents want her to work with her aunt?

2. If the narrator wanted a job as she claims, why hadn't she looked for one yet? What kind of job did she want?

3. What were some of the "rules" at work that no one explained to the narrator? Why didn't her co-workers bother to tell her?

❖ Suggestions for Writing

1. Write a narrative about some of the people you have worked with. How did your relationships with them affect your attitudes toward your job and work in general?

2. Write an essay in which you compare the "rules" at your job with the "rules" of being a student. Which set of rules was easier to learn? Which "first day" was more comfortable?

Chris Llewellyn

March 25, 1911

Chris Llewellyn was born and raised in Fostoria, Ohio, and has lived in Washington, D.C., since 1970. She participated in the 1977 Jenny M. Moore Community College Writing Program taught by Marilyn Hacker at George Washington University and was a guest poet at the Festival of Poets and Poetry at St. Mary's College in Maryland. She is the recipient of a grant from the D.C. Commission on the Arts and Humanities, and her poems have been published in many journals and anthologies. Llewellyn has given poetry readings in the U.S. Congress, the Folger Shakespeare Library, and elsewhere.

I liked being able to work out my ideas in a notebook.

—Lauren Johnson

Prereading Reflection

Write about what you think life might have been like for a young woman in 1911 who lived in a large American city.

It was Spring. It was Saturday.
Payday. For some it was Sabbath.
Soon it will be Easter. It was
approaching April, nearing Passover.
It was close to closing time.

The heads of trees budding
in Washington Square Park.
The sun a hot flywheel spinning
the earth's axle. The days long
enough for leaving in light.
It was Spring.

Can you remember a spring day like this?

America's sweethearts—the ladies—
stroll in shirtwaists of lawn and lace,
mimic Charles Dana Gibson's Girls.
They pose in finery cut from bolts of
flimsy and stitched by garment girls
on Gibbs, Wilcox, and Singer machines.
          It was Saturday.

Up in the Asch Building
in the Triangle Shirtwaist Company
Rosie Glantz is singing "Every Little
Movement Has a Meaning of Its Own."
Fixing hair, arranging puffs and tendrils,
the other girls in the cloakroom join in:
"Let me call you Sweetheart,
I'm in love with you."   How do you react when it is payday?
          It was Payday.

Attar-of-roses, lily of the valley,
still they smell of machine oil
that soaks the motors and floors.
The barrel in each stairwell
could fill a thousand lamps.
          For some it was Sabbath.

Here at Triangle, Sophie Salemi
and Della Costello sew on Singers.
Neighbors from Cherry Street,
they piecework facing each other,
the oil pan hitting their knees.
Tomorrow sisters will nail flowers
on tenement doors.
          Soon it will be Easter.

The machine heads connected by belts
to the flywheel to rotating axle
sing the Tarantella. Faster,
faster vibrate the needles, humming
faster the fashionable dance.
          It was approaching April.

Della and Sophie up on Ninth
piece sleeves, race the needle's pace
not knowing on Eighth, paper patterns
burn from the wire, fall on machines,
spark moths and pinwheels round the room.
Rockets push up cutting-tables.
          It was nearing Passover.

On Eighth, cutters throw pails of water
on the lawn of flame, and Louis,
holding the canvas hose, hollers:
"No pressure! Nothing coming!"

> What would you do if you were trapped in a fire?

It was close to closing time.

Down on Greene Street, Old Dominick
pushes his wheelbarrow, describes
"a big puff" when windows popped,
glittering showers of glass.
It was Spring.

Flaming swords, Pluto piles to Ninth.
Sophie and Della and dozens of others
jump on machine tables; the aisles jammed
with wicker workbaskets and chairs.
It was Saturday.

Mrs. Yaller testified: "Some froze at
machines. Others were packed in the cloakroom
filled with smoke. I heard them yelling
in Yiddish or Italian, crying out
the names of their children."

> How do the eyewitness accounts increase your understanding?

It was Payday.

Reporter Bill Shepherd is writing:
"I remember the great strike of last year,
these same girls demanding decent
working conditions."
For some it was Sabbath.

Rosie runs to the stairway. The door,
Locked! The telephone, Dead! Piling red
ribbons, fire backs girls into windows.
They stand on sills, see the room
a smashed altar lamp, hear the
screaming novenas of flame.
Soon it will be Easter.

Pleats of purple and gold wave,
incandescent filaments of lace snow
in shrapnel of needles and screws.
The blaze from molten bolts stains
glass, walls and lawns—on Cherry Street
sisters nail flowers on tenement doors.
It was approaching April.

"I could see them falling."
said Lena Goldman. "I was sweeping out
front of my cafe. At first we thought

it was bolts of cloth—till they opened
with legs! I still see the day
it rained children. Yes.
                  It was nearly Passover."

Sophie and Della stand on windowsill,
look out on the crazy quilt of town:
We will leave for our
block on Cherry Street,
leave these skeletons
leaning on machines,
the faces fixed on black
crucifix of cloakroom window.
                  It was close to closing time.

The *Times* quotes Mr. Porter: "The Triangle
never had a fire drill—only three factories
in the city have. One man I pleaded
with replied, 'Let em burn. They're
a lot of cattle anyhow.' "
                  It was Spring.

> Who is being blamed here?

Sophie and Della stand on sill:
We will leave, our arms
around each other, our only
sweethearts. Piling red roses
two white hearses pull up
Cherry Street and the Children
of Mary Society march
in banners of prayers.
                  It was Saturday.

Captain Henry was the first policeman to arrive:
"I saw dozens of girls hanging from sills.
Others, dresses on fire, leapt from the ledges."
                  It was Payday.

Sophie and Della look on crazy quilt of town:
Fifty of our schoolmates
sing in procession:
O Trinity of Blessed Light
Our Lady of Perpetual Help
Ave Maria, Ave Maria
Now and at the Hour
of the Tarantella.
                  For some it was Sabbath.

Ordering the nets and ladders, Battalion
Chief Worth explains, "I didn't know

they would come down three and even four
together. Why, these little ones went
through life-nets, pavement and all."
           Soon it will be Easter.

Sophie and Della stand on windowsill:
Look, the flywheel sun sinks
in the west. In the Winter
Garden, Mr. Jolson springs
and bows in blackface.
           It was approaching April.

At the Metropolitan Opera
George M. Cohan struts "The Rose
of Tralee" to the rich trailing
in diamond-sackcloth, rending
green ashes of dollar bills.
           It was nearing Passover.

Sophie and Della stand on sill,
look down crazy quilt of town:
Intertwined comets we will stream
the nightmares of Triangle Bosses
Joseph Asch
Max Blanck
Isaac Harris.
           It was close to closing time.

Our Bosses of the Locked
Doors of Sweetheart Contracts
who in puffs and tendrils
of silent telephones,
disconnected hoses, barred
shutters, fire escapes
dangling in perpetual no
help on earth in heaven.
           It was Spring.

The Lord is my shepherd
green pastures still
waters anointest heads
with oil overflowing
preparest a table—now
our arms around each other
we thread the needle where
no rich man can go spinning
the earth's axle we are
leaving in light.

O Lord my God, thou art very great!
Thou art clothed with honor and majesty,
who coverest thyself with
light as with a garment,
who stretchest out the heavens
like a curtain.

How does the inclusion of this psalm affect your reading of the poem?

—Psalm 104:1, 2

Final Reflection

After reading this poem, revise your first reflections about life for a young woman in 1911 America.

❖ *After You Read, Consider*

1. How do the lines in stanza 3 begin to increase the tension in the poem?

2. How does the author's emphasis on Sophie and Della help or hinder your reading of this poem?

3. Poetry often has multiple levels of meaning. What are some of the meanings or messages contained in this poem?

❖ *Suggestions for Writing*

1. Research a tragic event that could have been prevented. Using what you have learned, write a poem about the event.

2. Investigate working conditions or benefits in a local place of business and write a letter to the president that praises efforts or calls for change.

3. Using any medium you feel comfortable with, create the visual image suggested in stanza 16. Then write a reflective essay focusing on your image as well as the poem's imagery.

Melissa Graham

A World Painted John Deere Green

Melissa Graham grew up on a small farm in Rockledge, Georgia, and her experiences there have indelibly shaped how she sees the world. As a student at Wesleyan College, she is majoring in psychology and English with aspirations for graduate school coursework in both fields. "A World Painted John Deere Greene" reflects her childhood experience as well as the notions of practical psychology and a love for language.

❖

Prereading Reflection

Can you think of an invention that has dramatically changed your life?

❖

In 1837, a thirty-three year old blacksmith in Grand Detour, Illinois changed the world (Pete). His cast-iron plow was not the first steel blade destined to till the thick carpet of the American West, but the company he built ten years later now paints the world John Deere Green (Pete; "Deere & Company").

Why does Graham begin by telling us about paint? Why is this paint important?

Coating tractor steel, this paint is rust-resistant. Slathered over American culture, this paint is rust-actuating.

The mid-1800s found Americans moving West, searching for new lives of prosperity with "squatter's rights" firmly clutched in work-calloused hands (Conlin, 210). The indomitable spirit of the American farmer grasped the awkward handlebars of a plow—produced by a burgeoning company—without realizing that he was breaking up the grassroots not only of the soil, but also of the culture beneath his feet. What the plow and tractor did to make small farming productive and

Do you agree with Graham's perspective of the American farmer?

efficient, it simultaneously did to make small farming ineffective and non-existent. In desiring bigger and better, the proverbial "eat my dust"—accomplished with tractors and not shovels—is hurled at the ideology of small and adequate. The "American rush of consumerism, elitism, (and) status" unfortunately "runs like a Deere" (Richards, 23; "Deere & Company").

The brink of a new millennium finds America moving, searching for new lives of prosperity with college degrees firmly clutched in hands cramped by carpal tunnel syndrome. How many of those degree-holders are small farmers? 1.1 million ("Small Farmers," 107). How do these small farmers fare in our global economy? They, sixty-percent of all American farmers, "only make up 4% of all US agricultural sales" ("Small Farmers," 107). When 60% of a population produces merely 4% of the product of that population, something revolutionary has occurred to corrode the framework of the society in which that population exists. That revolution has painted our world John Deere Green.

Like the precious flecks of a crumbling monument, this corruption is fit for a museum, specifically the Smithsonian Institute. On June 10, 1997, the Deere & Company Collection was formally included in the Smithsonian Institution's Permanent Research Collection of Information Technology Innovation at the National Museum of American History ("Deere & Company Honored"). This distinction is the result of the company's use of the Genetic Algorithm Based Scheduling Optimization (GABSO)—a computer program designed to maximize production and minimize resources ("Deere & Company Honored"). In regards to their inclusion in this exclusive collection, Deere touts its innovation as becoming "part of a national treasure which documents how information technology is being used to shape society and improve our world." As scientists, students, and economists, the GABSO is a paradigm because it facilitates the bigger-and-better-with-minimal-resources philosophy. But, is something with the potential to reduce the efficacy of 60% of a population below their already meager 4% production rate a national treasure? Technological change demands cultural change, but technological progression does not preclude cultural progression. The issue in agricultural industrialization is not so much where the product comes from or how much is produced; rather, what matters is how much it will cost in terms of cultural lag.

Do you think all technology creates a cultural lag?

The cultural lag created by agricultural industrialization or "modern farming" appears in multiple forms. Among hundreds, three symptoms are central. First, a kind of phobia for a John Deere Green world indicates that society has not fully embraced all that technology makes available. Second, a contemplation of the dangers of consumption manifest a wariness about the direction of these technological changes. Third, a sub-cultural rejection of society and its standards alludes to an undercurrent of disquiet concerning these rapid innovations. These occurrences imply that, even to star-spangled eyes, John Deere Green lacks its promised shine.

> Does premodern farming have a "pristine record"?

The marvels of modern farming do not have pristine records. Yet, the "green revolution," as an article in *Economist* describes, surprised even the most optimistic forecasters with its resultant farm productivity. The abundance of affordable foods has kept hundreds of people from starving and bettered the nutritional balance of thousands more ("Growing Pains," 71). However, technological advancement has not solved either starvation or vitamin deficiencies; this is true namely because our system of distribution does not equal our production capabilities: it is a cultural lag. On a different note, the scientific manipulations of nature's own processes are not infallible. That the terms Mad cow disease (BSE) or growth hormone injection need no explanation attest to the public's fear of the glories of science. When produce was picked from a backyard garden or meat purchased from a next door neighbor, these words were never whispered much less spoken. While it is not reasonable to believe that "modern farming is a subversion of nature and that plants and animals would in general do much better without human interference," it is reasonable to question the safety of the food supply and the validity of a "symbiotic relationship between humans and animals" ("Growing Pains," 73). The elimination of the small farmer ultimately means that the common man knows neither what he is consuming nor what the repercussions of his consumption are. In a world of machine-driven farming, corporations have power, efficiency, and knowledge, not individuals.

Biographies like John Deere's reflect the American dream: an individual achieving success through capitalism under the banner of democracy. Yet, as our society has become more heterogeneous and exponentionally more stratified, individuals are significant because of the corporations they build or aspire to manage. This phenomenon stimulates anomie or normlessness: individuals no longer participate in communities, but they are tenuously connected to corporations. In contrast to the small farm family of the mid-1800's who ate, worked, slept, and worshipped together, "the average American now spends six hours a week shopping and ... the average couple only spends about 12 minutes per day talking together!" (Brandt, 28). American society is being consumed by its own consumption, hooked on the lure of bigger and better with minimal resources. This trend is not being ignored. One of the combatant approaches is a "new nonprofit organization whose goal is to promote 'sustainable consumption' " called, appropriately, "the Center for a New American Dream" (Brandt, 28). Ellen Furnari, director of the organization, states:

> The problem is that most of us are not living according to what we really value. It's not that people want to go back to the Stone Age; they don't want to give up material things. But, they want more of a balance between material things and those non-material things which give real meaning to life (Brandt, 29).

In a sense, this organization and countless others like it are reseeding the grass carpet which has been trampled by a world painted John Deere Green.

Awareness of the problem and interest in the solution does not satisfy everyone who has experienced the steel blade of cultural lag; some are ready for definitive action. The by-word in many circles recently is "voluntary simplicity." This philosophy "isn't some radical 'let's get back to the land' dropout movement"; rather it is a term that was coined to explain why "nearly one-third of (the American corporate population) voluntarily changed the way [they] lived and worked because of new priorities" in 1995 (Richards, 21). With farms maximizing their resources through scientific innovations, the last thing needed is more produce. Instead, the notion involves refocusing your lifestyle against "everything [you've] been taught about how people should live in the 20th century" (Richards, 23). Richards boldly asserts that "simple living is much more intentional, deep, and complex than buying into the American dream" (23). In fact, the principles advocated by this growing movement redefine the American Dream as something that cannot be bought. It, instead, must be a chosen alignment of what is internal with what is external. This lifestyle is possible "only in a community of faith [where there is] found an obvious and deep-seated explanation for our lives [that will stand opposite to] the individual progress, ambition, and acquisition of what is bigger and better" (Richards, 22). An increasing number of individuals are redefining what it means to be small farmers, for they are planting what needs to be planted and painting what needs to be painted ... even in John Deere Green.

John Deere, neither the man nor his company, is the grim reaper of American culture. Rather, John Deere, as an icon of the self-made man and corporate America, represents a distinctive episode in the dissolution of the American Dream. He was one man who made a plow, and, because he did it on a bigger scale, his plow was deemed better by a people eager to tame new territory. The trouble isn't the inventor or the invention or even the desire to dominate; contrastly, the quandary is a society which simultaneously exalts the accomplishments of the individual and lauds the power of the corporation. The acid of American society is the underlying belief that "bigger is better with minimal resources" when, in actuality, "small and adequate with appropriate investment" suffices nicely. Not even John Deere Green can protect steel from the elements in the presence of an acid.

Do you believe that smaller and adequate is better? That corporations have hurt individuals?

Neither John Deere nor his company is to blame for the ills or glories of agricultural industrialization. The problem is that society has not assimilated well into the scientific farming corporation. By emasculating the small farmer, agricultural industrialization reeks economic havoc, yes; but, more importantly, it violates the grassroots community which germinated the American Dream. By tilling the carpet of American culture, capitalism of the kitchen makes anomie, isolation, and powerlessness the foundation of society as compared with the bedrock of stability, connection, and opportunity nurtured by "one nation under God."

Why doesn't Graham blame John Deere?

The recreation of the American Dream doesn't need a new color scheme. More tools and toys will neither help nor hurt the re-carpeting of America. Technological progress, economic differentiation, or administrative hierarchies are neither the answers to nor the causes of the crisis of American society. Attention to the evils of outrageous consumption will not circumvent the impending collapse of a mud-based monument. Instead, in a world painted John Deere Green, small farmers—who plant what needs to be planted and paint what needs to be painted—grasp the awkward handlebars of the only philosophy sure to sustain cultural growth.

How does the color work in this essay? Do you think it is effective?

WORKS CITED

Brandt, Barbara. "Can We Build a New American Dream?" *Dollars & Sense* 217 (May 1998): Harcourt Brace, 28–29.

Conlin, Joseph R., ed. *The American Past: A Survey of American History*. 4th ed. Fort Worth: Texas: Harcourt Brace, 1984.

"Growing Pains." *Economist* 339.7962 (20 April 1996): 71–73.

John Deere & Company. "Deere & Company." Online. Internet. 19 Sept. 1998. Available: www.chadlittle.com/JDInfor.html.

John Deere & Company. "Deere & Company Honored by Smithsonian Institute." Online. Internet. Available: www.chadlittle.com/JDInfor.html.

Pete, J. "John Deere." Online. 19 Sept. 1998. Available: www.-users.itlabs.umn.edu/~east0029/deere/jd_hist.html.

Richards, Ramona. "Held Hostage by the American Dream." *Home Life* 51.7 (July 1998): 21–23.

"Small Farmers Pay for the Privilege." *Countryside & Small Stock Journal* 82.4 (July 1998): 107.

Final Reflection

What other inventions have both benefited and hurt American culture?

❖ *After You Read, Consider*

1. How did the tractor hurt American agriculture? What exactly changed when agricultural technology advanced?

2. Graham blames technology for changes in the American family. Is this blame justified?

3. Can you think of other inventions that changed the shape of American families? Graham claims technology has changed communities into corporations. Is this change always negative, as Graham suggests?

Just one more revision, just one more week! I really dislike deadlines.
—Marybeth Housman

❖ *Suggestions for Writing*

1. Write an essay in which you explore whether computer technology has made communities into corporations. You might want to look at how computers have affected your work or educational environment.

2. Write an essay in which you argue with Graham by showing the benefits of agricultural technology. You might want to be more specific with your examples than Graham is, for example, by looking at a particular crop or at how modern ranches are managed.

3. Explore the different degree programs in an agricultural college in your state or in another. Why would these courses be useful to a small farmer? Explore the benefits of studying in a school of agriculture.

Collaborative Assignments for Work Literacy

1. With a small group, make a list of jobs that you find interesting. Discuss what skills or attributes would be necessary for one to be successful in those occupations and why you find those particular occupations attractive.
2. As a class, discuss the different meanings of the words *job, career,* and *profession*. List the kinds of work that fall under each category and your reasons for placing them there.
3. In small groups, research the average national salary of several different careers, for example software designer, pediatrician, elementary school teacher, nurse, social worker. Do you think these salaries are fair? Is there any correlation between salary and education? List other motivations for choosing particular careers besides income.
4. Individually list all the reasons you can think of to choose a particular career or profession. Rank your list from most important to least important. In small groups, share your individual lists with each other and attempt to make a group list.
5. Go to your school library and research the local paper's want ads from 25 years ago. What do you notice about these ads? Compare them to the Want Ads in a recent newspaper. What do you attribute to the change? In small groups, discuss which careers are predominantly chosen by women. Which by men? Why do you think this happens?

Home Literacy

*Making something out of
almost nothing, some
new patterns from
a ball of yarn takes
hours. Days. Takes dawn
till dark.*

—Kathryn Stripling Byer

KITCHEN TABLE TALK

One day, my five-year-old son sat at the kitchen counter watching me concoct dinner. Behind me, the Utah sunset blazed its peaches, golds, pinks, and vermillions. Jeff looked wistfully out the window and said, "Mom, you know my favorite place in the whole world?"

"No, where?"

"It's on our mountain. I go to a special spot to pick flowers for you and to watch the sun go down; it's the best sun-going-down there is."

I had never known where Jeff found the flowers that he held out proudly for me at those Sunday picnics on our mountain; I had never known that he watched the setting sun while I was stirring stew over the campfire or boiling water to wash dishes after meal's end. I did know that his spot was part of his history, though, part of the connection he had with nature and with our family. Years later, he would write about our weekends on the property in poems with vivid descriptions that reawakened my lost memories of our time together and of what each of us learned through the experience.

Oftentimes we fail to realize that much of our education, our honest knowing, does not occur in the typical school setting—at a desk with book opened, paper smoothed, and pen poised. The first, and perhaps more important education, is made up of who we are—the where's and who's we came from. We must honor that education, the places where the learning occurred, and the people who remain our first and last teachers. These learning moments help us make sense of what we learn in the more formal settings of school and work. In many ways, our home learning refines our understanding and sharpens our critical thinking. But this learning does more: It adds the color and the connections to the words we read, the formulas we memorize, the facts we recite.

Not long ago, I was reminded of the ways we learn and the subtle shifting to and from student to teacher that occurs in every family as I taped up a box of mementos collected during a trip to Disney World with my twin two-year-old granddaughters. I had packed the mouse ears, the ticket stubs, the deflated helium balloons, and a letter to each child reminding them of how many times grandpa and I had held them close and listened to "It's a Small World After All," sung during their favorite ride. I wrote of our meeting with Mickey, of their fear on first meeting this life-sized mouse, of how that fear was put to rest when Mickey asked grandma to sit on his lap and to give him a kiss on his cheek. And I wrote about the magic that each of them helped me rediscover as we visited this Florida theme park. Years from now when they open the box, I hope they understand that even at two years of age they were teachers, and good ones too. For as most of us know, in a family, learning and teaching do not stop; each continues as long as family members remain receptive to the possibilities that sit around and cover up our kitchen tables.

Once we grasp the concept of what it means to be a lifelong learner in our family, we recognize those learning moments everywhere, every day—at home, at the kitchen tables of our grandmothers and the basement workbenches of our grandpas, in the gardens of our mothers and the garages of our dads, at the births of our children and the deaths of our parents. And when we begin to evaluate the education we have acquired, we may find, just as my young son did that evening so long ago, that the best we have come to know grew out of those secret places where the wildflowers bloom year round and the sun-going-downs are the most vivid.

"Kitchen Table Talk" begins with Les Wade's poem, "Grandma's Fruitroom," where the jars of peaches, apricots, and beans stay stacked along dusty shelves. Should the fruit be tossed, or do the bottles hold more lessons from Grandma? Marti Baker examines how having a child at sixteen has forced her into the parental teaching role, leaving little time for the student who remains committed to getting her education. "Talk Is the Thing" extends the family beyond the immediate and into the community, where residents of Trackton help their neighbors decipher the messages found in the daily newspaper. In the preface to *Fannie Flagg's Original Whistle Stop Cafe Cookbook*, readers are introduced to comfort foods, those meals designed to bring people together and make them content not just with the meal but with those with whom the meal is shared. In Whitney Otto's chapter "Instructions No. 3," from *How to Make an American Quilt*, readers learn the importance of binding the edges of a quilt, of the women of the quilting circle, and of a couple in a relationship. Her "Grandmother's Kitchen" is where Kim King experienced the valuable lessons that continue to serve her well even though the days spent in the kitchen classroom have ended.

In her poem, "Why I Read," Jeanne Leiby remembers her first reader, her father, and credits him with her continual love affair with words. In J. Nozipo Maraire's *Zenzele: A Letter for My Daughter*, a mother worries that the teaching and learning within her home has not been enough to prepare her daughter for the world she is about to enter. Often it is not simply words that we read or hear in our homes as described by Jenny Joseph in her poem, "Warning." In "Zoo Welcomes New Arrival" Pat Rushin's narrator contemplates the changes his child will make in his life, and whether or not the world is a safe enough place to raise a child. *Native Speaker* by Chang-rae Lee examines what can be learned from lists, in particular the one that the narrator's wife hands to him on the day she leaves for good. Eudora Welty's reading was enhanced by parents who budgeted for books, and she shares how those subsequent purchases expanded her world in her essay, "Wordstruck."

Les Wade

Grandma's Fruitroom

Born in 1951 in Ogden, Utah, Les Wade began writing poetry at a young age and had his first poem published during the eighth grade. He began college in 1969, but soon dropped out and didn't return until 1982. After taking his first Introduction to Poetry class, he quickly changed his major from accounting to English. He graduated with his MA in English in 1992 and has taught at the college level ever since. He currently teaches at Weber State University, Utah State University, and Park College. He is the father of five children.

Prereading Reflection

Write about a family heirloom or possession that you have kept but probably will never use.

Downstairs in my basement,
around the corner and
down a dark bare-earth hallway
hides a fruitroom,   Have you ever been to such a
Grandma's fruitroom.   room? What was it used for?
The shelves, rising from
the earthen floor,
are filled with dusty bottles
filled with home-canned, home-grown pickles,
juices, jellies and jams, fruits and vegetables.

A pull on the string hanging from a lone light bulb
reveals row after row, shelf after shelf
bottle after bottle of
pickles, both dill and sweet,
grape juice and jelly, berry jams
peaches, pears, green beans, raspberries,
and strange mysterious yellowish fluidy stuff.

We had a family party,
a-come-get-Grandma's-stuff party,
after we bought the house,
but nobody wanted anything,
not even a baby-food jar
of homemade plum jelly,
from the dark, damp, and musty fruitroom.

> How would you suspect the author's grandma would react if she knew no one wanted her canned food?

So what if it's old.
Don't my cousins, aunts, and uncles know
how hard Grandma worked to grow,
pick, and process all those bottles,
all those bottles that nobody wants.

"Just dump the stuff down the disposal,"
my mom says, "and wash the bottles."
But I can't.

It hurts too much to feed
that hungry disposal the contents
of those bottles, all those bottles,
or flush it, or even empty the bottles
on the compost pile,
so on the dusty shelves
the dusty, webby,
bottles sit waiting
waiting someday to be opened.

> The author does not want the canned fruit. Why can't he throw the fruit away?

Final Reflection

Write about how keeping the preserved fruit might also be preserving the grandma's memory.

> *Sometimes when we go off topic in class discussions, the discussions get more interesting.*
>
> —Tom Bailey

❖ *After You Read, Consider*

1. The author lists the contents of the bottles in the fruitroom, including "strange mysterious yellowish fluidy stuff." How does this phrase impact the rest of the list?

2. The author is told, "Just dump the stuff down the disposal . . . and wash the bottles." Why can't he?

3. What do you suppose will happen to the jars of fruit?

❖ *Suggestions for Writing*

1. Research products in your area that are still preserved in homes either by canning, freezing, or drying. Then do a cost comparison between the home preserving process and the commercial preserving process and determine which is most cost efficient. Write an essay that explores why a person might can fruit or vegetables at home. Would cost be the only factor in whether to can at home? What other factors might be more important?

2. Plot out a vegetable garden that would provide enough food for a family of four for six months. Write a pamphlet or newsletter to share your plan.

3. The author writes of pouring the fruit on a compost pile. Investigate how to create such a pile and write an article for your local newspaper or college magazine not only explaining the process, but arguing why composting is desirable.

Marti S. Baker

Circle of My Womanhood

Marti S. Baker is a secondary education major at Armstrong Atlantic State University in Savannah, Georgia. "I consider myself a well-rounded individual. At the time I wrote this piece, I had many concerns with being a single African-American mother because of the social stereotypes that often frame my life. I have now overcome most of the negative feelings associated with being a single parent thanks to support from family and friends who wish to see me succeed in life."

Sometimes my journal reflections were very private. Thank you for not reading them.

—Priscilla Bakerson

Prereading Reflection

Write about an event that made you realize that you had become an adult.

It has taken me five years to fully understand the validity of being a woman, my purpose for living, and my self as a young African-American single mother. The birth of my son, rejection from society, and being overlooked by society has helped me realize and be fully aware of my womanhood. The rejection by some segments of society is the result of what I had to do to provide for my son and myself.

> Recall a time when you faced rejection.

With this realization came the desire to complete the circle of becoming a woman.

I did not know what to do when I became pregnant at sixteen, and telling my mother was the very last option. After realizing that coming up with the money for an abortion was a myth, I had to face the fact that I was going to be another statistic. I eventually told my mother and my siblings. Of the four, only one brother accepted the situation I was in and was willing to help. He bluntly told me, "You are not the first teenager to have a child, and you will not be the last." There was one brother who said I should have an abortion (at five months) and a sister who was willing to take me to have the abortion. My oldest sister literally sat back and watched with disappointment, and rarely commented on the situation. They all basically said, except for the one brother who understood, the choice of having an abortion or keeping the child was mine. To make the decision to not have an abortion was step one of my awareness of being a woman.

I gave birth to Maurice on May 23, 1992. Ironically, my mother, who also wanted me to have an abortion, begged me to give him her maiden name, so I did in hopes for a reconciliation between us. As Maurice grew, my womanhood became even more defined. I had to raise a child alone, with limited help from family members, who had families of their own. Unfortunately with becoming a mother too soon came the rejection and the ridicule, especially from family members. They assumed that my son and I would be a financial burden on them. I did not want to place any more pressure on my family, so I decided to look for financial assistance. Becoming a provider for my son was a step toward womanhood.

Soon after Maurice's birth, I saw welfare as an option. Welfare provided money and health care for my child and myself. I was able to purchase things I needed and wanted for my son. I wanted him to have nice clothes to wear and to always have a decent haircut. I am glad to say that I did not get caught up in the fashion trend that was going on at the time. All of the other girls who were on welfare always had acrylic nails and new hairdos every week. Not me. If I was able to get a perm, that would have been alright for me. If my son had decent clothes to wear, even if they came from K-Mart, that was fine with me, too. My mother, my sister, and my brother made sure that Maurice had new clothes to wear, and they contributed greatly to his sense of well being. But along with this government help, which I thought was a plus, came the label of being another welfare statistic. I found myself stereotyped as another African-American teenage mother who would do nothing with her life and receive ADFC checks for shopping purposes only. I was perceived as a woman who did nothing with her life but collect a check and wait for the food stamps to come. Every time I went to the AFDC, WIC, or a doctor's offices, I got negative looks from the workers. When I reapplied for food stamps, AFDC, or pulled out my Medicaid card, I felt they would assume I was lazy and unwilling to work. It was common in the city that I lived in for teenagers to become pregnant. Unfortunately, the stereotype did have some foundation in reality. It was very common that these teenagers

Have you ever felt stereotyped? When?

did nothing with their lives and only waited for a government check to arrive every month.

Being seen in the grocery store with food stamps was not always fun. Sure they were good to have because I was able to provide for my household. Making sure food was in the house was a form of rent I had to pay my mother. However, the looks I received from people standing behind me and the looks from the people behind the desk at the Department of Family and Children Services began to disturb me, so I did something about being uncomfortable about the "help" the government was giving me.

I decided to get a job during the summer of my son's birth. I was making $191.40 a week as a desk clerk. At the time, I thought this was good. It was another step towards fully becoming a woman because I was in the working world, even if it was temporary. This made me feel independent because I provided for my child on my own without the government's help. I earned money the way I felt was appropriate, and I did not have to rely on the government or solely on my family for help. I also felt responsible for caring for my son. Yes, I still received the food stamps, but I did not have to stand in the welfare line downtown. The government stopped giving me money, but I still received Medicaid for Maurice and myself. This did not last long, because in September of that same year, I had to return to complete high school. I was happy to return to school and complete my education; however, getting back on welfare and being dependent on the government for the next two years was a step down.

> Recall a job that you held that seemed to pay good money.

The following spring my secondary education ended, and I was on my way to college. I did not want to immediately find a job and support my son. I felt that if I did not have a college degree my life would be meaningless because I would not have a stable career. Having a college degree would give me a sense of achievement. This was yet another step to completing the circle of my womanhood. I believe that some women who have children while in high school don't really become women until they are able to take care of their children without the help of the government. Of course, this is only a part of possessing the qualities of being a woman. I was graduating from high school and closer to getting out of my mother's house, and away from her rules. Only four years to go.

My mother offered to keep Maurice during the week, if I wanted to attend Georgia Southern University. But I didn't because I wanted to be close to my son and opted to stay in Savannah and attend a local college. With the goal of becoming a nurse like my mother, my dream of completing a post-secondary education was better focused. I still felt stereotyped because I had to depend on the government to help raise my child. The idea of the government paying me was not in my best interest because the government was not the father of my child, but instead took his place. I realized that I was not a woman by allowing the system to pay my way. This would have been the easy way out. *Yeah, thanks for the help, but I think I can do it on my own.*

While in college I was able to maintain a part-time job at a grocery store, and later at a K-Mart. I was also able to get a work-study job with the help of a professor who saw my potential. This was definitely a positive step in completing my circle of becoming a woman. I was less rejected and ridiculed by family members because they saw that I was determined to make something of myself and not just stay on welfare, like the other girls who went to college, had a child, and collected a check from the government. I no longer got nasty looks from people behind me in the grocery store line because I no longer got food stamps. The government cut me off because they said I made too much money in one month's time. Fortunately, Maurice still receives Medicaid because of his age.

I felt more independent and more in touch with myself because I was able to make decisions on my own. Since I have been off the welfare system, I do not feel like there is a weight holding me down from accomplishing my goals of becoming a teacher and a good provider for my son. I also do not feel limited. While on the welfare system I had to make sure I did not work too many hours on my job. If I did, I would not receive any more checks. I am now able to work the way I want to and own things in my name (like a bank account, and one credit card). I can determine what is best for my son without any intervention from the caseworkers at the welfare office.

My circle of becoming a woman is almost complete. I am still a full-time college student who is anticipating graduating in June of 1999. My college career is almost over. My relationship with my family is stronger than ever, partly because I moved out of my mother's house and into my father's house. The brother who wanted me to have an abortion now gives my son educational toys for Christmas. The relationship with my mother is no longer one filled with heated debates on how to raise my son. I look at her lectures now as good advice and helpful tips for properly raising a boy alone. The sisters who were disappointed are some of my best friends and help me by giving my son the things he needs (and one even takes him to Chuck E. Cheese's occasionally). My purpose for living is clearer than ever due to the experience of being a single black mother. If I had not gone through this cycle, I don't think I would be as well rounded as I am now, and I probably would still be living with my mother.

How might the author's own educational experiences prepare her for her career as a teacher?

There was a time when I questioned my worth and my purpose for being here. I now know my purpose is to raise my son the best way I can and give back to society by becoming an educator. I am worthwhile because I can make a difference in the world. The definition of *being* a woman is the same as having what it takes to be a man. Women must face the consequences associated with being looked over and stereotyped. With each passing day, I become more aware of the obstacles in my path and I am learning how to deal with them so they won't hold me back. I realize that I can overcome the obstacles and complete my circle of *womanhood*.

Final Reflection

The author writes about her changing relationship with other members of her family. Consider what might be causing the changes.

❖ *After You Read, Consider*

1. The author states, "I believe that some women who have children while in high school don't really become women until they are able to take care of their children without the help of the government." Do you agree with the author's point of view? Why or why not?

2. After a brief period where the author was able to support her son, she decides to return to school to obtain her high school diploma. Her return to school meant she would have to rely on government help to support her son. Why do you believe getting a high school diploma is so important? Do you think that getting a GED might have served her as well?

3. The author writes, "I felt they would assume I was lazy and unwilling to work. It was common in the city that I lived in for teenagers to become pregnant.... It was very common that these teenagers did nothing with their lives and only waited for a government check to arrive every month." No concrete examples support the writer's assertions. What do you think caused her to feel as she did?

   All the revisions usually made me re-think my position. Sometimes I even changed my mind!

   —Anne Welsch

❖ *Suggestions for Writing*

1. Investigate the types of services available for single mothers in your community. Then write a letter to the editor of your local newspaper

that demands an increase or a decrease in the amount and types of services available.

2. Much current research suggests that children of single parents are at higher risk of dropping out of school and getting into trouble with the law. Examine the effects of single parenting on children from a group of single parents that you know and write a paper that illustrates the effects using narratives from the children and the parents.

3. Compare and contrast the lives of college students who do or do not have children to support. Consider the areas of time spent working, studying outside of class, and engaging in extracurricular activities. Draw conclusions and present the information to fellow class members in oral or written form.

Shirley Brice Heath

Talk Is the Thing

Shirley Brice Heath spent ten years in the Piedmont Carolinas studying the daily activities and conversations of "ordinary folk" in Trackton, a black community, and Roadville, a white community. The result of her ethnographic research was shared in Ways with Words: Language, Life, and Work in Communities and Classrooms *(1983). In this book, Heath combines her skills as an ethnographer, social historian, and teacher to raise fundamental questions about the nature of language and development, the effects of literacy on oral habits, and the sources of communication problems in schools and workplaces. Heath is currently a Professor of Anthropology and Linguistics in the School of Education at Stanford University.*

❖

Prereading Reflection

Write about a time that you talked with others after you read a particular piece of writing.

❖

In almost every situation in Trackton in which a piece of writing is integral to the nature of the participants' interactions and their interpretations of meaning, talk is a necessary component. Knowing which box of cereal is Kellogg's raisin bran does little good without announcing that choice to older brothers and sisters helping pour the cereal. Knowing the kind of bicycle tire and tube on one's old bike is translated into action only at Mr. Green's bicycle shop or with a friend who has an old bike he is not using. Certain types of talk describe, repeat, reinforce, frame, expand, and even contradict written materials, and children in Trackton learn not only how to read print, but also when and how to surround the print in their lives with appropriate talk. For them there are far more occasions in the community

What is Heath telling us about language and meaning?

which call for appropriate knowledge of forms and uses of talk around or about writing, than there are actual occasions for reading and writing extended connected discourse.

For Trackton adults, reading is a social activity; when something is read in Trackton, it almost always provokes narratives, jokes, sidetracking talk, and active negotiation of the meaning of written texts among the listeners. Authority in the written word does not rest in the words themselves, but in the meanings which are negotiated through the experiences of the group. The evening newspaper is read on the front porch for most months of the year. The obituaries on the back page are usually read first, followed by employment listings, advertisements for grocery and department store sales, and captions beneath pictures and headlines. An obituary is read for some trace of acquaintance with either the deceased, his relatives, place of birth, church, or school; active discussion follows about who the individual was and who he might have known. Circulars or letters to individuals regarding the neighborhood center and its recreational or medical services are read aloud and their meanings jointly negotiated by those who have had experience with such activities or know about the forms to be filled out to be eligible for such services. Neighbors share stories of what they did or what happened to them in similar circumstances. One day when Lillie Mae had received a letter about a daycare program, several neighbors were sitting on porches, working on cars nearby, or sweeping their front yards. Lillie Mae came out on her front porch, read the first paragraph of a letter, and announced:

Do you have a precise routine that you follow when you read the daily newspaper? How does it compare to the routine followed by citizens of Trackton?

Trackton Text X

How does the use of dialogue help you visualize the townspeople?

Lillie Mae: You hear this, it says Lem [then two years old] might can get into Ridgeway [a local neighborhood center daycare program], but I hafta have the papers ready and apply by next Friday.

Visiting friend: You ever been to Kent to get his birth certificate? [friend is mother of three children already in school]

Mattie Crawford: But what hours that program gonna be? You may not can get him there.

Lillie Mae: They want the birth certificate? I got his vaccination papers.

Annie Mae: Sometimes they take that, 'cause they can 'bout tell the age from those early shots.

Visiting friend: But you better get it, 'cause you gotta have it when he go to school anyway.

Lillie Mae: But it says here they don't know what hours yet. How am I gonna get over to Kent? How much does it cost? Lemme see if the program costs anything. (She reads aloud part of the letter.)

How does reading the letter to her neighbors help Lillie Mae problem solve?

Conversation on various parts of the letter continued for nearly an hour, while neighbors and Lillie Mae pooled their knowledge of the pros and cons of such programs. They discussed ways of getting rides to Kent, the county seat thirty miles away, to which all mothers had to go to get their children's birth certificates to prove their age at school entrance. The question "What does this mean?" was answered not only from the information in print, but from the group's joint bringing of experience to the text. Lillie Mae, reading aloud, decoded the written text, but her friends and neighbors interpreted the text's meaning through their own experiences. The experience of any one individual had to become common to the group, however, and that was done through the recounting of members' experiences. Such recounting re-created scenes, embellished the truth, illustrated the character of the individuals involved, and to the greatest extent possible brought the audience into the experience itself. Beyond these recountings of episodes (such as one mother's efforts to get her doctor to give her "papers" to verify her son's age), there was a reintegration of these now commonly shared experiences with the text itself. After the reading episode, Lillie Mae had to relate the text's meaning to the experiences she had heard shared, and she checked out this final synthesis of meaning for her with some of the group. Some members did not care about this final synthesis and had wandered off, satisfied to have told their stories, but others commented that they thought her chosen course of action the right one, and her understanding of the letter to fit their interpretations.

About the only material not delivered for group negotiation is that which involves private finances or information which members feel

Have you ever withheld information from family members, friends, or acquaintances because sharing the information might increase the competition?

might somehow give them an opportunity their neighbors do not have. A postcard from a local mill announcing days on which the mill will be accepting new employment applications will not be shared aloud, but kept secret because of the competition for jobs. On the other hand, a newspaper story about the expansion of the mill will be read aloud, and all will pool information in general terms.

Tables 1 and 2 show that the uses of writing and reading in the community are multiple, though there are few occasions for reading of extended connected discourse and almost no occasions for writing such material, except by those school children who diligently try to complete their homework assignments. Foremost among the types of uses of reading and writing are those which are *instrumental*. Adults and children read what they have to read to solve practical problems of daily life: price tags, traffic signs, house numbers, bills, checks. Other uses are perhaps not as critical to problem-solving, but *social-interactional* uses give information relevant to social relations and contacts with persons not in Trackton's primary group. Some write letters; many send greeting cards; almost all read bumper stickers, newspaper obituaries and features, and church news bulletins. Other types of reading and writing are *news-related*. From the local newspaper, political flyers, memos from the city offices, and circulars from the neighborhood center, Trackton residents learn information about local and distant events. They rarely read much more than headlines about distant events, since the evening news programs on television give them the same national or metropolitan news. Stories about the local towns are, however, read, because there is often no other source of information on happenings there. Some individuals in Trackton read for *confirmation*—to seek support for beliefs or ideas they already hold. Miss

Table 1. Types of Uses of Reading in Trackton

Instrumental:	Reading to accomplish practical goals of daily life (price tags, checks, bills, telephone dials, clocks, street signs, house numbers).
Social-interactional/ recreational:	Reading to maintain social relationships, make plans, and introduce topics for discussion and story-telling (greeting cards, cartoons, letters, newspaper features, political flyers, announcements of community meetings).
News-related:	Reading to learn about third parties or distant events (local news items, circulars from the community center or school).
Confirmational:	Reading to gain support for attitudes or beliefs already held (Bible, brochures on cars, loan notes, bills).

Note. Listed in relative order of frequency of occasions when time on these types of tasks exceeded five minutes per day.

Table 2. Types of Uses of Writing in Trackton

Memory aids: (primarily used by women)	Writing to serve as a reminder for the writer and, only occasionally, others (telephone numbers, notes on calendars).
Substitutes for oral messages: (primarily used by women)	Writing used when direct oral communication was not possible or would prove embarrassing (notes for tardiness or absence from school, greeting cards, letters).
Financial:	Writing to record numerals and to write out amounts and accompanying notes (signatures on checks and public forms, figures and notes for income tax preparation).
Public records: (church only)	Writing to announce the order of the church services and forthcoming events and to record financial and policy decisions (church bulletins, reports of the church building fund committee).

Note. Listed in relative order of frequency of occasions when time on these types of tasks exceeded five minutes per day.

Lula reads the Bible. When the mayor maintains that one kind of car gets better mileage than another, and others disagree, he has to produce a brochure from a car dealer to prove his point. Children who become involved in boasts often called on written proof to confirm their lofty accounts of themselves or others. Every home has some permanent records—loan notes, tax forms, birth certificates—which families keep, but can rarely find when they are needed. However, if they can be found and are read, they can confirm an oral statement.

The most frequent occasions for writing are those when Trackton family members say they cannot trust their memory (*memory-supportive*), or they have to write to substitute *for an oral message*. Beside the telephone, women write frequently called numbers and addresses; they tack calendars on the kitchen wall and add notes reminding them of dates for their children's vaccinations and the school holidays, etc. Some few women in the community write letters. Lillie Mae often writes relatives up-North to invite them to come home and to thank them for bringing presents. Women sometimes have to write notes to school about children's absences or tardiness or to request a local merchant to extend credit a few weeks longer. Men almost never write except to sign their paychecks, public forms, and to collect information for income tax preparation. One exception in Trackton is the mayor who meets once a month with a group of other church members to prepare Sunday church bulletins as well as to handle business related to the building fund or to plan for revival meetings. These written materials are negotiated cooperatively at the meetings; no individual takes sole responsibility.

Community literacy activities are public and social. Written information almost never stands alone in Trackton. It is reshaped and reworded into an oral mode by adults and children who incorporate chunks of the written text in their talk. They often reflect their own awareness that print imposes a different kind of organization on written materials than talk does. Literacy events in Trackton which bring the written word into a central focus in interactions and interpretations have their rules of occurrence and appropriateness, just as talking junk, fussing, or performing a playsong do. The group activities of reading the newspaper across porches, debating the power of a new car, or discussing the city's plans to bring in earthmoving equipment to clear lots behind the community, produce more speaking than reading, more group than individual effort. There are repeated metaphors, comparisons, and fast-paced, overlapping language as Trackton residents move from print to what it means in their lives. On some occasions, they attend to the text itself; on others, they use it only as a starting point for wide-ranging talk. On all occasions, they bring in knowledge related to the text and interpret beyond the text for their own context; in so doing, they achieve a new synthesis of information from the text and the joint experiences of community members.

I like writing reflections before and after I read. It helps me question what I thought I knew already.

—Allen Berman

Final Reflection

How has talking about a piece of writing with others helped you understand or interpret what you read?

❖ *After You Read, Consider*

1. The information presented in Tables 1 and 2 is also presented in the narrative. Is one method of presentation superior to another?

2. The author relates, "When the mayor maintains that one kind of car gets better mileage than another, and others disagree, he has to produce a brochure from a car dealer to prove his point." This is an example of providing support to back up an assertion. Have you ever needed to provide proof for an opinion you held? What were the circumstances, and what type of support did you present?

3. Heath writes, "Community literacy activities are public and social. Written information almost never stands alone in Trackton. It is reshaped and reworded into an oral mode by adults and children who incorporate chunks of the written text in their talk. They often reflect their own awareness that print imposes a different kind of organization on written materials than talk does." Define what *awareness* might mean as it relates to our reading of and writing about new ideas.

I still don't like to write, but at least I don't have as much trouble getting started.

—Michelle Holloway

❖ Suggestions for Writing

1. Make a chart listing the ways that you and your family members use reading and writing. How does it compare or contrast with the citizens of Trackton? Hypothesize why it may be the same or different.

2. Write a character sketch of someone you feel might fit in well with the residents of Trackton.

3. Write an essay that illustrates the ways reading and writing changed for you when you began taking college courses.

Fannie Flagg

Preface from Fannie Flagg's Original Whistle Stop Cafe Cookbook

Fannie Flagg began writing and producing television specials at age nineteen and went on to distinguish herself as an actress and writer in television, films, and the theater. Her first novel, Daisy Fay and the Miracle Man, *spent ten weeks on the* New York Times *paperback best-seller list, and her second novel,* Fried Green Tomatoes at the Whistle Stop Cafe, *spent thirty-six weeks on the same list. It was produced by Universal Pictures as the feature film* Fried Green Tomatoes. *Flagg's script was nominated for both the Academy and Writers Guild of America awards and won the highly regarded Scripters Award. Flagg narrated both novels on audiotape and received a Grammy Award nomination for best spoken word. Flagg currently lives in California.*

❖

Prereading Reflection

Tell the story behind your favorite recipe.

❖

"A *cookbook!* Why in the world are *you* of all people going to write a cookbook?" That was the response when I told my friends what I was doing. You would have thought that I had just announced my attempt to overthrow a foreign government with a fork. "Why not?" I asked somewhat defensively, considering that most of them had been to my home for dinner. I turned to my friend. "Mickey, how can you say that? Why just the other night your very own husband, Bob, just raved and raved about my pork chops and black-eyed peas!" She paused. "Now, Fannie. I didn't say they weren't good; it's just that they are the only thing you ever serve."

Would you buy a cookbook written by someone who can cook only a few types of food?

"That's not true," I cried. "Remember the year before last when I had the pork chop and turnip greens instead?"

Anyway, I guess by now you can pretty much get the picture. My culinary skills are somewhat limited. To tell you the truth, I was surprised myself when my publisher called. "A *cookbook!* ... Why in the world would you want *me* of all people to do a cookbook?"

Then I thought, Hey, wait a minute ... why *not* me? After all, doesn't my relationship with food go way back? But then, whose doesn't? But I am a Southerner and everyone knows we have all been preoccupied with food and stories since birth. Me, perhaps, more than most. I have always loved to eat, loved to be around other people eating; why I even love to see *pictures* of people eating. Besides, I have written two entire novels, both of which revolve around restaurants, one a malt shop and one a cafe. So, why not me indeed?

What makes Flagg a food expert?

As the only child of a mother who did not like to cook, I have eaten out almost every day of my life and enjoyed myself immensely, so I certainly know good food when I see it. Better still, when I taste it. Anyhow, they say you should only write about things that you are interested in and care about, and I certainly qualify on both counts.

So I knew right off the bat that this book would be great fun. But there was another reason I wanted to do this book. Since the novel and the film version of *Fried Green Tomatoes at the Whistle Stop Cafe* were released, I have received thousands of letters from sweet people all over the world, asking me if there really was a Whistle Stop Cafe. Did I have one in mind when I was writing the book, and if so could they please have some of the original recipes?

The answer is yes. There really was such a cafe. The Irondale Cafe was started by my great aunt Bess in the thirties and she ran it for over fifty years. It is located in Irondale, Alabama, a small town just outside my hometown of Birmingham. The good news is that it is thriving, doing a roaring business, with people still coming from miles around to enjoy those same hot delicious meals. Not only that, Virginia Johnson, that fabulous cook who first went to work for my aunt when she was eleven, can still be found in the kitchen, happily frying up a fresh batch of fried green tomatoes every day, the same kind that I, along with generations of others, have enjoyed since we were children. And the best news of all is that the McMichaels family, who bought the cafe from my Aunt Bess and continue to run the cafe so successfully, are dear friends and the nicest people you will ever meet.

So I am delighted to share their original recipes with you, just in case you can't make it down to Alabama anytime soon. We all want you to be able to enjoy and have the fun of making and tasting real downhome cafe cooking in your own kitchen. Not only can you fix and serve it, you can be right in style, foodwise. The marketing people tell me that these recipes fall into the category of "comfort food" that has suddenly become very In and Trendy. When I heard that, I surely had to laugh. Just think... I had been In and Trendy all my life and just didn't know it, because I have *always* been comfortable eating a good meal.

> Hasn't comfort food always been trendy? What other kinds of food are trendy?

Which brings me to the main reason I wanted so much to write this book. Lately it seems everyone is mad at someone, with groups on every corner, on the radio, on television, screaming about something or someone or other they don't like. And there is so much anger in the air that you almost see it like a thick fog. In times like this, I think it is particularly important to try to be as calm and happy as possible. And I don't know about you, but, I have always been happiest where food was concerned. Some of the best times in my life have revolved around meals. Let's face it—eating is fun. I like everything about it. I particularly like the sounds and the smells and the friendly atmosphere. People laughing, dishes rattling, and glasses tinkling are music to my ears, and I find it impossible to be miserable and angry and enjoy a good meal at the same time. Everybody could use a little comfort these days and is there any place better for a little comfort than a cafe?

> What do you think of Flagg's purpose for writing a cookbook?

So come on back with me if you will, to a time when people were as sweet as the tea they served and everyone knew you and liked you, even knew your daddy's daddy. To a time that no matter how poor you were or what hard times you might be going through, nothing could make you feel better than a side of creamy hot mashed potatoes served with a smile. When the cafe was your home away from home, the center of town where you could always find a friend and have a laugh. Down at the cafe, where the food always tasted better than it looked and somebody was always around, morning, noon, and night, and after church on Sundays; where you had your favorite table, a place you were always welcome, as familiar as your own living room; where if they were busy, you helped yourself to more iced tea or hot coffee; where you sometimes just left your money on the counter and never counted your change.

No matter where you come from, East or West, North or South, and no matter if your cafe was called the Whistle Stop, the Busy Bee, the Melrose Diner, or the Chatter Box, close your eyes, forget your troubles, and come on back home with me for just a little while....

It is sunrise. The birds are just starting to chirp, the dogs begin to shake themselves and let out a bark or two, and kitchen lights start to come on one by one all over town. There is an early morning chill in the air. But over at the cafe the kitchen is warm, the radio is playing, bacon is frying and biscuits are being cut, and the cooks are wide awake. One by one, sleepy-eyed customers stumble in the door with their newspapers and hot steaming coffee is placed in front of them by waitresses who know just how they take it, cream no sugar, sugar no cream, or just plain black. . . .

> Why is Flagg describing a diner here? What does she want us to see? To feel?

As the morning progresses the dishes slowly start to clatter and as the kitchen door opens and closes you can hear the sounds of eggs and bacon frying and the warm rich smell of fresh biscuits baking wafts through the room. The pace gets faster, more coffee is poured, eyes brighten, laughs start, and pretty soon the whole place is humming and rattling like a cage full of happy finches chirping away. And then, after a couple of hours, it slowly calms down into that soft quiet non-time between breakfast and lunch, that lull until the lunch bunch suddenly comes slammin' and bangin' in the door, once more loud and ravenous, calling out for the Blue Plate Special. . . .

> Have you ever worked in a restaurant? Was it always as happy as Flagg describes?

This happy scenario goes on day after day, week after week, year after year, and no matter if you wander away for a day or a decade, when you come back it is always the same over at the cafe. Like a good play that has been running for years, the cast may change a little from time to time but the storyline remains the same, feed the people with love, a smile, and good food.

And although the word *cafe* is French, I'm sure that most little lean-to shacks that have popped up all over the country would be surprised to learn of their origins. These little cafes were not always grand but they were the very heart of the town, with personalities of their own. And when one closed down it was mourned for generations. For weeks afterward, you could see lost old men still peering inside the boarded up windows, hoping that maybe, somehow, it could come back to life. Conversations start with "Remember when the cafe was still running, that time we had lunch with Memaw or supper with Uncle Buddy?" Or: "Remember when we used to have the Rotary's meeting over at the cafe?" People still can't believe it's closed and none of the new, cold, operating room sterile, orange plastic fast food joints can ever take the place of the old cafe, where the silverware never matched and more often than not was bent and covered with water spots. But still, it felt like silverware and it was silverware with a past. That spoon you are stirring your coffee with may have been used by your grandmother thirty years ago, and that knife by your first cousin just yesterday; not some flimsy white plastic "knives and forks" in a cellophane package to be thrown away. And oh, if only those old chipped plates could talk. How many faces have they looked up at through the years, how many pretty young girls have they seen grow into beautiful old women, soldier boys come and go, handsome cowlicky boys turn into grandfathers, and how many babies have they seen cry or laugh with delight? And those poor old chairs. How many times have they been kicked by children, knocked over by people in a hurry, pushed and pulled and dragged around the room, joining other tables for conversations about not much of anything, I suspect, nothing less than the everyday lives of a town full of people trying to do their best day after day, year after year.

So my hat's off to you, all you old cafes that are gone now, and to the ones still going. You made life a little easier for all of us: simple, clean, steady, and honest . . . just like a good friend.

Fried Green Tomatoes I

To keep the cooked tomatoes from getting soggy before they are served, stand them up like wheels in the serving dish instead of stacking them.

3/4 cup self-rising flour
1/4 cup cornmeal
1/4 teaspoon salt
1/4 teaspoon pepper
3/4 cup milk
3 to 4 green tomatoes, cut into 1/4-inch slices
Vegetable oil

Combine first 5 ingredients; mix until smooth. Add additional milk to thin, if necessary; batter should resemble pancake batter. Working in batches, dip tomato slices into batter, allowing excess batter to drip back into bowl. Fry in 2 inches hot oil (375° F.) in a large heavy skillet until browned, turning once carefully with tongs. Transfer to a colander to drain.   Yield, 3 to 4 servings

Final Reflection

How much of this piece is about cooking? What else is this piece about? Why are there other subjects in a cookbook?

❖ After You Read, Consider

1. How is learning to cook part of learning a culture?

2. Flagg's definition of community is very much wrapped up in eating meals with others. Can you think of ethnic or religious traditions where food and community are equally as important?

3. Flagg makes fun of herself throughout this piece. Is this effective?

> *I think I wrote better essays when I wrote about my family.*
> —Donna Michaels

❖ Suggestions for Writing

1. Write a story about a diner or restaurant that you like to eat in. What are the owners and staff like? What kinds of people eat there? Why do you eat there?

2. Find a favorite "original" recipe from one of your family members. What memories does the recipe bring back? Why is the recipe important to you? Write an essay that shows your rememberances and insights.

3. Write about planning a dinner for your closest friends. Who would you invite? What would you cook? How would you decorate?

Whitney Otto

Instructions No. 3

Whitney Otto has a BA in history and an MFA in English from the University of California at Irvine. She is a native of California and currently lives with her husband, John, and son, Sam, in Portland, OR. In her novel How to Make an American Quilt *(1991), Otto crafts the framework of quilting to illuminate the lives of her characters. The patterns of the quilts the women sew reflect the patterns of their stories, their histories, and their gender. Otto is also the author of* Now You See Her *(1994) and* The Passion Dream Book *(1999).*

❖

Prereading Reflection

Write about a handcraft that either you or someone in your family does.

❖

Do not underestimate the importance of the carefully constructed border in the quilt. Its function is to keep the blocks apart while binding the entire work together both literally and thematically. But before you are ready with needle and thread, it is best to experiment with the layout of the blocks.

Characterize the voice of the narrator.

As you prepare to join your blocks, affix them to the dining-room wall or pin them to a set of drapes or arrange them upon the bed you share with your husband. You want to imagine how they will look once bound together. Think about what binds you to your husband and he to you. Marvel at the strength of that bond, which is both abstract and concrete, spiritual and legal.

Who is the *you* the author is addressing?

A nineteenth-century Englishman said that marriages made in Heaven are subject to the will of the angel or the will of Heaven. And when a couple passes into the next world, they will become the angel. That is their fate, their destiny. This carries a certain appeal for you.

Consider the courtship of lovers. The way in which you imagined how the marriage would look before it took place. But perhaps you had other things on your mind before you tied the knot.

Think of how it all began with that first kiss.

Klimt's surrendering golden kiss that shimmered on the canvas. The kiss of reverence, of desire. The kiss of the wave as it slaps the shore. Neruda wrote, *In love you have loosed yourself like sea water; I can scarcely measure the sky's most precious eyes and I lean down to your mouth to kiss the earth.* Your sun-kissed garden. The kiss that first united your body to his.

Meditate on the soul-kiss, which, prior to the twentieth century, meant that the souls of lovers were exchanged; mouth to mouth, tongue to tongue; transferred from one to the other as a great gift and act of faith. But the body grows lonely for its old soul (even as it loves the new one) and longs to have it returned. A quilt, though stitched together, will always be separate, individual parts.

What is the purpose for making this quilt?

You understand this loneliness of giving a part of yourself away to the man to whom you are wed, the man who is sometimes called away, the man who is seldom home. Though the exchange of souls carries with it the promise of return.

Take special care when arranging your blocks; be sympathetic to harmonies of color, fabric, and form. Do not be hesitant in devising new, different ways to link the patches to each other; what works for one quilt may not be successful for another. Keep this in mind should you find yourself doubting your design.

Why is this advice important? What else is the narrator talking about?

Use only the highest-quality thread when piecing your quilt together. Remember, your intention is to make the quilt last forever. Traditionally, quilts are stitched with white thread, but if you feel the addition of color would enhance the work, you are encouraged to do what you must, though it is a good idea to test for color fastness before you incorporate it into the work. Once bound, it is difficult to undo without reducing your finished quilt to separate and myriad pieces. Avoid embroidery yarn, which has been known to ravel and fray.

Watch for breakage.

You must decide between two main types of sashing: *one-strip sashing* or *piece sashing*. Sashing is the interior border between each block; the border encompasses the entire work—in much the same way that the marriage vow encompasses your life together. One-strip sashing is fabric all of one piece, while pieced sashing allows for more than one fabric within the border. One-piece sashing is not for beginners. But, of course, you may be feeling particularly ambitious and lucky.

It is only in recent times that the bride has felt fortunate in marriage. Because she is encouraged to marry for love, not for family name or political alliance or wealth. No longer is she the unwilling spoil of war. The breathing tribute of a conquering tribe. No longer is she the stolen prize, crying for rescue, arms outstretched to her defeated kinsmen as she is spirited away. Yet, there are echoes of this theft today: the ritual bridal costume, the father relinquishing his daughter before the invited witnesses; the bride quietly leaving her own marital celebration while the guests continue to feast and dance. The cloister of the honeymoon, with its secret location that no one is privy to lest they track down and disturb the couple.

The narrator has discussed America, England, and now Africa—why the more global perspective?

Many years ago, somewhere in Africa, the groom would prowl the bride's home, as if to kidnap her. Her response was to cry for help, to only pretend to resist. In other places she was exchanged for movable property.

Study the colors of the blocks. Do not be hasty when deciding on a border, as you will have to live with this choice the rest of your quilt's life. Some sashes and borders will be more complementary to the blocks than others. All sashing will divide, but some will enhance, bring out the best in the blocks, while others will dull the blocks, hide their original beauty. Marriage, too, can heighten the wife's colors or consign her to listless hues and shades.

Is the narrator talking about quilting here or something else?

Often, there is no way to know until you are joined. All you really have to go on is the faith of the kiss.

As you stitch the top cloth to the batting to the back work, paste all three layers together—for security and accuracy. Do not skimp on these steps. A little effort now will save you a great deal of effort later. You know that marriage and friendship require effort.

Pioneer quilts were bound, front to back, by knots with dangling strings.

The rose is bound to the earth by the dangle of its roots. Without roots, you are milkweed to the wind, drifting from place to place and never really arriving. On your bad days, this thought keeps you in bed longer than you should be in the mornings. On your good days, you revel in the lightness of wind-drifting because you understand that for a plant to survive its soil (a house to remain in good repair; a friendship to remain close), it must be carefully tended. Which adds up to a good deal of attention paid; attention you are sometimes not prepared to give.

How important is friendship to marriage?

Still, you are drawn to the bond of friendship, the marriage pact.

Drawn and repelled, as if you do not know the difference (the benefits and hardships) between leaving and staying.

A bride carries a floral bouquet as she travels down the aisle. Castilian girls wear white flowers at their bosom; Andalusian girls with their hair alive with wreaths of small roses; the Hawaiian girl gently tucks a hibiscus behind one ear; the right means "spoken for," the left open to promises.

Your garden contains love-in-a-mist and honey-bear roses, which fill the air with an exceptionally sweet scent; only a few people are able to tolerate such a honey-sweetened atmosphere. And the climbing roses making their ascent toward sun and sky, bound at the root to the earth but longing for the sky.

Binding the quilt is not the same as laying the borders. Binding encompasses the entire work and may be achieved a couple of ways. You can turn the back edge forward. Be sure to leave a generous excess on the back work, enough to frame the top material. Or you can stitch on a separate edge. The separate edge is often recommended since it can be replaced if the quilt suffers from tension, stretching, age, or accident. Sometimes, a quilt can benefit from an attached border; can make the fusion whole yet relaxed.

The bride of one hundred years ago was often given a bridal friendship quilt on the day she was wed. Bringing something of value and use to the marriage, some little bit of personal property.

In America and England there were marriages known as "shift" or "closet" marriages, which protected a bride's property from her new husband's debtors. No one could show himself on the day after the wedding and say, with authority, to the newlyweds, *This is mine. This is what I am owed*. In the shift marriage the bride is systematically stripped to her undergarment as she approaches the altar, leaving her in a state of false poverty, as she stands, ashamed of her near nakedness, before her husband and minister. In the closet marriage, she is secreted in a closet with only her hand coming through a hole in the door to receive the ring.

The friendship quilt should have inked messages written upon its patches: wishing the woman well; good fortune for the newly married; quoting poetry or a wise saying or a bit of advice. Offering a warning or an admonition to be safe, to take care, and so long. Quoting scripture is common and not seen by the quilter as blasphemous.

Leaving or staying forces you to face the presence or absence of friends. The quilters will probably piece together a friendship quilt one day. It seems logical and correct. Historically it has its place for women who quilt. Peaking in popularity as American families pushed west, having already claimed the East, and friends said good-bye, certain not to meet again in this hard life. These journeys were uncertain, fraught with mystery. Manifest Destiny being all the rage in 1845.

You know, too, about pushing west and looking for fresh territory. You know about friendship and loss. Neruda has a second poem, written to his wife, regarding the earth but unlike the other earth poem, which relies on the sweetness of a kiss. This one says, *And each wound has the shape of your mouth.* But all you will remember when he is gone and you are almost friendless, is the mention of the kiss.

When you are making the friendship quilt you are declaring love and faithfulness in the face of parting, perhaps forever.

Say it with your hands.

Then wave good-bye.

Final Reflection

How does the craft you wrote about in your initial reflection tell a story of your family?

Small groups were easier for me than a whole class discussion. I didn't have to fight to get a word in.

—Frank Morrison

❖ *After You Read, Consider*

1. Think about the process of making a quilt. Why should so much time be spent on planning?

2. Imagine the audience for this piece. Who is Otto writing to?

3. Otto includes lines of poetry by Neruda. What is the poetry's effect on you?

❖ *Suggestions for Writing*

1. Write an essay in which you explore how the process of making a quilt or how the parts of the quilt are a metaphor for married life.

2. Write an essay in which you discuss how quilts represent American culture and American families.

3. Otto writes that marrying for love has made marriage easier on wives: "It is only in recent times that the bride has felt fortunate in marriage." Write an essay in which you explore how husband and wife may perceive their marriages differently.

Kim King

Grandmother's Kitchen, My Classroom

> *Kim King earned her English degree at Armstrong Atlantic State University in Savannah, Georgia. She works in marketing services for a large corporation by day, and by night is a reader, an entrepreneur, a confectioner, and a wife. She lives with her husband Matt, an aerospace engineer, in Richmond Hill, Georgia.*

❖

Prereading Reflection

Write about a room, a house, or a person that taught you some life-changing lessons.

❖

Daddy says I've been going to Richmond Hill since I was knee high to a grasshopper. And I must admit, there is almost no more comforting a sight than the little white house on Magnolia Street. The weathered green shutters, red brick chimney, and crooked cement steps detail the fifty-five year old house nestled amongst fragrant pink and white azaleas and green shiny-leafed holly bushes. On family visits to this house, I was always the first one to reach the back door—running inside to find my grandmother who was usually in the kitchen. My grandfather would meander in from his wood-working shop to say hello, but it was always my grandmother who I ran to first. She was usually stirring gravies or test-tasting vegetables and would turn around in such surprise to see me and my siblings. Grandma would drop what she was doing and give me a hug, then send me to the sink to wash my hands and help prepare the meal. My grandmother made so many good things in her kitchen, from banana pudding to chicken and dumplings, but that kitchen served a far greater purpose than cooking and dish

How do these details help you visualize the type of people who live inside the house?

washing. Grandma's kitchen was her workshop where she laughed with me, taught me, spanked me, molded me, shaped my mind, and enlightened my soul.

Grandma's kitchen/workshop served as the stage for lessons of all types. I baked my first batch of chocolate-chip cookies there; I sewed my first Barbie doll clothes there, and I used my first sets of watercolor and acrylic paints there, on everything from canvas to china. My grandmother was a true craftswoman. Her paintings adorn all the walls of our family's homes and her dolls have sat in all her grandchildren's laps. Her love of crafting not only produced all of these wonderful keepsakes, it also helped develop my creativity and my confidence in what I could make with my hands and with my heart. Grandma allowed me to cook when I wanted and did not mind the floury mess. She helped me pick out patterns for skirts and dresses, and beautiful rolls of material to transform into a wardrobe. We pulled out twenty colors of paint, spread newspaper on the table, and filled several Mason jars with rinse water every time we felt the urge to paint a lone flower on scrap wood.

> Why would King's mother not have the time to "play" with King as her grandmother did?

These adventures were never explored in my mom's kitchen. She was usually too busy or too finicky to pull out materials and clean up spills. I never made cookies in mom's kitchen and she only let me get crafty with Crayola markers. I would draw things for Grandma and save them up till I got to see her again. I felt so comfortable at her house, so welcome, and so very loved. I would cry every time I had to leave because I felt like I was leaving not only my Grandma, but I was leaving a part of me. I was leaving my hands that knew how to pull a needle through dainty dresser scarves. I was leaving my arms that knew how to hold the yards of material we selected at the remnant table. I was leaving my smile that knew how to appreciate any art we turned out of that kitchen. Grandma knows she created many things in her kitchen, but I don't know if she realizes one of those things is me.

My "artsy" self was not created without some mental stimulation. Grandma would fill quiet time with stories of family, friends, and life.

> What is the importance of King's grandmother's stories?

Many of those stories related to cooking and sewing, arts that her mother and grandmother passed down to her. "Kimmie," she said as we made an apron out of pink flowered material, "I can remember my mama going out the back door of her house, filling her apron up with chicken feed, and coaxing the chickens out into the middle of the yard. They would come out for that corn, and she'd grab one up and prepare it for dinner. That boilin' chicken was the worst smell I ever smelled.

But she fried the best chicken you've ever had." I learned how she and her mother and family lived through the Depression, planting Victory gardens and making "skating skirts" out of flour sacks. I learned the importance of saving every scrap of food and material, because it was a blessing for us to have it. I learned how important children were by helping grandma take care of the little ones at church and do crafts with them. I learned the importance of giving from the heart, whether it was time or money, or something handmade (which is usually the best gift!). I learned how important it was to visit the old folks around the neighborhood as we made breads and sweets to take to their homes. I learned the importance of emotion, as we visited my great-grandmother in the nursing home, so affected by Alzheimer's disease, we could do nothing but talk about how pretty she looked and then cry about it later. I recently learned the meaning of marriage as we prepared for my wedding, making the silk roses to hold birdseed and making my veil out of fine beaded material and delicate tulle.

> Can you remember a handmade gift that meant more to you than a gift that was store-bought?

Through all of this crafting, from doll clothes to wedding trinkets, I have learned many morals, values, meanings, and reasons. I have learned the concrete chores and skills of cooking, sewing, and cleaning, but as I reflect on the twenty-one years I have known my grandma, I see that those arts and crafts were more than trinkets and gifts. They were our way of bonding. We expressed our loves, our hates, strengths, weaknesses, and friendship for each other. When her arthritis didn't allow her to pull the needle through the cross-stitch, I pulled it through. When I couldn't tie the apron we just made around my waist, she tightened it into a beautiful bow. When her oldest son went through a divorce, I listened to her worries. And when my mom doubted my choice of man to marry, she wiped away the tears on late nights in the kitchen. My grandmother has helped me through life by giving me both concrete and abstract lessons. She has used her art and her love of crafts to guide me down life's roads, painting in happy times and erasing tears of pain. My grandmother's kitchen has served thousands of meals to hundreds of people, family and friends alike. But it has never served a greater purpose to me than being the workshop and classroom I studied in.

Final Reflection

Add to your initial reflection, including more concrete details about the room, the house, or the person.

❖ *After You Read, Consider*

1. The writer describes some of her grandmother's crafts: "Her paintings adorn all the walls of our family's homes and her dolls have sat in all her grandchildren's laps." How might these paintings and dolls be used after King's grandmother is gone?

2. King writes, "Grandma would fill quiet time with stories of family, friends, and life." How might the stories add to the writer's creativity?

3. In the conclusion, King details the ways her grandmother helped her and the ways she helped her grandmother. Do you think that King's grandmother was getting back as much as she gave in the relationship? Why or why not?

I felt best when I wrote about things I was very familiar with.
—Marianne Smith

❖ *Suggestions for Writing*

1. Write a narrative about where or from whom you learned a most important lesson, talent, or skill.

2. Visit a nursing home and collect stories from residents about how things used to be done (for example, cooking, farming, hunting, fishing, and so on). Compare then and now and draw conclusions about which way you consider better.

3. Choose a skill in which you feel competent. Write out the process that you incorporate and have a younger family member follow the written instructions trying to duplicate what you are able to do. Then share what happened with members in your class.

Jeanne Leiby

Why I Read

> "When I was living in Knoxville, Tennessee, I saw an advertisement for a writing contest sponsored by a great local bookstore. The topic was 'Why We Read' and the prize was $50 worth of books. Yes—I wanted the books, but I'm also a writer who craves assignments and deadlines—anything to kill the panic of the blank page." Jeanne Leiby was born and grew up in Detroit, MI. She earned an MFA from the University of Alabama in 1997 and teaches fiction and screen writing at the University of Central Florida. Ms. Leiby is interested in and writes about urban landscapes.

Prereading Reflection

Write about your first reading memories.

Gray winter evenings my father comes home,
lips and hands blue with cold, his days
spent far away from me setting glass panes
in the big building, downtown Detroit.
He turns blue for glazier's wages, but his dues
buy no friends, no community on the job
because no, he doesn't understand football,
hockey, NASCAR, and speed boats.
My father dresses as prescribed by weather
and work: brown Wrangler jeans, heavy
boots studded with caulk and putty, thick
hands scarred by broken panes and stray nails.
Now twenty years removed from this memory,
he is safe and warm in dry retirement,
but still I weather his lonely coffee breaks:
his strong shoulders supporting rusty girders,
a white-tipped Tipperello between his lips,
puffs of smoke sending silent thoughts
into near-dark, scoria-thick skies.

Have you ever lacked an interest or hobby shared by your friends, family, or colleagues that caused you to feel separate?

This man never finished high school,
grew up picking asparagus on the South side,
never once received a book for his birthday.
But he thaws his hands over stove burners,
and when his thick fingers can turn pages,
when the dinner dishes have been cleared away,
he settles into a leather chair molded over years
to fit the contours of his body alone.
In this memory, I am only six years old,   Briefly describe a person
and I don't know how to read, but he does,   who used to read to you.
and I watch the color rise in his lips and cheeks;
he's touched by the warm glow of things
I will only struggle to understand.

Final Reflection

How have your early reading experiences shaped the reader you've become?

❖ *After You Read, Consider*

1. The poet gives no clues about what her father reads. Using the poem and your own experiences with a friend or family member, predict what the father in this poem might choose to read.

2. The poet writes, "he is safe and warm in dry retirement but still I weather his lonely coffee breaks." Why do you believe she still recalls how her father's life used to be?

3. How do the vivid descriptions of clothing and surroundings help you visualize the poet's father? Write a physical description of the man you envision.

❖ *Suggestions for Writing*

1. In this textbook, several different authors share early reading experiences. Choose at least two of these pieces and compare or contrast the pieces you have chosen.

2. Choose an elementary school in your community and collect early reading memories from some of the students. (*Note*: You must first get their parents' permission for this project.) Then prepare a presentation for language arts class in your college or university that illustrates the stories and analyzes what these memories mean in terms of students in a classroom setting.

3. Begin or enter a children's reading circle in a local preschool, after-school program, day care, or library. Keep a journal of the books you or another reader presents and the children's reaction to the reading. Share your experiences with your classmates and prepare a pamphlet for the local library detailing the stories and reactions to assist parents as they choose books for their children.

J. Nozipo Maraire

From Zenzele: A Letter for My Daughter

J. Nozipo Maraire was born in Harare, Zimbabwe, in 1966 during the transition of the country from colonial Rhodesia under Britain to the independent country now called Zimbabwe. Maraire's grandparents, parents, and other close family members were directly involved in the war for independence from both the British and the white elite. Maraire left Zimbabwe during the war. She lived and went to school in Canada, the United States, and Jamaica. "I saw the world as vast and magical with so many different cultures and people," she says. "It opened me up and made me very adaptable to change. It also meant that I was not afraid to be in strange places, to experience, and to learn." Maraire returned to Zimbabwe before the war ended during the height of racism and fear. Despite their small numbers, the white inhabitants of Zimbabwe governed over the country and over the black majority. Maraire stayed in Zimbabwe until she was eighteen when she moved to Boston to study at Harvard University. While growing up, she had dreamed about studying medicine in America. However, her plan had been and still is to return to Zimbabwe as a doctor who could help improve Africa's health care and economy. Maraire's dream came true when she went to Columbia Medical School after receiving an undergraduate degree from Harvard. Currently, she is a fourth-year resident in neurosurgery at Yale University. In 1995, she was published in the Neurosurgery journal for her work on intercranial cavernous malformations that lead to many neurological disabilities, hemorrhages, and seizures.

Writing in a journal gave me the chance to explore all kinds of ideas and work out some things I wasn't sure I knew enough about.

—Karen Lanuette

Prereading Reflection

Write about a place near your home that reminds you of someone special to you.

Today is the first day of winter, I believe. There is a thin frost on the ground that makes the white wall almost silver and casts a pallor on the garden. Not a single bloom remains; they all shuddered and collapsed as the air grew cool. Even the shrubs and trees are curling back their leaves in retreat, huddling together and bending low, close to the earth, to seek refuge. There is a ghostly glow and a glacial stillness all around, outside and within. There is something mournful about a winter dawn. It is a time of death, of loss, of flight.

> Why does Maraire open with descriptions of winter? What mood is she creating?

It is still early—not even Samuel is awake—and I am sitting in the kitchen, sipping my morning tea, looking out at the backyard. As my strength falters, I love to spend the early hours of the morning in the orange glow of the dawn that fills the kitchen. I look out at the garden, whose face changes in subtle and beautiful ways every day. I have a most privileged seat at the season's opening of nature's theatrics. But perhaps the real reason that I creep quietly down in the mornings is that here I am reminded of you. This was your stage and my refuge. It is here that we encountered each other. I have a vivid image of you on the day you announced your plans: glowing brown skin that defies the indignities you subject it to (chlorine pools, Chimanimani winds, and Chakowa sun) and that lively tangle of black curls cropped short, as you insisted. You, with restless confidence, expounding on the necessity of going abroad for university. For months, you toted that bright red prospectus like a new Bible. There was undeniable proof of the merits of an American college education. During my spring cleaning, I was tempted (with fervent urging by your siblings) to discard it accidentally. We watched keenly as it grew more and more tattered from constant use. We patiently waited. It was simply a matter of time before it disintegrated and our sermons would cease. Until then, any heretic was immediately set aright by the printed word, the gospel truth of higher education, as proclaimed by that book. I became the unfortunate target of your crusade.

"Mama, they have so many subjects. Look, the psychoanalytic theories of political anthropology! I don't even know what that means. And twenty libraries, for *one* university. They even have museums, Mama, full of art, and it's *on the campus*." You gushed, already picking up the jargon.

Why is Zenzele's mother not excited about her daughter's college plans?

"Look here, Mama, the professors are from all over the world. Here's one—Professor Dao Wong Ng from Vietnam, and get this—Professor Miguel Rodrigues Carrera Maria de dos Santos from Argentina. I'll bet he thanks his parents for that! Just imagine, Mama. Oh, look, I could even learn Polish. Ha-ha. There is no limit, Mama, don't you see?"

You looking up at me, eyes wide and round like the globe you long to conquer. I heard no more. Your mind is set, I see. You are going to fly away and leave my nest.

"I am not going to war, Mama; don't look like that." Softly now, taking my arm. "It is only a four-year program.

"I will call every week and every holiday I shall hop on the first plane headed for Harare. Promise."

Ah. But I know better. There will be summer writing workshops, dancing classes, and bicycle tours; there will be Paris and London waiting to be discovered by you. I begrudge you not one single joy of youth, especially you who have such energy to embrace life. I finally gave in. But all I could think was, America? Harvard? Thousands of miles from Harare. I took up my ironing board, leaving you dancing to your chant of opportunities. America—so far away.

Why does her mother imagine her daughter's future as far away from her family?

Was I too distant? Perhaps. I was often bewildered by the task of motherhood, that precarious balance between total surrender and totalitarianism. How could I prepare you for a world that I did not even understand? I was struck by the absurdity of my predicament as a woman. I had been excluded from the social contract that drafted and perpetuated those very rules that it fell to my lot to inculcate in you. Had it been up to me, I would have constructed a very different world for you. There would have been more laughter, more color, less struggle. But despite my reality, you have made your own world. Of all of my children, you are the only one who has created yourself.

Now that her daughter is grown, why is she questioning her mothering?

Mine was a simple life. As the eldest of five children, I had many chores to do, and one duty: to make mother's load easier. Together, we calculated school fees, allotted the household spending money, bought uniforms and stationery. We pooled our earnings, subtracted the food and rent, and hid the remainder in an earthen jar behind the maize sacks in the pantry. We saved for birthdays and Sunday dresses. Ours was a close but practical relationship. We were allies in a battle against hunger and squalor. I did not weep over the starving in Ethiopia, the refugees in Mozambique, the students of Soweto, nor did it ever occur to me to lend my fury to a march against rape and sexual violence. I signed no appeals to politicians; I did not sit on cold pavements, with fingers frozen and my toes numb, to denounce neocolonialist foreign domination. I have watched in wonder as you did all of these. In my days, I yearned for little else than my own room with pretty blue curtains and a bedspread to match, where I could sleep alone instead of listening to Farai's snoring and suffering the bruises of Linda's flailing limbs. I wanted only peace. I yearned to escape from the world and its hardships. You mustn't wonder, then, that I am startled when you burst into the kitchen, demanding, "Mother, what do you think of global warming?" My mind flashes a picture of a beach in Jamaica, then goes blank. I often feel compelled to prepare for a conversation with you. But I could never keep up. You weave so many subjects into one, then, having thoroughly dissected one issue, you launch with equal passion into another. I am not only defeated; I am exhausted.

> Why does she want to tell her daughter about her own growing up?

Nothing gives me greater pleasure, therefore, than to sit with my knitting and watch you debating with your father. I am reassured to see that even the internationally renowned lawyer is vulnerable. I inwardly delight to see him falter to keep pace with your sharp wits. I can see you, on those evenings, your features distorted from the consolidation of mental faculties, merciless, ready to pounce on any minor flaw in his argument.

We have the same eyes, you and I. But yours are still vulnerable. They are candid and honest; like a scrupulous documentary, they take note of all of the details of life. And all of the world is reflected there— the beautiful and wretched alike. My eyes are resigned to observe, detached, from some distance. They want no part; they do not take in. They keep out. In your company, I often feel blind, groping for firm objects, hesitant lest I collide with some obstacle I cannot characterize, let alone surmount. Ah. But your fingers are truly mine, long, dark, and graceful. And those clumsy lips, those are mine, too. They fall and tense and bend into every shape. They are never still, never without expression.

The world is full of so many more illustrious and better-qualified women—bankers, lawyers, doctors, and presidents—who would have served as far superior role models. But I alone had the responsibility of being your mother, and so, by default, your guide and mentor. I have learned something in my awkward journey through womanhood. The lessons are few, but enduring. So I hope that you will pardon this curious distillation of traditional African teaching, social commentary, and maternal concern. These are the stories that have made me what I am today. It is just that you are my very own, and it is an old woman's privilege to impart her wisdom. It is all that I have to give to you, Zenzele.

Final Reflection

What would be the best advice you could give a younger family member?

❖ *After You Read, Consider*

1. Why would the mother's stories be the most important thing she could give her daughter?

2. In a few places in the letter Zenzele's mother compares her life to the possibilities in her daughter's life. Why would she do this?

3. Is Zenzele's mother proud of her? How does she feel about her going to America to attend college?

> *I liked when we wrote letters instead of essays. It was easier to see my audience in a letter.*
> —Tom Bryant-Smith

❖ *Suggestions for Writing*

1. Write a letter to your child or a child you might have. Address your life and the life you hope your child might lead.

2. Write an argument for or against going to school and living near your family.

3. Maraire writes, "You weave so many subjects into one, then, having thoroughly dissected one issue, you launch with equal passion into another. I am not only defeated; I am exhausted." Write an essay in which you explore how education can separate you from your family even if you live in the same town.

Pat Rushin

Zoo Welcomes New Arrival

Pat Rushin's stories have appeared in the North American Review, Indiana Review, Kansas Quarterly, Quarterly West, *and in* Sudden Fiction: American Short Stories *(1987). His short story collection,* Puzzling Through the News, *was published in 1991. He currently lives with his wife and daughters near Orlando, where he teaches creative writing at the University of Central Florida.*

❖

Prereading Reflection

Describe how you feel when you are waiting for something important.

❖

Maybe it's the combination of changes in his life—starting a new job, moving downtown, Celia getting pregnant, all in the first year of their marriage—but Casey hasn't been sleeping well lately.

It doesn't help that the city is suffering record-high temperatures, either. What with the hazy sun baking the streets all day and no air conditioning in their two-story row house, Casey and Celia have been sleeping with the bedroom windows open, and all the noises outside filter up and in through the whirring box fan. Bottles breaking, drunks raging, sirens shrieking, kids screaming: these things startle Casey out of sleep. Quiet, ghostly voices drift by, discussing lives Casey has no part in: they nag him awake.

Why is Casey uncomfortable?

Meanwhile, Celia sleeps through damn near anything. Fitfully, at times, now that she's into her third trimester and can't seem to toss and turn her way into a position comfortable enough to last her ten minutes on end, but she sleeps. Casey lies awake next to her, waiting for her to stir and settle, listening for more noises from the street.

"What singing?" she says in the morning when Casey complains of some wino glee club on the corner that kept him awake half the night. "What gunshots?" she says, when they sounded so close his heart only stopped stuttering after he pulled his aluminum softball bat from beneath the bed, felt its reassuring weight tight in his grip. "Probably just a car backfiring," she says, massaging a sleepless night's stiffness from his neck. "My man, weapon in hand, protecting hearth and home. Relax," she says. "We're safe."

One night a street gang on the corner laughs and curses and shouts so loudly that even Celia wakes up.

"I'm calling the police," Casey says.

City girl born and bred, Celia's skeptical. "Cops can't do much but chase them off, and they'll come back and make more trouble when they find out somebody complained."

Casey calls the police.

"We can send somebody around in an hour or so," the desk sergeant tells him, "but I'll be honest, sir, we're very busy tonight and this is not a priority call unless you want to file a formal complaint, in which case you'd have to appear at a hearing, and God knows what kind of retribution some of these kids might plan for you and your family once they know who you are and where you live. I hope you understand me."

"Relax," Celia tells him. "You have to learn to live with street noises, kind of like living by a waterfall."

Is it just "street noise" that Casey is worried about?

A bottle shatters; a girl screams high and shrill, laughs wildly.

"Close the window if you want," she says. "You'll get used to it."

But it's too hot to close the window and Casey knows he'll never get used to the street.

Last year, right after they were married, when they were looking for a place to live, Casey suggested a country house he knew twenty minutes outside the beltway that needed caretaking. They'd get free rent in return for mowing a few acres of unused pastureland, feeding a dozen or so chickens, keeping the house clean and in good repair.

"Who has time for that?" Celia said. "We both work."

"It's not much, really. We could handle the chores on weekends."

"What do we know about farms?"

"It's not a farm. This is horse country, Celia."

"So what does a boy from the suburbs know about horses?"

"There aren't any horses. They don't use this place anymore."

She shook her head. "I couldn't live in the country. Too spooky. All alone out there like that?" She hugged his waist, ducked her head into his chest, shivered dramatically. "You ever see *In Cold Blood?*"

Instead she wanted to look at a bargain-basement-priced seventy-year-old row house just east of downtown in an area Casey would have thought twice about *driving* through let alone *living* in.

"It's the perfect starter house," Celia explained. "It's cheap, it's in decent shape, it's a step away from gentrification. Trust me. I know for a fact the gay community's got an eye on this neighborhood. Five years from now there'll be health food shops and gift boutiques on every corner. They'll strip the street and sandblast the original cobblestone. It'll be a showplace, believe me, I heard them talking about it at the office. This place is a renovator's dream. Tear up the linoloeum and we have hardwood floors, some paint and polish here and there and we can sell for three times what we buy for."

> How does Celia talk Casey into buying a house in the city? Are her reasons all financial?

Besides, the location was a short bus ride, no transfer, to Celia's office downtown where she worked as a receptionist for one of the more successful real estate agencies in town.

So they bought.

And now Casey drives an hour each way in rush hour traffic to and from the manufacturing plant in the suburbs where he works in computer aided design, doodling out low-tolerance specifications for machining little parts of defense industry products he never sees. Mornings he picks his way through the trash on the street, unlocks his car, locks it behind him as soon as he's in. Evenings he parks his car as close as he can, walks briskly to his door, head down, avoiding eye contact with any of the bums and street punks who are starting to come alive with the setting sun.

One evening, as he locks his car, he sees a half-a-dozen teenagers loitering on the sidewalk a couple of houses down from his. They're laughing, smoking, passing around a paper-bagged bottle. Don't they have parents? he thinks. One girl, no more than thirteen or fourteen, lounges against an older boy, her thumb hooked in his back pocket, her fingers spread across the cheek of his ass. They look at him as he approaches. The older boy tilts his head, says something too low for Casey to hear, and the whole group snickers.

"Nice car," one of them calls, and they all grin at him like piranha. Casey nods in their direction, tries to smile, turns to his front door. Hands tremble, breath comes short, and the piercing laughter behind him reddens his neck as he unlocks three locks, enters, locks three locks, throws two deadbolts, latches a chain. He takes a deep breath.

"I'm home," he calls.

The next morning his tape player is gone, wires snaking out of the hole in the dashboard.

"You shouldn't park on the street," Celia says.

"There's no place else to park."

"Maybe we can rent a garage somewhere." She looks at her watch, kisses him quickly. "My poor baby, I'm late for work. Better report this to the police before you go."

"What's the use? They'll never get it back."

"Insurance report."

Why is Casey afraid of the teenagers? Why doesn't he replace his tape player?

"Oh," Casey says, but he doesn't bother calling the police or replacing the tape player. The hum of tire on pavement is his only music this summer.

"Oh!" Celia says one night, sitting up suddenly in bed. "That was a big one."

Casey opens bleary eyes.

"He kicked me," Celia says. "Feels like he's playing soccer in there. Want to feel?" She grabs his hand, places it hard against her rounded belly. "Wait. He stopped. Wait a minute."

Casey waits, yawns, waits.

Why doesn't Casey feel the same elation Celia does when their baby kicks?

"There," he says finally. "I felt it."

"No, that was me. Wait."

He toys with the line of coarse, dark hairs that have recently sprouted below her navel, takes his hand away to rub his eyes.

"There!" she says, grabbing his hand again. "That was a whopper. Did you feel it?"

"Missed it."

"Wait, he'll do it again."

Casey waits and waits. Suddenly her stomach bulges and rolls beneath his hand. He still can't get over how strange it feels, like holding a live fish in a plastic bag full of water.

"Wow," Celia says, "he's doing back flips. Did you feel it?"

"Yes, I felt it."

"Isn't that wild, how hard he kicks?"

Casey pats her stomach. "High point of my night."

"Well, you don't have to be so sarcastic."

"I'm just tired, honey, please." Casey rolls over, closes his eyes. "I love you, I love our baby, I need some sleep, okay?"

"Okay." Celia snuggles up to his back. "Sorry for waking you."

"You didn't wake me," Casey says.

As the summer wears on, it gets to the point where even when the street *is* quiet, even when he *does* fall off to sleep, he dreams he's awake, sweating, nagged by a muggy, cramped oppressiveness. He dreams that Celia's leg is draped heavy over both of his, that her arm coils around his throat like a boa constrictor, squeezing the breath out of him, that her swollen belly presses skin-to-skin tight against his ribs, that the baby is kicking, kicking at him.

What other things in his life are making Casey feel oppressed?

He awakens hanging half off the bed, Celia wedged hard against him, a wealth of vacant mattress to the other side of her. He lifts her arm from his chest, slides out from beneath her leg, gets up, walks around to the other side of the bed, gets in. The sheets are cool beneath him. He stretches out, closes his eyes, listens to the street a minute or two before he hears her whimper in her sleep like a child denied, feels her weight shift, her body roll until it finds him again.

He kids her about it the next morning, her hogging the bed.

"Do I really?" she says, eyes wide, head tilted. "Come on, I don't do that, do I?"

He smiles. "You snore, too."

"Oh, come on, I do not," she says, grinning and blushing, delighted with her own mischief. "Do I?"

"What's the matter?" his boss says one afternoon. "Too much partying last night?"

Casey blinks at his screen, tries to bring the blurry curving green lines into focus. He's been revising the design of a cylindrical casing since lunch, rotating it this way and that on its axis, looking for the right perspective. He moves his stylus on the menu board.

"Oops," his boss says, leaning over his shoulder. "That doesn't belong there, does it?"

"No," Casey says. "I don't know," he says. "What I'm trying to do, I guess," he says, and forgets what he's trying to do. "I've been under a lot of pressure lately," he says, and wishes immediately he hadn't.

His boss's face softens. "Hey, that's okay. This part isn't critical. I'll give it to somebody else."

"At home," Casey says quickly. "I mean at home. We're having our first baby pretty soon, you know, my wife and I."

"Hey, that's right, congratulations, I forgot to tell you." He puts a hand on Casey's shoulder. "When's she due?"

"End of the summer."

"Sure picked a hot one. Well, hey, that's just wonderful. Best of luck to you both." He slaps Casey's back. "Listen, hey, I know what you're going through, but appreciate your time together now, a baby doesn't give you a minute's rest. Believe you me, I know, I got four of my own. They take up all your time. Me and my wife used to hire a sitter and rent a room at the Holiday for the evening, just to get some peace and quiet sometimes." He laughs. "You think you got pressure now, wait'll the midnight feedings start, wait'll the potty training starts, wait'll the first day of school. Are you in a good school district?"

"I don't know," Casey says. "I don't think so."

"Where do you live again?"

Casey tells him.

Predict how Casey might feel after the conversation with his boss?

His boss frowns. "None of my business, but I don't even know if they *have* schools there. No offense, it's your life, but I wouldn't raise a *dog* in that part of town. Believe you me, that is *not* a safe place for children. Believe you me," he says, and he walks off shaking his head.

The instructor of their childbirth class at the hospital downtown tells all the daddies to be especially patient with the mommies during the final month of pregnancy. "Mommy is feeling cranky right now, Daddy," the instructor says. "It's hot and sticky, and Mommy is feeling terribly blue. Take Mommy someplace nice, Daddy. Go dancing, get out of the house, go to the beach, get some fresh air. Mommy needs to get her mind off her body."

Casey suggests a picnic in the country somewhere, a state park, maybe, or maybe just some open meadowland off some winding back road.

"Let's go to the zoo," Celia says. "I haven't been to the zoo since I was a kid. I read in the paper they have a new baby gorilla there. They say it looks just like a human baby, almost."

Casey heads for the car when they hit the street, but Celia stops him. "You and that car," she says, "Don't you get sick of driving? Let's take the bus."

A couple of bums are dozing in the kiosk at the end of their block—taking a break from a hard morning's begging, Casey figures—so he steers Celia up the street to the next stop. The bus driver smiles at Celia, lurches off while Casey's still counting out change. Celia grabs the handrail to keep from falling.

"Hey," Casey says sharply. "She's *preg*nant."

The driver shrugs. "So?"

"So be careful."

"Sure," the driver says.

"If she fell and hurt herself or the baby—"

"Okay, okay, sit down, Jesus."

"Forget it Casey, come on," Celia says, and she leads him unsteadily to a seat.

At the zoo, Casey buys two popcorns, one plain, one caramel, and though the animal stench is strong in the afternoon heat, the sun brings color to Celia's high, plump cheeks, and she laughs and flirts with him as they walk hand in hand.

"Apple cheeks," Casey tells her. "They look so good I want to take a bite out of one." He nips at her and she squeals and jumps like a skittish kitten.

There's a crowd at the gorilla cages. Celia squeezes her way through, pulling Casey behind her. "Pregnant lady," she says. "Excuse me, mother with child." People mostly smile and laugh as they move aside, though Casey hears a high school girl mumble, "I'm sure, like I care a *lot*," to her gum-chewing companion, who looks sideways at Casey and rolls her eyes.

Mother and daughter gorillas have a cage to themselves. Mother gorilla sits in the back corner, rocking her daughter in one arm and picking at her coat of fine brown fuzz. She eats what she picks. Baby gorilla sucks her thumb, eyes darting wide and wild from face to face outside the cage. Casey meets the eyes for a moment, but they quickly move on. The crowd behind them presses and jostles; a tall man to Casey's right, camera hanging from sunburnt neck, jabbers loudly in high-pitched monkey chatter: the baby gorilla twists her head, eyes moving, moving.

"God," Celia breathes. *"She's adorable."*

The tall man snorts. "Got a face only a mother could love."

Celia looks at him, dark eyes burning. "Asshole," she says.

Why does Celia get so angry?

Casey pulls her from the crowd, hugs her, rubs her back. He wipes the tears from her eyes.

"Casey, I can't wait anymore," she says. "I want our baby *now*."

"Shoosh," he tells her. "It's okay, that's all right."

"The joys of pregnancy," he hears someone say behind him, and he turns to see a sharp-faced woman with long black hair smirking at them. The big dumb-looking guy holding her by the arm lowers his head, shrugs, lets her lead him away.

There are people in this world, Casey realizes, who should never have children. There are people who make this world a shitty place to bring children into.

Casey hugs Celia closer, stares into the cage behind her. A hulking male gorilla rocks on his haunches in the corner, scratches his groin, peers through the chain-link mesh separating him from mother and daughter gorillas in the adjacent cage. Casey knows that gorillas only *look* human, but he can't help noticing a sad, almost wistful expression on the ape's face.

"Hey!" he says, turning Celia around and pointing. "Do you think he might be the father?"

She wipes her eyes, grins suddenly. "How can you say a thing like that?" she says, winking. "Trust me, you're the father."

Casey laughs loud and long, sinks to his knees. He wraps his arms around her wide, full hips and nuzzles her belly, telling her how much he loves her again and again. Celia giggles—*Casey, people are watching*—but he doesn't care. She pushes him away, laughing and blushing and as beautiful as he's ever seen her.

"Control yourself!" she says. "That's the kind of wild passion that got us into trouble in the first place."

"No trouble," Casey says. "My pleasure."

And for the rest of the day, as they stroll from cage to cage, Casey can't keep his hands off her, as though she might slip out of sight, out of his life, if he's not touching her.

Why have Casey's feelings changed?

He finds himself smiling mawkishly at babies in strollers, trading due dates and Lamaze tips with other pregnant couples, bragging about the force of his baby's kicks, and feeling proud, so proud and happy that he doesn't want the day to end.

That night, after they've made love—slowly, patiently, carefully, at first, and then more and more recklessly—and after Celia has talked herself to sleep counting off all the things that still need to be done before the baby comes—the nursery needs painting, the crib they bought last month must be put together, they still have to buy a car seat—Casey lies on his side staring at Celia. Suddenly her belly rolls. Casey puts his hand beneath her nightgown, feels the warm bulge moving, turning, kicking. It won't be long, he thinks. And the more he thinks it, the less the thought scares him, until, like a mantra, it soothes him to sleep.

"So why didn't you?" a sharp voice says.

Casey springs up in bed.

"I was going to," a girl's voice says. "I was all ready to."

"So why didn't you?"

"I don't know."

"You don't know," the first voice says, and Casey recognizes now that it's the voice of a boy trying to sound like a man. The boy curses, and Casey hears a sharp slap, the girl crying out. His skin prickles, and he reaches for his bat. Another slap. Casey gets out of bed, turns off the fan, takes it out of the window, and peers down at the street. On the sidewalk just below, a tall lean boy in sneakers, torn jeans, and a tanktop tee-shirt holds a girl by the arm. He shakes her. She lowers her head, doesn't resist. The streetlight down the block casts vague shadows, but Casey thinks he's seen these two before with the rest of their gang on the corner.

"You don't know," the boy's saying over and over, his voice rising to a mean, mocking falsetto now. He releases her, curses again, spits. "What's to know?" he says. "You go to the clinic, you get rid of it. What'd you do with the money?"

"I still got the money. I can still go."

"When?"

No answer.

"Casey?" Celia says behind him.

"Something's going on outside," he says.

"Come back to bed."

"There's some kids fighting down there."

"Close the window. Come to bed."

"*When?*" the boy shouts. He curses, holds the girl by the front of her shirt now, raises a fist, then pulls her sharply towards him.

"Please," she says, crying.

"Don't please me! What are you trying to do to me?"

"Hey!" Casey shouts, and the boy jumps, looks up.

"Hey what?" the boy shouts back, dark face gleaming in the soft light. Long lean muscles bunch and gather. "Hey *what!*" he screams up at the night.

Casey's heart jumps. "Knock it off," he calls down, and the weakness of his voice angers him.

The boy curses, curses, curses, vile raging nonsensical curses, threats, curses that make Casey back away from the window.

"Don't!" the girl says, and the boy suddenly swings at her, knocks her to the ground. "Is this what you want?" he says, voice shaking. "Is this what it takes?"

And Casey feels the heat surge from his chest to his head, his throat tightening, his grip burning the bat. He pulls on a pair of jeans, Celia telling him no, no, Casey, wait, I'll call the police, don't go, but it's too late now as Casey races down the stairs. He pulls open the front door, slams it tight behind him.

> Does Casey get involved because the girl is pregnant? Do you think he would have reacted this way if two boys were fighting?

The girl lies on the sidewalk, moaning. The boy stands beside her, fists raised, tears streaming down his face.

"Leave her alone," Casey says.

"Stay out of this!" The boy grabs the girl by the arm, yanks her to her knees. "Let's go," he says, but she slumps to the ground. He yanks her up again, "Come *on!*"

"Enough!" Casey yells, bat raised.

The boy turns to him, eyes wild. "You want some of this?" He whirls suddenly and punches her, knocks her sprawling against the house, and Casey feels a growling bellow of fear and hate rising in his throat to a roar as he springs forward swinging and the bat connects. The boy falls and rolls, holding his shoulder, howls and howls, cries no, no, no in a high, heartbreaking whine that reminds Casey that this is, truly, just a boy, a child made of fragile bone and fledgling muscle.

"God," Casey says. "Oh, hey." He drops the bat, aluminum ringing on asphalt, and kneels to touch him, but the boy twists away, struggles to his feet, and stumbles off down the block, left arm hanging limp, the high, rasping sounds of his weeping fading as he turns the corner.

> Would you have reacted this strongly? How does Casey feel after hurting the boy?

"Casey," Celia calls from above. "Please come in. I called the police. Casey, please!"

"In a minute," he says. He walks to the girl, helps her up. "Are you all right?"

She won't look at him.

"Hey," he says. "You want to come in? You want to go to the hospital?"

She pulls back. "What are you doing here?" she says. "What do you want?"

Casey stands awkwardly, still panting. He's shirtless, shoeless, and suddenly doesn't know what to do with his hands. "I live here," he says. "I heard the trouble."

The girl shakes her head. "You don't know the trouble."

Casey takes a deep breath, hooks his thumbs in his belt loops. "I live here," he says, voice surer now. "He woke my wife. My wife needs her sleep. My wife's pregnant."

The girl looks up towards the second floor, dark eyes troubled, a purple blotch rising on her cheek, and she folds her hands across her stomach. Casey follows her gaze to where Celia stands in the window, hands pressed against the screen, crying low and soft.

"Casey, please, it's starting, I need you, it's starting."

"What's starting?"

"Contractions."

But it's too early, Casey knows, the baby's not due till end of summer, they'll have to weather the heat before they come to term. "You're kidding," he says.

"Casey, I mean it."

He feels the girl watching him, but when he looks at her, she turns away, begins walking slowly down the sidewalk.

"We can take you to the hospital," he calls after her, and a short convulsive giggle escapes him. "We're going anyway."

She glances back, tears shining in the streetlight's glow, looks back up to the window. Then she turns the corner and is gone.

Do what you want, Casey thinks. Just a child, the both of them, children left out to roam the night. The night is no time for children, no time at all, too dangerous, too stifling, too dark. It's just too late, he thinks, as he hears the door open behind him and turns to see Celia framed in the doorway, hands supporting the weight of her belly, teeth clenched and eyes narrowed to slits. She lets out a gasp, a whimper. "Jesus," she says. "What a night to start this."

Casey reaches for her. "Don't be scared," he says softly. "We're safe now. It's all over."

Final Reflection

What does it take for you to feel safe? For your home and neighborhood to feel comfortable?

❖ *After You Read, Consider*

1. Think about the differences between living in the country and living in the city. Where are you more comfortable? Why?

2. What kind of world does Casey think his child will be born in? Why is he less optimistic than Celia?

3. Why does Casey's mood lighten at the zoo? How does seeing the gorillas affect him?

> *I enjoyed writing about where I grew up, but I also liked analyzing why I don't like where I live now.*
>
> —Rose Cullen

❖ *Suggestions for Writing*

1. Narrate your experience with waiting for a major change in your life.

2. Write an essay in which you explore the zoo as a metaphor for Casey's life. In what ways is he as trapped as the father gorilla? Feeling separated from his wife's experience? How does Rushin let us know that Casey feels as if he is on the outside looking in?

3. Write a letter to the editor that responds to the problems in Casey's neighborhood.

Jenny Joseph

Warning

Jenny Joseph, a poet and writer from Gloucestershire, England, has published four volumes of poetry and six children's books. Persephone, a book of prose and verse, won her the James Tait Black Memorial Prize for fiction in 1986, and her Selected Poems *were published in 1993.*

Prereading Reflection

Write about what you hope you'll be like when you are elderly.

When I am an old woman I shall wear purple
With a red hat which doesn't go, and doesn't suit me.
And I shall spend my pension on brandy and summer gloves
And satin sandals, and say we've no money for butter.
I shall sit down on the pavement when I'm tired
And gobble up samples in shops and press alarm bells
And run my stick along the public railings   *How do you visualize*
And make up for the sobriety of my youth.   *Joseph as an old woman?*
I shall go out in my slippers in the rain
And pick the flowers in other people's gardens   *Why can she learn to*
And learn to spit.   *spit when she is old?*

You can wear terrible shirts and grow more fat
And eat three pounds of sausages at a go   *What positive things is Joseph*
Or only bread and pickle for a week   *telling us about growing old?*
And hoard pens and pencils and beermats and things in boxes.

But now we must have clothes that keep us dry
And pay our rent and not swear in the street
And set a good example for the children.
We must have friends to dinner and read the papers.

But maybe I ought to practise a little now?
So people who know me are not too shocked and surprised
When suddenly I am old, and start to wear purple.

Final Reflection

Why is Joseph warning us? What are elderly women usually like?

> *I hated, hated, hated class discussions when only a few people talked. But I know this is my fault as well.*
>
> —Tina Meyers

❖ After You Read, Consider

1. Why is Joseph choosing to be eccentric and mismatched in her old age?

2. Why does she find growing fat to be a relief?

3. How does one get ready to grow old?

❖ Suggestions for Writing

1. Write a portrait of an older person in your family or neighborhood that you admire. What makes this person appealing to you?

2. Write an essay in which you explore Joseph's choice of colors. Why does she find purple and red so outrageous that she warns us of their coming?

3. Write your own poem about growing old.

Chang-rae Lee

From Native Speaker

Chang-rae Lee was born in South Korea and at age three immigrated to the United States with his family. After receiving a degree from Yale University, he moved to the University of Oregon where he earned his MFA. He remained at the university after his graduation, accepting the position of assistant professor of creative writing. In 1995, Granta, *a prestigious British literary magazine, labeled Lee among the fifty best American writers under the age of forty.*

Prereading Reflection

Write about the value of lists in your life.

The day my wife left she gave me a list of who I was.

I didn't know what she was handing me. She had been compiling it without my knowledge for the last year or so we were together. Eventually I would understand that she didn't mean the list as exhaustive, something complete, in any way the sum of my character or nature. Lelia was the last person who would attempt anything even vaguely encyclopedic.

But then maybe she herself didn't know what she was doing. She was drawing up idioms in the list, visions of me in the whitest raw light, instant snapshots of the difficult truths native to our time together.

The year before she left she often took trips. Mostly weekends somewhere. I stayed home. I never voiced any displeasure at this. I made sure to know where she was going, who'd likely be there, the particular *milieu*, whether dancing or a sauna might be involved, those kinds of angles. The destinations were harmless, really, like the farming cooperative upstate,

> Predict the message sent when one member of a relationship begins to travel without the partner.

where her college roommate made soft cheeses for the city street markets. Or she went to New Hampshire, to see her mother, who'd been more or less depressed and homebound for the last three years. Once or twice she went to Montreal, which worried me a little, because whenever she called to say she was fine I would hear the sound of French in the background, all breezy and guttural. She would fly westward on longer trips, to El Paso and the like, where we first met ten years ago. Then at last and every day, from our Manhattan apartment, she would take day trips to any part of New York City, which she loved and thought she would never leave.

One day Lelia came home from work and said she was burning out. She said she desperately needed time off. She worked as a speech therapist for children, mostly freelancing in the public schools and then part-time at a speech and hearing clinic downtown.

> Have you ever felt "burned out"? What steps did you take to rejuvenate?

Sometimes she would have kids over at our place. The children she saw had all kinds of articulation problems, some because of physiological defects like cleft palates or tied tongues. Others had had laryngectomies, or else defective hearing, or learning disabilities, or for an unknown reason had begun speaking much later than was normal. And then others—the ones I always paid close attention to—came to her because they had entered the first grade speaking a home language other than English. They were nonnative speakers. All day she helped these children manipulate their tongues and their lips and their exhaling breath, guiding them through the difficult language.

So I told her fine, she could take it easy with work, that I could handle the finances, we were solid that way. This is when she professed a desire to travel—she hadn't yet said *alone*—and then in the next breath admitted she'd told the school people not to call for a while. She said she felt like maybe writing again, getting back to her essays and poems. She had published a few pieces in small, serious literary magazines early in our marriage, written some book reviews, articles, but nothing, she said harshly, that wasn't half-embarrassing.

She handed the list to me at the Alitalia counter at Kennedy, before her flight to Rome and then on to Naples and, finally, Sicily and Corsica. This was the way she had worked it out. Her intention was to spend November and December shuttling between the Italian islands, in some off-season rental, completely alone.

She was traveling heavy. This wasn't a trip of escape, in that normal sense. She was taking with her what seemed to be hundreds of books and notepapers. Also pads, brushes, tiny pastel-tinted sponges. Too many hats, I thought, which she wore like some dead and famed flyer. A signal white scarf of silk.

Nothing I had given her.

And maps. Here was a woman of maps. She had dozens of them, in various scales. Topographic, touristical, some schematic—these last handmade. Through the nights she stood like a field general over the kitchen counter, hands perched on those jutting hipbones, smoking with agitation, assessing points of entry and encampment and escape. Her routes, stenciled in thick deep blue, embarked inward, toward an uncharted grave center. A messy bruise of ink. She had already marked out a score of crosses that seemed to say *You Are Here*. Then, there were indications she was misreading the actual size of the islands. Her lines would have her trek the same patches of rocky earth many times over. Overrunning the land. I thought I could see her kicking at the bleached, known stones; the hard southern light surrendering to her boyish straightness; those clear green eyes, leveling on the rim of the arched sea.

Inside the international terminal I couldn't help her. She took to bearing the heaviest of her bags. But at some point I panicked and embraced her clumsily.

"Maybe I'll come with you this time," I said.

She tried to smile.

> What does he mean here? What island is she trading?

"You're just trading islands," I said, unhelpful as usual.

I asked if she had enough money. She said her savings would take care of her. I thought they were *our* savings, but the notion didn't seem to matter at the moment. Her answer was also, of course, a means of renunciation, itself a denial of everything else I wasn't offering.

When they started the call for boarding she gave me the list, squeezing it tight between our hands.

"This doesn't mean what you'll think," she said, getting up.

"That's okay."

"You don't even know what it is."

"It doesn't matter."

She bit her lip. In a steely voice she told me to read it when I got back to the car. I put it away. I walked with her to the entrance. Her cheek stiffened when I leaned to kiss her. She walked backward for several steps, her movement inertial, tipsy, and then disappeared down the telescoping tunnel.

I read through the list twice sitting in our car in the terminal garage. Later I would make three photocopies, one to reside permanently next to my body, in my wallet, as a kind of personal asterisk, I thought, in case of accidental death. Another I saved to show her again sometime, if I wanted pity or else needed some easy ammunition. The last, to historicize, I sealed in an envelope and mailed to myself.

The original I destroyed. I prefer versions of things, copies that aren't so precious. I remember its hand, definitely Lelia's, considerable, vertical, architectural, but gone awry in parts, scrawling and windbent, in unschemed colors of ink and graphite and Crayola. I could tell the page had been crumpled up and flattened out. Folded and unfolded. It looked weathered, beaten about her purse and pockets. There were smudges of olive oil. Maybe chocolate. I imagined her scribbling something down in the middle of a recipe.

Why does he imagine what his wife is doing when she writes the list? Why would this matter?

My first impression was that it was a love poem. An amnesty. Dulcet verse.

But I was wrong. It said, variously:

You are surreptitious
B+ student of life
first string hummer of Wagner and Strauss
illegal alien
emotional alien
genre bug
Yellow peril: neo-American
great in bed
overrated
poppa's boy
sentimentalist
anti-romantic
_____ analyst (you fill in)
stranger
follower
traitor
spy

For a long time I was able to resist the idea of considering the list as a cheap parting shot, a last-ditch lob between our spoiling trenches. I took it instead as one long message, broken into parts, terse communiqués from her moments of despair. For this reason, I never considered the thing mean. In fact, I even appreciated its count, the clean cadence. And just as I was nearly ready to forget the whole idea of it, maybe even forgive it completely, like the Christ that my mother and father always wished I would know, I found a scrap of paper beneath our bed while I was cleaning. Her signature, again: *False speaker of language.*

Before she left I had started a new assignment, nothing itself terribly significant but I will say now it was the sort of thing that can clinch a person's career. It's the one you spend all your energy on, it bears the fullness of your thoughts until done, the kind of job that if you mess up you've got only one more chance to redeem.

I thought I was keeping my work secret from her, an effort that was getting easier all the time. Or so it seemed. We were hardly talking then, sitting down to our evening meal like boarders in a rooming house, reciting the usual, drawn-out exchanges of familiar news, bits of the day. When she asked after my latest assignment I answered that it was *sensitive* and *evolving* but going well, and after a pause Lelia said down to her cold plate, Oh good, it's the Henryspeak.

> Why wouldn't he want his wife to know what he did for a living?

By then she had long known what I was.

For the first few years she thought I worked for companies with security problems. Stolen industrial secrets, patents, worker theft. I let her think that I and my colleagues went to a company and covertly observed a warehouse or laboratory or retail floor, then exposed all the cheats and criminals.

But I wasn't to be found anywhere near corporate or industrial sites, then or ever. Rather, my work was entirely personal. I was always assigned to an individual, someone I didn't know or care the first stitch for on a given day but who in a matter of weeks could be as bound up with me as a brother or sister or wife.

I lied to Lelia. For as long as I could I lied. I will speak the evidence now. My father, a Confucian of high order, would commend me for finally honoring that which is wholly evident. For him, all of life was a rigid matter of family. I know all about that fine and terrible ordering, how it variously casts you as the golden child, the slave-son or daughter, the venerable father, the long-dead god. But I know, too, of the basic comfort in this familial precision, where the relation abides no argument, no questions or quarrels. The truth, finally, is who can tell it.

> Have you ever allowed someone's opinion of you to alter how you see yourself?

And yet you may know me. I am an amiable man. I can be most personable, if not charming, and whatever I possess in this life is more or less the result of a talent I have for making you feel good about yourself when you are with me. In this sense I am not a seducer. I am hardly seen. I won't speak untruths to you, I won't pass easy compliments or odious offerings of flattery. I make do with on-hand materials, what I can chip out of you, your natural ore. Then I fuel the fire of your most secret vanity.

Final Reflection

The author leaves you with questions about his job. Predict what the author's work involves.

I will never like speaking in class, but at least I tried.

—Donna Morris

❖ *After You Read, Consider*

1. The author's wife handed her husband the list "at the Alitalia counter at Kennedy." Why hand the list to him at that moment?

2. What is the significance of setting off the line "Nothing I had given her" as a paragraph?

3. Why do you believe the author saves three copies of the list? Would you have thrown away the original? Why or why not?

❖ *Suggestions for Writing*

1. Create a detailed list of how you see yourself. Ask a close friend or family member to do the same. Write an essay that examines what the two lists help you to understand about yourself.

2. The author seems to have a secret life. His partner develops one through her frequent trips. Argue for or against whether the hidden elements of an individual's life might impact the ability to form or keep close relationships with others.

3. Create an in-depth character sketch of a person with secrets.

Eudora Welty

Wordstruck

Eudora Welty was born in Jackson, Mississippi, on April 13, 1909, and attended the public schools there. She published several pieces in magazines for children before she reached her teens. From 1925–1927, she attended Mississippi State College for Women in Columbus, but transferred for her final two years of college to the University of Wisconsin in Madison. She spent an academic year in New York City, studying at the Columbia University School of Business but attended lectures, plays, concerts, and art exhibitions as well. The untimely death of her father in 1931 prompted her return to Jackson, where she worked for the local radio station and wrote Jackson and Delta society news for the Memphis, Tennessee, Commercial Appeal, *a major newspaper for northwest Mississippi. In 1935 and 1936, she worked for Franklin Roosevelt's New Deal program, the Works Progress Administration (WPA), serving as a "junior publicity agent" and traveling to many parts of Mississippi to promote road building, new airstrips, canning factories, and other efforts to bring economic progress to poor and remote rural areas of the state. In 1936 she published her first important short story, and from that time onward her writing career expanded and found considerable success.*

❖

Prereading Reflection

What is the experience of reading like for you?

❖

I learned from the age of two or three that any room in our house, at any time of day, was there to read in, or to be read to. My mother read to me. She'd read to me in the big bedroom in the mornings, when we were in her rocker together, which ticked in rhythm as we rocked, as though we had a cricket accompanying the story. She'd read to me in the diningroom on winter afternoons in front of the coal fire, with our cuckoo clock ending the story with "Cuckoo," and at night when

I'd got in my own bed. I must have given her no peace. Sometimes she read to me in the kitchen while she sat churning, and the churning sobbed along with *any* story. It was my ambition to have her read to me while *I* churned; once she granted my wish, but she read off my story before I brought her butter. She was an expressive reader. When she was reading "Puss in Boots," for instance, it was impossible not to know that she distrusted *all* cats.

> Why is learning that writers were people disappointing for Welty?

It had been startling and disappointing to me to find out that story books had been written by *people*, that books were not natural wonders, coming up of themselves like grass. Yet regardless of where they came from, I cannot remember a time when I was not in love with them—with the books themselves, cover and binding and the paper they were printed on, with their smell and their weight and with their possession in my arms, captured and carried off to myself. Still illiterate, I was ready for them, committed to all the reading I could give them.

Neither of my parents had come from homes that could afford to buy many books, but though it must have been something of a strain

> Why did Welty's parents think it important to spend some of the family budget on books?

on his salary, as the youngest officer in a young insurance company, my father was all the while carefully selecting and ordering away for what he and Mother thought we children should grow up with. They bought first for the future.

Besides the bookcase in the livingroom, which was always called "the library," there were the encyclopedia tables and dictionary stand under windows in our diningroom. Here to help us grow up arguing around the diningroom table were the Unabridged Webster, the Columbia Encyclopedia, Compton's Pictured Encyclopedia, the Lincoln Library of Information, and later the Book of Knowledge. And the year we moved into our new house, there was room to celebrate it with the new 1925 edition of the Britannica, which my father, his face always deliberately turned toward the future, was of course disposed to think better than any previous edition.

> Why does Welty describe her family "library" so carefully? What does this say about what is important to her?

In "the library," inside the mission-style bookcase with its three diamond-latticed glass doors, with my father's Morris chair and the glass-shaded lamp on its table beside it, were books I could soon begin on—and I did, reading them all alike and as they came, straight down their rows, top shelf to bottom. There was the set of Stoddard's Lectures, in all its late nineteenth-century vocabulary and vignettes of peasant life and quaint beliefs and customs, with matching halftone illustrations: Vesuvius erupting, Venice by moonlight, gypsies glimpsed by their campfires. I didn't know then the clue they were to my father's longing to see the rest of the world. I read straight through his other love-from-afar: the Victrola Book of the Opera, with opera after opera in synopsis, with portraits in costume of Melba, Caruso, Galli-Curci, and Geraldine Farrar, some of whose voices we could listen to on our Red Seal records.

My mother read secondarily for information; she sank as a hedonist into novels. She read Dickens in the spirit in which she would have eloped with him. The novels of her girlhood that had stayed on in her imagination, besides those of Dickens and Scott and Robert Louis Stevenson, were *Jane Eyre, Trilby, The Woman in White, Green Mansions, King Solomon's Mines.* Marie Corelli's name would crop up but I understood she had gone out of favor with my mother, who had only kept *Ardath* out of loyalty. In time she absorbed herself in Galsworthy, Edith Wharton, above all in Thomas Mann of the *Joseph* volumes.

St. Elmo was not in our house; I saw it often in other houses. This wildly popular Southern novel is where all the Edna Earles in our population started coming from. They're all named for the heroine, who succeeded in bringing a dissolute, sinning roué and atheist of a lover (St. Elmo) to his knees. My mother was able to forgo it. But she remembered the classic advice given to rose growers on how to water their bushes long enough: "Take a chair and *St. Elmo.*"

To both my parents I owe my early acquaintance with a beloved Mark Twain. There was a full set of Mark Twain and a short set of Ring Lardner in our bookcase, and those were the volumes that in time united us all, parents and children.

Reading everything that stood before me was how I came upon a worn old book without a back that had belonged to my father as a child. It was called *Sanford and Merton.* Is there anyone left who recognizes it, I wonder? It is the famous moral tale written by Thomas Day in the 1780s, but of him no mention is made on the title page of *this* book; here it is *Sanford and Merton in Words of One Syllable* by Mary Godolphin. Here are the rich boy and the poor boy and Mr. Barlow, their teacher and interlocutor, in long discourses alternating with dramatic scenes—danger and rescue allotted to the rich and the poor respectively. It may have only words of one syllable, but one of them is "quoth." It ends with not one but two morals, both engraved on rings: "Do what you ought, come what may," and "If we would be great, we must first learn to be good."

This book was lacking its front cover, the back held on by strips of pasted paper, now turned golden, in several layers, and the pages stained, flecked, and tattered around the edges; its garish illustrations had come unattached but were preserved, laid in. I had the feeling even in my heedless childhood that this was the only book my father as a little boy had had of his own. He had held onto it, and might have gone to sleep on its coverless face: he had lost his mother when he was seven. My father had never made any mention to his own children of the book, but he had brought it along with him from Ohio to our house and shelved it in our bookcase.

My mother had brought from West Virginia that set of Dickens; those books looked sad, too—they had been through fire and water before I was born, she told me, and there they were, lined up—as I later realized, waiting for *me*.

I was presented, from as early as I can remember, with books of my own, which appeared on my birthday and Christmas morning. Indeed, my parents could not give me books enough. They must have sacrificed to give me on my sixth or seventh birthday—it was after I became a reader for myself—the ten-volume set of Our Wonder World. These were beautifully made, heavy books I would lie down with on the floor in front of the diningroom hearth, and more often than the rest volume 5, *Every Child's Story Book*, was under my eyes. There were the fairy tales—Grimm, Andersen, the English, the French, "Ali Baba and the Forty Thieves"; and there was Aesop and Reynard the Fox; there were the myths and legends, Robin Hood, King Arthur, and St. George and the Dragon, even the history of Joan of Arc; a whack of *Pilgrim's Progress* and a long piece of *Gulliver*. They all carried their classic illustrations. I located myself in these pages and could go straight to the stories and pictures I loved; very often "The Yellow Dwarf" was first choice, with Walter Crane's Yellow Dwarf in full color making his terrifying appearance flanked by turkeys. Now that volume is as worn and backless and hanging apart as my father's poor *Sanford and Merton*. The precious page with Edward Lear's "Jumblies" on it has been in danger of slipping out for all these years. One measure of my love for Our Wonder World was that for a long time I wondered if I would go through fire and water for it as my mother had done for Charles Dickens; and the only comfort was to think I could ask my mother to do it for me.

> Why was it important to Welty to own her own books?

I believe I'm the only child I know of who grew up with this treasure in the house. I used to ask others, "Did you have Our Wonder World?" I'd have to tell them The Book of Knowledge could not hold a candle to it.

I live in gratitude to my parents for initiating me—and as early as I begged for it, without keeping me waiting—into knowledge of the word, into reading and spelling, by way of the alphabet. They taught it to me at home in time for me to begin to read before starting to school. I believe the alphabet is no longer considered an essential piece of equipment for traveling through life. In my day it was the keystone to knowledge. You learned the alphabet as you learned to count to ten, as you learned "Now I lay me" and the Lord's Prayer and your father's and mother's name and address and telephone number, all in case you were lost.

My love for the alphabet, which endures, grew out of reciting it but, before that, out of seeing the letters on the page. In my own story books, before I could read them for myself, I fell in love with various winding, enchanted-looking initials drawn by Walter Crane at the heads of fairy tales. In "Once upon a time," an "O" had a rabbit running it as a treadmill, his feet upon flowers. When the day came, years later, for me to see the Book of Kells, all the wizardry of letter, initial, and word swept over me a thousand times over, and the illumination, the gold, seemed a part of the word's beauty and holiness that had been there from the start.

Learning stamps you with its moments. Childhood's learning is made up of moments. It isn't steady. It's a pulse.

In a children's art class, we sat in a ring on kindergarten chairs and drew three daffodils that had just been picked out of the yard; and while I was drawing, my sharpened yellow pencil and the cup of the yellow daffodil gave off whiffs just alike. That the pencil doing the drawing should give off the same smell as the flower it drew seemed part of the art lesson—as shouldn't it be? Children, like animals, use all their senses to discover the world. Then artists come along and discover it the same way, all over again. Here and there, it's the same world. Or now and then we'll hear from an artist who's never lost it.

> How does Welty connect her home learning and school learning?

In my sensory education I include my physical awareness of the *word*. Of a certain word, that is; the connection it has with what it stands for. At around age six, perhaps, I was standing by myself in our front yard waiting for supper, just at that hour in a late summer day when the sun is already below the horizon and the risen full moon in the visible sky stops being chalky and begins to take on light. There comes the moment, and I saw it then, when the moon goes from flat to round. For the first time it met my eyes as a globe. The word "moon" came into my mouth as though fed to me out of a silver spoon. Held in my mouth the moon became a word. It had the roundness of a Concord grape Grandpa took off his vine and gave me to suck out of its skin and swallow whole, in Ohio.

This love did not prevent me from living for years in foolish error about the moon. The new moon just appearing in the west was the rising moon to me. The new should be rising. And in early childhood the sun and moon, those opposite reigning powers, I just as easily assumed rose in east and west respectively in their opposite sides of the sky, and like partners in a reel they advanced, sun from the east, moon from the west, crossed over (when I wasn't looking) and went down on the other side. My father couldn't have known I believed that when, bending behind me and guiding my shoulder, he positioned me at our telescope in the front yard and, with careful adjustment of the focus, brought the moon close to me.

The night sky over my childhood Jackson was velvety black. I could see the full constellations in it and call their names; when I could read, I knew their myths. Though I was always waked for eclipses, and indeed carried to the window as an infant in arms and shown Halley's Comet in my sleep, and though I'd been taught at our diningroom table about the solar system and knew the earth revolved around the sun, and our moon around us, I never found out the moon didn't come up in the west until I was a writer and Herschel Brickell, the literary critic, told me after I misplaced it in a story. He said valuable words to me about my new profession: "Always be sure you get your moon in the right part of the sky."

> Why do you think Welty tells us that her mother sang to her?

My mother always sang to her children. Her voice came out just a little bit in the minor key. "Wee Willie Winkie's" song was wonderfully sad when she sang the lullabies.

"Oh, but now there's a record. She could have her own record to listen to," my father would have said. For there came a Victrola record of "Bobby Shafftoe" and "Rock-a-Bye Baby," all of Mother's lullabies, which could be played to take her place. Soon I was able to play her my own lullabies all day long.

Our Victrola stood in the diningroom. I was allowed to climb onto the seat of a diningroom chair to wind it, start the record turning, and set the needle playing. In a second I'd jumped to the floor, to spin or march around the table as the music called for—now there were all the other records I could play too. I skinned back onto the chair just in time to lift the needle at the end, stop the record and turn it over, then change the needle. That brass receptacle with a hole in the lid gave off a metallic smell like human sweat, from all the hot needles that were fed it. Winding up, dancing, being cocked to start and stop the record, was of course all in one the act of *listening*—to "Overture to *Daughter of the Regiment*," "Selections from *The Fortune Teller*," "Kiss Me Again," "Gypsy Dance from *Carmen*," "Stars and Stripes Forever," "When the Midnight Choo-Choo Leaves for Alabam," or whatever came next. Movement must be at the very heart of listening.

Ever since I was first read to, then started reading to myself, there has never been a line read that I didn't *hear*. As my eyes followed the sentence, a voice was saying it silently to me. It isn't my mother's voice, or the voice of any person I can identify, certainly not my own.

It is human, but inward, and it is inwardly that I listen to it. It is to me the voice of the story or the poem itself. The cadence, whatever it is that asks you to believe, the feeling that resides in the printed word, reaches me through the reader-voice. I have supposed, but never found out, that this is the case with all readers—to read as listeners—and with all writers, to write as listeners. It may be part of the desire to write. The sound of what falls on the page begins the process of testing it for truth, for me. Whether I am right to trust so far I don't know. By now I don't know whether I could do either one, reading or writing, without the other.

My own words, when I am at work on a story, I hear too as they go, in the same voice that I hear when I read in books. When I write and the sound of it comes back to my ears, then I act to make my changes. I have always trusted this voice.

> *Sometimes I just copied passages from texts into my journal, but they were the phrases that were important to me and made me think.*
>
> —Kathy Finley

Final Reflection

Have you ever read a book the way Welty describes?

❖ *After You Read, Consider*

1. How did being read to as a child inspire Welty to write?

2. Why are books and reading important to a child's imagination?

3. What different purposes for reading does Welty describe?

❖ *Suggestions for Writing*

1. Write an essay about an experience you recall from childhood in which you felt that your imagination was opening up through reading a particular book.

2. Discuss a writer whose work has had an influence on your sense of self and values.

3. Welty writes how books and reading made her family close to each other, but have you ever found that what you learned from reading separated you from the people and community around you? What were you reading? How did you integrate your new knowledge into your daily life and way of thinking? Write about the experience.

Collaborative Assignments for Home Literacy

After forming groups of three or four students, consider the cultural history that has been handed down to each of you through some activity or hobby that your family is involved with (i.e. cooking, woodworking, participating in sports). Individually or as a group trace the roots of the involvement, and present the information to the entire class in a poster presentation format.

1. As a group, visit a local nursing or assisted care home several times. Collect stories of the residents. Find a consistent theme within the stories (i.e. going to war, dating, jobs, or education) and share both the themes and versions of the stories with your class.
2. As individuals, make a list of the reading materials available in each of your homes. As a group, meet and share the lists compiled and discuss how reading and writing are valued in your homes. Then establish a plan to enhance reading and writing activities in the home of each group member. Present your plans to the other members of the class.
3. As a group, create a list of want-to-read books. Select one or two novels or works of nonfiction as a focus. Have individual members of the group choose one of the works to read at home. In addition, have each member keep a journal of reflections, recollections, or questions about the reading. As the reading progresses, share and discuss your journal entries with group members who are reading the same work. Then as a group, prepare book reviews for your class and for members of your family.
4. Collect family stories. After each individual collects the stories, have the group analyze the stories to discover common threads among the different families represented; then, prepare a written paper that shares what you found.
5. Research rites of passage or celebratory events in several cultures. As a group, design a pamphlet that incorporates illustrations and narratives that your group found through their investigation and distribute to local high schools and libraires.
6. As a group, script a one-act play or scene that involves a family conflict, a family conversation, or a family celebration. After writing the play, rehearse and present the program to the class. This performance could be presented as a reader's theater or a stage production.
7. Have individual members of the group interview their own family about the importance of life-long learning. Compare and

contrast the results of the interview with members of your group. Based on the information, consider ways to enhance the importance of lifelong learning in your individual families and share the information with class members.
8. Have the group divide into pairs. Visit several different home settings in your community (i.e. foster homes, group homes, college dormitories, or long-term care facilities). After considering the needs in several of the home settings, create a program that has the potential of meeting some of the needs that are currently going unmet. As you design the program, consider possible sources for funding (if needed) as well and incorporate suggestions for obtaining the necessary funding in your final program proposal.
9. As a group, create a list of recommended reading or writing activities for the parents and children in various age groups including preschool, K–3, elementary, middle, or high school. Distribute the pamphlet throughout the community.
10. Create a calendar of reading and writing events throughout your community that includes library reading circles, puppet shows, book store readings, poetry slams, play productions etc. Also include information on special discount rates for children or families who attend these events. Distribute the calendar throughout your community.
11. Conduct a panel discussion on the various roles that families play in the success of traditional and return-to-school students.
12. Create a series of ads designed to increase community awareness of education opportunities for return-to-school students. Include services and programs available to the students with young children or those who are homebound as well as funding sources for the potential student population.

Alternative Literacy

Surface is the great revealer. Both poetry and painting have surface, but with poetry the location of surface is harder to pin down.

—Bill Berkson

OTHER LITERACIES

The real voyage of discovery consists not in seeking new landscapes but in having new eyes.

—Marcel Proust

Now we have come to the end. We've read how school, work, and home shape our knowing. *What else is there* might be one question that comes to mind. The world, our world, is much more than those first sections we have read and talked about. It is everything we see, whether we attend to what passes before our eyes or not. And so in this section, we are going to read, respond, reflect, and discuss other ways we experience life, other ways we come to know.

Over the past fourteen years, I have learned through a variety of experiences. The person who taught me to see with "new eyes" became my husband. Just before Bill and I married, a good friend invited me out for coffee and conversation. Our afternoon talk went something like this: "Peg, you have your degree; he's a high school dropout. You're making a terrible mistake. Don't settle for this. In a few years you'll be wondering what you ever had in common with a man who doesn't see life in the same way you do."

I thought about her warning for just a moment and then responded, "I like to watch him work on cars; I like to watch the way the cold, steel wrenches warm and come to life with his twistings and turnings of the engine's nuts and bolts. I like to hear the audible clicking of his mind when he hears a noise that should not be, to watch his eyes focus on horizons I cannot fathom while he tries to figure out why something doesn't respond the way he expects it will. You think that we are different because I have a formal education, and he doesn't. You're right, we are different. He knows how to use his knowledge, his skill to create something out of nothing. I know how to analyze poetry, a kind of creating nothing from something."

My friend stopped trying to convince me after that, and I am still married to Bill, perhaps in part because I still enjoy watching my husband find method in chaos; his is a creative genius that sees gaskets in cardboard boxes, fuel filters in pen parts, and rolling stages in flatbed trailers.

I have come to know the world better because I have started reviewing what has always been in front of me. I have "relived" experiences with my husband and through him. One of those occasions presented itself just after we met when I invited him to attend a play for which I had tickets. Prior to asking him, I considered my choice of productions carefully and picked *Harvey*.

He agreed with just one condition, "Okay, I'll go, but don't tell anyone I did." After the performance, he was boasting to all his friends that "plays are about real people—drunks whose best friends are invisible white rabbits." Since that first play, Bill and I have seen many productions, and for the most part, he's enjoyed them as much as I have. And I've attended car races, with the noisy engines roaring and smoking, with the fiberglass bodies chasing each other around dirt-packed circles while splattering mud on captivated audiences who stand for each corner turn, pass around, or through that occurs during the course of the lap.

And I have learned of peace from warm summer days as I walked the river flipping flies close to shaded river banks and of excitement when the line tugs with more than the movement of the current. And we have both learned from the majestic elk who stared down from our mountain top, daring us to climb even one step higher. And, if we are very lucky, we might finish out our days looking at this old world with new eyes.

In section 4, we offer opportunities to "review" what has always been. In Lillian Hellman's "Turtle," readers learn how great the will to live can be through the death of a snapping turtle. In "The Whole Pot," a chapter from *María: The Potter of San Ildefonso*, Alice Marriott records the first efforts of María and Julián Martinez in 1908 to reproduce the kind of pottery that anthropologists working in New Mexico had unearthed in the form of shards or broken clay pieces. "Graffiti: Tunnel Notes of a New Yorker," written by Leonard Kriegel, gives a close-up view of what the color-filled designs on the sides of buildings and walls of cities tell us about the artists and the lives they lead. Timothy Guidera checks out sports in "Bowl's Eye View." Jane Martin-Brown experiences a sense of isolation from her family and fiancé as she evaluates what she and others read and choose to do with their lives. In a scene from Rita Nachtmann's play *Pee Wee and the Wheelman*, Liza and Ruben are drawn together as each discloses an individual talent that has gone unrecognized or been hidden from Pee Wee, the man they both serve. For Liza, her art lies in her approach to studying; for Ruben, his gift is composing music.

Mary Sterner Lawson's pen and ink drawing entitled "Reading Faces" illustrates yet another way we come to know: the facial expressions from those with whom we come in contact. The work in oils "I Am What I Am" by Libby Bailey asks the viewers to consider how often individuals are judged by what they wear rather than who they are, and we are left to consider how much we lose in the judging.

"The Bracelet," a multigenre piece by Nancy Hemingway, focuses on how our discoveries of even a simple piece of jewelry can continue to impact us throughout our lives. And Dorothy Allison writes, in *Bastard Out of Carolina*, of how little is known when individuals are lumped into larger groups where labels replace names. In a chapter from bell hooks's novel, *Bone Black*, a young girl discovers the futility of having knowledge without having power. And finally, in Fernando La Rosa's photograph, "The Man," viewers are faced with the idea that no matter how far we have traveled, no matter how much we have learned, we still are not finished with the journey.

Lillian Hellman

Turtle

Lillian Hellman established herself as one of America's leading dramatists with The Children's Hour *(1934),* The Little Foxes *(1939), and* Watch on the Rhine *(1941). Hellman was active in anti-fascist work during the Spanish civil war and World War II, and was blacklisted for her left-wing politics during the McCarthy era. In* Pentimento *(1973), in which "Turtle" appears, she provides portraits of several family friends, of the friend she called "Julia," who worked against fascism in the European resistance, and of her numerous literary acquaintances.*

--- ❖ ---

Prereading Reflection

Write about your relationship to the natural world.

--- ❖ ---

I had awakened at five and decided to fish for a few hours. I rowed the dinghy out to the boat on that lovely foggy morning and then headed around my side of Martha's Vineyard into the heavy waters of West Chop. Up toward Lake Tashmoo I found the quiet rip where the flounders had been running, put out two lines, and made myself some coffee. I am always child-happy when I am alone in a boat, no other boat to be seen until the light breaks through. In an hour I had caught nine flounders and a couple of tautogs that Helen would like for chowder and decided to swim before going home to work. The boat had drifted out, down toward the heavy chop, but there was nothing new in this, and I was never careless: I tied my two-pound stone to a long rope, carried it down the boat ladder with me, and took it out to where I would swim near it. I don't know how long it took me to know that I wasn't swimming but was moving with incredible swiftness, carried by a tide I had never seen before. The boat had, of course, moved with me, but the high offshore wind was carrying it out of the rip into deep water. There was no decision to make: I could not swim to the boat, I could not force myself against the heavy tide. I have very little knowledge of the next period of time except that I turned on my back and

249

knew that panic was not always as it has been described. For a time I was rigid, my face washed with water; then I wasn't rigid and I tried to see where the tide would take me. But when I turned to raise my head, I went down, and when I came up again I didn't care that I couldn't see the shore, thinking that water had been with me, all my life, and this wasn't a bad way to die if only I had sense enough to go quietly and not make myself miserable with struggle. And then—I do not know when—I bumped my head against the pilings of the West Chop pier, threw my arms around a post, and remembered all three of us, and the conversation that took place four days after the turtle died when I said to Hammett, "You understood each other. He was a survivor and so are you. But what about me?"

> Why might Hellman be recalling this conversation?

He hadn't answered and so I repeated the question that night. "I don't know," he said, "maybe you are, maybe not. What good is my opinion?"

Holding to the piling, I was having a conversation with a man who had been dead five years about a turtle who had been dead for twenty-six.

Even in those days, 1940, it was one of the last large places in that part of Westchester County. I had seen it on a Tuesday, bought it on Thursday with royalties from *The Little Foxes*, knowing and not caring that I didn't have enough money left to buy food for a week. It was called an estate, but the house was so disproportionately modest compared to the great formal nineteenth-century gardens that one was immediately interested in the family who had owned it for a hundred and twenty years but who had, according to the agent, disappeared. (This was not true: eight or nine years later a young man of about sixteen or seventeen came by and asked if he could see the house and picnic at the lake. He said he had been born in the house and he took with him a giant branch of the hawthorn tree he said his mother had planted to celebrate his birth.)

> This "estate" is important to Hellman. Does the fact that she links it to the dramatic opening event cause you, as a reader, to recognize its importance as a setting for her story?

In the first weeks, I closed the two guesthouses, decided to forget about the boxwood and rare plants and bridle paths, and as soon as Hammett sold two short stories we painted the house, made a room for me to work in, and fixed up the barn. I wanted to use the land and would not listen to those who warned me against the caked, rock-filled soil. I hired Fred Herrmann, a young German farmer, because I had an immediate instinct that his nature was close to mine, and together, through the years, we drove ourselves to the ends of weariness by work that began at six in the morning and ended at night. Many of our plans failed, but some of them worked fine: we raised and sold poodles, very fashionable then, until we had enough profit to buy chickens; I took the money I got from the movie script of *The Little Foxes* and bought cattle and three thousand plants of asparagus we bleached white and sold at great prices. We cross-bred ducks that nobody liked but me, stocked the lake with bass and pickerel, raised good pigs and made good money with them and lost that money on pheasants; made some of it back with the first giant tomatoes, the sale of young lambs and rich unpasteurized milk. But all that was in the good years before the place had to be sold because Hammett went to jail in the McCarthy period and I was banned in Hollywood after I was called before the House Un-American Activities Committee. The time of doing what I liked was over in 1952.

I have a jungle of memories about those days: things learned and forgotten, or half remembered, which is worse than forgetting. It seems to me I once knew a lot about trees, birds, wildflowers, vegetables and some animals; about how to make butter and cheese and sausage; how to get the muddy taste out of large-mouth bass, how to make people sick with the weeds I would dig and boil up according to all those books that say you can. The elegant Gerald and Sara Murphy grew very ill on skunk cabbage I had disguised according to an eighteenth-century recipe.

But the day I remember best was in the first spring I owned the place. The snow had gone on the bridle paths and, having finished with the morning's work at the barns, I took Salud, the large poodle, and four of his puppies on an early morning walk to the lake. As we reached the heavily wooded small hill opposite the lake, Salud stopped, wheeled sharply, ran into the woods, and then slowly backed down to the road. The puppies and I went past him to the lake and I whistled for him, sure that he had been attracted by a woodchuck. But when I looked back he was immobile on the road, as if he had taken a deep breath and had not let it out. I called to him but he did not move. I called again in a command tone that he had never before disobeyed. He made an obedient movement of his head and front legs, stared at me, and turned back. I had never seen a dog stand paralyzed and, as I went back toward him, I remembered old tales of snakes and the spell they cast. I stopped to pick up a heavy stick and a rock, frightened of seeing the snake. As I heard Salud make a strange bark, I threw the rock over his head and into the woods, yelling at him to follow me. As the rock hit the ground, there was a heavy movement straight in front of the dog. Sure now that it was a snake about to strike, I ran toward Salud, grabbed his collar, and stumbled with the weight of him.

How would you categorize Hellman's first encounter with the turtle?

He pulled away from me and moved slowly toward the sound. As I picked myself up, I saw a large, possibly three-foot round shell move past him and go slowly toward the water. It was a large turtle. Salud moved with caution behind the turtle and as I stood, amazed at the picture of the dog and the slowly moving shell, the dog jumped in front of the turtle, threw out a paw, and the jaws of the turtle clamped down on the leg. Salud was silent, then he reared back and a howl of pain came from him that was like nothing I had ever heard before. I don't know how long it took me to act, but I came down hard with my stick on the turtle's tail, and he was gone into the water. Salud's leg was a mess but he was too big for me to carry, so I ran back to the house for Fred and together we carried him to a vet. A week later, he was well enough to limp for the rest of his life.

Have you ever been afraid of an animal? Why?

Hammett was in California for a few weeks and so I went alone almost every day to the lake in an attempt to see the turtle again, remembering that when I was a child in New Orleans I had gone each Saturday with my aunt to the French market to buy supplies for her boardinghouse. There had been two butchers in the market who had no thumbs, the thumbs having been taken off as they handled snapping turtles.

Hammett came back to the farm upset and angry to find his favorite dog was crippled. He said he had always known there were snappers in the lake, and snakes as well, but now he thought we ought to do something, and so he began his usual thorough research. The next few weeks brought books and government publications on how to trap turtles and strange packages began to arrive: large wire-mesh cages, meant for something else but stared at for days until Hammett decided how to alter them; giant fishhooks; extra heavy, finely made rope; and a book on tying knots. We both read about the origin of snapping turtles, but it didn't seem to me the accounts said very much: a guess that they were the oldest living species that had remained unchanged, that their jaws were powerful and of great danger to an enemy, that they could do nothing if turned on their backs, and the explanation of why my turtle had come out of the woods—each spring the female laid eggs on land, sat on them each day, and took the chance that the hatched babies would find their way to water.

What do you think about the way Hammett solves problems?

One day, a month later perhaps—there was never any hurrying Hammett when he had made up his mind to learn about something—we went to the lake carrying the wire cages, the giant fishhooks, fish heads and smelly pieces of meat that he had put in the sun a few days before. I grew bored, as I often did, with the slow precision which was part of Dash's doing anything, and walked along the banks of the lake as he tied the bait inside the traps, baited the hooks, and rowed out with them to find heavy overhanging branches to attach them to.

He had finished with one side of the lake, and had rowed himself beyond my view to the south side, when I decided on a swim. As I swam slowly toward the raft, I saw that one limb of a sassafras tree was swinging wildly over the water, some distance from me. Sitting on the raft, I watched it until I saw that the movement was caused by the guyline that held one of the hooks Hammett had tied to the branch. I shouted at Hammett that he had caught a turtle and he called back that couldn't be true so fast, and I called back that he was to come for me quick because I was frightened and not to argue.

As he came around the bend of the lake, he grinned at me.

"Drunk this early?"

I pointed to the swinging branch. He forgot about me and rowed over very fast. I saw him haul at the line, have trouble lifting it, stand up in the boat, haul again, and then slowly drop the line. He rowed back to the raft.

"It's a turtle all right. Get in. I need help."

I took the oars as he stood up to take the line from the tree. The line was so heavy that as he moved to attach it to the stern of the rowboat he toppled backward. I put an oar into the center of his back.

He stared at me, rubbing his back. "Remind me," he said and tied the line to the stern. Then he took the oars from me.

"Remind you of what?"

Why doesn't Hammett want her to save him?

"Never to save me. I've been meaning to tell you for a long time."

When we beached the boat, he detached the rope and began to pull the rope on land. A turtle, larger than the one I had seen with Salud, was hauled up and I jumped back as the head came shooting out. Dash leaned down, grabbed the tail, and threw the turtle on its back.

"The hook is in fine. It'll hold. Go back and get the car for me."

I said, "I don't like to leave you alone, you shouldn't be handling that thing—"

"Go on," he said. "A turtle isn't a woman. I'll be safe."

We took the turtle home tied to the back bumper, dragging it through the dirt of the mile to the house. Dash went to the toolhouse for an axe, came back with it and a long heavy stick. He turned the turtle on its stomach, handed me the stick, and said, "Stand far back, hold the stick out, and wait until he snaps at it."

I did that, the turtle did snap, and the axe came down. But Dash missed because the turtle, seeing his arm, quickly withdrew his head. We tried five or six times. It was a hot day and that's why I thought I was sweating and, anyway, I never was comfortable with Hammett when he was doing something that didn't work.

He said. "Try once more."

I put the stick out, the turtle didn't take it, then did, and as he did, I moved my hand down the stick thinking that I could hold it better. The turtle dropped the stick and made the fastest move I had ever seen for my hand. I jumped back and the stick bruised my leg. Hammett put down the axe, took the stick from me, shook his head and said, "Go lie down."

I said I wasn't going to and he said I was to go somewhere and get out of his way. I said I wasn't going to do that either, that he was in a bad temper with me only because he couldn't kill the turtle with the axe.

"I am going to shoot it. But that's not my reason for bad temper. We've got some talking to do, you and I, it's been a long time."

"Talk now."

"No. I'm busy. I want you out of the way."

He took my arm, moved me to the kitchen steps, pushed me down and went into the house for a rifle. When he came out he put a piece of meat in front of the turtle's head and got behind it. We waited for a long time. Finally, the head did come out to stare at the meat and Hammett's gun went off. The shot was a beauty, just slightly behind the eyes. As I ran toward them the turtle's head convulsed in a forward movement, the feet carried the shell forward in a kind of heavy leap. I leaned down close and Hammett said, "Don't go too near. He isn't dead."

Then he picked up the axe and came down very hard on the neck, severing the head to the skin.

"That's odd," he said. "The shot didn't kill it, and yet it went through the brain. Very odd."

He grabbed the turtle by the tail and carried it up the long flight of steps to the kitchen. We found some newspapers and put the turtle on top of the coal stove that wasn't used much anymore except in the sausage-making season.

I said, "Now we'll have to learn about cutting it for soup."

Dash nodded. "O.K. But it's a long job. Let's wait until tomorrow."

I left a note under Helen's door—it was her day off and she had gone to New York—warning her there was a turtle sitting on the stove and not to be frightened. Then I telephoned my Aunt Jenny in New Orleans to get the recipe for the good soup of my childhood and she said I was to stay away from live turtles and go back to fine embroidery like a nice lady.

The next morning, coming down at six to help Fred milk the cows, I forgot about the turtle until I started down the kitchen steps and saw blood. Then, thinking it was the blood that we had spilled carrying the turtle into the house the evening before, I went on toward the barns. When I came back at eight, Helen asked me what I wanted for breakfast, she had made corn bread, and what had I meant by a turtle on the stove?

Going up to have a bath, I called back, "Just what I said. It's a turtle on the stove and you must know about snappers from your childhood."

After a few minutes she came upstairs to stare at me in the bathtub. "There ain't no turtle. But there's a mess of blood."

"On top of the coal stove," I said. "Just go have a look."

"I had a lot of looks. There ain't no turtle on top a stove in this house."

"Go wake Mr. Hammett," I said, "right away."

"I wouldn't like to do that," she said. "I don't like to wake men."

I went running down to the kitchen, and then fast back upstairs to Hammett's room, and shook him hard.

"Get up right away. The turtle's gone."

He turned over to stare at me. "You drink too much in the morning."

I said, *"The turtle's gone."*

He came down to the kitchen in a few minutes, stared at the stove, and turned to Helen. "Did you clean the floor?"

"Yes," she said, "it was all nasty. Look at the steps."

He stared at the steps that led to the cellar and out to the lawn. Then he moved slowly down the steps, following the path of blood spots, and out into the orchard. Near the orchard, planted many years before I owned the house, was a large rock garden, over half an acre of rare trees and plants, rising steep above the house entrance. Hammett turned toward it, following a path around the orchard. He said, "Once, when I worked for Pinkerton, I found a stolen ferris wheel for a traveling country fair. Then I lost the ferris wheel and, as far as I know, nobody ever found it again."

> Why do they believe someone stole the turtle?

I said, "A turtle is not a ferris wheel. Somebody took the turtle."

"Who?"

"I don't know. Got a theory?"

"The turtle moved himself."

"I don't like what you're saying. He was dead last night. Stone dead."

"Look," he said.

He was pointing into the rock garden. Salud and three poodle puppies were sitting on a large rock, staring at something in a bush. We ran toward the garden. Hammett told the puppies to go away and parted the branches of the bush. The turtle sidling in an effort at movement, was trying to leave the bush, its head dangling from one piece of neck skin.

"My God," we both said at the same time and stood watching the turtle for the very long time it took to move a foot away from us. Then it stopped and its back legs stiffened. Salud, quiet until now, immediately leaped on it and his two puppies, yapping, leaped after him. Salud licked the blood from the head and the turtle moved his front legs. I grabbed Salud's collar and threw him too hard against a rock.

> Why is it important to Hellman that the turtle is dead? To Hammett?

Hammett said, "The turtle can't bite him now. He's dead."

I said, "How do you know?"

He picked up the turtle by the tail.

"What are you going to do?"

"Take it back to the kitchen."

I said, "Let's take it to the lake. It's earned its life."

"It's dead. It's been dead since yesterday."

"No. Or maybe it was dead and now it isn't."

> What are they arguing about?

"The resurrection? You're a hard woman for an ex-Catholic," he said, moving off.

I was behind him as he came into the kitchen, threw the turtle on a marble slab. I heard Helen say, "My goodness, the good Lord help us all."

Hammett took down one of the butcher knives. He moved his lips as if rehearsing what he had read. Then he separated the leg meat from the shell, cutting expertly around the joints. The other leg moved as the knife went in.

> Why does Hellman think this animal is different than the other farm animals they eat?

Helen went out of the kitchen and I said, "You know very well that I help with the butchering of the animals here and don't like talk about how distasteful killing is by people who are willing to eat what is killed for them. But this is different. This is something else. We shouldn't touch it. It has earned its life."

He put down the knife. "O.K. Whatever you want."

We both went into the living room and he picked up a book. After an hour I said, "Then how does one define life?"

He said, "Lilly, I'm too old for that stuff."

Toward afternoon I telephoned the New York Zoological Society of which I was a member. I had a hard time being transferred to somebody who knew about turtles. When I finished, the young voice said, "Yes, the *Chelydra serpentina*. A ferocious foe. Where did you meet it?"

"Meet it?"

"Encounter it."

"At a literary cocktail party by a lake."

He coughed. "On land or water? Particularly ferocious when encountered on land. Bites with such speed that the naked human eye often cannot follow the movement. The limbs are powerful and a narrow projection from each side connects them to the carapace—"

"Yes," I said. "You are reading from the same book I read. I want to know how it managed to get down a staircase and up into a garden with its head hanging only by a piece of skin."

"An average snapper weighs between twenty and thirty pounds, but many have weighed twice that amount. The eggs are very interesting, hard of shell, often compared with ping-pong balls—"

"Please tell me what you think of, of, of its *life*."

After a while he said, "I don't understand."

"Is it, was it, alive when we found it in the garden? Is it alive now?"

"I don't know what you mean," he said.

"I'm asking about life. What is *life*?"

"I guess what comes before death. Please put its heart in a small amount of salted water and be kind enough to send us a note reporting how long the heart beats. Our records show ten hours."

"Then it isn't dead."

There was a pause. "In our sense."

"What is our sense?"

There was talk in the background noise and I heard him whisper to somebody. Then he said, "The snapping turtle is a very low, possibly the lowest, form of life."

I said, "*Is it alive or is it dead?* That's all I want to know, please."

There was more whispering. "You asked me for a scientific opinion, Miss Hellernan. I am not qualified to give you a theological one. Thank you for calling."

Ten or twelve years later, at the end of a dinner party, a large lady crossed the room to sit beside me. She said she was engaged in doing a book on Madame de Staël, and when I had finished with the sounds I have for what I don't know about she said, "My brother used to be a zoologist. You once called him about a snapping turtle." I said to give him my regards and apologies and she said, "Oh, that's not necessary. He practices in Calcutta."

But the day of the phone call I went to tell Hammett about my conversation. He listened, smiled when I came to the theological part, went back to reading an old book called *The Animal Kingdom*. My notation in the front of this book, picked up again on a July afternoon in 1972, is what brought me to this memory of the turtle.

Toward dinnertime, Helen came into the room and said, "That turtle. I can't cook with it sitting around me."

I said to Hammett, "What will we do?"

"Make soup."

"The next time. The next turtle. Let's bury this one."

"*You* bury it."

"You're punishing me," I said. "Why?"

"I'm trying to understand you."

"It's that it moved so far. It's that I've never before thought about *life,* if you know what I mean."

"No, I don't," he said.

"Well, what is life and stuff like that."

"Stuff like that. At your age."

I said, "You are much older than I am."

"That still makes you thirty-four and too old for stuff like that."

"You're making fun of me."

"Cut it out, Lilly. I know all the signs."

"Signs of what?"

He got up and left the room. I carried up a martini an hour later and said, "Just this turtle, the next I'll be O.K."

"Fine with me," he said, "either way."

"No, it isn't fine with you. You're saying something else."

"I'm saying cut it out."

"And *I'm* saying—"

"I don't want any dinner," he said.

I left the room and slammed the door. At dinnertime I sent Helen up to tell him to come down immediately and she came back and said he said he wasn't hungry immediately.

During dinner she said she didn't want the turtle around when she came down for breakfast.

About ten, when Helen had gone to bed, I went upstairs and threw a book against Hammett's door.

"Yes?" he said.

"Please come and help me bury the turtle."

"I don't bury turtles."

"Will you bury me?"

"When the times comes, I'll do my best," he said.

"Open the door."

"No. Get Fred Herrmann to help you bury the turtle. And borrow Helen's prayer book."

But by the time I had had three more drinks, it was too late to wake Fred. I went to look at the turtle and saw that its blood was dripping to the floor. For many years, and for many years to come, I had been frightened of Helen and so, toward midnight, I tied a rope around the turtle's tail, took a flashlight, dragged it down the kitchen steps to the garage, and tied the rope to the bumper of the car. Then I went back to stand under Hammett's window.

I shouted up. "I'm weak. I can't dig a hole big enough. Come help me."

After I had said it twice, he called down, "I wish I could help you, but I'm asleep."

I spent the next hour digging a hole on the high ground above the lake, and by the time I covered the turtle the whiskey in the bottle was gone and I was dizzy and feeling sick. I put a stick over the grave, drove the car back towards the house, and when I was halfway there evidently fell asleep because I woke up at dawn in a heavy rain with the right wheels of the car turned into a tree stump. I walked home to bed and neither Hammett nor I mentioned the turtle for four or five days. That was no accident because we didn't speak to each other for three of those days, eating our meals at separate times.

Then he came back from a late afternoon walk and said, "I've caught two turtles. What would you like to do with them?"

"Kill them. Make soup."

"You're sure?"

"The first of anything is hard," I said. "You know that."

"I didn't know that until I met you," he said.

"I hurt my back digging the grave and I've a cold, but I had to bury that turtle and I don't want to talk about it again."

"You didn't do it very well. Some animal's been at your grave and eaten the turtle, but God will bless you anyway. I gathered the bones, put them back in the hole, and painted a tombstone sign for you.

For all the years we lived on the place, and maybe even now, there was a small wooden sign, neatly painted: "My first turtle is buried here. Miss Religious L.H."

Final Reflection

Why couldn't Hellman eat the turtle after it was dead?

❖ *After You Read, Consider*

1. What did Hellman mean when she told Hammett he and the turtle were survivors? Why couldn't Hammett answer her question about whether she was a survivor?

2. Why does the turtle become so important to Hellman?

3. Hammett and Hellman seem to have a contest of wills over the turtle. What does Hammett want her to learn? What does Hellman want him to understand?

Writing in class gave me a chance to consider things I'd never thought of before.
—Margaret Austen

❖ Suggestions for Writing

1. Reread back over those parts of the story that illustrate Hellman's changing reaction to the turtle. Why do you think she found the turtle so difficult to kill? Why did she think it had earned its life? What was so important about her phone conversation with the naturalist at the New York Zoological Society? Why did Hellman feel it was necessary to bury the turtle? Write an essay in which you explore Hellman's relationship with the turtle.

2. Narrate a story about your own encounter with an animal. What did you learn about nature from the encounter? What did you learn about yourself?

3. Research what happened to Hellman and Hammett during the McCarthy years. Report on what you find and then see if you can answer the initial question about whether Hellman is a survivor.

Alice Marriott

The Whole Pot

Alice Lee Marriott was born in Wilmette, Illinois, but has lived most of her life in Oklahoma. She earned a BA in English and French at Oklahoma City University in 1930, and another BA in anthropology at the University of Oklahoma in 1935. Since then, she has combined her work as an anthropologist and a writer. She has been a consultant to the Oklahoma Indian Council since 1962, has taught anthropology at the University of Oklahoma, and has been artist-in-residence at Central State University in Edmond, Oklahoma, since 1968. Her awards and honors include the University of Oklahoma Achievement Award and membership in both the Oklahoma Hall of Fame and the Oklahoma Literary Hall of Fame. Since 1945, Marriott has published more than two dozen books and innumerable essays and stories in periodicals.

❖

Prereading Reflection

Write about a time you enjoyed making something with your hands.

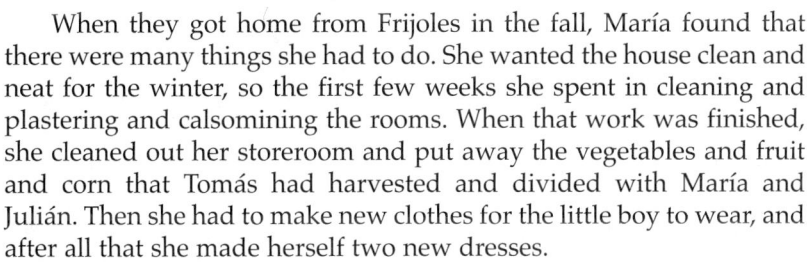

❖

When they got home from Frijoles in the fall, María found that there were many things she had to do. She wanted the house clean and neat for the winter, so the first few weeks she spent in cleaning and plastering and calsomining the rooms. When that work was finished, she cleaned out her storeroom and put away the vegetables and fruit and corn that Tomás had harvested and divided with María and Julián. Then she had to make new clothes for the little boy to wear, and after all that she made herself two new dresses.

All the time the old potsherd was in the back of her mind. She was thinking about it as much as she was about her other work. Every time that she was conscious of thinking about the pottery, she put the thought away. It was like fruit ripening on a tree. You could go out a few times in the season and look at it on the branches, but you could not do anything until the fruit was really ripe. María let the thought of the potsherd ripen slowly in her mind. When the time came and she and the thought had ripened, she would be ready to work.

Once or twice Julián spoke about the sherd to María. He asked her once where it was, and if she would mind letting him see and handle it. Another time he asked her when she was going to start making the pot.

"When the time comes," she told him.

"It's a long time coming," said Julián.

"I'll be ready for it," María answered, and that was all that either of them said.

Soon after that, the first boy was named in English. Julián wanted to name him Adam, and María asked if it were because Adam was the first man.

"No," Julián said, "it's for Adams, that worked on the job last summer. I like that Adams, and he's got a good name. I'd like to call my boy for him."

"Why don't you call him Adams?" Tomás asked when he heard this.

"Because everybody always forgets about that extra 's' anyway," said Julián. "If we call him Adam to start with, they won't have to forget."

So there was the first new man of the family. Somehow, when she looked at him now, María knew that she was never again going to have to worry about this child. He ate and slept, and when he waked, he laughed. He needed hardly any care.

So, one morning, María awoke with all her other jobs finished and was ready to begin on the pottery. After breakfast she got out the potsherd and sat down by the fire with the fragment in her hand. She sat and looked at the sherd for a long time. The clay was so thin and hard that she had to study the broken edge for a long while to find out whether anything had been mixed with the paste. She wished that she had a little glass that folded out of a case, like one the head man had, to make small things look larger. At last, by tipping the broken edge of the sherd towards the firelight, she caught a small, bright shine on one spot in the sherd. That was it, then. There was fine sand mixed with the clay.

> Why did María need to finish everything else before she could begin making the pot?

María went out to the storeroom and looked at her own supply of clay and sand carefully. She had good, fine clay, but no sand that was hard and small enough. She wrapped her shawl around her and went over to Tía Nicolasa's house, taking the piece of pottery with her.

When María showed her the sherd, Tía Nicolasa grew most excited.

"This is beautiful," she kept saying. "I never saw pottery like this before. It's very beautiful."

"The sand is so fine," said María. "I don't know where to get fine sand like that."

"The blue sand bed on the way to Española has fine sand in it," Tía Nicolasa answered. "Not everywhere, but in some places. That's where you should go to get your fine sand."

"I could sift it and get out the finest part," said María thoughtfully.

"That would be a good thing to do," Tía Nicolasa agreed. "You ought to do the same thing with the clay, too. Then that will be fine and hard and right."

Why is it important to have just the right sand and clay?

Since it was winter and most of the work in the fields was finished, Julián could take María to get the sand. The trip was not long; about two hours each way in the wagon was all. One day would do it. They left Adam with Desidéria, who promised to take good care of him. María packed *tortillas* and beans and milk for lunch, and she and Julián started out.

It was the first time they had been away from the pueblo and alone together since they had gone to St. Louis. At first María felt shy and almost as if she were traveling with someone she did not know well. Then Julián began to sing, drumming with his hand on the wagon seat beside him, and the horses started to trot uphill, and she was happy. It was a warm day for December, with lots of sun and a little wind that picked heavy thoughts from your heart and carried them away. Riding together and being together was good, and it seemed a short trip to the sand bed.

María remembered what Tía Nicolasa had told her.

"The finest sand is just in certain places," she told Julián.

"We'd better hunt for a place, then," he said.

They separated, and went back and forth across the surface of the sand dune, looking for the best place to dig. At last María called, "Here it is. I think this is a good place to start."

"All right," said Julián. "I can't seem to find anything special. It all just looks like sand to me."

He brought the shovel from the wagon and peered doubtfully down at the place where María was standing.

"It doesn't look much different from the rest," he said.

"It is, though," María insisted. "It's finer. I can feel it with my fingers. You can dig here."

How does María know that this is the place to dig?

"Well," said Julián, "all right."

He still looked doubtful.

María brought the two flour sacks she had packed in the wagon, and Julián began to dig up sand to fill them. María watched him closely, and when she thought he was getting near the coarser sand, she warned him about it.

"I still don't see any difference," Julián protested. "You must have good eyes to be able to tell."

"I'm watching," said María, and Julián laughed.

"You must be," he said, and finished filling the sacks, taking the sand only from the places where she told him to dig.

When they lifted the filled sacks into the wagon, though, they could both tell the difference in the sand. The sacks were heavier than they would usually be and little rings of sand sifted out through the cloth onto the floor of the wagon. These were good, new flour sacks that María had bought at the store for just this trip. There were no holes in the bags, but the sand came through the cloth as if they had been coarse bran sacks.

"That sand is the right kind," said María contentedly.

They rested and ate their lunch on the sunny side of the sand dune, where the wind could just touch the tops of their heads but not get down around their shoulders or blow sand at them to make them uncomfortable. When they had finished eating, they sat on, looking out across the valley to the river and to the rim of Pajarito Plateau beyond.

"This is good country," said Julián, and María agreed, "I never want to live anywhere else in all my life."

Julián laughed at her a little, nicely. "You won't," he said. "Pueblo Indians belong here. This is their country. They'd better like it, because it's all they have."

Going back to the pueblo, María thought about what Julián had just said. He was a man who liked to be going, to be seeing new places and meeting new people. He was a man who had a need for that in his life. She liked doing that herself; but if she knew that she would never go anywhere again, she could be happy still, with Julián and Adam and her father and mother.

Anyway, just this little trip was like going through new country, from the first time she remembered. Things had changed. There were houses where once there had been fields, and fields where once there had been marshlands along the river. Most of all, there were bare spots on the mountains, where there had once been dense, heavy coverings of big trees. That was the biggest change; it was because that change had taken place that the others had come about. Maybe if there were some way to stop the timber companies from cutting off the big trees, the other changes would stop of themselves. That would hold back time, so that they would all be young a long time together, and babies would be little and soft. Then she shook her head.

"What are you thinking about?" Julián asked.

"That maybe there might be a way to stop changes."

Why doesn't María want change?

"There isn't any way," said Julián. "That's the way things are. That's part of living."

"That's what I thought, too," María said.

They went along towards home then, and when they had almost reached the pueblo, Julián said, "I want to stop here. I need some of that yucca."

"To wash your hair? We have plenty for that at home. This kind doesn't make very good suds."

"To wash the pot's hair, said Julián, handing her the reins. He climbed down from the wagon, and went over to the yucca plant. It was one of the long, tall, spindly kind with leaves like narrow knives. Julián did not dig up the whole plant but just cut the main stem through above the root and brought the top of the plant back to the wagon.

"There," he said, "that ought to make me some good paint brushes."

The next morning María had Julián bring one of the new sacks of sand into the storeroom, where she could get at it easily. She thought for a while, as she washed the dishes, about how she was going to sift the sand. The flour sifter was the only real sifter that she had, and it was too coarse to use. Then she remembered how the sand had worked its way through the sacks, and she decided to use a cloth for a sifter. She stretched a piece of an old shirt over a bowl, and poured the sand on the cloth. Gently, she worked the sand back and forth with her fingers and watched the pile on the cloth grow smaller as she worked. The sand was sifting through, steadily and slowly.

After that, María started in to sift the clay. It was finer than the sand to begin with, so she began by sifting it through a piece of flour sack. She needed much more clay than sand and it went through the cloth very slowly, but by noon she had a pile in the bottom of a dishpan. She thought it would be enough. Julián came in for dinner, and found her cooking and smiling.

"What's the joke?" he asked her. He was a man who always loved jokes.

"I was remembering," María replied. "I was remembering when Desidéria and I were little girls and made ourselves toy dishes. Tía Nicolasa made us sift the clay and sand for them then. I wouldn't think anything about it any more, but then it was just as hard work as sifting these things was this morning."

What is the difference between play and work? Do you remember activities that felt like play but now seem like work?

"Well," said Julián, helping himself to the beans, "if you keep on making fine pottery, maybe you'll get so this won't be anything to think about, either."

"Maybe," said María, and sat down beside him to eat her own lunch.

After they had eaten, Julián got out his new clump of yucca. He sat and looked at it for quite a while. Then he cut off a piece about six inches long from one of the heaviest leaves. He trimmed the blade of the leaf back to the stem, so that all that was left was a narrow, three-sided little stick.

"It looks like the quill of a feather," Julián said, holding the stick out on the palm of his hand, and studying it.

"Miss Grimes told us once that the white people used to write letters with feather quills," said María. She was sitting on the opposite side of the fireplace, mixing sand and clay together, getting ready to add the water to them.

"Maybe they were smart," said Julián. "I'll have to try a feather quill for this some time." He put the yucca quill in his mouth, and began to chew its thicker end, so that bits of the hard, stiff part came away from the long fibres. When he had his mouth full of the scraps he looked at María suddenly, startled.

"Spit it in the fireplace," she said. "You can't go running to the door every time you get a mouthful. Next time you'd better do it outdoors, where you can spit as much as you like."

"Thanks," said Julián, when his mouth was empty and he could speak. "I'll remember about that," he went on. "This stuff doesn't have much taste, but it's puckery."

María brought some water and began to mix it with her clay and sand. The stuff was so fine that it made only a small ball in the bottom of the mixing pan, instead of the big pile she had expected.

"I can make just one pot this time," she said, looking at the mixture.

"That's all they want of this kind," said Julián. "They didn't tell you to go on making a lot of these pots. Just one was all."

"Well," said María, "I thought as long as we were at it we could make four or five. Then maybe they could sell the extra ones, the way they said."

"Maybe," said Julián. "I think we ought to wait and see how the first one turns out. Are you going to start now?"

"Not this afternoon," María answered. "Good clay is better if it rests overnight. I'll start in the morning, and then the pot will have all day to dry."

She went ahead with the work that she had to do in the house, while Julián sat and looked at the potsherd and tried to draw its designs on a clean board with his new brush. Finally he put the brush away and shook his head. "I can't make it come out right," he said. "Besides, how can I know what kind of design to make till I see the pot?"

> Why does Julián need to see the pot before he can make a design?

María started in shaping the pot the next morning. From the way that the sherd curved, she thought it must have come from a big bowl, although she could not be sure. Besides, she did not have enough fine clay ready to make a very big piece of pottery. She patted out a clay *tortilla* for the base, and then pinched off a small piece of the clay, punched it thoroughly to get out the air bubbles, and began rolling it between her hands to make the first coil.

The fine mixture rolled and worked more easily than any clay she ever remembered handling. She was surprised at how quickly she could build the bowl, and how thin she could make it. Before noon the shaping and polishing were finished, and she set the bowl on the kitchen table to dry. It was round and firm and lighter than any piece of pottery she had seen made in San Ildefonso.

When Julián came in, he stood and looked at the bowl for a long time. "Is it dry enough to paint?" he asked.

"I don't think so," María answered. "It ought to dry overnight, I believe."

"That's all right anyway," Julián said. "I've got to figure out what to paint it with."

"What did they use on the old pots?" María inquired.

"Jack said probably guaco," answered Julián. "He said they made a syrup out of guaco, like sugar syrup, and boiled it down till it got thick. Then when the pot was fired, the guaco burned and made a black design."

"We haven't got any guaco," María said.

"I guess I'll have to go out and look for some this afternoon," replied Julián.

"It's pretty late in the year to find any growing," María reminded him. "It all dries up in the fall."

"Well, I'll ask around," said Julián. "Maybe somebody will have some syrup made up to use for tea, or something."

When he came back late in the afternoon, he had a little jar in his hand.

"Where did you get it?" María demanded.

"Your Tía Nicolasa had it," Julián answered with a grin. "When you want to know anything about pottery, you go to your Tía Nicolasa. So did I. She said she made it up a long time ago, to decorate a storage jar. Then she put it away and forgot about it, so it dried out. She says if we grind the dry syrup up fine and boil it down again with lots of water, it will be just as good as ever."

"Well, we can try," said María. She put the hard little black cake that she found in the bottom of the jar on the fine *metate*, and ground it until it was a powder she could have sifted through a cloth like the clay. Then she put the powder, mixed with water, in a bowl by the fireplace, and let it cook slowly. There was a faint, plantlike smell all through the house in a little while and by bedtime they could smell nothing else.

While María ground and cooked the guaco, Julián sat by the fire. Sometimes he looked at the bowl, and sometimes he looked at the potsherd in his hand. He was studying them both together, one with the other, and he never moved or spoke until María gave him a bowl of *atole* for supper. Then he ate it, and said, "That was good. What was it?"

"Coffee," María told him.

"I'd like another cup, please," said Julián. This time she did give him coffee, and he drank it and never knew the difference. At bedtime he got up, stretched, and said, "It will fit," and they went to bed without another word.

The next morning Julián took his bowl of guaco and his yucca brush into the living room as soon as he had finished his outdoor work. Then he took the new bowl from the kitchen table. Last of all, he got the potsherd and set it beside the bowl on a stool. Then he sat down on the floor, with the pot of guaco beside him, dipped the brush into the paint, and went to work. María went away and left him. She wanted to sift some more sand and clay and get ready to begin another bowl.

When María went to call him to lunch, Julián had finished his part of the work. He was still sitting on the floor in front of the stool, and before him was the bowl, covered with fine gray lines. They made a pattern of a water snake, with square, even designs for the pueblo and the fields around it. María had never seen a bowl like this before.

"It's beautiful," she said, when she had looked and looked.

"It's all right," said Julián. "It came out all right. The lines matched."

"It looks as if the design grew on the bowl," María said.

"It's all right," Julián repeated. "I like it. I like this sort of work. It's like making saddles. You think what you're doing, and that makes your hands do it. It's good. Everything goes with you. Not like plowing, when everything can go against you."

María laughed. "You'd better be a potter," she said. "It's better to do something you like than something you don't like."

"Men aren't potters," said Julián, putting his brush down on the floor beside the pot of guaco, carelessly. "Is lunch ready?"

Final Reflection

Was it important to María that she have just the right kind of sand to mix with the clay? Are you this exacting when you make things? Why or why not?

❖ *After You Read, Consider*

1. Is creating art work? What is the same and different about this kind of labor?

2. Julián tells María, "Pueblo Indians belong here. This is their country. They'd better like it, because it's all they have." What does he mean?

3. Why does Julián say, "Men aren't potters"? Do men and women approach art differently?

❖ Suggestions for Writing

1. Write about a time when you created something special. Narrate the process with all the details, including conversations you had with and advice you got from others about what you were making. Then think about the pot that María makes. How many people are involved in the making of her pot? Is art always an individual vision?

2. Write about someone you know who "makes art." Using this person's work as an example, write about the difference between fine art and functional art and argue the merits of one over another. Should art include things that people only look at? Should art include things that are only useful?

Leonard Kriegel

Graffiti: Tunnel Notes of a New Yorker

Leonard Kriegel is an essayist and novelist who currently lives in New York City. He is the author of nonfiction: Working Through: A Teacher's Journey in the Urban University *(1986),* On Men and Manhood *(1989), and* Falling into Life *(1989). He has also published novels, including* Flying Solo: Reimagining Manhood, Courage, and Loss *(1998).*

I used my journal as space to re-define what I read and thought about, what I saw and heard every day, what others in class thought and said. It is probably a good thing that we didn't have to share our journals.

—Kristi McCollum

Prereading Reflection

How have you learned to define art? Where did you learn this definition? What do you think should be the purpose of art?

When I was eight, I loved to run with my friends through the tunnel leading into Reservoir Oval in the North Central Bronx. The Oval occupied the site of a former city reservoir dredged by the WPA and then landscaped with playgrounds, wading pools, softball fields, a quarter-mile dirt track, and some of the finest tennis courts in the city—all ringed by attractive bush-and-tree-lined walks that provided a natural shield for the sexual probings of early adolescence. Nothing else that bordered our neighborhood—not the wilds of Bronx Park or the chestnut trees of Van Cortlandt Park or the small camel-humped rock hill in Mosholu Parkway down which we went belly-whopping on American Flyer sleds in winter—fed us so incontrovertible a sense that America's promise now included us as did the long green and gray sweep of Reservoir Oval.

We would run through that entrance tunnel like a pack of Hollywood Indians on the warpath, our whoops echoing off the walls until we emerged from its shadows into the lush green lawns and brick walks and playing fields. Our portion of the Bronx was an ethnically mixed stew of immigrant families and their children, many of whom had fled Manhattan's crowded Lower East Side tenements for the spacious, park-rich green borough where Jonas Bronck had followed his cow across the Harlem River three hundred years earlier. The Bronx was still the city's "new" borough in 1941. Sparsely settled until after World War I, our neighborhood contained typical New York working- and lower-middle-class families on the rise in an America emerging from the Depression.

How does Kriegel's description of his childhood neighborhood affect you?

We children had already been assimilated into the wider American world. All of us—Irish and Italian Catholic as well as Eastern European Jew—believed we could ride the dream of success to a singular destiny. We were not yet of an age where we could physically journey into that wider America the books we read and the movies we saw told us was ours for the taking. The Oval was where we played together. It was also where we sometimes fought each other over myths that grew increasingly foreign and more raggedly European with each passing day. (Not that we were unaware of our parents' cultural baggage: marriage between Italian and Irish Catholics was still considered "mixed" in 1941.)

How innocent was Kriegel's childhood?

Occasionally, I would chance the Oval alone, in search of more solitary adventure. A curious metamorphosis would envelope me at such times: the entrance tunnel seemed darker and more threatening, the shadows warning me to move cautiously past walls peppered with graffiti. Alone, I let loose no war whoops to echo through that emptiness. Instead, I picked my way carefully through that dark half-moon of enclosed space, as if the graffiti scrawled on its surface held the clue to my future. There was something menacing about words scrawled on walls. Like an archaeologist probing ruins, I might turn in terror at any moment and run back to the security of my apartment three blocks south of the Oval.

Most of the graffiti was of the "John loves Mary!" kind, no different from the scribbled notes we passed one another in the P.S. 80 school yard down the hill. But it was also on that tunnel's walls that I first read the rage and fury of those who stained the world with conspiratorial fantasies. As rage exploded like bullets, words burrowed into my consciousness. "Roosevelt Jew Bastard!" "Unite Unite/Keep America White!" "Father Coughlin Speaks Truth!" "Kill All Jews!" In the raw grasp of age-old hatreds, politics was plot and plot was history and that reality seemed as impregnable as it was inescapable.

Like adults, children learn to shape anger through the words they confront. The graffiti on that tunnel wall mobilized my rage, nurturing my need for vengeance in the midst of isolation. It wasn't simply the anti-Semitism I wanted vengeance upon; it was my own solitary passage through that entrance tunnel. As I moved through it alone, the tunnel was transformed into everything my budding sense of myself as embryonic American hated. Walking through it became an act of daring, for graffiti had converted its emptiness into a threat that could only be taken the way it was offered—a threat that was distinctly personal.

Why does Kriegel feel personally threatened by the graffiti he encounters in the tunnel?

In no other part of that huge complex of fields and walks was graffiti in great evidence. Other than the occasional heart-linked initials carved into the green-painted slats of wooden benches, I remember nothing else defacing the Oval. One emerged from that tunnel and the graffiti disappeared—all of it, "John loves Mary!" as well as "Kill All Jews!" It was as if an unwritten compact had been silently agreed upon, allowing the tunnel leading to the Oval to be scrawled over (despite occasional whitewashing, the tunnel was dark and poorly lit) while the rest of that huge recreation complex remained free of the presence of graffiti. Running that tunnel alone was an act of purgation, rewarded when one was safely home with the illusion (and occasionally the reality) of ethnic harmony.

Other than that tunnel, the presence of graffiti was localized to a few alleys and subway stations and public urinals in the New York I remember from the forties and fifties. Until the sixties, even chalk and paint adhered to the unwritten laws of proportion in neighborhoods like mine. Buildings had not yet been crusted over with curlicued shapes and exploding slashes, zigzagging to a visual anarchy that testified to a love of color and line overwhelmed by hatred of the idea that color and line do not dictate the needs of community. Even the anti-Semitic graffiti of that tunnel remains in my memory as less the product of hatred than an expression of the distance existing between groups struggling to claim a portion of the American past.

What does Kriegel see as the origin of graffiti?

In an essay published in 1973, Norman Mailer labeled graffiti a "faith," a word that struck me even back then as an odd use of language when applied to what a graffiti writer does. From the perspective of that eight-year-old child moving through that tunnel entrance, graffiti was the very antithesis of faith. It embodied a poetics of rage and hatred, a syntax in which anyone could claim the right, if he possessed the will, to impose his needs on others. But rage is not faith, as even an eight-year-old knew. It is simply rage.

In today's New York—and in today's London and Paris and Amsterdam and Los Angeles—the spread of graffiti is as accurate a barometer of the decline of urban civility as anything else one can think of. Paradoxically, even as it spread, graffiti was hailed as one of the few successful attempts the voiceless in our nation's cities made to impose their presence on urban culture. If graffiti is now the most obvious form of visual pollution city landscapes are forced to endure (even more polluting than those paste-up false windows with flower pots that grow like urban ivy on the deserted apartment houses fronting the Major Deegan Parkway in the East Bronx), it has assumed for New Yorkers the shape and frame of this city's prospects. Where expectation is confused with coherence, those savage slashes on brick and sidewalk embody our idea of all that city life is and all that we can now expect it to be.

Do you agree that graffiti measures the decline of urban life?

In books and photographic essays, graffiti is heralded as the art structuring the real urban landscape that the poor confront in their daily lives. "Graffiti makes a statement!" is the rallying cry of those who defend its presence. True enough—even if one believes that the statement graffiti makes chokes the very idea of what a city can be. One can argue that it is not what the statement says but the style the statement employs that lends graffiti its insistent singularity. But the evidence of the streets insists that graffiti is an urban statement whose ultimate end is nothing less than the destruction of urban life. Regardless of whether it is considered art or public nuisance, graffiti denies the possibility of an urban community by insisting that individual style is a more natural right than the communitarian demands of city life.

Do you think this voice is important?

Defenders of graffiti may insist that its importance lies in the voice it gives to anger and that its triumph resides in the alternative it offers to rage. Perhaps so. But anyone who walks through the streets of today's New York understands that the price graffiti demands is an emotional exhaustion in which we find ourselves the victims of that same rage and anger supposedly given voice—*vented* is today's fashionable word—by these indiscriminate slashes of color plastered against brick and wall and doorway and telephone booth.

Contemporary graffiti is not particularly political—at least not in New York. On those few times when one spots graffiti that does seek to embrace a message, the politics seem prepubescent sloganeering.

Few openly political sayings are lettered onto these buildings and walls. Even the huge graffiti-like wall mural of a small Trotskyite press that one sees driving north on West Street in lower Manhattan speaks not of politics but of a peculiar Third World clubbiness more characteristic of the early 1970s than of our time. Malcolm X, Che Guevarra—originally offered as a pantheon of Third World liberators, the faces over the years have taken on the likeness of the comic-book superheroes in whose image one suspects they were originally conceived and drawn. The future they appeal to is curiously apolitical, as if the revolution they promise lies frozen in a nineteenth-century photograph in which reality assumes the proportions of myth. One has the impression that these are icons that have been hung on the wall for good luck, like a rabbit's foot or one of those plastic Jesuses one sees hanging from the rear-view mirrors of battered old Chevys.

The single most effective political graffito I have seen over the past few years was not in New York. Last summer, as I drove through streets filled with the spacious walled-in homes and immaculate concrete driveways of a wealthy Phoenix suburb, on my way to visit Frank Lloyd Wright's Taliesin West, I came across "Save Our Desert" slashed in large dripping red letters across a brown sun-drenched adobe wall surrounding one of the huge sun palaces that root like cacti in the nouveau riche wilds of Goldwater County. Here was a graffito in which politics was central, a gauntlet thrown at the feet of developers for whom the Arizona desert is mere space to be acquired and used and disposed of for profit.

<small>Why is this graffiti political?</small>

Perhaps because it is more traditional, political graffiti seems more understandable than these explosions of line and color and ectoplasmic scrawl now plastered like dried mucus against New York's brick and concrete. "Save Our Desert!" may be simplistic, but at least it expresses a desire to right a balance deemed unjust and unnecessary. Political graffiti intrudes on privacy by voicing a specific protest. This alone serves to distinguish it from the public stains New Yorkers now assume are as natural as blades of grass growing between the cracks in a sidewalk.

To deny this city's painful decline over the past three decades is to deny the obvious. One can measure that decline through the spread of graffiti. The process began with the insistence that these mindless blotches and savage strokes embodied a legitimate, if admittedly different, sense of fashion, that they could be viewed—indeed, they had to be viewed—as a "natural" expression of the new and daring.

Like everything else in this city, graffiti demands an emotional investment from those who defend it. One can only vindicate these slashes and blobs of color because their presence is so overwhelming. What choice do we have but to demand that the world recognize the "art" in these urban voices? Anything else forces us to examine the consequences of what we have allowed through the intimidating fear of not being in fashion. Even as acceptance is demanded, graffiti continues to pound against the city, having grown as mechanical and fixed as the sound of the boom boxes in the streets below our windows. We label graffiti "real," we label it "authentic," we label it "powerful." Like true pedants, we discuss the nuances of these different voices. We create graffiti martyrs from Keith Haring, dead of AIDS, and from Basquiat, dead of a drug overdose. In their deaths, we tell ourselves, our city lives. For their art is "urban." And urban counts. Urban must count. If not, why have we permitted what has been done to this city we claim to love?

If the graffiti plastered first on subway cars and then on billboard and doorway and brick truly constitutes an art form, then it is an art that seeks to rip out the root idea of what supposedly created it—the idea that a specifically urban culture exists. Defended as a creative act in which the city itself becomes the artist's canvas, the paradox of graffiti is the extent to which its existence connotes an implicit hatred of what a city is and what it can offer its citizens. At the core of graffiti's spread lurks the dangerously romantic notion that the city is a place of such overwhelming evil that it must be torn apart, savaged into its own death, its residents given a "voice" in the irrational hope that in this way its more urbane voices will be stilled. Graffiti slashes at the heart of New York, the heart of urbanity, by attacking the city's splendid nineteenth-century monuments of cast-iron architecture in the resurrected Soho neighborhood of lower Manhattan as indifferently as it attacks the playful 1930s art deco apartment house façades that once made the now-dingy Grand Concourse in the Bronx so singularly playful an example of urban aspiration.

New Yorkers stand like helpless mannequins before the onslaught. Graffiti does not, after all, destroy lives. It is not like the scourge of crack, or the horrendous spread of AIDS, or the rising tension in our neighborhoods between blacks and Jews and between blacks and Asians. Graffiti is no more than a background for the homeless who cage themselves in makeshift cardboard boxes or laundry baskets at night or the crazies who walk the streets engaged in heated dialogues with Jesus or Lenin or Mary Baker Eddy or George Steinbrenner or the dead yet still-celebrated Basquiat. Graffiti is innocent, or so we continue to tell ourselves even in the face of powerful evidence to the contrary. "No one ever died from graffiti!" a friend impatiently snaps, as I point out a deserted bank on the northwest corner of Fourteenth Street and Eighth Avenue, its once-attractive façade gouged and stabbed by slashes of black spray paint. "There are more important problems in this city."

Of course, there *are* more important problems in this city. Yet none speak more directly to the true state of affairs in this New York than the mushrooming graffiti in our streets. And nothing traces the actual state of those streets better than the insistence graffiti makes that there are neither rules nor obligations for the survival of urban hope and aspiration. The prospect of a voice for the voiceless illuminates every dark alley in the New Yorker's mind, like the reflection of one of those stars already extinguished millions and millions of light years away. But is that to be all those of us who claim to love this city are finally left with, these dead light gleanings of one false revolution after another, beneath whose costly illusions—in the name of fashion—we have bent this great and wounded metropolis out of time and out of function and perhaps even out of its future?

Why does Kriegel think graffiti is an important urban problem?

Final Reflection

How do you feel about Kriegel's definition of *art*? Do you think other kinds of public art are more effective?

❖ *After You Read, Consider*

1. What do you think of the distinction Kriegel makes between political graffiti and the graffiti he sees every day in New York?

2. Do you respond differently to art that is housed in a museum, and so traditionally presented as an art object, than to art that is part of an urban environment?

3. Do you believe, as Kriegel does, that graffiti only serves to highlight the decline of urban life? That it only serves to give voice to an individual's rage and anger and so creates an emotional exhaustion in the community?

I'm glad you liked the pictures I drew on my drafts.

—Terry Williamson

❖ *Suggestions for Writing*

1. Find some examples on your campus or in your city of different kinds of graffiti. Carefully analyze the message that is communicated, and then write an essay that either defends or supports the distinction between political and nonpolitical graffiti. Discuss whether Kriegel is right in saying that the politics expressed are "prepubescent sloganeering" or, as in the case of murals of Malcolm X and Che Gue-

varra, that the future they promise is "apolitical." What is the social significance of graffiti if not to question or comment on contemporary politics?

2. How does Kriegel distinguish between the graffiti he saw in his youth and more contemporary graffiti? Write an essay in which you explore why and how graffiti has changed since World War II from "the rage and fury of those who stained the world with conspiratorial fantasies" to an art form that many critics now claim is the voice of urban culture.

3. Collect examples of public art that you consider marginal. Write a biography for each piece you collect: What is the art's message? Where did you find it? Why do you consider this piece art?

Timothy Guidera

Bowl's Eye View

Tim Guidera is a sports writer who lives in Savannah, Georgia. Most of the time he covers sporting events like the Masters Tournament in Augusta, Georgia.

I thought I'd be happy when I got to my last journal entry.

—Anne Johnson

Prereading Reflection

When you go to sporting events, how important do you find the halftime activities?

It wasn't as dark as I thought it would be. Nor as damp. And, to tell the whole truth, it didn't smell anything like I feared it might. Actually, my first trip inside a toilet was not at all what I had expected. Just everything I had hoped.

It should come as little surprise that I am a big fan of the running toilet promotion at Savannah Sand Gnats games. I have written about the Chatham County Ground Water Guardian Program's stadium gag often enough to concern friends. I've spoken highly of it to anyone polite enough to listen and cheered it unashamedly on occasional trips to Grayson Stadium this season.

What I hadn't done was reveal that, from the first time I saw the running toilet on opening night, I knew I had to be it. Immediately, I had felt a compelling desire to slip on the oversized tank-and-bowl contraption and trot around the field. When it came to this toilet, I had to go.

Why do you think Guidera wants to play this part?

Saturday night, I got the chance.

With the Gnats playing the Asheville Tourists, I played Less Waters in the Ground Water Guardian Program's nightly promotion. And

I was perfectly flushed with excitement to have my career suddenly go in the toilet.

But, there's more to using this bowl than simply getting the urge.

Permission is required, which I received from Mary Elfner, the Water Conservation Planner for Savannah/Chatham County, whose office manages the Ground Water group. And there is a mandatory briefing on the rigors of the position, the responsibilities of the character and proper toilet behavior.

This is the part I found most curious.

I mean, I know my way around a toilet. I have been using one since, like, high school. And, if I may say, I have become pretty familiar with the procedure. Through the years I had stood in front of them, sat on them, knelt before them and, on a few particularly rough nights, slept under them. I thought I knew my end of the toilet business pretty well.

Why did Guidera need to learn to play this part?

Turns out, I knew nothing.

The Preparation

The identity of who is usually inside the running toilet is a stringently guarded secret. And protecting that information was part of the deal in getting inside the costume. But, because reference to the person who regularly plays Less Waters will be necessary, I will have to call him—or her—something. And "John" seems appropriate enough.

My biggest night at the bowl since that last unfortunate trip to the Mexican buffet, started when I met John at the toilet's secret hideaway about 90 minutes before gametime.

There I was told that I would take the field at the top of the third inning, walk to home plate and race a randomly chosen youngster around the bases. I was informed that John would be transporting the toilet to the park, which was good, because the first thing I noticed about the commode was that it is half the size of my compact car. Most importantly, I was instructed on how to get into the costume, a complicated, but easily understood series of twists, reaches and bends.

The interior plumbing of this particular toilet contains a large harness—like you'd see on an oversized camper's pack—that rests on your back, two padded straps that allow you to support most of the weight on your shoulders and a belt attachment that keeps the costume from wobbling as you run. It's as easy to wear as such a complex outfit could be, thanks to the professional design of Angela Beasley, who owns and operates Puppet People in Thunderbolt.

And getting into the toilet becomes equally simple after you do it once.

> Why is Guidera explaining how to put the costume on? What does he want us to know about the job?

Starting with the costume laying parallel to the ground, you lean in and put it on backward. Holding an aluminum crossbar at the top of the suit, you slip your left arm into one strap, twist the whole costume to face forward, slide in your right arm, buckle the belt and you're toilet-ready.

"It took a lot of trial and error to figure out the best way to get it on, especially when you have to do it by yourself sometimes," said John, who did not warn me about knocking my head on the cross beam, which I did immediately.

But the full-time innards of the toilet did give me some valuable tips.

John told me to do a little dance once I got out on the field, to wave in acknowledgment to the fans and the public-address announcer and to watch out for Nick the Gnat, the Sand Gnats mascot who sometimes ambushes Less during the race.

Everything seemed pretty straightforward. In fact, about the only problem I had was with the costume's shoes, which were considerably larger than mine. And, not thrilled with the prospect of flopping around the bases with my size-9 feet inside the costume's boat-like 12.5s, I made a quick trip home to get a pair of my own black loafers. (This will be worth remembering later.)

The Wait

Once at the stadium, the excitement started to build. As did a little unexpected nervousness.

John had told me that it's tougher to be the toilet on nights when the Gnats draw larger and younger crowds. And, of course, I had chosen to be Less Waters on Kids Jersey Night at Grayson, meaning there would not only be more people there than usual, but many more kids. Oh great!

> Why is it tougher to be Less Waters when there's lots of children in the crowd?

But, since it was too late to back out, I headed outside of the ballpark in the middle of the second inning and got dressed out of the back of the costume's transport van. The striped thigh-high socks went on first, then the black shoes (my own) and then it was time to get into uniform. Diving into the base of the bowl up to my waist, I lifted the suit out of the truck, flipped it around in one easy move and strapped myself in. Nothing to it.

After a few quick practice runs and checking the position of the hand-operated arms in the reflection of the van's windows, I waited for my cue to enter the stadium with two outs in the bottom of the second.

Given the Sand Gnat offense, this is typically a short wait. The home team can often be expected to make two outs with great swiftness. But, not Saturday. Savannah sent 10 batters to the plate in the bottom of the second, scored four runs and left the bases loaded—all with my head deep inside a huge toilet that I was discovering is hotter than its burgeoning national reputation. Thanks guys.

The extended rally at least helped me appreciate that there is more than glamour and glean to the toilet business.

For one thing, it's hot in there. Real hot. And, just standing around the park on the warmest night of spring, I was sweating more than Patrick Ewing in a playoff game.

"In all my years in baseball," Sand Gnats assistant general manager Dave Maloney told me later, "I've never seen an overweight mascot. It's rough inside those suits." Now he tells me.

It is also difficult to maneuver through a crowd inside something the size of a refrigerator box when your only line of vision is through a painted screen that serves as the costume's eyes. This is why the Less Waters gig is often a two-person job and why John advised me to bring along someone to serve as a toilet's little helper. For this chore, I enlisted the kindness—and unsuspecting nature—of my wife, Anne.

Now, I'm sure somewhere in the back of her mind, Anne feared there might come a time when she would have to help me in the toilet. I'm equally certain, though, that she probably thought that would occur as we approached our 60th anniversary, not our first. But she was a good sport, and a big help in thwarting the munchkin swarm that was in full attack mode from the moment I stepped inside the stadium.

The Reaction

Even with my new, inside look at Less Waters, I haven't quite figured out the phenomenon, except to understand that there truly is one. Kids are fascinated with the running toilet, even when it's only walking or even standing still.

Immediately upon entering the park through a side entrance, I was besieged with little ones wanting to get close to, touch and tug on the toilet.

It's a fairly strange obsession when you think about it, but a heartwarming one when you're the man inside.

Most of the kids wanted me to wave or shake hands. Almost all of them wanted to look inside the bowl and tugged the seat down to their low eye level. The resulting physics of this nearly pulled me over on top of them, but I managed to avoid flattening any of the little fans.

There was also this universal preoccupation with gender.

"Wave sideways if you're a boy or up and down if you're a girl," the gathering crowd asked repeatedly.

One little girl deduced that Less must be a boy because "I heard his laugh."

One boy—who would have gotten a lid across the back of the neck if I thought I could have gotten away with it—had his own reasoning. "He's got to be a girl," he yelled.

"Look at those shoes. They're girls' shoes." Where's the traffic when you need it?

Why does it bother Guidera when a child thinks he's a girl?

Working through the miniature mob, I settled into a roped-off area behind third base and, until it was time to take the field, withstood the steady chorus coming from behind me of "toilet, toilet, hey toilet! Look over here toilet! We love you toilet!"

Why is the toilet so popular?

Call it Poop-arazzi.

The Race

When the final out of the second inning was recorded, a gate opened and I was escorted onto the field by Chris, a Sand Gnat employee, and introduced to Gregory Shafer, my competition for the race around the bases.

Starting to the catcher's left, I would run clockwise, heading the third-base line and make right-hand turns along the way. Gregory would get to run the bases the proper way. It was a disadvantage I was determined to overcome.

The keys to successful toileting, as earlier explained by John, were: 1. Don't fall. 2. Don't make too much a fool of yourself, and 3. Don't win.

Why is it important that Less Waters lose the race?

I thought I should be able to handle the first, couldn't help the second and would ignore the third. The kid unfortunate enough to be picked when I was Less Waters, I told myself, was going down in a swirl of defeat.

And this shouldn't have been too difficult. The team usually finds a tiny, bewildered tyke who takes more time to get around the bases than Babe Ruth after a big meal. But, I learned, I was going up against a 10-year-old speedster intent on putting this bowl in its place.

It was no contest.

I started unsurely and, by the time I reached third base, Gregory was already rounding second. I was getting dusted, embarrassed, flushed like a used goldfish.

If I was to save any respectability at all, I would have to slow down this little spitfire that was in full-bore pursuit of a toilet-race speed record. I tried to derail him by getting in his way around where the shortstop would be standing, even bumping him onto the infield grass—a move that sounded slightly unpopular with the crowd.

This kid was like a miniature Michael Johnson. Or Secretariat. He was a racing machine and I was just carrying one. Before I had reached the midpoint of the race, I had conceded defeat. Problem was, I still had to complete the run.

It was at this point I discovered something. Of all the suggestions and helpful information that John had given me, the one thing he never mentioned was just how difficult it is to run while carrying a giant toilet. A convenient omission, I thought at the time.

You see, Less Waters weighs about 20 pounds, but is more cumbersome than heavy. To negotiate the race's circular route, you pretty much have to take the tiny steps you do when trying to carry all the groceries in from the car in one trip. Leg extension is less an option than in the backseat of a Hyundai. But you can still be nimble when necessary.

Shortly after rounding second, I got my first glimpse of Nick the Gnat, who had come out to compound my humiliation by further slowing down my rain-delay trip around the bases. But, determined not to be shown up by someone who wears one of these mascot costumes as a career, I gave him a little inside-out move—a real head fake, you might say—and scooted past. But he caught me coming around first and thoughtfully guided me the final 90 feet to home plate, where I arrived to an it's-about-time look from the catcher.

As bad as I felt about my performance, my pain was multiplied later when friends in the press box told me with great glee that this was the first time all season they could recall the challenger being across home plate before the commode had reached first. Nice guys, huh?

The Aftermath

When I left the field at the end of my brief shining moment in the bowl, I realized that I had forgotten to dance, forgotten to lift the lid with the lever inside the suit and forgotten to bow. And, with my full range of vision restored when out from under the toilet, I realized something else far more disturbing.

Behind the third-base stands, I saw John cavorting with Gregory. My teacher to my torturer were laughing and slapping hands. I think I saw cash being exchanged.

I'd been set up.

It turns out, John knew this kid and had hand-selected him for the race to ensure his standing as Savannah's master toilet man. He had sneakily picked Gregory knowing that he would run right off the base path anyone fool enough to stand in as the guest bowl. I knew I would smell something afoul.

"I knew he was fast," said John. "He plays Little League."

Foiled by a toilet, how embarrassing.

But that's OK. I understood John wanting to protect his professional reputation as the best toilet in town. I actually respected the pride he took in his dirty job that someone has to do.

Besides, he was right all along. Winning wasn't important. Even being beaten so soundly didn't diminish my day in the throne. The experience was worth all the sweat, the exhaustion, the shame.

"Come back and do it any time," offered John, still snickering.

But, I don't know. I think I've got to move on to bigger and better things in this bathroom business. Maybe a weekend as a Port-a-John should be next. I could have a future in masquerading as fixtures, a real career movement, you might say.

But I don't have time to worry about that now. I've got to get to the men's room.

Me and the urinal are going to do the town.

Final Reflection

What did Guidera learn about work after completing his run as Less Waters?

❖ *After You Read, Consider*

1. Have you ever wanted to try something like this? Work as a Disney character? Dress up as a clown for a children's party? How do you imagine the work to be?

2. Why is the identity of Less Waters a secret?

3. Why did Guidera find it more effective to use a sense of humor when he wrote this piece?

I find it easier to be funny when I write. I'm not too good at being serious.
—Kevin Bradford

❖ *Suggestions for Writing*

1. Interview someone who wears a costume for a living. Then write a profile on that person and his or her job.

2. How does Less Waters establish a relationship with the crowds at Grayson Stadium? Why is that relationship important in his or her job? Write about other occupations in which it is important to establish rapport with an unknown audience.

3. Research the groundwater situation in southeastern Georgia. Then create a pamphlet that explains why using "less water" is important in that area.

Jane Martin-Brown

Paths of Loss and Liberation

Mother, student, and amateur philosopher, Jane Martin-Brown lives and works in Savannah, Georgia, where she is completing an undergraduate degree in English. "Writing, for me, has always involved conflict, an attempt to reconcile divergent feelings and values. I spend time searching for the voices who will tell the stories."

❖

I hate to admit it, but I began to like writing in my journal.

—Mike Tilson

Prereading Reflection

Write about an educational experience that left you disenchanted.

❖

My mother was and is an avid reader. As a small child I loved to watch her read, sitting on the back porch, a rake at her feet, leaves neglected in the yard. She would take long pulls off her cigarette in between pages. I figured she was pretty wise, and many years later, I would take my own books and cigarettes into the woods behind the house in order to study when I couldn't find a quiet place inside. Of course now I realize those books she read were romance novels—a fact I wish I had never learned, for learning it did more to divide us than unite us. My mother was not to be my reading companion or fellow journeyer, as I had hoped. She felt no need to delve beneath the surface of the world as I did. I wanted to know more about everything from lasers to Lincoln to Lichtenstein. I read voraciously, especially biographies and literature. But my mother's reading was quite limited, and her interests were, and remain, in other areas—a fact that I cannot help but regret. My growth, my education, has separated me from my mother, from my parents.

When have you been disappointed in your parents when one or both failed to meet your expectations?

My parents believed mostly in work, and they worked and worked and worked, at night, on the weekends, off-hours. For them, my work was school. In retrospect, I think they valued education, but they were often antagonistic toward any voice that threatened their position as middle-class consumers. They objected to my ultra-short haircut, my music (*The Sex Pistols* and *Violent Femmes*) and my dress, which for them was either too unkempt or too provocative. Most of all, they bristled at my ideas, which more and more began to challenge their conservative political views as well as their materialistic values. My behavior and my choices were not merely an expression of individuality, but were, to them, an attack on their way of life. The unspoken message at my house was "we work to gain possessions and leisure time," a life that affords us a good house, jet skis and appropriate acceptance at church on Sundays. My father in particular viewed reading as play. He would tease me about reading fiction when I should have been memorizing the states and their capitals—in other words, gaining *useful* information.

But when I was in grade school my parents supported my reading, which was good because I hated the work we did at school. An ambivalent child in some respects, not easy to impress, I turned to fiction as a way to escape the duty-filled days of school. The book mobile replaced the ice cream man, and trips to the library with my mother became prized adventures. I would sit on the rough carpet at the Bull Street Library, flipping through dozens of worn pages, making sure to pick out the right books.

At school I was deemed gifted in the third grade by a fifteen-minute session with a school psychologist wherein I repeated lists of numbers in reverse, connected lines to form a perfect kite on a sheet of paper, eyes closed, pencil not lifting. I and the other students (mostly white and suburban) were placed in a SEARCH program, dismissed from mainstream class participation, and sent off to the library to write dry little reports on subjects like "Our Amazing Solar System," and "The Eating Habits of Polar Bears." For the most part we educated ourselves in a program that to me seemed designed to take the burden of teaching away from teachers and give it to us. We had a box of lessons labeled SRA, color-coded by level, red being the lowest, brown the highest. It was obvious who was ahead of whom. We pulled the lesson cards, read the assignment, answered the multiple-choice questions, graded our own answers. I longed for the ends of days when I could go home, curl up in my walk-in closet, and read my books. In that same closet my mother had stored a great many old books, books passed on from her family, books from her college nursing program, books no one now cared to read, saved only because someone, I can only guess who, felt too guilty to throw them away. Anatomy books. Some Greek tragedies. Freud. They made little sense to me, but I could sound out a lot of the words, and I recognized them as part of some mysterious future, a future where I would know things, a future I could make complete by the words' absorption into my consciousness. I read out loud, savoring the feeling it gave me just repeating the words—*trachea, tragedy, transference.*

This pattern continued into high school. I was pulled from the public school system and attended a Christian high school. We were educated to take tests. We were allowed to discuss books in class as long as we didn't threaten the authority of the teachers, which was somehow attached to the authority of God. I was supposed to pick up some basic information in order to do well on tests, strange tests made up by invisible knowers who would determine intelligence, predict my future, reward my memorization, condemn any forays into imagination. My parents became more shrill in their instructions: *if you don't get good grades and scores, you won't get a good job. If you waste time reading books not assigned for class, your grades will suffer.*

> Can you relate to education that does not threaten authority?

Following their instructions more or less, I began college as a nursing major, but by this time I had little or no respect for educational systems. I hated the rote memorization in chemistry class and anatomy. While my friends spent their free periods in intense sessions differentiating the clavicle from the scapula, I was wandering the stacks in the library, checking out books I didn't know anything about. Once, on a whim, I checked out an anthology of British poets. "You're not really going to read it," my boyfriend sneered.

Unable to bear another minute of school or my parents or my boyfriend, I just quit, and left school to work. It was the best decision I ever made for my education. I made friends with whole new sets of readers, poets, cultural critics. We waited tables at Miss Billie's and Archibald's, and stayed late afterwards, eating the leftovers and drinking beer, talking about reading, music, movies, politics—anything we wanted. Conversation became our curriculum, and our books had no library—they were strewn on the floor, loaded on tables in our apartments, tossed in the backseats of cars. In those days, getting a ride with the right person could mean meeting a new author.

My educational history is made up of a lack of professional ambition, a disregard for institutions, a distrust of middle-class expectations. But with that has come loss, alienation from family and religion. Those whose opinions I once valued—parents, grandparents, and church members—I no longer have in my life. It is not without pain that I say this. I respect their dedication to natural law, Christianity, patriotism, but I cannot conform to please them. And though I see them on holidays and anniversaries and birthdays, we are not close.

> Have you challenged your parents' views at times? What topic caused the dissention?

I think of my mother's romance novels. They were not the books I wanted her to read. I wanted her to read serious literature, Woolf's *A Room of One's Own* or Joyce's *Ulysses*. I wanted her to read Kant and Nietzsche. It pains me to say that. I think of my high school textbooks, books no one would ever read unless they were assigned. And even now, today, back in school, I find myself in the stacks, ignoring the reading list, ignoring (at my own peril) my assignments, putting off homework, choosing books that satisfy my interests, not the institution's. I'm going to follow the rules this time around, but only because I have to.

Final Reflection

Do you believe the author's educational experience will be different this time? Why or why not?

> *I found it difficult at first to talk about the essays we read. I had to start really thinking and taking notes while I read.*
>
> —Darrell Kowalski

❖ After You Read, Consider

1. The author writes, "My father in particular viewed reading as play. He would tease me about reading fiction when I should have been memorizing the states and their capitals—in other words, gaining *useful* information." Why would the father tease his daughter's choices of reading material?

2. How or why does education serve to separate or divide the student from parents, other family members, and friends?

3. In what ways do choices of reading material color the way friends, family members, and teachers view an individual?

4. The author writes about class discussion of books that do not threaten the authority of the teachers. How would such a discussion of any topic serve to threaten authority of teachers or a school?

❖ Suggestions for Writing

1. Consider the rules that bind you in your current educational endeavors. Write an essay that supports or denounces those rules as important to your reasons for coming back to school.

2. Reflect back on an education rule that you were required to follow that seemed senseless at the time but that you later discovered had merit. Write a cause and effect paper based on that rule.

3. Make a list of readings that have caused you to question the status quo in your life. Then write an essay that examines the changes that might have occurred, or actually did occur, based on those readings.

Rita Nachtmann

From Pee Wee and the Wheelman

Rita Nachtmann is a recipient of the PEN Center USA West Literary Award for her play How I Spent My Life's Vacation, *the Berrilla Kerr Award, a Hawthornden fellowship at the writer's retreat in Scotland, and a John Anson Kittredge Educational grant. Her BFA is from the University of Illinois and her MA (twenty-five years later) is from New York University. Nachtmann is a member of the Dramatist's Guild.*

❖

Prereading Reflection

Recall a time when you had to convince yourself to visit a friend, companion, or family member.

❖

Pee Wee and the Wheelman was first performed at the Passage Theatre in Trenton, New Jersey with the role of LIZA played by Donna Daley and the role of RUBEN played by Paul Romero.

Introduction to Act II. Scene One: **Ruben**, a man in his mid-thirties, is the new home attendant to Pee Wee, a paraplegic man in his early sixties. Ruben, who wears a temporary patch over one eye, is a tall, strapping man with just the muscle needed to navigate the obese Pee Wee in, out and around in his wheelchair. Like most evenings, Ruben has taken Pee Wee to a music club in the Village in New York City. Pee Wee, who has a penchant for women and a passion for power, is a crude, foul-mouthed man with an acid wit whose fear of displaying any fragility makes him at moments all the more irascible. On this particular evening, he has been especially ornery with Ruben who is beginning to question the worth of his newfound and fairly lucrative job. But the evening of the Grammy Awards is only days away and Ruben is to accompany Pee Wee. A songwriter who found his fame in the 1960's, Pee Wee nervously hopes to win for Best Song and reclaim a bit of fame. Pee Wee has a policy of never hiring musicians as home attendants. Because of this, Ruben has kept from Pee Wee the fact that he is a composer. Ruben is extremely talented but lacks the shrewdness or fearlessness needed to attain any significant success in the world of music. When Ruben mentions a "she" in the scene he is referring to Cactus, his live-in girlfriend who is constantly throwing in his face his inability to make significant money. Theirs is a volatile relationship. Cactus is a sculptor, a fiery woman who is finally reaping hard-earned success in the art world. **Liza** is Pee Wee's girlfriend. Younger by two decades, Liza has returned to school (after many years) to get her Master's degree—an education that Pee Wee has been funding but mildly resents as she achieves a greater sense of self. At this point in the play, Liza suspects Pee Wee of being infatuated with Cactus. Scene II begins as Ruben, who has seen to Pee Wee's nightly ablutions and put him into bed, is exiting Pee Wee's apartment building when he discovers Liza sitting out front. This is the first time in the play that Liza and Ruben have spoken privately. . . .

> *(In front of PEE WEE'S apartment building. After midnight. The moon is almost full and spills down onto the sidewalk. LIZA sits on the low stone wall that surrounds the courtyard. RUBEN exits the building. He is in a dark mood, preoccupied. He sees LIZA in the shadows. She stares ahead as if in a dream.)*
>
> RUBEN
> He's waiting for you.
>
> LIZA
> I'm waiting for the aspirin to kick in.
>
> RUBEN
> Stop me if I'm wrong about this . . . but when has it been safe for a woman to sit on a New York street after midnight?
>
> *(When he gets no answer, he starts to walk down the street. She stops him.)*
>
> LIZA
> How did Pee Wee find you?
>
> RUBEN
> Ad in the paper. Yes, I'm that easy to get. You could have placed an ad and gotten me.
>
> *(She smiles.)*
>
> RUBEN
> How did he find you?
>
> LIZA
> An ad.

Have you ever placed or answered an ad in the paper?

                        RUBEN
A singles thing?

                        LIZA
No, he'd never do that. An ad for an attendant, then . . . he turned me into a date.

(Again RUBEN starts to leave. Again, her words pull him back:)

                        LIZA
How was the club?

                        RUBEN
Full of important people, crowded, smokey.

                        LIZA
I used to go with him, but I decided to cut down on my cancer risk. Did they play his songs?

                        RUBEN
Not as many as he would have liked.

                        LIZA
So they didn't play his entire repertoire? Ow!   *(She grabs her hand.)*   It just starts shooting off like a gun. He's probably in a rotten mood, huh?

                        RUBEN
Did you see a doctor?

                        LIZA
Several. They all tell me something different—so I've done my own diagnosis.

              RUBEN   *(Walking Towards Her:)*
And?

                        LIZA
And what?

                        RUBEN
Diagnostically?

                        LIZA
Computer related . . . repetitive motion . . . problem.

                        RUBEN
That's smart.

                        LIZA
Who do you credit for your study   Me—smart? No, just good at
habits? Why?   studying. My father gets the

credit. He's the one who taught me good study—Ow!

(She grabs her hand.)

RUBEN
Have you ever been given a hand massage by a piano player?

LIZA
No.

RUBEN *(Gently:)*
Would you like one?

LIZA *(Surprised:)*
You're a—musician?

RUBEN
Yeah.

LIZA
You play—

RUBEN
I compose—on the piano.

LIZA
He shouldn't know.

RUBEN
So don't say anything.

LIZA
What's your style?

RUBEN
I'm figuring it out. So, how do you do it?

(He walks towards her.)

LIZA
What?

RUBEN
Study.

LIZA
That's not interesting.

RUBEN
Ah—*I'm* sure there's an art to it.

LIZA
So you're the product of the proverbial forced piano lessons?

RUBEN
No, my grandma—

(Again, she grabs her hand and applies pressure to the palm.)

RUBEN
You haven't lived until you've handed over your digits to a keyboard player.

LIZA
Your grandma was a music teacher?

RUBEN
No, she had a piano. Give me your ivories.

(He gently takes her hand.)

LIZA *(Guessing:)*
And your father was an . . . opera singer?

RUBEN
Cantor. And yours was a college professor—math.

LIZA
High school—history. Pee Wee needs a composer.

RUBEN
He needs a home attendant more.

(He begins massaging her hand.)

LIZA
I bet you're great.

RUBEN
I practice.

LIZA
When do you compose?

RUBEN
I'm composing right now.

LIZA *(Coyly:)*
I'm studying.

(They both smile.)

RUBEN
So if I were to practice the way you study, what would I do?

LIZA
Always review the material from class—daily.

RUBEN
I will.

LIZA
Always with your cat in your lap.

RUBEN
I'll have to get a cat.

LIZA
I stroke Phyllis as I stroke the ideas.

RUBEN
I envy Phyllis. *(He catches himself.)* I'm sorry.

LIZA
That sounded like Pee Wee.

RUBEN
I know. I've been working for the guy five days and already it's too long.

LIZA
Ohhh.

RUBEN
The aspirin kick in?

LIZA
Something did. *(Pause.)* Your parents—they bragged about you?

RUBEN
They didn't know.

LIZA
And it's still a secret?

RUBEN
Only to him.
(Indicates PEE WEE upstairs.)

LIZA
So when did you come out of the closet?

RUBEN
Why did you go back to school?

LIZA
In the high school play?

RUBEN
Temple Bethel. You went back because everyone else in your family had a graduate degree.

LIZA

It's part of the plan. And Grandma made you play?

RUBEN

Yes. I whispered to her, "What should I play?" She said "Play whatever you can remember."

LIZA

What did you remember?

RUBEN

Nothing.

(They laugh.)

LIZA

Exam time.

RUBEN

Yeah—I made up a tune that was a cross between Schumann and Kreutzer with a little Bach—no Burt Bacharach thrown in.

(LIZA laughs.)

RUBEN

Your father must be proud.

LIZA

He died when I was a sophomore in high school.

RUBEN

Oh.

LIZA

Can't show him my report card now. And your parents, how did they deal with the surprise?

RUBEN

Dad won by death default. Mom died three years later. I studied composition. At first, I felt like my piano playing had killed my mother. But Granny Rosen told me that was not possible—that I played too beautifully.

LIZA

Talent. It's a strange beast. I don't have it.

RUBEN

Everyone has it.

(RUBEN takes her hand, and with his over hers, begins to hum notes and press her fingers as if she is playing the piano. She smiles, then draws her hand back.)

LIZA

Not talented—not pretty—I was so damn ugly as a kid.

RUBEN

Then how nice for you to be an adult.

LIZA

Were you *ever* ugly?

RUBEN

I'll take that as a compliment.

LIZA

Have you been or do you remember someone like Liza?

"Always with her nose in a book," they would say. I hid. To this day I'm terrible at parties.

RUBEN

You've obviously been to the wrong parties.

LIZA

I'm the invisible type.

RUBEN

I pray for that.

LIZA

I should become a private detective—no one would notice me. A detective with a feminist twist—I could help women "find themselves."

(He laughs. She is pleased.)

LIZA

I made you laugh. I'm usually funnier when I'm alone. (Pause.) Ruben, do you know what it's like to be supported by someone?

RUBEN

There are all different kinds of support. (Pause.) When I was sixteen I got a job working in a department store on Saturdays. Minimum wage and I was thrilled. The manager offered me a couple of evenings and my parents nixed it—they said that I needed to concentrate on my studies. Since then, I've never been good at making money. But that is going to change.

LIZA

Yes. I am going to get that Master's. I am going to march down that aisle in cap and gown—with all thirty-thousand other graduates and I am going to hold that diploma up (she begins to cry.) ... and I am going to yell up to my father that I HAVE DONE IT.

And he'll forgive me my mistakes—all my mistakes—and I have made many! But I will be forgiven!

(Pause.)

RUBEN
I think you've just given yourself absolution.

(Pause. RUBEN tenderly puts his arm around her.)

LIZA
What happened to your eye?

RUBEN
We were arguing . . .

LIZA
About . . .

RUBEN
Probably money. *(Tears well up in his eyes, his voice falters:)* Without any warning, she fired up her work and wheeled around to make a point. She made her point. I took a hot spark a little too close to the cornea.

(We hear the neighbors arguing again. RUBEN and LIZA look up at the window above. Then, we hear PEE WEE yelling to the neighbors:)

PEE WEE
SHUT THE FUCK UP!

LIZA
Tell me, how is it possible to be so sweet one moment and so nasty the next?

RUBEN
Too much sugar?

(She smiles. They look up at each other and are drawn into a slow kiss.)

RUBEN
That shouldn't have happened.

LIZA
No.

RUBEN
It won't—again.

LIZA
You're rock steady, aren't you?

RUBEN
No, but I'm working on it.

Final Reflection

In the introduction, Nachtmann explains that Pee Wee has been funding Liza's education but mildly resents the change in Liza, her "greater sense of self." Think about how the process of getting an education has changed you over time. How are you different now? Then consider whether you have ever felt that a friend or family member has resented that change in you.

❖ *After You Read, Consider*

1. Liza wants her father to know when she receives her masters. What doesn't that desire indicate about how important school is to her?

2. Consider how you study. Think about your process, which would begin with preparing the area where you study. Then ask yourself if studying is an art and provide support for your answer using your own experiences as evidence.

3. Although Pee Wee appears only briefly in this scene (when he yells out the window to the neighbors), his presence is felt from the beginning of the scene through the end. Create a character sketch of Pee Wee and compare your sketch with other class members. Discuss how textual clues and personal experiences affect the character descriptions that individual class members create.

> *Writing about an issue that makes you angry is a lot easier than writing about something you don't really care about.*
> —Karen Miller

❖ *Suggestions for Writing*

1. Design a series of classified advertisements that reach a variety of potential applicants for a particular position or relationship.

2. Ruben's grandmother had a piano, and he became a composer. Liza's father was a high school teacher, and she is continuing her education. Research the role of modeling in a child's life and write a paper that examines what you found through the research.

3. Write a thank you letter to the person who had the single greatest influence on your decision to enroll in a college or university course or program.

Mary Sterner Lawson

Reading Faces

Ohio native Mary Sterner Lawson has taught English courses at Albany State University in Albany, Georgia, since 1973. Although her PhD is in Victorian literature, her serious avocation and vacation-time profession is art. The accessibility of pen and ink coupled with a desire to capture people's expressions, moods, and attitudes on paper has made character drawings her forte. This talent aids Lawson in recording personal responses to new faces and scenes and in enduring long meetings.

❖

Prereading Reflection

Write about a person whose face you consider distinctive.

❖

Which of the five faces do you relate to the most? Why?

Which of the five faces do you consider least captivating? Why?

Which face conveys strong emotion? What emotion does the face convey?

Final Reflection

Write about what you believe a person who sees you for the first time can read from your face.

❖ *After You Read, Consider*

1. What lifestyles do you believe the faces convey? What details lead you to these particular choices?

2. What characteristics or features make you notice a face in a crowd?

3. How do you read people's faces? What are some of the stories you have read?

> *I tend to think visually, but that actually helped me write better.*
> —Adam Lawrence

❖ Suggestions for Writing

1. Create a dialogue between two or more of the people you predict these sketches represent. Incorporate setting and storyline into the dialogue to create a scene. Cast your scene using class members and present your production to the class.

2. Collect stories from a specific group of individuals and photograph members whose stories you gather. Present the stories to your class and have students identify which face belongs to which story. Conduct a class discussion on what clues led individual members to choose the pairings they did.

3. Write a biography of a person whose distinctive facial features affect how you relate to the individual.

Libby Bailey

I Am What I Am

Libby Bailey is an associate professor of art at Wesleyan College. She is an artist and an art historian, and received training in both areas at the University of Georgia. Her specialty in art history is early fifteenth-century painting in Florence. Her love of art history and travel is revealed in her large oil paintings. She also does watercolors, etchings, and woodblock prints. Her paintings have been shown in solo and group shows in the Southeast, most recently at the Parthenon in Nashville, Tennessee.

Prereading Reflection

When you meet people for the first time, how does what they are wearing influence your perception of who they are?

How do you feel when you get really dressed up?

Have you ever made a change in your appearance that you considered very bold (like dyeing your hair purple)? What did you do?

How do others around you react when you dress or act differently than they expect you to?

Final Reflection

The model is dressed up for a role in a play. Consider what internal changes might be necessary for a man or woman to make to effectively play a character of the opposite sex.

Class discussions helped me to understand people who were different from me. I always thought I was tolerant before, but I found that I really didn't know anyone different well enough to be tolerant or intolerant.

—Marybeth Markman

❖ After You Read, Consider

1. What are the most striking details of this portrait for you? Why are you drawn to those details?

2. Look closely at the picture. The model is playing the part of a drag queen. If you had not been given that information, would you have recognized that the model is a male? Why or why not?

3. Oftentimes, we are expected to play roles, whether on stage or in our individual lives. Think about the roles that you have played and identify the most difficult ones. Why were those harder than the rest?

❖ Suggestions for Writing

1. Create a character who must appear to be something he or she is not. Then place that character within a story or play.

2. Consider the many stereotypes in our society and the negative connotations that are attached to such classifications. Write a paper that examines a particular group. As part of your research, interview individuals who might fall within the parameters of the group, incorporating what you learn through the interviewing process into your paper.

3. Investigate the role of art or music in a student's education. Prepare a presentation for a local school board that supports incorporating or excluding art or music in the district's curriculum.

Nancy Hemingway

The Bracelet

Nancy Hemingway is from Madison, Georgia, a small town noted for its historic old homes and traditions. She graduated from Wesleyan College in 1999 with a BA in communication and a minor in political science. Her outside interests include reading, hiking, scuba diving, singing, and playing volleyball. Hemingway is working for a business solution firm in Atlanta, Georgia.

Prereading Reflection

When you keep a diary, who are you writing to?

January 1981

Dear Diary,

> How old do you think the narrator is? Why?

I made momma real mad today. I didn't mean to. I was helping her make up her bed, but she got weird. There was a bracelet in there. I found it. It was pretty. I knew it wasn't momma's. She never wears jewelry. I didn't know whose it was, but I liked it. I almost told momma it wasn't mine, but I think she would've been real mad so I told her that I found it on the playground and I turned it in to Miss Jenkins but that nobody said it was theirs so I got to keep it. She almost cried. I think she knew it wasn't mine. I hope it wasn't another lady's. I don't want a new momma. Lots of kids have new mommas and daddys, but I don't want one. I want to stay with momma, but I wouldn't like her very much without dad. I heard her crying after she told me to go to my room. I hear lots of stuff in there. Our rooms are right next to each other. I know when dad got home she was yelling, and then she told me to go outside and play. Yesterday she told me not to go outside cause it was too cold out there. So I found Foxy and I petted her for a while, but my bike was too cold to ride. My cheeks got all red and stingy. So I came back inside and sneaked in my room. Jason wasn't home, but I knew I had to get back outside before Dad went to get him from Scouts. When I heard momma call him a word I heard on the soap the other day—basterd—that's a funny word, I laughed but I don't think it was really funny. Dad didn't say anything back. Momma said bracelet. I told her it was mine before, dad said it was probly mine too. I think I'll keep it. I just won't wear it around momma.

August 1983

Dear Diary,

> Why did the narrator keep the bracelet?

I found the bracelet that I found in my parent's room a long time ago today. Mom said I had to get rid of some of the junk or she'd get rid of it for me. I'll be cheerleading next week for the Junior Football team. I'm a Cowboy. The cutest boy in my class, Charlie McClain, is on my team!! Maybe he'll be my escort in the Homecoming parade. I don't chase him on the playground like other girls do. Mom says that's not ladylike. Dad doesn't say anything. Mom and Dad espeshally don't talk about my cheering. Daddy knows my coach Miss Jennie, but mom hates her. I don't know where they met, but when I talk about Charlie, mom sometimes says mean things about her. She says she thinks I must be learning things from her. I did learn a herkie yesterday, but that's about all. I already know most of the cheers cause I sit and watch the high school girls on Friday nights. I went last week with Anne from church. Her mom, Miss Frances, said she thought my mom and dad needed to spend a night together without us—me and Jason. We had fun. I got to spend the whole weekend playing their Atari. I didn't get home until last night, and mom didn't say anything about making sure I did my homework. Her eyes were all puffy, like the time I hit Jason real hard and broke my arm and cried cause it hurt so bad but nobody believed it was really broke. Dad wasn't here when I got back. Mom said he was out. I hope he gets back soon. Our favorite show comes on tonight. But anyway, bout that bracelet. I put it on tonight with the dress I'm gonna wear in the Homecoming parade. Mom busted out crying like I socked her. I don't get it. I hope I don't get goofy like that when I get old.

April 1988

> Do you remember your first kiss? Date? How does the narrator's relationship help her realize the significance of the bracelet?

I got my first kiss tonight! Me and Steve Fairchild were running around upstairs in the fellowship hall and he grabbed me and pulled me into a closet. I like him sooo much. He's so cute and he's in the 8TH GRADE!!! The girls in homeroom are going to die in the morning when we have rap session. But I thought he had another girlfriend. Jamie is her name. She's in the 7TH grade. She's okay, but I want to go with Steve. My mom just said to be careful and not to get hurt. She said first loves are the worst. Then she smiled and said that later loves aren't always easy either, but that if you work on it it gets better. But she said that trust is the most important thing in a relationship and then she said that one day I would understand. "I quote" Mrs. Harris says that all the time "I quote" Mom said and i "quote"—"you will have your heart broken and then you will get over it. Then it will break again and you will get over that too. Sometimes it takes longer and you will want to make it work and it will be the hardest thing you have ever done. But if it's meant to be it will be. Your dad and I have had our problems, and there was a time when I didn't trust him. But Marlene, trust is the most important thing and it has to be earned. You may think Steve Fairchild is yours forever, but if you think he has another girlfriend then you have to respect that. If you can remember that then you're way ahead of some people in this world." And then I was like . . . Oh my god! Dad cheated on her. That's what the big deal was all about. I know all about sex and stuff now, so I have an idea of some stuff that was the problem. I will never cheat on anybody. Mom had a terrible time getting over it. I would never want that to happen to me. But I'm sure Steve is for me. If not, then Jeffrey is pretty cute too.

May 1991

Marlene's mother worried about her daughter too much. There were so many things to learn about life. The world was a different place than it had been when she was Marlene's age. Just today she had opened the paper and seen a report on one of the issues that had troubled her, and she only wanted the best for her daughter. Marlene's personality and her relationships with boys her age (she was almost 16!) made her think ahead to the times when her daughter would surely encounter difficulty. Where was that paper? She would have to clip that report and share it with her daughter when she got home from school.

AP—Troubling statistics for America were released today by an independent polling agency. According to a nationwide survey, over 65% of women and 72% of married men admitted to committing adultery on his or her spouse. This corresponds with the increasingly high divorce rate that was reported during the last national census. According to governmental estimates, around 56% of all marriages are now expected to end in divorce. Conservative groups are blaming the phenomenon on households in which both spouses work full-time jobs, as well as the glorification of extramarital affairs and sex in the media. Long time conservative leader Jerry Falwell reasoned, "What do you expect in a society that allows television to teach our children that sex is the only worthwhile goal other than money and that it does not matter where the sex comes from. We have to be concerned about this, and we have to lead by example and show that a relationship takes work and perseverance. In our society we have lost the incentive to work hard for anything. Divorce rates and infidelity are just the tip of the iceberg." Politicians are jumping on the proverbial bandwagon as well, with President Bush announcing today a renewal by the Republican Party of its family values campaign and incentives to working families to make economic situations a little easier. The hope is to "take some of the pressure off of families so that they are better able to focus on the most important thing—remaining a family."

How do you read the inclusion of this article?

June 1998

Location: Sports Spot Bar, Macon, GA

Amy looked around the bar. It was getting late, and smoky. It felt so good to be out again after the month she'd spent on the coast recovering from mono. She hadn't gotten to see David for almost that whole time. But they had a wonderful dinner tonight at Downtown Grill with Jef and Susan and John and Leigh and had then come to this wonderfully familiar place. She sighed and put down her glass. She frowned. Water. David was pretty adamant that she not drink. He probably just needed a driver. No, she knew that wasn't true. He was so protective of her now that she was sick. She'd thought things were going downhill but since she hadn't seen him for a while this was a great reunion. She was finally feeling better and was ready to show it. She pulled her pack of Merit Menthols out of her purse and drew out a long slim cigarette. David gave her one of those looks, then grabbed her and spun her around playfully. She didn't know what she had been worried about. After all, they had been going out for two years. Rumor had it they were going to be engaged within the next two.

Why is Amy suspicious?

Occasionally she got a sixth sense when she saw one particular girl walk into the bar, but David never talked to her and Amy was sure she kept pretty close tabs on both of them when they were in the same place. There were just too many nights the phone went unanswered, entire weekends when David was unavailable to talk to her. Amy batted his hand away and gave him a quick kiss on the cheek. Then she looked down to get her lighter, but Jake was standing behind her with one ready to go. Such a gentleman, she thought to herself. But as she spun, she recognized the blonde that had frozen on the other end of the bar. Amy thought she might have been looking in a mirror. The look of pain on the other girl's face caused one on Amy's. Nothing had to be said— that look said it all. And all Amy knew was that her name was Marlene, and that she was in love with David.

    Marlene had busted her ass to get off work tonight in time to head to the Spot before last call. She helped Hanna close the bar. On the drive over, she tried to fix her makeup but without having changed clothes, it really didn't matter what she looked like. In fact, it was to her advantage that her clothes were stained with A1 and smelled of beer—she had an excuse to look bad and if she happened to look decent, more power to her. She couldn't wait to see David. It had been almost a week since they had left the lake where they had spent the last three weekends. The "Spot" was their second home during the week. She thought on the drive over that life was too good. She had a hundred and thirty dollars in her pocket, a full pack of Ultra Lights, and an hour to drink. Of course the night never ended there. There were still Krystal runs to make and last dashes to the convenience store to beat the two am deadline. As she pulled into the bar she spotted it. The dirty red Acura with the dilapidated Ole Miss parking sticker from at least three years ago was sitting in the lot and she got the tingly feeling that she always did when she thought about him. She didn't know exactly when she stopped caring that he had a girlfriend. Marlene thought it must have been when she felt no guilt about cheating on her own boyfriend to see David. He was like an obsession to her. They had such a good time when they were together. Marlene didn't know Amy. Even when her friends had become involved in the David-Amy-Todd-Steve-Mike crowd, she had never wanted to be introduced to the girl. From the moment she saw David during the second quarter of the SuperBowl, she had felt a strong attraction to him. It had only taken about three weeks before they were sneaking around and telling lies, checking caller ids and leaving coded messages. The danger had attracted her at first as much as anything else, and Lord knows things hadn't been going well with Clif, and their relationship had ended only a month after she met David. She felt like she really knew David. Their goals were one and the same. Their intelligence was equal, although she thought he may have even been brighter than she was. They were both cool, a little withdrawn, but together they were magic. She couldn't imagine what he saw in Amy. She was your typical spoiled Stratford girl, whiny and dependent. David had confided that it drove him crazy, but she had been there when he had needed her and he simply couldn't abandon her now. Marlene was pretty skeptical about that, but it was easier to have someone else's boyfriend than to have her own. It was a lot less trouble with all the benefits. Sometimes at night when she was alone she felt a deep longing, but she knew she could never trust him if he was actually hers. What was it mom had said years ago, she thought as she opened the door to the bar; oh yes, "Trust is everything." Maybe so, but she didn't have time for a real relationship right now. Anyway, now that Amy was sick she'd had him all to herself for the last month. She was sure that as soon as Amy was strong enough to hear it, David would leave her.

Marlene made her way to the bar and flagged Drex for a beer. God that Bud Light tastes good. She scanned the bar for familiar faces. She hated coming here alone this late, but she had a feeling she wouldn't be alone for very long. She saw him. He looked great in the deep blue shirt that she told him made his eyes the color of a June sky and khakis. She preferred his suits, but he could look good in anything. He hadn't seen her yet, so she slid off the barstool and took about half of a step before she noticed who he was with. The girl kissed him and he smiled. Marlene knew that look. When the girl spun around to get a light, Marlene felt her heart drop to a place beneath the sticky floor. The room disappeared and tunnel vision set in. The honeymoon was over.

Obsession

The bottle smooth
Smoky gray and cool,
The words white-pure,
The idea behind them stark contrast
Not of white on gray but White on Black—
They want to be noticed.

Pieces of glass on the floor,
The smell so strong you taste.
The shards arranged in chaotic anger.
They beg to tell their story.

It begins with lust,
Then vanity, pride, obsession leads to inevitable anger
and introduces you to Guilt.
He is worst of all.
He clings—a constant companion.

The pieces are swept away—
But still there are more.
You find them in the dark of night,
Or on lazy coffee and bagel Sundays.
They find you when you dress,

ruin your hose.
They are his little army, created by Him.

You may think you have cleaned, swept them away,
But those slivers saturated in Obsession,
Created by your own hand
Will never go away.

They linger—lurking, watching, waiting.
They never let you forget their story.
Guilt has taught them well.

October 6, 1998

To my darling daughter Marlene,

What is her mother trying to teach the narrator?

I hope this reaches you on your twenty-third birthday. I have spent so much time thinking about you lately, and I want you to know how proud your father and I are of all your accomplishments. You have grown into a beautiful person. The hardest part about actual "life" will be finding a partner, having a good relationship and raising a family. It's all trial and error and always remembering to trust your judgment, your own moral and ethical background and having faith. Without Faith, life is at best routine and devoid of real joy. I want you to think about several things. First, I love you very much, and I want you to know that no matter what decisions and choices you make they are your decisions. I am not going to tell you that they are wrong or bad because I want you to always feel free to come to me with anything. But I have to comment on this relationship that you have formed with David. I know you care about him a great deal, but you deserve so much more. You deserve someone who will honor and respect you, and who will make you number one in his life. From what I have gathered from our conversations, and when you call in tears and in need of consolation, that is not the case. I know that David and his girlfriend are not married, but understand that although I have never met him I know that you will not marry him either. You need to put your trust in God and really evaluate where you want your life to go. You may think you are grown, but you are still our baby. And you have seen the hurt that it causes in a relationship when one of the partners is unfaithful. I want for you above all things to have a clear conscience and to be available when the right man for you comes along. I wish you the best, My Baby, a life filled with Love, and Joy, and Laughter. Thanks for all the memories.

Mother

October 28, 1998

6:45 p.m.

Marlene finished brushing her hair, sprayed it into place, and waited. She lit a shaking cigarette and took a deep breath as she looked at the dusk sky. This was her favorite time of day. Everything was kind of murky, nothing was very clear, but it was so beautiful. It reminded her of her relationship with David. Then she took a long drag from her cigarette. That would be over tonight. She had her letter written and tonight was going to be her last night with him. They had never even been on a real dinner date alone, they always had one of his partners in crime with them. Tonight was going to be special. She had made them reservations at the best restaurant in town and it was to be a joint celebration of their birthdays. Amy was in the apartment that she and David now shared in Atlanta, and he had made arrangements for them to stay in his old place in Macon. She watched as the clean Acura pulled into her yard. He stepped out and she melted. She didn't think she could go through with it but she had to.

October 29, 1998

7:15 am

Marlene heard him get out of bed and go into the bathroom. She wanted to allow herself the luxury of waiting until he was done and watch him put on his suit, but that would be too painful. She sat up as she heard the bathroom door close. She quickly dressed, thankful that she had thought to bring a change of clothes for work so that she didn't have to go back to her own lonely apartment. She had left her jewelry on last night; they'd had a little too much sweet red wine for her to think about taking it off. She took her letter out of the bag as she ran the compact over her face and sprayed a little perfume. She hoped the scent would linger in the room while he was reading. She read silently in an attempt at proofreading, although she had read it a million times:

Dear David,

I wanted last night to be perfect. I wanted to spend an evening alone with you. I wanted to look my best for you; I had to do this so I could remember the way you looked at me. I need to remember every word, every look, the way you felt when I touched you and the way you made me feel when you touched me. I had to memorize every detail of your face because it was the last time I would ever see it. I wanted to have one perfect night to hold on to, because I never want to see you again. I think I would probably marry you tomorrow if you asked and that scares me because we have only seen each other on stolen time. If you added all the hours we have spent together since January, it would probably only equal about ten days. I grew attached to you when I thought I wouldn't, I believed you when you said that you wanted to spend the next sixty or so years with me and that you wanted me to be the mother of your children. I felt a real connection to you, but it was easier to grow close to you than to find someone else that I really cared about. There are no surprises here—I knew I would get hurt. I have come to the point in my life when I am afraid of two things. The first one is leaving you and never finding that kind of love again, and the second is waking up and realizing I am dating a married man and two or three years have passed with nothing to show for my time.

I know now that no matter what you say or how unhappy you claim to be, you will never break up with Amy. The only thing you ever promised me was that when you moved to Atlanta you wouldn't have her there and me here. Although you deny it, I know you live together. I thought I could be patient and let her drive you crazy, but you need her dependence. I am too independent for you. You don't think that I need you. Maybe not in the same way that she does, but I do. The difference is, I am strong enough to get over you. I can do better. She can't. Even if you did choose me, I would never be able to trust you. I believe that you love me as much as you can love anyone, but I need more than that. I need to love you in a way that you're not ready for and I need to be loved in a way that you never can. I know that if this was really a reciprocal relationship, then it would not take you nine months to realize what I've felt all along. It just doesn't work that way.

I hope last night was as special for you as it was for me, and I hope that you remember me in a favorable way. I am not abandoning you, I am abandoning what you can never be. I don't want you to call me, I don't even want you to ask your friends in Macon about me. When you visit town, and if you see me out, please act like you don't know me. When you read this, I will have walked out the door. I will never walk in it again. I wish you all the best in the world, and I hope you find the thing that makes you happy. When you do, cherish it.

Always,

Marlene

There. That was about all that needed to be said. She had a lot more she could say, but that was all he needed to know. She heard the water from the shower turn off and she made a frantic grab at her bag, her clothes, her keys. She touched the pillow where his head had been resting ten minutes before. It was still warm, and she leaned into it and took in its scent. She stored it into her memory the way she had done everything the night before. She placed the letter carefully on the pillow, the contrast of the white paper and the black sheets leaving another lasting impression. She took one last look around the room, smiled when she thought about how happy she'd been there, and then stopped smiling when she thought of how much pain that happiness had brought to herself and others. She closed the door to the bedroom and crept through the cluttered living room to the door. This time she did not look around. She just opened the door and left, never looking back.

As she was driving to work, she turned her cell phone off in case he tried to reach her. She knew that at this stage in the game she'd turn around and go back, like she'd done so many times before. She pressed on and got to her desk a little earlier than usual. She fixed her coffee as always. Just another day. This is where she had started, in remembering how she got here. When she looked up, the girl in the mirror was finally able to look back at her with a clear conscience. She looked down at her hands, and knew that the ring that would be on her left hand one day would not come from David Delaney, but she had accepted that. She pushed her sleeves up and turned the water on, almost not noticing the lack of resistance on her right arm. She began to laugh. It was the crazy, delirious laugh of those that have lost touch with reality or have just realized a tragic irony. Somewhere in the night, she had lost her bracelet.

Marlene stood in the bathroom of her efficient, clean office building. She watched the water run into the cool smooth gray sink, and reflected on how each individual stream of water came together at the bottom. She laughed as she thought how they came together just before they all went down the drain. She tried to think if there was ever a time in her life when everything didn't seem to be directed down the drain, as it was right now. She stared down into the bottom of the sink and then let her eyes wander to the unforgiving mirror in front of her. As the seconds ticked by, she let her mind drift back so she could remember exactly how she came to be in her current situation. . . .

Final Reflection

What can you learn from reading other people's journals and letters?

❖ *After You Read, Consider*

1. How difficult was it to read a piece written in several styles? Could you make connections between the different parts? How did you do this?

2. Could you tell how old the writer was in each part?

3. How did the writer's understanding of an "adult world" develop?

❖ Suggestions for Writing

1. Write a letter to your child (real or imagined) in which you explain a mistake you made and how you lived through it.

2. Write your own mixed genre piece that focuses on one life experience and includes your child, teenage, and adult voice. You can include poems, letters, narrative, drawings, and whatever else you think is necessary to give a full perspective.

3. Collect newspaper or magazine articles that focus on some issue that you have made a choice about in your own life (for example, marrying, raising children, buying a home, choosing a career). Narrate your story and include voices from other sources.

Dorothy Allison

From Bastard Out of Carolina

Dorothy Allison gained acclaim and audience outside the lesbian and gay community for her National Book Award Finalist novel Bastard Out of Carolina *(1992). Prior to her novel, she published a volume of poetry,* The Women Who Hate Me *(1983), and a collection of short stories,* Trash *(1988), which later became the basis for her full-length work. Since the novel, Allison has published a collection of essays,* Skin *(1994), and most recently,* Two or Three Things I Know for Sure *(1995).*

❖

Prereading Reflection

Write about a time when you used your birth certificate (for example, to get a driver's license or a marriage license, to enroll in school, and so on).

❖

I've been called Bone all my life, but my name's Ruth Anne. I was named for and by my oldest aunt—Aunt Ruth. My mama didn't have much to say about it, since strictly speaking, she wasn't there. Mama and a carful of my aunts and uncles had been going out to the airport to meet one of the cousins who was on his way back from playing soldier. Aunt Alma, Aunt Ruth, and her husband, Travis, were squeezed into the front, and Mama was stretched out in back, sound asleep. Mama hadn't adjusted to pregnant life very happily, and by the time she was eight months gone, she had a lot of trouble sleeping. She said that when she lay on her back it felt like I was crushing her, when she lay on her side it felt like I was climbing up her backbone, and there was no rest on her stomach at all. Her only comfort was the backseat of Uncle Travis's Chevy, which was jacked up so high that it easily cradled little kids or pregnant women. Moments after lying back into that seat, Mama had fallen into her first deep sleep in eight months. She slept so hard, even the accident didn't wake her up.

My aunt Alma insists to this day that what happened was in no way Uncle Travis's fault, but I *know* that the first time I ever saw Uncle

Travis sober was when I was seventeen and they had just removed half his stomach along with his liver. I cannot imagine that he hadn't been drinking. There's no question in my mind but that they had *all* been drinking, except Mama, who never could drink, and certainly not when she was pregnant.

> What tone does the author use here when she speaks about her Mama not drinking? Why?

No, Mama was just asleep and everyone else was drunk. And what they did was plow headlong into a slow-moving car. The front of Uncle Travis's Chevy accordioned; the back flew up; the aunts and Uncle Travis were squeezed so tight they just bounced a little; and Mama, still asleep with her hands curled under her chin, flew right over their heads, through the windshield, and over the car they hit. Going through the glass, she cut the top of her head, and when she hit the ground she bruised her backside, but other than that she wasn't hurt at all. Of course, she didn't wake up for three days, not till after Granny and Aunt Ruth had signed all the papers and picked out my name.

> Think back to an accident you were involved in. How vivid are the details?

I am Ruth for my aunt Ruth, and Anne for my mama. I got the nickname Bone shortly after Mama brought me home from the hospital and Uncle Earle announced that I was "no bigger than a knucklebone" and Aunt Ruth's youngest girl, Deedee, pulled the blanket back to see "the bone." It's lucky I'm not Mattie Raylene like Granny wanted. But Mama had always promised to name her first daughter after her oldest sister, and Aunt Ruth thought Mama's child should just naturally carry Mama's name since they had come so close to losing her.

Other than the name, they got just about everything else wrong. Neither Aunt Ruth nor Granny could write very clearly, and they hadn't bothered to discuss how Anne would be spelled, so it wound up spelled three different ways on the form—Ann, Anne, and Anna. As for the name of the father, Granny refused to speak it after she had run him out of town for messing with her daughter, and Aunt Ruth had never been sure of his last name anyway. They tried to get away with just scribbling something down, but if the hospital didn't mind how a baby's middle name was spelled, they were definite about having a father's last name. So Granny gave one and Ruth gave another, the clerk got mad, and there I was—certified a bastard by the state of South Carolina.

> How important is the spelling of your name to you?

Mama always said it would never have happened if she'd been awake. "After all," she told my aunt Alma, "they don't ask for a marriage license before they put you up on the table." She was convinced that she could have bluffed her way through it, *said* she was married firmly enough that no one would have questioned her.

"It's only when you bring it to their attention that they write it down."

Granny said it didn't matter anyhow. Who cared what was written down? Did people read courthouse records? Did they ask to see your birth certificate before they sat themselves on your porch? Everybody who mattered knew, and she didn't give a rat's ass about anybody else. She teased Mama about the damn silly paper with the red stamp on the bottom.

"What was it? You intended to frame that thing? You wanted something on your wall to prove you done it right?" Granny could be mean where her pride was involved. "The child is proof enough. An't no stamp on her nobody can see."

If Granny didn't care, Mama did. Mama hated to be called trash, hated the memory of every day she'd ever spent bent over other people's peanuts and strawberry plants while they stood tall and looked at her like she was a rock on the ground. The stamp on that birth certificate burned her like the stamp she knew they'd tried to put on her. *No-good, lazy, shiftless.* She'd work her hands to claws, her back to a shovel shape, her mouth to a bent and awkward smile—anything to deny what Greenville County wanted to name her. Now a soft-talking black-eyed man had done it for them—set a mark on her and hers. It was all she could do to pull herself up eight days after I was born and go back to work waiting tables with a tight mouth and swollen eyes.

Mama waited a year. Four days before my first birthday and a month past her sixteenth, she wrapped me in a blanket and took me to the courthouse. The clerk was polite but bored. He had her fill out a form and pay a two-dollar fee. Mama filled it out in a fine schoolgirl's hand. She hadn't been to school in three years, but she wrote letters for everyone in the family and was proud of her graceful, slightly canted script.

"What happened to the other one?" the clerk asked.

Mama didn't look up from my head on her arm. "It got torn across the bottom."

The clerk looked at her more closely, turned a glance on me. "Is that right?"

He went to the back and was gone a long time. Mama stood, quiet but stubborn, at the counter. When he came back, he passed her the paper and stayed to watch her face.

It was the same, identical to the other one. Across the bottom in oversized red-inked block letters it read, "ILLEGITIMATE."

Mama drew breath like an old woman with pleurisy, and flushed pink from her neck to her hairline. "I don't want it like this," she blurted.

"Well, little lady," he said in a long, slow drawl. Behind him she could see some of the women clerks standing in a doorway, their faces almost as flushed as her own but their eyes bright with an entirely different emotion. "This is how it's got to be. The facts have been established." He drew the word out even longer and louder so that it hung in the air between them like a neon reflection of my mama's blush—*established.*

The women in the doorway shook their heads and pursed their lips. One mouthed to the other, "Some people."

Mama made her back straighten, bundled me closer to her neck, and turned suddenly for the hall door. "You forgetting your certificate," the man called after her, but she didn't stop. Her hands on my body clamped so tight I let out a high, thin wail. Mama just held on and let me scream.

She waited another year before going back, that time taking my Aunt Ruth with her and leaving me with Granny. "I was there," Aunt Ruth promised them, "and it was really my fault. In so much excitement I just got confused, what with Anney here looking like she was dead to the world and everybody shouting and running around. You know, there was a three-car accident brought in just minutes after us." Aunt Ruth gave the clerk a very sincere direct look, awkwardly trying to keep her eyes wide and friendly.

"You know how these things can happen."

"Oh, I do," he said, enjoying it all immensely.

The form he brought out was no different from the others. The look he gave my mama and my aunt was pure righteous justification. "*What'd you expect?*" he seemed to be saying. His face was set and almost gentle, but his eyes laughed at them. My aunt came close to swinging her purse at his head, but Mama caught her arm. That time she took the certificate copy with her.

> Can you remember a time when how an individual responded to you was more important than what the individual said?

"Might as well have something for my two dollars," she said. At seventeen, she was a lot older than she had been at sixteen. The next year she went alone, and the year after. That same year she met Lyle Parsons and started thinking more about marrying him than dragging down to the courthouse again. Uncle Earle teased her that if she lived with Lyle for seven years, she could get the same result without paying a courthouse lawyer. "The law never done us no good. Might as well get on without it."

Mama quit working as a waitress soon after marrying Lyle Parsons, though she wasn't so sure that was a good idea. "We're gonna need things," she told him, but he wouldn't listen. Lyle was one of the sweetest boys the Parsonses ever produced, a soft-eyed, soft-spoken, too-pretty boy tired of being his mama's baby. Totally serious about providing well for his family and proving himself a man, he got Mama pregnant almost immediately and didn't want her to go out to work at all. But pumping gas and changing tires in his cousin's Texaco station, he made barely enough to pay the rent. Mama tried working part-time in a grocery store but gave it up when she got so pregnant she couldn't lift boxes. It was easier to sit a stool on the line at the Stevens factory until Reese was born, but Lyle didn't like that at all.

"How's that baby gonna grow my long legs if you always sitting bent over?" he complained. He wanted to borrow money or take a second job, anything to keep his pretty new wife out of the mill. "Honey girl," he called her, "sweet thing."

"Dumpling," she called him back, "sugar tit," and when no one could hear, "manchild." She loved him like a baby, whispered to her sisters about the soft blond hairs on his belly, the way he slept with one leg thrown over her hip, the stories he told her about all the places he wanted to take her.

"He loves Bone, he really does," she told Aunt Ruth. "Wants to adopt her when we get some money put by." She loved to take pictures of him. The best of them is one made at the gas station in the bright summer sun with Lyle swinging from the Texaco sign and wearing a jacket that proclaimed "Greenville County Racetrack." He'd taken a job out at the track where they held the stock-car races, working in the pit changing tires at high speed and picking up a little cash in the demolition derby on Sunday afternoon. Mama didn't go out there with him much. She didn't like the noise or the stink, or the way the other men would tease Lyle into drinking warm beer to see if his work slowed down any. As much as she liked taking pictures, she only took one of him out at the track, with a tire hugged against his left hip, grease all over one side of his face, and a grin so wide you could smell the beer.

It was a Sunday when Lyle died, not at the track but on the way home, so easily, so gently, that the peanut pickers who had seen the accident kept insisting that the boy could not be dead. There'd been one of those eerie summer showers where the sun never stopped shining and the rain came down in soft sheets that everybody ignored. Lyle's truck had come around the curve from the train crossing at a clip. He waved at one of the pickers, giving his widest grin. Then the truck was spinning off the highway in a rain-slicked patch of oil, and Lyle was bumped out the side door and onto the pavement.

"That's a handsome boy," one of the pickers kept telling the highway patrolman. "He wasn't doing nothing wrong, just coming along the road in the rain—that devil's rain, you know. The sun was so bright, and that boy just grinned so." The old man wouldn't stop looking back over to where Lyle lay still on the edge of the road.

Lyle lay uncovered for a good twenty minutes. Everybody kept expecting him to get up. There was not a mark on him, and his face was shining with that lazy smile. But the back of his head flattened into the gravel, and his palms lay open and damp in the spray of the traffic the patrolmen diverted around the wreck.

Mama was holding Reese when the sheriff's car pulled up at Aunt Alma's, and she must have known immediately what he had come to tell her, because she put her head back and howled like an old dog in labor, howled and rocked and squeezed her baby girl so tight Aunt Alma had to pinch her to get Reese free.

Mama was nineteen, with two babies and three copies of my birth certificate in her dresser drawer. When she stopped howling, she stopped making any sound at all and would only nod at people when they tried to get her to cry or talk. She took both her girls to the funeral with all her sisters lined up alongside of her. The Parsonses barely spoke to her. Lyle's mother told Aunt Alma that if her boy hadn't taken that damn job for Mama's sake, he wouldn't have died in the road. Mama paid no attention. Her blond hair looked dark and limp, her skin gray, and within those few days fine lines had appeared at the corners of her eyes. Aunt Ruth steered her away from the gravesite while Aunt Raylene tucked some of the flowers into her family Bible and stopped to tell Mrs. Parsons what a damn fool she was.

Aunt Ruth was heavily pregnant with her eighth child, and it was hard for her not to take Mama into her arms like another baby. At Uncle Earle's car, she stopped and leaned back against the front door, hanging on to Mama. She brushed Mama's hair back off her face, looking closely into her eyes. "Nothing else will ever hit you this hard," she promised. She ran her thumbs under Mama's eyes, her fingers resting lightly on either temple. "Now you look like a Boatwright," she said. "Now you got the look. You're as old as you're ever gonna get, girl. This is the way you'll look till you die." Mama just nodded; it didn't matter to her anymore what she looked like.

A year in the mill was all Mama could take after they buried Lyle; the dust in the air got to her too fast. After that there was no choice but to find work in a diner. The tips made all the difference, though she knew she could make more money at the honky-tonks or managing a slot as a cocktail waitress. There was always more money serving people beer and wine, more still in hard liquor, but she'd have had to go outside Greenville County to do that, and she couldn't imagine

How has location influenced your choice of jobs?

moving away from her family. She needed her sisters' help with her two girls.

The White Horse Cafe was a good choice anyway, one of the few decent diners downtown. The work left her tired but not sick to death like the mill, and she liked the people she met there, the tips and the conversation.

"You got a way with a smile," the manager told her.

"Oh, my smile gets me a long way," she laughed, and no one would have known she didn't mean it. Truckers or judges, they all liked Mama. Aunt Ruth was right, her face had settled into itself. Her color had come back after a while, and the lines at the corners of her eyes just made her look ready to smile. When the men at the counter weren't slipping quarters in her pocket they were bringing her things, souvenirs or friendship cards, once or twice a ring. Mama smiled, joked, slapped ass, and firmly passed back anything that looked like a down payment on something she didn't want to sell.

Reese was two years old the next time Mama stopped in at the courthouse. The clerk looked pleased to see her again. She didn't talk to him this time, just picked up the paperwork and took it over to the new business offices near the Sears, Roebuck Auto Outlet. Uncle Earle had given her a share of his settlement from another car accident, and she wanted to use a piece of it to hire his lawyer for a few hours. The man took her money and then smiled at her much like the clerk when she told him what she wanted. Her face went hard, and he swallowed quick to keep from laughing. No sense making an enemy of Earle Boatwright's sister.

> Why has eliminating the word from Bone's birth certificate become so important to her mother?

"I'm sorry," he told her, handing half her money back. "The way the law stands there's nothing I could do for you. If I was to put it through, it would come back just like the one you got now. You just wait a few years. Sooner or later they'll get rid of that damn ordinance. Mostly it's not enforced anymore anyway."

"Then why," she asked him, "do they insist on enforcing it on me?"

"Now, honey," he sighed, clearly embarrassed. He wiggled in his seat and passed her the rest of her money across the desk. "You don't need me to tell you the answer to that. You've lived in this county all your life, and you know how things are." He gave a grin that had no humor in it at all. "By now, they look forward to you coming in."

"Small-minded people," he told her, but that grin never left his face.

"Bastard!" Mama hissed, and then caught herself. She hated that word.

Family is family, but even love can't keep people from eating at each other. Mama's pride, Granny's resentment that there should even be anything to consider shameful, my aunts' fear and bitter humor, my uncles' hard-mouthed contempt for anything that could not be handled with a shotgun or a two-by-four—all combined to grow my mama up fast and painfully. There was only one way to fight off the pity and hatefulness. Mama learned to laugh with them, before they could laugh at her, and to do it so well no one could be sure what she really thought or felt. She got a reputation for an easy smile and a sharp tongue, and using one to balance the other, she seemed friendly but distant. No one knew that she cried in the night for Lyle and her lost happiness, that under that biscuit-crust exterior she was all butter grief and hunger, that more than anything else in the world she wanted someone strong to love her like she loved her girls.

"Now, you got to watch yourself with my sister," Uncle Earle told Glen Waddell the day he took him over to the diner for lunch. "Say the wrong thing and she'll take the shine off your teeth."

It was a Thursday, and the diner was serving chicken-fried steak and collard greens, which was Earle's excuse for dragging his new workmate halfway across Greenville in the middle of a work day. He'd taken a kind of shine to Glen, though moment to moment he could not tell what that short stubborn boy was thinking behind those dark blue eyes. The Waddells owned the dairy, and the oldest Waddell son was running for district attorney. Skinny, nervous little Glen Waddell didn't seem like he would amount to much, driving a truck for the furnace works, and shaking a little every time he tried to look a man in the eye. But at seventeen, maybe it was enough that Glen tried, Earle told himself, and kept repeating stories about his sister to get the boy to relax.

"Anney makes the best gravy in the county, the sweetest biscuits, and puts just enough vinegar in those greens. Know what I mean?"

Glen nodded, though the truth was he'd never had much of a taste for greens, and his well-educated mama had always told him that gravy was bad for the heart. So he was not ready for the moment when Mama pushed her short blond hair back and set that big hot plate of food down in front of his open hands. Glen took a bite of gristly meat and gravy, and it melted between his teeth. The greens were salt-sweet and fat-rich. His tongue sang to his throat; his neck went loose, and his hair fell across his face. It was like sex, that food, too good to waste on the middle of the day and a roomful of men too tired to taste. He chewed, swallowed, and began to come alive himself. He began to feel for the first time like one of the boys, a grown man accepted by the notorious and dangerous Black Earle Boatwright, staring across the counter at one of the prettiest women he'd ever seen. His face went hot, and he took a big drink of ice tea to cool himself.

"Her?" he stammered to Earle. "That your sister? That pretty little white-headed thing? She an't no bigger than a girl."

Earle grinned. The look on Glen's face was as clear as the sky after spring rain. "Oh, she's a girl," he agreed, and put his big hand on Glen's shoulder. "She's my own sweet mama's baby girl. But you know our mama's a rattlesnake and our daddy was a son of a gun." He laughed loud, only stopping when he saw how Glen was watching Anney walk away, the bow of her apron riding high on her butt. For a moment he went hot-angry and then pulled himself back. The boy was a fool, but a boy. Probably no harm in him. Feeling generous and Christian, Earle gave a last hard squeeze to Glen's shoulder and told him again, "You watch yourself, son. Just watch yourself."

Glen Waddell nodded, understanding completely the look on Earle's face. The man was a Boatwright, after all, and he and his two brothers had all gone to jail for causing other men serious damage. Rumor told deadly stories about the Boatwright boys, the kind of tales men whispered over whiskey when women were not around. Earle was good with a hammer or a saw, and magical with a pickax. He drove a truck like he was making love to the gears and carried a seven-inch pigsticker in the side pocket of his reinforced painter's pants. Earle Boatwright was everything Glen had ever wanted to be—specially since his older brothers laughed at him for his hot temper, bad memory, and general uselessness. Moreover, Earle had a gift for charming people—men or women—and he had charmed the black sheep of the Waddell family right out of his terror of the other men on the crew, charmed him as well out of his fear of his family's disapproval. When Earle turned that grin on him, Glen found himself grinning back, enjoying the notion of angering his daddy and outraging his brothers. It was something to work for, that relaxed and disarming grin of Earle's. It made a person want to see it again, to feel Earle's handclasp along with it and know a piece of Earle's admiration. More than anything in the world, Glen Waddell wanted Earle Boatwright to like him. Never mind that pretty little girl, he told himself, and put his manners on hard until Earle settled back down. Glen yes-ma'amed all the waitresses and grabbed Earle's check right out of Anney's hand, though it would take him down to quarters and cigarettes after he paid it.

But when Earle went off to the bathroom, Glen let himself watch her again, that bow on her ass and the way her lips kept pulling back off her teeth when she smiled. Anney looked him once full in the face, and he saw right through her. She had grinned at her brother with an open face and bright sparkling eyes, an easy smile and a soft mouth, a face without fear or guile. The smile she gave Glen and everyone else at the counter was just as easy but not so open. Between her eyes was a fine line that deepened when her smile tightened. A shadow darkened her clear pupils in the moment before her glance moved away. It made her no less pretty but added an aura of sadness.

"You coming over tonight, Earle?" she asked when he came back, in a voice as buttery and sweet as the biscuits. "The girls miss you 'bout as much as I do."

"Might be over," Earle drawled, "if this kid here does his job right and we get through before dark this time." He slapped Glen's shoulder lightly and winked at Anney. "Maybe I'll even bring him with me."

Yes, Glen thought, oh yes, but he kept quiet and took another drink of tea. The gravy in his stomach steadied him, but it was Anney's smile that cooled him down. He felt so strong he wanted to spit. He would have her, he told himself. He would marry Black Earle's baby sister, marry the whole Boatwright legend, shame his daddy and shock his brothers. He would carry a knife in his pocket and kill any man who dared to touch her. Yes, he thought to himself, oh yes.

Mama looked over at the boy standing by the cash register, with his dark blue eyes and bushy brown hair. Time was she would have blushed at the way he was watching her, but for that moment she just looked back into his eyes. He'd make a good daddy, she imagined, a steady man. He smiled and his smile was crooked. His eyes bored into her and got darker still. She flushed then, and smelled her own sweat, nervously unable to tell if it came from fear or lust.

I need a husband, she thought, turned her back, and wiped her face. Yeah, and a car and a home and a hundred thousand dollars. She shook her head and waved Earle out the door, not looking again at the boy with him.

"Sister Anney, why don't you come over here and stand by my coffee cup," one of her regulars teased. "It'll take heat just being next to your heart."

Mama gave her careful laugh and pulled up the coffeepot. "An't got time to charm coffee when I can pour you a warm-up with one hand," she teased him back. Never mind no silly friends of Earle's, she told herself, and filled coffee cups one at a time until she could get off the line and go take herself a break.

"Where you keep that paper, Ruth Anne's birth certificate, huh?" they'd tease Mama down at the diner.

"Under the sink with all the other trash," she'd shoot back, giving them a glance so sharp they'd think twice before trying to tease her again.

"Put it away," Granny kept telling her. "If you stopped thinking about it, people would too. As long as it's something that'll get a rise out of you, people're gonna keep on using it."

The preacher agreed. "Your shame is between you and God, Sister Anne. No need to let it mark the child."

My mama went as pale as the underside of an unpeeled cotton boll. "I got no shame," she told him, "and I don't need no man to tell me jackshit about my child."

"Jackshit," my aunt Ruth boasted. "She said 'jackshit' to the preacher. An't nobody says nothing to my little sister, an't nobody can touch that girl or what's hers. You just better watch yourself around her."

You better. You better. You just better watch yourself around her.

Watch her in the diner, laughing, pouring coffee, palming tips, and frying eggs. Watch her push her hair back, tug her apron higher, refuse dates, pinches, suggestions. Watch her eyes and how they sink into her face, the lines that grow out from that tight stubborn mouth, the easy banter that rises from the deepest place inside her.

"An't it about time you tried the courthouse again, Sister Anney?"

"An't it time you zipped your britches, Brother Calvin?"

An't it time the Lord did something, rained fire and retribution on Greenville County? An't there sin enough, grief enough, inch by inch of pain enough? An't the measure made yet? Anney never said what she was thinking, but her mind was working all the time.

Glen Waddell stayed on at the furnace works with Earle for one whole year, and drove all the way downtown for lunch at the diner almost every workday and even some Saturdays. "I'd like to see your little girls," he told Anney once every few weeks until she started to believe him. "Got to be pretty little girls with such a beautiful mama." She stared at him, took his quarter tips, and admitted it. Yes, she had two beautiful little girls. Yes, he might as well come over, meet her girls, sit on her porch and talk a little. She wiped sweaty palms on her apron before she let him take her hand. His shoulders were tanned dark, and he looked bigger all over from the work he had been doing with Earle. The muscles bulging through his worn white T-shirt reminded her of Lyle, though he had none of Lyle's sweet demeanor. His grip when he reached to take her arm was as firm as Earle's, but his smile was his own, like no one else's she had ever known. She took a careful deep breath and let herself really smile back at him. Maybe, she kept telling herself, maybe he'd make a good daddy.

Mama was working grill at the White Horse Cafe the day the radio announced that the fire downtown had gone out of control, burning the courthouse and the hall of records to the ground. It was midway through the noon rush. Mama was holding a pot of coffee in one hand and two cups in the other. She put the cups down and passed the pot to her friend Mab.

"I'm going home."

"You what?"

"I've got to go home."
"Where's she going?"
"Trouble at home."

The cardboard box of wrinkled and stained papers was tucked under the sheets in the bottom of Aunt Alma's chifforobe. Mama pulled out the ones she wanted, took them into the kitchen, and dropped them in the sink without bothering to unfold them. She'd just lit a kitchen match when the phone rang.

"You heard, I suppose." It was Aunt Ruth. "Mab said you took off like someone set a fire under you."

"Not me," Mama replied. "The only fire I got going here is the one burning up all these useless papers."

Aunt Ruth's laughter spilled out of the phone and all over the kitchen.

"Girl, there an't a woman in town going to believe you didn't set that fire yourself. Half the county's gonna tell the other how you burned down that courthouse."

"Let them talk," Mama said, and blew at the sparks flying up. "Talk won't send me to jail. The sheriff and half his deputies know I was at work all morning, 'cause I served them their coffee. I can't get into any trouble just 'cause I'm glad the goddam courthouse burned down."

She blew at the sparks again, whistling into the phone, and then laughed out loud. Halfway across town, Aunt Ruth balanced the phone against her neck, squeezed Granny's shoulder, and laughed with her. Over at the mill, Aunt Alma looked out a window at the smoke billowing up downtown and had to cover her mouth to keep from giggling like a girl. In the outer yard back of the furnace works, Uncle Earle and Glen Waddell were moving iron and listening to the radio. Both of them grinned and looked up at each other at the same moment, then burst out laughing. It was almost as if everyone could hear each other, all over Greenville, laughing as the courthouse burned to the ground.

Reflecting on my own life helped me to write about the pieces we read.
—Morgan Phipps

Final Reflection

Bone's birth certificate was the pivotal element of this reading. Write about an important physical piece of your history.

❖ *After You Read, Consider*

1. Anney is careful about who she lets into her life. Using specific examples from the text, consider why this might be so.

2. How does Lyle's death make Bone's mama "as old as [she's] ever gonna get"?

3. What does the lawyer mean by "you know how things are"?

❖ Suggestions for Writing

1. Using specific examples, write an essay that illustrates the potential effect of labels on an individual or a specific group of individuals. Then envision a world in which labels do not exist. What might be the problems or possibilities in such a world?

2. How Anney smiles at her customers and acquaintances is an essential element of her personality. Consider how a specific physical characteristic of someone you know illustrates a part of his or her personality and write an essay about the characteristic.

3. Career choice and income and educational levels appear to impact the treatment of Bone and her family by government officials. Conduct a series of interviews of individuals in your community who represent a variety of socioeconomic positions. Then analyze the information and write a paper that addresses what conclusions you drew from the interviews.

bell hooks
From Bone Black

A professor of English at Oberlin College where she teaches English and African American literature, bell hooks is also a poet and activist. Throughout her career she has written extensively on the politics of race, gender, and class. Her works include Talking Back: Thinking Feminist, Thinking Black *(1989) and* Feminist Theory: From Margin to Center *(1984). hooks always reflects on her own experiences in her writing.* Bone Black *is hooks's 1996 autobiography.*

Prereading Reflection

What part does television play in your life?

Television belonged to him. He not only owned it, it existed for his pleasure. Sitting directly in front of it with his can of beer he would slowly release the hard lines like shadows covering his face, keeping the smiling happy self from showing through. They liked staring at him at these times, watching the changes. They liked seeing that he could feel pleasure, that he was not all hard, not all made of concrete. If they got in his way while he watched television his mood would suddenly change. The harsh angry side of him would emerge. Usually he would yell at their mama telling her that she was too soft with them, that she didn't teach them how to mind. Mama would begin to fuss and yell at them to show that she wasn't soft, that she was willing to punish, would punish any minute. When her punishments did not work she would threaten them with telling him, with Wait 'til daddy comes home.

> The author speaks of "he" and "they." Whom do you suspect the pronouns represent?

Daddy came home to his chair, his beer, and his television. He liked watching sports, cheering on his favorite team. Saturdays and Sundays were the days for sports. They were not good days for children. There was no school, no one to play with, no *where* to go. They would be fine as long as the cartoons were on and he was outside washing his car, mowing the yard, working in the shed. When the time came to watch sports they would go outside but not if it was rainy or too cold. Her brother it seemed had all the fun games to play inside. He had coffee cans and mason jars filled with marbles. He would spread them on the floor making different patterns, shooting them with his favorite, his lucky one.

> Do you know someone who likes to watch sports? What influence does his or her passion have on family or friends?

The father was busy watching the game, while the boy played marbles on the floor. She did not want to play with her sisters, she wanted to play with the marbles. The boy said no. She hated the way he could assert these boy rights and not include them in games. They were always being told to share. Angry at his refusal to let her play, she threatened to walk right into the marbles, scattering them everywhere. The boy dared her. Mama had already begun to encourage her to leave the boy alone. Several times the father had interrupted his game to tell her to leave him alone, that he did not want to tell her one more time to leave him alone. Again the boy dared her. She hesitated only a few seconds before stomping her feet onto his marbles. Jumping from his chair the father began to hit her—not wanting to damage his hands since he needed them for work, he tore a piece of wood from the screen door that kept flies out. As he hit her with the wood he kept saying Didn't I tell you to leave those marbles alone? Didn't I tell you? The mama stood watching, afraid of this anger, afraid of what it might do, but too afraid to stop it. The spectators knew not to cheer this punishment or they might be next. They would cheer afterward, they would tease her afterward when he could not hear, when they did not need to fear being next.

> Have you experienced a double standard such as this? How did you react?

She was sent to bed without dinner. She was told to stop crying, to make no sound or she would be whipped more. No one could talk to her and she could talk to no one. She could hear him telling the mama that the girl had too much spirit, that she had to learn to mind, that that spirit had to be broken.

Final Reflection

What does "breaking the spirit" represent to the young girl in this piece?

Small groups were the best!

—Anne Margaret Adamson

❖ *After You Read, Consider*

1. How might the last two sentences of the first paragraph cause confusion for a reader?

2. This piece does not appear to use character descriptions. What strategies does the author use other than vivid descriptions to help the reader empathize with the characters?

3. What is significant about the violent action that takes place during such a passive activity as television viewing?

Revising often felt like being in a tornado—cleansing and destructive at the same time.

—Brad Bailey

❖ *Suggestions for Writing*

1. Create a scene between the father and daughter ten to fifteen years later where they discuss his behavior when she was a child.

2. Write an editorial, discussing the mother's role in the father's violent behavior.

3. Research the long-term effects of family violence on individual family members. Present your research findings to a group of teenagers enrolled in a parenting class.

Fernando La Rosa

The Man

Fernando La Rosa was Peru's most influential photographer in the early 1970s, providing inspiration to a host of photographers who matured by his side. He remains one of the most respected and collected photographers not only of his native Peru, but also of Latin America. La Rosa's photographs are included in numerous private and public collections, including the Art Institute of Chicago and the Metropolitan Museum of Art in New York.

❖

Prereading Reflection

Recall a favorite photograph. What do you remember most about the picture?

❖

What can you discern from a photograph of a person without a face?

What details draw your attention when you look at the photograph? Why these?

How do the lights and shadows within the photograph impact the details that you attend to as you view the photo?

LA ROSA ❖ The Man 333

Final Reflection

Recall your favorite photograph from the initial reflection. What was happening around the subject when the picture was taken?

❖ *After You Read, Consider*

1. What might the man in the photograph do for a living? How do you know this?

2. Without the title, would you know this person is male?

3. What feature in the photograph is most noticeable to you? Why?

> *I would much rather write about photographs and art. When I write about stories, I always compare my writing with the author's.*
> —Kathy Klein

❖ *Suggestions for Writing*

1. Create a character sketch of a man who fits the description of the man in the photograph.

2. Write a poem that highlights a component found in this photograph or another photograph of your choice.

3. Create a collection of photographs that share a common theme. Title each photograph and write a short description to include with the individuals' pictures.

Suggestions for Group Literacy Work

1. In a small group, choose a topic of interest and research various aspects of the topic; then develop a creative way of presenting the information you discover (for example, public service announcement, dramatic reading, pamphlet, and so on).
2. Visit a local museum or gallery. Individually select pieces of work that interest you and, while in the museum or gallery, write a response to the selected piece of art. Then begin researching the art, the artist, the style, the design, or other element of the subject you selected. As a group, create a panel presentation that details what you learned. This assignment would also work well if the group attended a concert, play, or other cultural event.
3. Visit a local bookstore and browse through the children's section. Choose a topic that interests the group. Research the topic; then create a fully illustrated children's book on the topic. Include a section that explains how parents or teachers might most effectively incorporate the book into their children's reading sessions.
4. Research a local issue and prepare an ad campaign that argues for or against the issue.
5. Create a newspaper edition that focuses on one issue. In the edition, include editorials, feature stories, news reports, advertisements for products—all of which must be appropriate to the issue selected.
6. Write a song (lyrics and music) on a topical issue. Perform the song for a group concerned with the topic you've chosen.
7. Create a comic strip that would appeal to a specific audience. Prior to creating the strip, do an audience analysis that attempts to discover a population that is not currently being served by the local newspaper.
8. Create a mural that depicts the various literacies presented in this book or the various literacies represented within your group. Display the mural in a prominent area on your campus or in your community and be willing to address your work with interested individuals.
9. Have each member of your group become a mentor for new students on your campus. Teach them the literacy of the college or university you attend (for example, financial aid, registration, special learning labs or tutors, library, special services, and so on).
10. As a group, create a poetry or multigenre collection that details what each individual brought with her or him on entering college. Consider past experiences in homes, workplaces, and school. Share your work with your admissions representatives

and offer to serve as representatives for the school as the admissions staff begins recruitment activities.
11. Conduct a survey in your college and university that addresses what skills most prepared students to be successful in their current educational endeavors. Repeat the survey in a local high school. Analyze the responses received and present the information to the teachers and administrators in your school and the high school.
12. Evaluate the availability and cost of local day care, public transportation, or other need that a group of students who attend your institution would require. Then research funding sources to meet the identified need and write a proposal that details the requirements.
13. Contact several businesses in your community and discover what educational opportunities are available for employees of that company. Prepare an information sheet that details your findings for students who are interested in working while attending school.

Credits

Dorothy Allison. Excerpt from *Bastard Out of Carolina*. Copyright © 1992 by Dorothy Allison. Reprinted by permission of Dutton, a division of Penguin Putnam, Inc.

Libby Bailey. "I Am What I Am." Copyright © 1999 by Libby Bailey. Printed by permission of the artist.

Marti S. Baker. "Circle of My Womanhood." Copyright © 1998 by Marti S. Baker. Printed by permission of the author.

Elizabeth Berg. "Nurse Wonder" from *Range of Motion*. Copyright © 1995 by Elizabeth Berg. Reprinted by permission of Random House, Inc.

Sandra Cisneros. "First Job" from *The House on Mango Street*. Copyright © 1984 by Sandra Cisneros. Published by Vintage Books, a division of Random House, Inc., and in hardcover by Alfred A. Knopf in 1994. Reprinted by permission of Susan Bergholz Literary Services, New York. All rights reserved.

Jeremy Sanford and Johnny Connors. "The Man That Spelt 'Knife' Was a Fool" from *Gypsies*. Copyright © 1972. Reprinted by permission of Garland Publishing, Inc.

Michelle Cook. "The Great Blueberry War." Copyright © 1998 by Michelle Cook. Printed by permission of the author.

Fannie Flagg. "Preface" from *Fannie Flagg's Original Whistle Stop Cafe Cookbook*. Copyright © 1993 by Fannie Flagg. Reprinted by permission of Ballantine Books, a division of Random House, Inc.

Evelyn Freedman. "Ready for Anything." Copyright © 1998 by Evelyn Freedman. Printed by permission of the author.

Tiffany Gay. "Sugar, Spice, and Everything Nice: Just What Are Little Girls Made Of?" Copyright © 1998 by Tiffany Gay. Printed by permission of the author.

Melissa Graham. "A World Painted John Deere Green." Copyright © 1998 by Melissa Graham. Printed by permission of the author.

Katherine Grigg. "Frustration." Copyright © 1999 by Katherine Grigg. Printed by permission of the author.

Timothy Guidera. "Bowl's Eye View" from *The Savannah Morning News* (May 11, 1998). Copyright © 1998 by Timothy Guidera. Reprinted by permission of the author.

Bill Hall. "Toothmarks in the Table of Time" from *The Sandwich Man*. Copyright © 1988 by Bill Hall. Reprinted by permission of Bill Hall, *Lewiston Morning Tribune*.

Ben Hamper. "I, Rivethead" from *Mother Jones* (Summer 1986). Copyright © 1986 by *Mother Jones* Magazine. Reprinted by permission of *Mother Jones* Magazine.

Shirley Brice Heath. "Talk Is the Thing" from *Ways with Words*. Copyright © 1991 by Cambridge University Press. Reprinted by permission of Cambridge University Press.

Lillian Hellman. "Turtle" from *Pentimento*. Copyright © 1973 by Lillian Hellman. Reprinted by permission of Little, Brown and Company.

Nancy Hemingway. "The Bracelet." Copyright © 1998 by Nancy Hemingway. Printed by permission of the author.

Langston Hughes. "Theme for English B" from *Collected Poems*. Copyright © 1994 by the Estate of Langston Hughes. Reprinted by permission of Alfred A. Knopf, Inc.

bell hooks. Excerpt from *Bone Black*. Copyright © 1996 by Gloria Watkins. Reprinted by permission of Henry Holt and Company, Inc.

Jenny Joseph. "Warning" from *When I Am an Old Woman I Shall Wear Purple*. Copyright © 1991. Reprinted by permission of Paper-Mache Press.

Kim King. "Grandmother's Kitchen, My Classroom." Copyright © 1998 by Kim King. Printed by permission of the author.

Leonard Kriegel. "Graffiti: Tunnel Notes of a New Yorker" from *The American Scholar* 62.3 (Summer 1993). Copyright © 1993 by *The American Scholar*. Reprinted by permission of the author.

Fernando La Rosa. "The Man." Copyright © 1999 by Fernando La Rosa. Printed by permission of the artist.

Mary Sterner Lawson. "Reading Faces." Copyright © 1999 by Mary Sterner Lawson. Printed by permission of the artist.

Chang-rae Lee. Excerpt from *Native Speaker*. Copyright © 1995 by Chang-rae Lee. Reprinted by permission of Putnam Berkley, a division of Penguin Putnam, Inc.

CREDITS

Jeanne Leiby. "Why I Read." Copyright © 1999 by Jeanne Leiby. Printed by permission of the author.

Chris Llewellyn. "March 25, 1911" from *Fragments from the Fire: The Triangle Shirtwaist Company Fire of March 25, 1911*. Copyright © 1993 by Bottom Dog Press. Reprinted by permission of Bottom Dog Press.

J. Nozipo Maraire. Excerpt from *Zenzele: A Letter for My Daughter*. Copyright © 1996 by J. Nozipo Maraire. Reprinted by permission of Crown Publishers, Inc.

Jessica Marinara. "Christmas for the Colorblind." Copyright © 1998 by Jessica Marinara. Printed by permission of the author.

Alice Marriott. "The Whole Pot" from *María: The Potter of San Ildefonso*. Copyright © 1948 by the University of Oklahoma Press. Reprinted by permission of the University of Oklahoma Press.

Jane Martin-Brown. "Paths of Loss and Liberation." Copyright © 1998 by Jane Martin-Brown. Printed by permission of the author.

John McPherson. Selections from "Close to Home" cartoons. Copyright © 1999 by John McPherson. Reprinted by permission of the author.

Rita Nachtmann. Act II, scene 2 from *Pee Wee and the Wheelman*. Copyright © 1999 by Rita Nachtmann. Reprinted by permission of the author.

Tim O'Brien. "The Things They Carried" from *The Things They Carried*. Copyright © 1990 by Tim O'Brien. Reprinted by permission of Houghton Mifflin Co./Seymour Laurence. All rights reserved.

Tillie Olsen. "I Stand Here Ironing" from *Tell Me a Riddle*. Copyright 1956, 1957, 1960, 1961 by Tillie Olsen. Reprinted by permission of Delacourt Press/Seymour Laurence, a division of Bantam Doubleday Dell Publishing Group, Inc.

Susan Orlean. "Beautiful Girls" from *The New Yorker* 73.22 (Aug. 4, 1997). Copyright © 1997 by *The New Yorker*. Reprinted by permission of the author.

Whitney Otto. "Instructions No. 3" from *How to Make an American Quilt*. Copyright © 1991 by Whitney Otto. Reprinted by permission of Villard Books, a division of Random House, Inc.

Mike Rose. "I Just Wanna Be Average" from *Lives on the Boundary: The Struggles and Achievements of America's Underprepared*. Copyright © 1989 by Mike Rose. Reprinted by permission of The Free Press, a division of Simon & Schuster, Inc.

Harold Rosen. "Comrade Rosie Rosen" from *Troublesome Boy*. Copyright © 1993. Reprinted by permission of English and Media Center, London.

Pat Rushin. "Zoo Welcomes New Arrival" from *Puzzling Through the News*. Copyright © 1991 by Pat Rushin. Reprinted by permission of the author.

Jane Smiley. "The Consequences" from *Moo*. Copyright © 1995 by Jane Smiley. Reprinted by permission of Alfred A. Knopf, Inc.

Nancy Sommers. "I Stand Here Writing" from *College English* 55.4 (April 1993). Copyright © 1993 by the National Council of Teachers of English. Reprinted by permission of the National Council of Teachers of English.

William Stafford. "At a Small College" from *Scripture of Leaves*. Copyright © 1989 by William Stafford. Reprinted by permission of Brethren Press, Elgin, IL.

Abraham Verghese. Excerpt from *My Own Country*. Copyright © 1994 by Abraham Verghese. Reprinted by permission of Simon & Schuster, Inc.

Les Wade. "Grandma's Fruitroom." Copyright © 1999 by Les Wade. Printed by permission of the author.

Eudora Welty. "Wordstruck" from *One Writer's Beginnings*. Copyright © 1983, 1984 by Eudora Welty. Reprinted by permission of Harvard University Press, Cambridge, MA.

Index

Allison, Dorothy, From *Bastard Out of Carolina* 316–327
At a Small College (Stafford) 46–47

Bailey, Libby, *I Am What I Am* 302–303
Baker, Marti S., *Circle of My Womanhood* 180–184
Beautiful Girls (Orlean) 81–93
Berg, Elizabeth, *Nurse Wonder* 108–115
Bowl's Eye View (Guidera) 278–284
Bracelet, The (Hemingway) 305–314

Christmas for the Colorblind (Marinara) 150–155
Circle of My Womanhood (Baker) 180–184
Cisneros, Sandra, *First Job* 157–158
Cook, Michelle, *The Great Blueberry War* 104–106
Close to Home (McPherson) 17–18
Comrade Rosie Rosen (Rosen) 10–15
Connors, Johnny, *The Man That Spelt "Knife" Was a Fool* 20–23
Consequences, from *Moo, The* (Smiley) 4–8

Ellington, Peggy, *Kitchen Table Talk* 174–176
Other Literacies 246–248

First Job (Cisneros) 157–158
Flagg, Fannie, Preface from *Fannie Flagg's Original Whistle Stop Cafe Cookbook* 193–197
Freedman, Evelyn, *Ready for Anything* 49–53
From *Bastard Out of Carolina* (Allison) 316–327
From *My Own Country* (Verghese) 95–102
From *Native Speaker* (Lee) 229–234
From *Pee Wee and the Wheelman* (Nachtmann) 289–298
From *Zenzele: A Letter for My Daughter* (Maraire) 211–215
Frustration (Grigg) 25–26

Gay, Tiffany, *Sugar, Spice, and Everything Nice* 28–31
Graffiti: Tunnel Notes of a New Yorker (Kriegel) 270–276
Graham, Melissa, *A World Painted John Deere Green* 166–170

INDEX

Grandma's Fruitroom (Wade) 177–178
Grandmother's Kitchen, My Classroom (King) 204–206
Great Blueberry War, The (Cook) 104–106
Grigg, Katherine, *Frustration* 25–26
Guidera, Timothy, *Bowl's Eye View* 278–284

Hall, Bill, *Toothmarks in the Table of Time* 55–57
Hamper, Ben; *I, Rivethead* 136–149
Heath, Shirley Brice, *Talk Is the Thing* 186–191
Hellman, Lillian, *Turtle* 249–259
Hemingway, Nancy, *The Bracelet* 305–314
hooks, bell, From *Bone Black* 329–330
Hughes, Langston, *Theme for English B* 33–34

I Am What I Am (Bailey) 302–303
I Just Wanna Be Average (Rose) 36–44
Instructions No. 3 (Otto) 199–203
I, Rivethead (Hamper) 136–149
I Stand Here Ironing (Olsen) 116–123
I Stand Here Writing (Sommers) 125–134

King, Kim; *Grandmother's Kitchen, My Classroom* 204–206
Kitchen Table Talk (Ellington) 174–176
Kriegel, Leonard, *Graffiti: Tunnel Notes of a New Yorker* 270–276

La Rosa, Fernando, *The Man* 332–333
Lawson, Mary Sterner, *Reading Faces* 299–300
Learning to Use Language (Marinara) 2–3
Lee, Chang-rae, From *Native Speaker* 229–234
Leiby, Jeanne, *Why I Read* 208–209

Llewellyn, Chris, *March 25, 1911* 160–165

Man That Spelt "Knife" Was a Fool, The (Connors) 20–23
Man, The (LaRosa) 332–333
Maraire, J. Nozipo, From *Zenzele: A Letter for My Daughter* 211–215
March 25, 1911 (Llewellyn) 160–165
Martin-Brown, Jane, *Paths of Loss and Liberation* 285–288
Marinara, Martha, *Learning to Use Language* 2–3
  Writing and Work 62–63
Marinara, Jessica, *Christmas for the Colorblind* 150–155
Marriott, Alice, *The Whole Pot* 261–268
McPherson, John, *Close to Home* 17–18

Natchtmann, Rita, From *Pee Wee and the Wheelman* 289–298
Nurse Wonder (Berg) 108–115

O'Brien, Tim, *The Things They Carried* 64–79
Olsen, Tillie, *I Stand Here Ironing* 116–123
Other Literacies (Ellington) 246–248
Orlean, Susan, *Beautiful Girls* 81–93
Otto, Whitney, *Instructions No. 3* 199–203

Paths of Loss and Liberation (Martin-Brown) 285–288
Preface from *Fannie Flagg's Original Whistle Stop Cafe Cookbook* (Flagg) 193–197

Reading Faces (Lawson) 299–300
Ready for Anything (Freedman) 49–53
Rose, Mike, *I Just Wanna Be Average* 36–44
Rosen, Harold, *Comrade Rosie Rosen* 10–15
Rushin, Pat, *Zoo Welcomes New Arrival* 216–225

INDEX

Smiley, Jane, *The Consequences*, from *Moo* 4–8
Sommers, Nancy, *I Stand Here Writing* 125–134
Stafford, William, *At a Small College* 46–47
Sugar, Spice, and Everything Nice (Gay) 25–26

Talk Is the Thing (Heath) 186–191
Theme for English B (Hughes) 33–34
Things They Carried, The (O'Brien) 64–79
Toothmarks in the Table of Time (Hall) 55–57
Turtle (Hellman) 249–259

Verghese, Abraham, From *My Own Country* 95–102

Wade, Les, *Grandma's Fruitroom* 177–178
Welty, Eudora, *Wordstruck* 235–241
Whole Pot, The (Marriott) 261–268
Wordstruck (Welty) 235–241
World Painted John Deere Green, A (Graham) 166–170
Writing and Work (Marinara) 62–63
Why I Read (Leiby) 208–209

Zoo Welcomes New Arrival (Rushin) 216–225